MEMORY AND ABUSE

Remembering and Healing the Effects of Trauma

CHARLES L. WHITFIELD, M.D.

Health Communications, Inc.
Deerfield Beach, Florida

Charles L. Whitfield
21 West Road
Baltimore, MD 21204
410-880-2538

also in Atlanta at:

Box 420487
Atlanta, GA 30342
410-880-2538
Send SASE for speaking and workshop schedule.

Library of Congress Cataloging-in-Publication Data

Whitfield, Charles L.
    Memory and abuse: remembering and healing the effects of
trauma / Charles L. Whitfield.
        p.   cm.
    Includes bibliographical references.
    ISBN 1-55874-320-0 (pbk.) : $12.95
    1. Adult child abuse victims—psychology.   2. Repression
(Psychology).   3. Memory.   4. False memory syndrome.   I. Title
RC569.5.C55W45   1995   94-23015
616.85'82239—dc20   CIP
©1995 Charles L. Whitfield
ISBN 1-55874-320-0

Publisher: Health Communications, Inc.
               3201 S.W. 15th Street
               Deerfield Beach, Florida 33442-8190

Cover design by Robert Cannata

I dedicate this book to all survivors of abuse
and to those who care for them.

I wish there was a way to make all this easier.

ACKNOWLEDGMENTS

Special thanks go to the following people for their contributions in editing and inspiration: Christine Courtois, Barbara Harris, James Cronin, Mary Cavanaugh, Jean Kiljian, Mary Anne Reilly, Lana Lawrence, Roland Summit, Christine Belleris, Matthew Diener, Homer Pyle, Jennifer Freyd, Robert Solomon, Duncan Bowen, Robin Bowen, Neil Shapiro, Richard Peterson, Kate Whitfield, Lloydd De Mause and Doreen DuPont. Also I thank the following people for interviews or answering specific questions: David Calof, Marche Isabella, Barbara Jo Levy, Lynn Crook, Holly Ramona, Stephanie Ramona, Kathy O'Connor, David O'Connor, Connie Kristiansen, Connie Maggio, Richard Peterson and also George Ganaway, Elizabeth Loftus, Pamela Freyd, Richard Gardner, and Alan Feld. Finally, special thanks to Mary Johnston, who typed this book.

Grateful acknowledgement for permission to reprint material from their publications include: The University of Chicago Press to reproduce Figures 5.1 and 5.2 and Table 10.2 from Singer: *Repression and Dissociation,* © University of Chicago Press, 1990; Carol H. Neiman's painting "Equality" reproduced from *Psychological Perspectives,* issue 21, and the California Women's Caucus for the Arts © Carol H. Neiman, 1989; Michael Yapko to reproduce his suggestions of abuse from his book *Suggestions of Abuse,* © Michael Yapko, 1994; Thomas F. Nagy to reproduce Guidelines and direction when treating clients with repressed memories, from *The National Psychologist,* an independent newspaper for psychologists, 3(4): 8-9, 1994; Judith Herman's table on stages of recovery from her book *Trauma and Recovery,* © 1992 by Basic Books, a division of Harper Collins Publishers; Tables 3 and 4 from Roessler and Wind published in the *Journal of Interpersonal Violence,* © Sage Publications, 1994; Bremner et al's Table 3-1 from Pynoos (ed): *PTSD,* © American Psychiatric Press, 1993; V. J. Felitti to reproduce Figure 15.1 from his article from the *Southern Medical Journal,* 1991, © V. J. Felitti and *SMJ,* 1991; Robert L. Emrick to reproduce his material as the table in Appendix C, © Robert L. Emrick, 1994; Academic Press to reprint portions of "The Forgotten Difference: Ordinary Memory vs. Traumatic Memory" from *Consciousness and Cognition,* March 1995, © Academic Press; Michael Kerr for his Figure 17.1 on triangles, from Kerr and Bowen: *Family Evaluation,* © W. W. Norton, 1988; Roland Summit to quote from his article "The child sexual abuse accommodation syndrome," © Pergammon Press, 1983; George Ganatay to reproduce his long quote on page 168, personal communications, 1994; David Calof for quotes from his writings, including those published in *Treating Abuse Today,* on pages 189 and 190; Jennifer Freyd for quotes and ideas from her published work and from her forthcoming book on memory, *Betrayal Trauma,* © Jennifer Freyd; Ken Ring and Chris Rosing for a quote from their article in the *Journal of Near-Death Studies* 8 (4) 1990, © *Journal of Near-Death Studies,* 1990; and to Bruce Laflen and William Sturm for their figure reproduced in Appendix F on page 319 from their article in the *Journal of Child Sexual Abuse* 3(4):19-36, © Hawarth Press, 1994.

Except where referenced, I have changed the names and identifying characteristics of people in the case histories to protect their anonymity.

CONTENTS

Appendixes

FIGURES AND TABLES

Figures

Tables

FOREWORD

Dr. Charles Whitfield is a pioneer in assisting people in distress from addiction, co-addiction, family violence and trauma. His earlier works showed the common thread between these problems and the harm they inflict on individuals, relationships and the family unit. He also described the healing power of the recovery process in terms that were clear and helpful to both the lay person and the helping professional.

The effects of family violence and other trauma are difficult to identify and accept. Denial dies hard. Historically, social denial and ignorance have reinforced the problems of alcoholism and abuse in families and thus impeded recovery. It is only over the last 15 years that the prevalence and detrimental effects of these problems have been acknowledged and their causal association identified.

Recovery from addiction and trauma involves giving up denial and any other defenses used to keep the events and their associated pain at bay, in favor of accepting, remembering, feeling and resolving. It also involves taking personal responsibility for one's actions and developing spiritually.

Over the past five years, the "adult child" movement has been criticized for scapegoating families and for overusing past abuse to excuse present problems or behaviors. Three years ago that criticism began to consolidate around the possibility of "false memories" remembered by adults who did not previously talk about having been abused as children or who remembered after a period of forgetting. The critics of repressed memory champion parents and others who claim to have been falsely accused of molesting children based on flawed recall. They stress the damage caused by such a circumstance. They are especially concerned when the abuse memory returns during therapy, and they blame the therapist or the recovery process for it.

While false and inaccurate accusations are serious and should not be minimized, the reality of child abuse and the devastating toll of its untreated consequences must similarly not be minimized. It is to this end that *Memory and Abuse* has been written. In this important work, Charles Whitfield educates us about trauma and memory while simultaneously responding to the critics. He raises questions about the proponents of the false memory hypothesis regarding their knowledge of addiction, trauma and family violence and challenges their unquestioning support of anyone who claims to be falsely accused.

Denial, minimization and "false memories" are defenses used by many addicted and/or abusive individuals, even when their behavior is witnessed by others or corroborated in some way. Denial on the part of the abuser—and on the part of any other family member who should see and help but does not—creates a "conspiracy of silence," a vacuum that contributes to "not knowing." Defenses such as these are part of what impede disclosure at the time of the abuse as well as later, allow for the repetition of the abuse, and ultimately may affect the ability to recall the abusive experiences in a coherent way. Family attachment and loyalty also help in the cover-up. Children growing up in alcoholic or abusive homes suffer repeated traumas through their developmental years and learn to protect the family with silence and secrecy. To do otherwise might be too risky, including a feared loss or fragmentation of the family.

This book contains a wealth of information about the difference between ordinary and traumatic memory, the factors involved in remembering and forgetting one's personal history, the evidence in support of delayed memory and disclosure in child abuse, and characteristics helpful in sorting out true versus untrue memory. Traumatized people often have disturbances of memory that are shown in their symptoms, diagnoses and in what they remember and what they forget. While most seem to retain memory of the past trauma, they often have not identified it as being abusive, traumatic or even problematic, and may have never disclosed its occurrence. Others retain partial or selective memory and some have total amnesia.

Recovery is a process of facing and accepting what is known, as well as piecing together signs, symptoms and clues—both internal and external—about their personal meaning. The process is usually long and slow, requiring the person to remember and feel at a pace that is tolerable. Remembering is usually a struggle. The person defends against knowing and re-experiencing the trauma, for this brings great pain—but also the potential for repair and resolution. The most difficult circumstance, of course, arises for the person who has symptoms but no clear cognitive recall. Outside corroboration may or may not be available. In the absence of such evidence and memory, the person must proceed cautiously and may eventually have to accept the discomfort of uncertainty and of not knowing.

In this book, Dr. Whitfield argues that instead of the stridency and polemics which characterize much of the current controversy, we need a responsible and balanced discourse about memory and abuse. On the one hand, it must consider the concerns of the critics, and on the other it must not deny the reality of abuse or stifle those recovering from its aftereffects. It must expose the untrue and unacceptable claims of those who are anti-recovery, and it must be open to new information. At the same time, we need to learn more about family violence, its consequences, the similarities and differences between ordinary and traumatic memory, and individual and family healing. When dealing with this controversy surrounding "false memory syndrome," Charles Whitfield cautions against "throwing the baby out with the bathwater" and arguing the issue in the courts. We can only hope that the critics can respond to his challenge constructively.

Christine A. Courtois, Ph.D.
November 1994

Christine A. Courtois is the author of several articles on trauma and recovery and the book *Healing the Incest Wound.* She is a psychologist in private practice and is Clinical Director of the Center for Abuse Recovery & Empowerment of the Psychiatric Institute in Washington, D.C.

STATEMENT OF INTENTION

This book is not intended to replace the counsel of a licensed therapist and a qualified attorney in the matter of how to proceed when a person has memories of abuse. Each person's case is unique and deserves individual attention. Likewise, helping professionals should contact their clinical supervisor or attorney with questions about specific cases in which they are involved in assisting people with traumatic experiences. The references in the back of this book may assist the reader with the further exploration of this important issue. This information is not the final word on the subject and may be only the tip of the iceberg of the many dimensions of trauma.

INTRODUCTION

Memory is a double-edged sword. Most of the time it is useful. For instance, by reviewing past events we can gain insight into what works best for us in various areas of our life. Sometimes memory is painful. Traumatic events can haunt us for years. We suffer long-term from holding back a traumatic memory. Sometimes portions of a memory are untrue, and they may end up hurting us or another.

I hope this book will be useful to helping professionals and survivors of abuse as they sort out their memories, experiences and goals.

Helping professionals can use this book to update and expand their clinical skills when working with trauma survivors by appropriately facilitating their patients' or clients' memories of what happened.

Survivors of abuse can use this book to validate their personal experiences of abuse, to assist them in their recovery from the trauma and to help them form and set healthy personal boundaries.

Remembering and naming what happened is a crucial part of the process of healing from hurts, losses and traumas. But there may be obstacles along the way. Child abuse is such a painful act to contemplate that many people prefer to block out the possibility that it happens so often. It is hard to break out of the social trance that has so many of us hypnotized and sleepwalking.[48, 187] As a physician assisting people with the disease of alcoholism, I also observed many people who had memory blackouts while drinking and who truly believed they never did things that others observed them doing. Some may even pass a polygraph ("lie detector") test, believing that they did not do what others observed.

Despite the progress made in treatment for the effects of child abuse both for children or for adult survivors, there are many who doubt the problem exists, especially when it hits close to home. Culminating in a reaction from the most unbelieving among us, a group of accused parents, their lawyers and a few academics formed an organization in 1984 called Victims of Child Abuse Laws (VOCAL) and in 1992, the False Memory Syndrome Foundation (FMSF). Among their many claims—which I show in this book are mostly anti-recovery—are that delayed memories of sexual abuse are false. The media have spread their view, which has fueled the denial of many abusers and co-abusers as well as some victims and survivors. To understand the many dimensions and subtleties of what is known and what is controversial about memory and abuse we have to step back and look at the big picture. That big picture includes the politics involved, with all of its mental and emotional ramifications and reverberations.

No matter who is speaking or writing in this area today, it is difficult to avoid one's own point of view, experience and bias. I have seen no one in this controversy who is 100 percent neutral. A colleague and I attended a one-day seminar on this topic given by the FMS Foundation. We saw little or no compassion or concern for the adult children who had accused their parents or a relative of child sexual abuse. In fact, we saw no group support for any expressed emotions other than the parents' own anger. The focus was mostly on how to silence or punish the assumed "bad" outside influences that gave their accusing adult children their "false memories." Most attendees appeared to be confused, angry, numb or a combination of these.

The FMS advocates are playing an important role by pointing out to us the repercussions of any false accusation. We need to seriously consider what they are saying and at the same time not stifle those who were abused and are healing from the damaging effects of the abuse. To keep these two views in mind and heart is a delicate balance—whether we are a survivor, therapist or family member.

It would be devastating to be wrongly accused of such a serious charge as child abuse. Is it possible to sort out who is telling the truth? And if it is, can we do so without sacrificing individuals, destroying families and wasting millions of dollars in legal fees?

In trying to avoid both wrongful accusations and wrongful denials (which may stifle recovery from the effects of abuse), I have drawn on my 20 years of front-line clinical experience and on the expertise of numerous colleagues, plus the vast amount of literature on memory and trauma, both new and old. This book deals mostly with the clinical psychology of memory. Because the politics around memories of abuse have been so tumultuous, I have woven them into the story. These tactics of denial and attack by accused abusers have stirred us in two directions—one helpful and the other destructive. If this "false memory" debate stimulates appropriate research and encourages therapists to provide more helpful therapy, then it will be useful. But if it makes some therapists reluctant to assist survivors for fear of being harassed or sued, or if it pressures some survivors to doubt the validity of their memories, remain silent or recant, then the debate becomes destructive. If it draws attention away from the real social problem of child abuse and perpetuates the myth that women believe anything anyone tells them, then it is even more damaging.[389]

If there is a debate going on about memory of abuse, it appears to be lopsided. A minority, probably no more than a few thousand lay people, most of whom have been accused of child molestation, and a few hundred academics and psychologists are claiming that a majority, probably millions of sexual abuse survivors and a few hundred thousand helping professionals, are making up memories of having been sexually abused. But this minority and the media have acted as though the two opposing groups are equal in size and in accuracy. They are not.

It may be useful for the two sides of the memory controversy to eventually meet and have a dialogue addressing their mutual issues and concerns. If possible, they might then explore the possibility of working together to find some answers. However, from what we know about survivor and offender psychology, both have difficulty being open to what comes up for them in their inner life, which includes their memories, much less being able to take responsibility for exploring and expressing that often painful material. Those who address their pain and confusion in a recovery program can usually more easily expedite the healing process.

It is easy to ignore or deny the pain and to dissociate and separate from it. It takes great courage and humility for both the survivor and offender to risk being real with themselves and with the other. It is with a similar difficulty that I and other writers begin to describe our observations and experiences around this painful reality of memory and abuse.

To my knowledge, most of the books that are now being published on this topic represent the opposing point of view—that the abuse didn't happen. Or if it did, they don't tend to address its realities and how to heal from its harmful effects.

Denial of abuse, especially child sexual abuse, is as old as human history. Abusers come from all ethnic groups, socio-economic levels and professions. They are men and women who look like otherwise normal people. For example, the author Tennessee Williams' sister was repeatedly sexually abused as a child by her otherwise "upstanding" father who denied having committed the abuse. As an adult she spoke out in the only way that she could in a world that often invalidates these kinds of truths: she became mentally ill. So severe was her illness that she was lobotomized. Her father, her sexual abuser, signed permission for the lobotomy. This was clearly a double trauma, more severe but not unlike what countless other victims have experienced. This was a major "family secret" in the writings of Tennessee Williams,[524a] similar to the family secret that the "false memory syndrome" advocates and their enablers are trying to force us to keep as a nation.

At the same time that this is a painful topic, it is also exciting and healing if we open to the possibility of identifying and expressing the secret, and then grieving and finally letting go of its associated pain. The process of recovery works for most who have the courage to risk entering into and sticking with it.

In this book I confront the secret by exploring the world of traumatic memory and offer ways to heal from the otherwise crippling effects of the abuse and keeping it a secret. I would appeal to abusers and co-abusers who themselves may have traumatically forgotten or been in denial—let us not lobotomize another generation of our children.

Charles L. Whitfield
April 1995

1

THE "FALSE MEMORY" DEBATE

Imagine the following:

Jane is 35 years old, married, and has two children. Feeling irritable, sad and empty for several years, she began seeing a psychotherapist two years ago. While she had forgotten it for almost 20 years, during her recovery work she remembered that her father repeatedly sexually abused her from about ages 6 to 13 and that an uncle, who is now dead, did it once at age 11. In order to try to validate her experience and to heal the painful distance she has felt from her parents, she confronts them with this information, hoping for their acknowledgment that the abuse happened and an apology.

Instead, they both deny that the abuse ever happened. They tell her that she must have "false memory syndrome" and suggest that she leave psychotherapy and see the psychiatrist whom her mother had seen in the past for medication. Devastated and dejected, Jane questions the validity of her memories and slowly becomes unable to work at her part-time job. Still, she fears for her children's well-being when they are around her father, and decides to keep them away from him. Her mother sides with her father. Hurt and angry that they are not allowed to see their grandchildren, they file a lawsuit against Jane's therapist for malpractice and implanting "false memories" into their daughter. This causes Jane to stop attending her self-help group and become more self-doubting and withdrawn.

Since the early 1990s, this scenario—or a similar one—has been replayed thousands of times across the country. Sometimes an alleged abuse victim* changes their mind and retracts their story, and sometimes they stop seeing and rarely they even sue their therapist. There are now an estimated 4,000 lawsuits against psychotherapists related to this phenomenon,[518] and therapists across the country are rethinking their approaches to assisting people with these kinds of memories. Seeing the lawsuits publicized in the media and hearing stories from some of their peers, many survivors of child abuse are wondering where this backlash came from and whether their experience of having been abused is really true.

* * *

While there is no accepted diagnosis of "false memory syndrome" in any of the helping professional literature,[19, 34, 110, 113, 137, 216, 329a, 441, 661, 664, 693] a lay advocacy and lobby group—the False Memory Syndrome (FMS) Foundation, housed in an office in Philadelphia and headed by non-clinician Pamela Freyd — has stirred the media through networking and hype to publicize this alleged phenomenon as though it were common.** [215] Just how long the media will buy this idea is unpredictable. Attorney Sherry Quirk said, ". . . the majority of the members of the False Memory Syndrome Foundation are adults accused of [child] sexual abuse and experts who represent them in court—hardly a source of objective information on the veracity of memories of sexual molestation." [536]

Since the late 1980s there has been a backlash against the recovery movement.[137] It has taken many guises, and the most recent is the FMS claim, where parents accused of having sexually abused their children, their lawyers and a few academics are banding together and saying that the abuse "didn't really happen." Instead, they say that the memories of

---

* None of these kinds of terms is entirely satisfactory. Terms like *victim* can have an emotional charge to them. I here use victim to mean the person who is the target and experiencer of the abuse, although they might not so identify themself with this term in their words or behavior today. Abuse *survivor* is more often used, which implies that the person now identifies their experience of having been abused and they are attempting to heal from its painful after effects in some way. We are thereby aware that survival is a temporary state, one that we will replace with something healthier. See Lew for further discussion.[401] (To avoid the repeated he/she, her/his gender differentiations, in this book I have combined them into a "they" or "their" for a smoother reading flow.)
** See footnote on page 229 for comment on the term "lobby" in relation to the FMSF.

having been abused come from the effects of a pushy therapist on a vulnerable patient. They claim that most delayed memories of abuse are false. Their evidence appears to be based mostly on the denial of the alleged abusers and co-abusers, the stories of some retractors, and their interpretation of some of the literature on ordinary memory.

How Common is Abuse?

Two decades of research by psychologists, sociologists and government agencies have confirmed the existence of widespread dysfunction and violence within the American family. Part of what these studies show is that in the United States one girl in three or four has been sexually abused by age 18, and one boy in four to ten has been sexually abused. [21, 151, 199, 224, 349, 569, 570, 647, 706, 709] With a current U.S. population of about 260 million, this means that by using the most conservative figures, 50 to 80 million people now living in this country have been sexually abused. Others cite even higher figures. [174, 176] Addressing this high number, trauma therapists Judith Herman and Mary Harvey say that "Most abusers are known and trusted people in a position of authority over the child. Many are family members. This abuse is vastly underreported, because offenders usually succeed in silencing their victims. Probably less than 10% of child sexual abuse cases come to the attention of protective agencies or police." [328] Through the "false memory" claims, many perpetrators are trying to silence their victims again.

In spite of numerous studies that confirm these high numbers, FMS advocates (including the FMS Foundation's leader, Pamela Freyd) continue to ask: "Is the figure 50 million survivors accurate? Where does it come from?" (FMSF newsletter, 3 July 1993) Other critics are more subtle, attacking the therapists who assist survivors or casting doubt about the reality and natural history of abuse. FMS advocates say their organization was founded to protect the innocent against false accusations of abuse. By denying the existence of repressed memories of abuse they have, perhaps inadvertently, protected many abusers and also invalidated the painful experience of the victim. One example of their subtlety is their frequent qualifier: "We know that real abuse is bad and those abusers should be punished"—after which they usually proceed to invalidate survivors and attack their therapists. In spite of these almost patronizing statements, FMS advocates do not address "real abuse" or what to do about it.

The Usefulness of Critics

But critics can be helpful at times. At their best, they can encourage us to be more accurate and appropriate in our work. And at their worst they can push us to go deeper into ourselves and learn from the conflict that we have with them. Even though it may be painful to deal with people who deny and even attack the reality of our experiences, by working through our conflicts with them we can turn what appears to be a curse into a gift—the gift of our own personal empowerment and growth.

A Dysfunctional Family

The FMSF arose in the early 1990s with the beginnings of an explosive feud in the apparently dysfunctional family of Peter and Pamela Freyd.[238, 239, 240, 245, 248] While their younger daughter had long chosen to distance herself from them, their oldest daughter Jennifer, a psychology professor, had begun psychotherapy in 1990, and had remembered only hours after her second therapy session having been sexually abused as a child by her father, Peter.* [315, 238, 469] Jennifer's husband confronted her parents privately with this information. They both not only denied that the abuse had occurred, but—despite the fact that this information remained in the family—began to lash out at her with a series of personal attacks and personal boundary violations that have continued until the present. Some of the more serious ones include the following:

1) About six months after Jennifer began facing her painful childhood memories through psychotherapy, her mother began mailing a partially fictional and supposedly anonymous story of their denial that she had written under the name of "Jane Doe" [181] to many of Jennifer's colleagues at the University of Oregon, notably to full professors in her department. [238, 240] According to Jennifer, this was done "during the very year in which my promotion to full professorship was being considered." [The article untruthfully] ". . . states that I was denied tenure at a previous university

---

* During her second session, Jennifer's therapist asked if she had been sexually abused as a child. Jennifer said no, but afterwards memories began to come to her. She had always remembered her father's preoccupation with sex and inappropriate sexual behavior when she was a child, and her recovered memories that evolved only added to her experience that this was covert and at times overt sexual abuse.[19, 238] The Freyds claim that Jennifer's memories were "implanted". How could a simple question like "Were you sexually abused as a child?" have led Jennifer to make up these memories? She is clear that even when she wanted her therapist to help her have more memories, the therapist was unable to do so. [19, 238, 240]

. . ." [and it] ". . . also includes extensive discussion of my supposed sex life—a largely inaccurate discussion." Her mother phoned several of these colleagues, trying to tell them some of this story directly, and also contacted Jennifer's therapist and in-laws. [238]

2) Pamela and Peter brought together a small group of academics who supported their claim that memories of abuse were often false and implanted by psychotherapists. The Freyds incorporated the False Memory Syndrome Foundation in March of 1992. This group began contacting the media and Pamela traveled the country with her story, and to this date the FMSF functions mostly like a public relations firm.[315] Speaking about therapists who assist survivors of childhood sexual abuse in their healing while they recover their memories, Pamela Freyd said: "We are fighting an unproven radical revengeful therapy [sic] and intellectual garbage in terms of memory. If the mental health profession is unwilling to monitor itself . . . then we will have to shame them into it through the press." (December 8, 1991 FMS newsletter)

Judith Herman said that "false memory syndrome" ". . . sounded scientific. [But] few reporters bothered to find out that no such 'syndrome' has been shown to exist. The foundation further enhanced its image by recruiting a number of prominent psychiatrists and psychologists to serve on its advisory board. Some board members became zealous champions of the cause, giving frequent interviews to the media and testifying on behalf of accused perpetrators in court." [329a]

Many of the articles that appeared in the media and talks given by members of this group and its professional advisory board failed to mention their connection to the FMSF. Up to this point, there was no concept of "false memory syndrome" among mental health professionals, nor did it appear in their scientific literature. It is an FMSF term sometimes credited to Ralph Underwager, Ph.D.,[111] who was later pressured to resign from the FMSF Board, and to date it has no scientific credibility. [19, 34, 110, 111, 113, 172, 216, 329a, 393, 441, 661, 664, 693]

3) Just before the birth of her second child in July of 1988, nearly two years before she recovered her sexual abuse memories, Jennifer asked her mother to come and help her at the baby's birth, but please to come alone, without her father. She had long felt uneasy being around her father, and this was the first time that she explicitly asked her mother to help her in this way. But her mother did not honor that request, and her father's presence caused her much grief. [238]

4) Pamela invited her own personal psychiatrist, Harold Lief, M.D. of the University of Pennsylvania School of Medicine to join the FMSF Professional Advisory Board, and he did so.[63a, 215] He remains an active member and has denied any conflict of interest or dual relationship.[399, 403] Two ethics consultants considered this kind of interaction to be a dual relationship, and while it is neither illegal or unethical, they believe that it is unwise and may exploit the patient.[12, 35, 376, 479]

5) With no apparent consideration for Jennifer's experience and needs, Pamela and Peter also invited Jennifer to join the advisory board! Jennifer naturally declined.[54, 238]

6) Peter told Jennifer and her sister that the FMSF newsletter was a way to try to communicate with them.[238, 240]

Jennifer had wanted to keep the above information about her family private, but by early August 1993, because of the media focus that the FMSF had generated, she went public with her story, some of which is described above. In a memo to her colleagues, she said ". . . My parents' activities have been creating an atmosphere harmful to children as well as adult survivors of child abuse." In an attached statement, her colleague Pamela Birrell added that the situation ". . . was also creating an hysterical climate which prevented the free and unbiased exchange of ideas and research on the subject. . . .What has been presented by Jennifer's parents in the guise of scientific inquiry is actually a coverup for a vituperative attack. Now we can begin to engage in an honest intellectual dialogue and begin to deal more effectively with the pain created by child abuse."[54]

There are other old and new boundary distortions, such as the fact that Pamela and Peter are stepsiblings who grew up, for a short time, in the same family.*[248] Another is that two of the FMSF advisory board members published an interview advocating pedophilia as a potentially healthy lifestyle, although they had denied saying this in other interviews and a prior publication. Board member Ralph Underwager, Ph.D. who appears to have coined the term "false memory syndrome,"[111] was interviewed about pedophiles by the Netherlands publication, *Paidika: The Journal of*

---

* Peter was sexually abused for two years by a male family friend, starting when he was nine years old. Jennifer remembers him speaking of it as being "precocious sexuality" rather than abuse.[315] Other findings about the family are described elsewhere.[19, 63a, 111, 113, 181, 232a, 238, 239, 245, 248, 469]

Paedophilia, with his wife, Hollida Wakefield.[671] When asked "Is choosing paedophilia for you a responsible choice for the individual?", Underwager replied, "Certainly it is responsible . . . Paedophiles can boldly and courageously affirm what they choose. They can say that what they want is to find the best way to love. I am also a theologian and as a theologian I believe it is God's will that there be closeness and intimacy, unity of the flesh, between people. A paedophile can say: 'This closeness is possible for me within the choices that I've made.'" [671] When this article was made more widely available to people in the US, Underwager resigned from the FMSF professional advisory board, although exact reasons were not disclosed in their newsletter (FMSF newsletter July 3, 1993).[172, 398, 441]

The Freyd's two daughters are not the only family members to be alienated from them. Their mother (Peter's biological mother and Pamela's stepmother) and Peter's brother William have also chosen not to associate with Peter and Pamela for the past 20 years. After viewing a PBS Frontline documentary in April, 1995, that was biased in favor of "FMS" claims, William Freyd wrote the following letter to Frontline:

> Peter Freyd is my brother. Pamela Freyd is both my stepsister and sister-in-law. Jennifer and Gwendolyn are my nieces.
>
> There is no doubt in my mind that there was severe abuse in the home of Peter and Pam, while they were raising their daughters. Peter said (on your show, "Divided Memories") that his humor was ribald. Those of us who had to endure it, remember it as abusive at best and viciously sadistic at worst.
>
> The False Memory Syndrome Foundation is a fraud designed to deny a reality that Peter and Pam have spent most of their lives trying to escape. There is no such thing as a False Memory Syndrome. It is not, by any normal standard, a Foundation. Neither Pam nor Peter have any significant mental health expertise.
>
> That the False Memory Syndrome Foundation has been able to excite so much media attention has been a great surprise to those of us who would like to admire and respect the objectivity and motives of people in the media. Neither Peter's mother (who was also mine), nor his daughters, nor I have wanted anything to do with Peter and Pam for periods of time ranging up to more than two decades. We do not understand why you would "buy" such an obviously flawed story. But buy it you did, based on the severely biased presentation you made of the memory issue that Peter and Pam created to deny their own difficult reality . . .
>
> I would advance the idea that "Divided Memories" hurt victims,

helped abusers and confused the public. I wonder why you thought these results would be in the public interest that Public Broadcasting is funded to support.

Sincerely,

William Freyd

In my and others' opinion, this letter affirms and validates a part of Jennifer's experience and provides some external corroboration that the abuse happened. Even though this is a fairly strong testimony from an immediate family member, it is likely that Pamela and Peter Freyd, and other "FMS" advocates will try to invalidate it in some way.

After reading Jennifer's personal story, two additional FMSF professional advisory board members resigned.[240] In the ongoing politics of this fight there will likely be many more such developments, and since the information in this book is current to the best of my knowledge up to April 1995, I suggest that those interested in these developments look at the literature—anywhere from such sources as the FMSF newsletter to selected clinical and scientific journals.*

Our Greater Family

These are some clear examples of family dysfunction. They include boundary distortions within a pivotal current nuclear family and within the extended family of the FMSF. This dysfunction has extended further into our "greater family" via a dysfunctional media which has generally sided with the FMSF, although they have claimed to present a balanced view.[428] I have seen and read a number of these presentations, and only three were actually balanced—the "Oprah" show that aired in early August of 1993 and a few magazine articles. [153a, 155, 315, 342, 393, 469, 710]

---

* Examples that I am aware of include the *Journal of Child Sexual Abuse,* the *Family Violence and Sexual Assault Bulletin, Child Abuse and Neglect, The Advisor* (of the American Professional Society on the Abuse of Children), the *Journal of Interpersonal Violence, The Journal of Psychohistory, Treating Abuse Today, The Journal of Traumatic Stress, Dissociation,* the *American Journal of Psychiatry,* the *American Psychologist, Moving Forward, The Healing Woman, The Survivor Activist,* and *Truth About Abuse.* I will also be giving talks and workshops on this topic, as will others, in which we will provide an update of clinically important information.

The above is not surprising. Denial of child abuse, including child sexual abuse, is nearly as old as recorded time.[176] This denial is also reflected in the current resistance to children's rights, child abuse issues and to related recovery movements.

Nearly 20 years ago Christina Crawford, daughter of actress Joan Crawford, wrote *Mommie Dearest* and experienced great criticism for speaking her truth of having been abused as a child.[152a] Other celebrities and their children have written and/or spoken about similar experiences, such as Gary Crosby, Desi Arnaz Jr., Marilyn Van Derbur, Roseanne Arnold and LaToya Jackson, and in nearly all of these cases the parents and several relatives have denied the person's experience of abuse.[167, 168, 353, 618] The only exception was Suzanne Somers, whose parents validated her childhood and adult experiences. This validation and acceptance appears to have been remarkably healing for her and her family.[606]

Family Pain

The pain of child abuse is real for all people involved, from the survivor to the abuser and co-abusers, and it reverberates over time. One of these reverberations is the pain that other family members experience when survivors speak their own painful truth. From clinical experience and the literature on trauma and abuse, we know that most abusers were themselves abused as children, and that they may continue to be abused as adults.[176, 501, 623, 651]

While people are more familiar with news stories that paint abusers as solitary predators of others' children, most sexual abuse of children is incestuous, taking place within families.[425, 440, 515] In a vicious cycle of the victim sometimes becoming the abuser, the trauma is passed on from one generation to the next.

Interestingly, most survivors do not become abusers in a direct sense. They become co-abusers — overtly or covertly enabling other abusers to continue their perpetrations. Thus they may also be called passive abusers. The majority of all survivors are left with symptoms of post-traumatic stress, depression, dissociation, anxiety, difficulty maintaining a fulfilling relationship and other symptoms.[41, 43, 85, 86, 88, 92, 138, 140, 256, 323, 379, 516] One of these symptoms is not being aware of having any of these manifestations, which in essence becomes a denial of their emotional existence.[689]

When the abuse survivor speaks out the family's reaction is usually of shock, hurt and fear. The same reaction usually manifests whether the abuse was real or not. One accused parent writes, "We thought we were alone after being pushed into a bottomless pit by our accuser, aware of the stigma attached to such an accusation, yet resisting calling out for fear of further scarring of our troubled loved one" (FMSF newsletter July 3 1993). No doubt the family will suffer in these and other ways, often deeply, when confronted.[710] However, just what is meant by "further" and "troubled" depends upon the reality of the past abuse and the actual intent and meaning of the above speaker. Said with openness, humility and compassion, it can mean one thing, but said with denial, pity and anger, it means another.

In the fall of 1991 our nation witnessed the trauma of the Anita Hill/Clarence Thomas Senate hearings about an insidious form of sexual abuse — the covert kind called sexual harassment.[442, 521, 690] No matter where you may have sided on their conflict, Anita Hill's painful experience of having been doubly traumatized — once when the alleged abuse happened and again when she tried to share it — has been repeated in the lives of countless abuse victims, and it is continuing in the reverberations of the delayed memory controversy. When victims now risk speaking the truth of their experience to any of their families, they not only run the risk of being invalidated and denied by their abusers and co-abusers, but some of these perpetrators will also receive support for their denial from the FMSF and other enablers with similar views. These enablers are subtle and sophisticated.[689]

Addressing this "false memory" debate, psychotherapist and writer Mary Wylie writes in the *Family Therapy Networker,* "The question, 'Who do you believe?' strikes at the very heart of the American myth of innocence, our confidence in the fundamental goodness, fairness and justice of our civilization, our conviction that, for all our failings, we are a compassionate and honest people. How can we accept the possibility that hundreds of thousands, perhaps millions, of children have been and are being abused, tortured, even killed by the people most obligated to love and protect them? What does it mean to acknowledge that this is happening in virtually every American neighborhood by people who look and sound and dress exactly like us? They are our friends, our colleagues, our doctors, our lawyers, our politicians, our storekeepers, our plumbers. Perhaps they are our relatives, perhaps ourselves."[710]

2

THE PROCESS OF REMEMBERING: A PSYCHOLOGY OF MEMORY

Political Background

While most of my colleagues and I have not personally encountered people with completely untrue memories in our own practice, my sense from studying the literature and talking to numerous interested people about it and getting their feedback is that it happens rarely. Just how often it might occur is unknown, as there have been no clinical reports or scientific studies directed at this problem as yet. Until we learn more—no matter which side of the debate we may identify with—all conclusions are speculative.

Those who advocate the existence of "FMS" say it is common,[215, 417, 497] but most of them are not front-line clinicians who specialize in the long-term treatment of people with post-traumatic states, where a more accurate assessment and description of many of their dimensions may be found. The FMS advocates also argue that "repression" of memories has not been scientifically documented.[340, 413] This chapter and the following ones deal with memory, delayed memories and the "false memory" arguments in some detail. Memory is a complex, multilayered system that some critics may try to oversimplify. The word "repression" is often poorly defined and is used by psychology professionals in its most general sense

to cover a variety of memory processes, including repression, dissociation and denial. This causes some confusion that the following chapters
should relieve.

FMS advocates discuss only the repression of memory and avoid nearly a century of studies on dissociation and denial. In fact, most trauma
survivors with delayed memories are experiencing not a simple repression, but dissociative phenomena and often some degree of denial. Calof
shows how the FMS advocates set up their own definition of repression
as a straw man, and then proceed to knock it down. [113, 114] To the unso-
phisticated person their arguments can look good. But to the aware
observer they are limited and sometimes naive, as I explain in the next
several chapters.

FMS advocates base their claims that false memory exists mostly on a
combination of the denial of named or alleged perpetrators, the retraction of accusations by a few people, and a few anecdotal reports and
small research projects studying ordinary memory. [215, 413, 497] These projects
have generally not involved the study of the memories of sexual abuse
survivors or direct work with the psychotherapists who assist them in
their recovery. Traumatic memory differs greatly from ordinary memory,
but the FMS arguments are derived from studies on ordinary memory,
designed to examine such things as the memories of eyewitnesses in
legal cases. Examples include showing photographs of auto accidents or
videotapes of other scenes to college students, or having them read trial
transcripts, and then asking them misleading questions to see how the
details of their normal memories can be altered by others. [113, 114]

In their claims they use this deliberate narrowing of focus on the legit-
imately demonstrated errors of ordinary memory to try to transfer it to the
clinical and scientific area of traumatic memory. From this mistaken transfer, and from the fact that some of the peripheral details of traumatic
memory may also be in error, they then deny the essence or central core
of the memories of trauma survivors. In their claims they combine this
information with fragments of selected studies on abuse survivors and the
stories of "retractors"—people who suddenly change their minds about
having been abused, often saying they were manipulated by their therapist to make it up. They then argue their claims in the media, in court
and in some academic circles and journals. [411, 416-18, 496, 546, 572, 591] However,
most of these FMS advocates are not clinicians who specialize in the long
term treatment or study of people with post-traumatic states. [519, 620, 646, 718]

It is with trauma survivors, that a more accurate assessment and description of recovered memory may be found, not with college students looking at photos.[114, 156] In fact, there is a large body of research into traumatic memory which FMS advocates tend to ignore. In addition to the existing research with survivors, which I describe in Chapter 8, one reliable way to obtain a more accurate topography of traumatic memories will be to continue to study trauma survivors, and to survey and study the front-line clinicians who work with them.

My own opinion and that of numerous other clinicians[34, 328, 585, 641] is that the "FMS", i.e. a delayed memory of abuse that is not true, is rare. Just how unusual this phenomenon may be is difficult to estimate currently. My sense is that its incidence is minute when compared with the number of refutations by parents or other alleged perpetrators who actually are themselves in denial of their having mistreated or abused one or more of their accusing victims. When the first few survivors of sexual abuse by Father James Porter told of their memories, Porter denied having sexually abused any of them. And he had numerous enablers and co-abusers who supported his denial, including many authority figures in the Catholic Church. Over time, 130 of his victims had spoken up, and in 1993 he admitted to having abused at least 28 innocent children.[227, 528] We could even say that Porter and abusers like him, who are dissociated from their own pain or who deny their behavior, are the ones with the real "false memory syndrome."

A Simple View of Memory

How then can we begin to sort out some of the important factors and dynamics in our ability to remember our experiences? I will start by showing two "maps" of the process of remembering. The first map shows a simplified view of the process of remembering. There are six components: intake (or input), experience, encoding, rehearsal, storage, and output or retrieval, as shown in this diagram.

$$\text{In} \longrightarrow \text{Experience} \quad \begin{array}{c} \nearrow \text{Encode} \searrow \\ \\ \searrow \text{Store} \nearrow \end{array} \quad \text{Rehearse} \longrightarrow \text{Out (Memory Retrieval)}$$

Information comes in through our five or more senses—sight, sound, smell, taste, touch, position, and the like. Based on several factors within our own inner life, such as our beliefs, expectations and feelings, and on our past experience, we then begin to have a present *experience* of the event. Soon we begin to process the experience in various ways, the most important of which is rehearsal (thinking, talking or writing about it).[641]

Encoding is the process of how we lay down a memory trace into our recorded consciousness.* While simply having an experience of certain information taken in may be enough to encode it, rehearsing helps us to *store*, keep or retain it. Then, whenever we may need it or when something else may trigger it, we can retrieve it. *Retrieval* is how we activate our memory of the experience when triggered or required.[240]

In ordinary memory there may be no prominent blocks to remembering an experience. But in traumatic memory, blocks are common and they tend to occur most frequently in the area of *rehearsal* (thinking, talking or writing) and in retrieval. An important part of the genesis of traumatic forgetting is that the person is somehow inhibited or prohibited from completely processing and expressing their experience.

With this simple view, we can now expand our understanding of the process of remembering into a more detailed one. We can call this more expanded map of the memory process a "conventional view."

A Conventional View of Memory

Over the past 15 years a more expanded, "conventional view" of memory and the sequence of its stages of processing has been explored and re-evaluated.[489] This map is illustrated in Figure 2.1, and shows four clouds of components floating above several memory structures and concepts, which then interact with incoming signals and cues, internal processes, and outgoing expressions and actions. While this illustration or "map" is still simplified, it can give us an even broader understanding of the parts of the process of remembering.

These processes and functions are all part of a higher mental func-

---

*We don't know exactly how encoding occurs. One theory among many proposed is by psychology researcher Donald Hebb, who suggested that when groups of neurons are stimulated in ordinary memory, they form patterns of neural activity in the brain. If a specific group of neurons fires frequently, a reverberating and regular neural circuit is established. Hebb called this evolution of a temporary neural circuit into a more permanent circuit *consolidation*. He saw it as the basis of short-term memory, which permits the coding (encoding) of information into long-term memory. If Hebb is correct, when people first sense a new stimulus, only temporary changes in neurons occur.[313] But with repetition or rehearsal, consolidation occurs and the temporary circuit becomes permanent.[400]

tioning called *conscious awareness*, many of whose mechanisms are still unknown. These processes are complex and have more components and interconnections than are shown here. And they are not simply links or steps along the way. As memory researcher D.A.Norman described them, "They are active paths, with hills and brambles, magnets and highways." And they are often dynamic and may be laden with feelings.

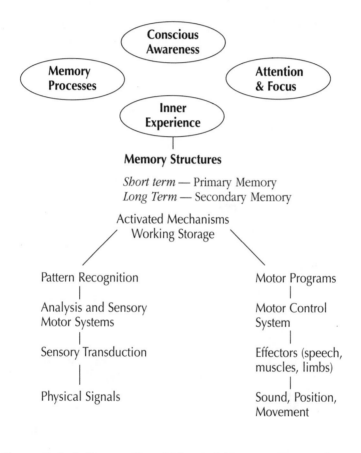

Figure 2.1. A Conventional View of Memory Processing
(modified from Norman 1981[489])

In 1890 the psychologist William James named primary memory as that which we most effortlessly remember of our present experience, and secondary memory as that which requires effort and search (for example, what did you eat for dinner three days ago?). Also called *short-term* memory, primary memory lasts for from seconds to minutes, while *long-term* or secondary memory lasts for from several minutes to hours to days or longer. Various "memory processes" (upper cloud on the left of Figure 2.1) can help strengthen secondary memory, and include searching, interpreting, structuring, constructing and rehearsing.

Rehearsal, the deliberate act of repeating the material that is in primary memory, appears to be the strongest of these, and it is illustrated in Figure 2.2. A common problem for abused children and adults is that they do not get to adequately rehearse their experience of being abused.

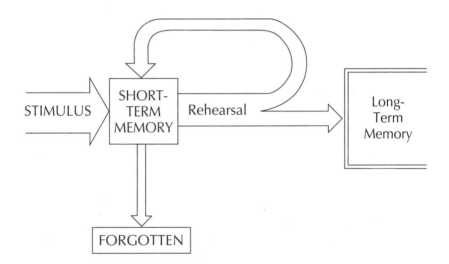

Figure 2.2. The Short- and Long-Term Memory System. (All experience enters our primary or short-term memory, where it is either rehearsed or forgotten. Rehearsed material may enter our long-term or secondary memory.
(Modified from Waugh and Norman, 1965).[679a]

And even if they do, they may not feel safe enough to be validated. I will describe the need to feel safe in the next chapter and throughout this book.

With this introduction to the process of remembering, we can now further expand on our knowledge of its components.

3

MEMORY AND
EXPERIENCE

Memory is an amalgam of components from our inner life, made up of experiences that are stored in our conscious and unconscious awareness. Memory is both cognitive and experiential, and it depends on the quality, quantity and interaction of several factors, which I describe below and summarize in Table 3.1.

Traumatic experiences are nearly always encoded and stored in long-term memory, although they are frequently forgotten, whereas our experiences of ordinary events are usually not encoded or stored unless they are notable in some way. These following 16 factors apply to both ordinary and traumatic memory:

Meaning and Processing

Because of the complex nature of human experience and the way that it is processed in our psyche, the memory of any event cannot be exactly like a movie or a videotaped version of the experience. Most memories contain only one or two fragments of the actual scene. But they may also contain some of the essential elements of the person's individual experience and the (1) *meaning* that it has for them. That meaning may change over time, varying with the quality and quantity of their (2) *processing* of the experience. That processing may include any one or usually a combination of several additional factors that are involved in the dynamics of remembering. A review of some of these follows.

Inner Life Experience

Whether we remember an experience or not may also depend on:

(3) The *emotional impact* of the event — whether it is painful, joyful, or in between. This includes the crucial part of our inner life that we call our *feelings*.[687-689]

(4) *Other components* of our inner life, such as our beliefs, thoughts, decisions and choices — and more. It is from the interaction of these components, over time, within our inner life, that the memories of our life experiences are processed, encoded and stored. While memories are also a distinct part of our inner life, we can also consider them to be an amalgam which includes many of the components shown in Figure 3.1.

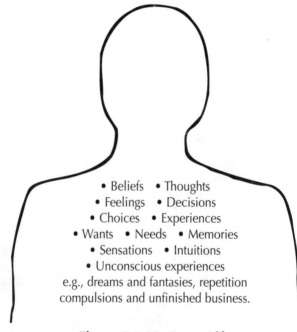

• Beliefs   • Thoughts
• Feelings   • Decisions
• Choices   • Experiences
• Wants   • Needs   • Memories
• Sensations   • Intuitions
• Unconscious experiences
e.g., dreams and fantasies, repetition
compulsions and unfinished business.

Figure 3.1 My Inner Life

(5) We may have *other ways of experiencing* than feeling, especially through our *senses*—e.g. sight, hearing, touch, smell, movement, intuition and others. Most of our experiences include a combination of these.

Sharing or Not

(6) *Sharing* our experiences is a specific and useful kind of rehearsal. Remembering our experiences may depend on whether or not we shared them. And if so, to what extent did we share? Did we simply mention, discuss, argue about, write it down, or express or document it in some other way? As research psychologist Jennifer Freyd describes, it is through this process of expressing and sharing an experience that we can recode the material that is happening in our inner life to be clearer and more discrete,[241] memorable and meaningful, as shown in Figure 3.1 above.* For example, it appears that Anita Hill's ability to remember was probably improved by sharing some of her experience with some of her trusted friends around the time that she was allegedly mistreated.[690]

Different families may vary in the kind of memories they share among their members and to what extent they share them, as the following history shows.

> Anne is a 38-year-old elementary school teacher. In group therapy one day she said, "I remember a few things from my childhood, but my family didn't talk much about things from their past. While my husband's family was also dysfunctional, they talked a lot about their ordinary memories, and that felt strange to me. I liked it, but also was confused, since I wasn't used to it. I'm talking more about my past now in my recovery program, and that is helping me a lot. I'm beginning to notice that what my husband's family talks about are more superficial things. I'm trying to talk about and remember deeper and more real things that involve my recovery, and while that is easier for me to do in my therapy group, it's harder to do with my husband.

A healthy family tends to share about both ordinary *and* extraordinary and traumatic experiences and memories, as long as appropriate boundaries are respected. An unhealthy family tends not to share emotional

---

* It is perhaps synchronistic that Jennifer Freyd Ph.D., the daughter of the two founders of the False Memory Syndrome Foundation, and who they accuse of having "false memories" of being abused by her father and co-abused by her mother when she tried to share her experience with them, is a professor of psychology at the University of Oregon and specializes in the psychology of memory.[241, 242]

experiences, especially traumatic experiences and their associated painful feelings. In abusive families, there is often additional emotional and physical abuse, including direct threats to the lives of abused children or people they love in order to prevent the abuser from being exposed.

If full or complete sharing with a safe person helps to encode an experience in our memory, *not* sharing tends to inhibit or prevent remembering. Memory is greatly impaired by threats and acts of physical violence that commonly accompany sexual abuse. Trauma psychiatrist Roland Summit said, "Contrary to the general expectation that the [abuse] victim would normally seek help, the majority of the victims in retrospective surveys had never told anyone during their childhood."[629] This observation is one of several factors that help us understand why forgotten or delayed memories of abuse are so common. The inability to rehearse, through thinking, talking and writing about our traumatic experiences, is instrumental in the genesis of traumatic forgetting.[641]

Safety

(7) Also important is *whether it feels safe* or not to remember all or parts of the experience in our conscious awareness. Clearly, abusive parents do not provide a safe environment for a child, and may instead make what a child experiences as a kind of combat zone, fraught with peril. If I feel unsafe with you, I may be inhibited in talking about my experiences with you, and traumatic experiences are more difficult to talk about than ordinary ones. I discuss some principles of how to differentiate safe from unsafe people in Chapter 24.

Validation

(8) Also affecting our ability to remember is to what extent impactful others around us *validate* or *invalidate* our experience, which I discuss further in Chapter 27. Validation is a crucial part of processing and completing our "unfinished business" around a memory. One of a child's deepest developmental needs is validation, which is a form of mirroring. In this process, a child is supposed to receive a loving and accurate reflection that their experience of self and life is valid. Abuse is the polar opposite of validation, and often includes deeply traumatic messages, including lies ("You haven't got the sense God gave a goose!"), shaming of children's attributes and experiences, and emotionally disrupting,

contradictory messages called double binds that cause a child to be conflicted and confused about reality itself. In these circumstances, memory can be profoundly affected.

Usefulness

(9) Also important is *how useful* it might be, from a personal and environmental functioning and survival perspective, *to remember* part or all of an experience. For example, it may be more useful for a child to forget (dissociate, suppress, repress or not remember in some way) part or even all of being repeatedly abused than to remember it and thereby be overwhelmed by the experience or become dysfunctional from it. Even if it is "forgotten" and the person is then amnestic about the experience for a time, the impact of the traumatic experience usually remains encoded and stored in their unconscious mind and may also be manifested somatically in some way. For instance, a person who was sexually abused may gag or feel nauseated or numb when having sexual feelings or experiences.

Other Similar, Associated or Anticipated Events

(10) Also effecting our ability to remember is the *memory of past* similar or associated events or experiences and/or *the anticipation of future such events* or experiences. This is one of several roles that time can play in the encoding and processing of an experience.

Awareness

(11) The *degree of conscious awareness* that we have during the experience is another important factor in our ability to remember (as shown in Figure 2.1 above). If I am not aware of something, how can I retain it in my conscious memory? Most children, adolescents and adults who are being mistreated or abused frequently become numb to much of their inner life. With no one safe to talk to and validate their experience, the pain of their trauma and isolation mounts, and can become overwhelming. As I describe in the next chapter, when this happens, to survive, the person's True Self defensively submerges deep within an unconscious part of itself: "the child goes into hiding" (Figure 4.1 on page 33). From this point on, during many life events—traumatic or otherwise—the person may have little or no awareness.

Table 3.1. Factors involved in remembering, and their association with promoting or inhibiting the memory of an experience

Factors	Promoting and Reinforcing	Inhibiting and Blocking
1) **Meaning** of the experience	Meaningful	Not meaningful
2) **Processing** of the experience	Present	Absent
3) **Emotional impact** of event	Joyful or Painful	Painful
4) **Other inner life** components	More than one component	Limited to one or two
5) **Sensory ways** of experiencing	More than one sense	Limited to one or two
6) **Sharing** the experience	Shared and expressed	Not shared or expressed
7) **Safe** to remember	Safe	Unsafe
8) Our experience is **validated**	Validated	Not validated, or invalidated
9) **Usefulness** to remember it	Useful	Not useful, or counterproductive
10) Memory of **associated experiences**	Can promote if conscious and appropriate	May inhibit, esp. if unconscious or inappropriate
11) **Awareness** during experience	High and clear	Low and/or blurred
12) **Focus** or selective attention	Strong to moderate	Weak to none
13) **Parallel** ways of thinking	Conflicted or not	Conflicted
14) **Divided ways** of thinking	In sync, integrated	Out of sync, not integrated
15) **Internal conflict**	Conflicted or not	Conflicted or not
16) **Conscious effort** to remember	Present	Absent

Our awareness may be affected by psychological factors such as those described above and by physical factors, such as using psychoactive drugs that may alter our awareness by depressing, stimulating or otherwise distorting it. Also, if we are in a trance or confused during an experience, which is common in those of us who have been abused, this may inhibit our ability to remember an experience.

Some Variations in Awareness

Memory researchers use specific terms to describe various aspects of memory. They call our conscious memories explicit (i.e. simple, clear and uncomplicated) and those that are not conscious implicit (hidden, entangled or entwined).[241, 662] They also divide conscious memories into three kinds: episodic, semantic and autobiographical. Episodic knowledge in memories is time-dated and/or place-located, as occurs in a specific event. By contrast, semantic knowledge is not time-dated, for example as in our knowledge of a language.[241] Similarly, "generic event" memory is also not time or place-associated, but is instead a memory of a familiar pattern or event, such as driving to work.[241]

Autobiographical or "Story" Memory

Autobiographical memory is part of our life story and depends upon the structure of our language.[96, 487] This fact may explain in part why expressed or shared and correctly named experiences are more often remembered. In summarizing some of the developmental origins of autobiographical memory, memory researcher Katherine Nelson said:

> ...research indicates that children learn to share memories with others, that they acquire the narrative forms of memory recounting, and that such recounts are effective in reinstating experienced memories only after the children can utilize another person's representation of an experience in language as a reinstatement of their own experience.[487]

Nelson clarifies that while episodic memory is sometimes a part of autobiographical memory, it is often not a part of it:

> To take a simple example, what I ate for lunch yesterday is today part of my episodic memory, but being unremarkable in any way, it will not, I am quite sure, become part of my autobiographical memory. It has no significance to my life story beyond the general schema of lunch. In contrast, the first time I presented a paper at a conference is part of my autobiographical memory: I remember the time, place, and details of the program and participants, and I have a sense of how that experience fits into the rest of my personal life story. It is important to make this distinction at the outset, because, as recent research has established,

very young children do have episodic memories, but do not yet have autobiographical memory of this kind.[487]

The "Infantile Amnesia" Claim

Expanded from Freud's notion of "infantile amnesia," the current belief among memory researchers is in keeping with their observations, mostly on ordinary memory, where before age three or four children do not have full verbal or story (autobiographical) memory.*

However, some people can remember some impactful episodes from when they were very young children, such as their having been mistreated or abused, as Nelson,[487] Terr,[637, 641] Bruhn,[93, 97] Hewitt,[331] Ainsworth et al,[6] Meyers et al,[463] and Burgess et al[102] describe.

Every traumatic memory from before age three or four cannot be automatically dismissed as being invalid. Many of these are real memories, some may be metaphorical or "screen" memories, and—related to these — others may result from various "cumulative strain" traumas** as described by analyst Lawrence Hedges,[316] while still others may be partly or completely untrue. Without a careful assessment over time by a therapist who is skilled and experienced in working with trauma, one cannot categorically rule out the veracity of an early traumatic memory based only on a theory such as "infantile amnesia" or "childhood amnesia." The following is one of many examples.

> Tom is a 46-year-old electrician who always remembered a traumatic experience when he was two years and three months old, when his mother dropped him and his sister at an orphanage and did not return for four years. His sister also had always remembered that painful day, although neither had ever spoken to the other about it until over forty years later, when Tom started recovery. She later validated his experience and several details that had stuck in his memory.

---

* Freud also postulated that some early memories may be "screen memories," which gather many emotional details into a single picture, narration or "screen" and cover or hide emotionally impactful events with trivial ones.[316] Terr gives an example as part of a lengthy case history of a man named Ross whose brother was killed when he was four and he had not been able to grieve his loss: "If Ross...had written to me that he had a clear memory of burying a pet fish when he was seven, but not of the earlier interment of his brother, the fish memory would have been a screen memory standing for lost memories of his brother's burial."[641] However, as Hedges points out, a screen memory may also be a *reasonably accurate rendition of what actually happened.*[316]

A common tactic of FMS advocates is to attack the credibility of survivors who remember having been abused before age three or four—
whether or not they have always remembered it.[17, 417, 497, 572] They use the
"infantile amnesia" variation of the "false memory" defense. But many
people can and do remember traces, fragments or even the majority of
traumatic experiences from this early age.[22, 53, 127, 312, 331, 332, 460, 463, 637-9] For example, professor of psychiatric nursing and trauma researcher Ann Burgess
and her colleagues prospectively studied 34 children who had been
repeatedly sexually abused by day-care staff.[102] The children's ages at the
time of the abuse ranged from three months old to about four-and-a-half
years old, with an average age of two-and-a-half years old. Nineteen of
these 34 children were subsequently evaluated in follow-up by three
independent observers at five and ten years after the abuse, and the plan
is to continue the follow-up. The results suggest that children remember
traumatic experiences in at least four dimensions, including the somatic,
behavioral, verbal and visual. Eleven (58 percent) of the children always
verbally remembered the abuse, five (26 percent) partially remembered
and three (16 percent) totally forgot experiencing any abuse. Other
observers have reported similar results.[53, 331, 637-639]

What would happen if as children or adults they told helping professionals, authorities or the courts of their experiences and they were invalidated by the "infantile amnesia" claim? How would that negative response
to their true experience affect their well-being and the after effects of the
abuse? Would it re-traumatize them? If so, how much? I believe, as do oth-
ers,[22, 53, 97, 127, 312, 331, 332, 347a, 637-639] that people can remember or recover traumatic
memories of abuse from this early age, as this study demonstrates. We
need more trauma therapists and researchers to study and report their
observations, whether on individuals or groups of survivors.

Much before age three children cannot talk clearly about their experiences. They tend to act out or "act in" their traumatic experiences to

---

** Hedges says that based on psychoanalytic theory "cumulative strain" traumas may occur
from many different kinds of painful experiences, such as early illness or hospitalization,
prolonged absence of important others, early feeding or interacting difficulties, or family
stresses. To the child the pain feels overwhelming and may be attributed later in life to faulty
or abusive parents or others. (Hedges 94) This must be balanced by the possibility of *accuracy*, based on the clinical observation of the child's and the adult's somatic, behavioral,
visual and verbal expressions, in remembering one or more traumatic experiences before
age three or four.

express their pain—somatically, behaviorally or visually. In the Burgess et al study cited above, 100 percent of the 34 children manifested *somatic* memories, 82 percent showed *behavioral* associated memories, and 59 percent had *visual* memories shown through art therapy.[102, 103]

Terr calls our autobiographical or story memory a verbal system, which comes in around age three as part of our conscious or explicit memory. She says that, "It operates through sensory pathways that lead to the hippocampus and medial thalamus and then runs up to the cerebral cortex for associations and long term processing. Implicit [including traumatic] memory is earlier in appearance, different in anatomical distribution [see also pages 246 & 7] and very reliable. This is why, though we have no words for our infantile connections to our parents, those old nonverbal memories from our infant and toddler stages often predict the strength of our connections to others as we grow older."[641]

Terr studied 20 children who suffered documented psychic trauma before age five at an average age of three years and ten months (ranging from six months to four years old) at the time of their traumas. She found that *visual* and *behavioral* memory are stronger and more influential and enduring than is verbal memory.[637] *Verbal memory is not the most sophisticated manifestation of memory,* nor is memory a solely verbal system. No matter the age that a person may suffer *abuse,* their *memory* of it *includes several components,* including any from their inner life (Figure 3.1) plus the physical, behavioral, visual and verbal. Each of these may be a part of one's story memory.

Autobiographical memory, our "story" or parts of it, is usually specific, personal, long-lasting, and often has practical usefulness.[487] However, with a history of having been mistreated, abused or traumatized in another way, that memory may be dissociated and split off from our ordinary consciousness and memory. Only when the person feels safe enough and has triggers or cues to assist them in remembering a forgotten traumatic experience will they be able to bring it into their conscious awareness.*

---

*To help us remember early memories more easily, Bruhn has developed a useful booklet called the Early Memories Procedure in which we can explore and write some of our memories[94, 95] (discussed further on pages 187 and 267).

Focus

The degree to which the person (12) *focuses* their *awareness* upon or *selectively attends* to the incoming and evolving information of an experience will also affect the quantity and quality of their memory, as shown in Figure 2.1 in the previous chapter. But even when information is not entering fully into conscious awareness, we can still be processing it — at times even deeply. For example, if we are at a party and attending to one speech stream and ignoring another, we may suddenly become aware of the unattended one when our name or something else of interest to us is mentioned. [241, 242]

Ways of Thinking

(13) We each possess *ways of thinking* and organizing our thoughts, called by memory researchers *cognitive mechanisms* or "mental modules." Each of these ways of thinking can process information simultaneously and in parallel, although each of these ways may also process the same information differently. [241] For example, if you are hungry and see some food sitting in a dangerous place, a part of your mind may tell you to go for the food. At the same time, another part of your mind is concerned about safety and may tell you to avoid the danger, which brings about an approach-avoidance conflict. [241, 242] Approach-avoidance conflicts are common experiences in the life of a child or adult who is mistreated or abused in a dysfunctional environment.

(14) These ways of thinking or cognitive mechanisms may also *divide automatically*, as when we drive a car at the same time that we are talking to a passenger. Another example is a person whose "dividing mechanism" is out of sync, saying "I'm not angry!" in an angry voice and posture. [241] This kind of dividing is one example of what clinicians call *dissociation*.

Internal Conflict

(15) An *internal conflict*, whether similar to or different from either of the two examples above, may also affect our memory of an experience. For example, a child may be conflicted over the pain of being mistreated or abused by a parent, while at the same time needing to be dependent on and nurtured by the parent. To cope with and handle it, the child may shut the conflict and its associated pain out of its conscious awareness,

which may manifest in several ways, including feeling numb and even forgetting about the experience of the abuse. The conflict is then buried and unresolved. The child is left wounded and with a decreased awareness and sense of self, and thus with a lower self-esteem. Memory researcher Jennifer Freyd calls this dynamic the *betrayal trauma* theory, which explains the conflict of the two realities: that of abuse and that of the need for nurturing from a caregiver.[241, 242]

Other factors may be at play in such a conflict, for example:

- Demands from the abuser (e.g., "This didn't happen," "This is our little secret," or "Something bad will happen if you tell";[202, 241, 629]
- Alternate realities occurring (e.g., abuse that occurs later at night, while the family may look "normal" during the day);[241, 641, 680]
- Isolation during the abuse experience, with no sharing or validation of it with anyone;[202, 241]
- A young age at the onset of and/or during the abuse (their reality being usually defined by older people, plus a lack of integrative functions that occur in an immature nervous system)[241, 242]; and
- Others shame and invalidate the child or adult (e.g., "What's wrong with you?" and "You're the problem in this family").[687, 691]

Any one or a combination of these factors may contribute to and aggravate the *conflict* that develops within the person's conscious and unconscious mind. To survive, it may thus be easier to try to separate or distance oneself from the painful experience—including to partially or completely forget it. Jennifer Freyd expands on these dynamics of traumatic forgetting in her betrayal-trauma theory:

> Betrayal-trauma theory suggests that psychogenic amnesia is an adaptive response to childhood abuse. When a parent or other powerful figure violates a fundamental ethic of human relationship, victims may need to remain unaware of the trauma not to reduce suffering but rather to promote survival. Amnesia enables the child to maintain an attachment with a figure vital to survival, development, and thriving. Analysis of evolutionary pressures, mental modules, social cognitions, and developmental needs suggests that the degree to which the most fundamental human ethics are violated can influence the nature, form, processes, and responses to trauma.[241, 242]

Conscious Efforts to Remember

(16) Also helping us remember an experience is whether the person is making a *conscious effort to remember and heal* by using some kind of

recovery aid, such as group or individual psychotherapy, or a combination of such aids in a program that is safe, supportive and validating of their experience and that nurtures their personal growth.[149, 151, 326, 430, 447, 687, 689, 691, 692] This is an important factor in strengthening the ability of abuse survivors to speak about their experience.

Sorting Out These Factors in a Memory

All of the above are factors that may influence the process of remembering one or more of our experiences. Knowing about these 16 factors can be useful in sorting out—i.e., evaluating and explaining—how the memory of a traumatic experience can be either inhibited and blocked or promoted and reinforced, as shown in Table 3.1.

Inhibiting and Blocking a Memory

As an example, if the child or adult's experience of an event is painful and they try to express their pain — including their associated wants and needs — in an unsafe environment and they are then invalidated, they will tend to have a harder time processing the traumatic experience than were they able to express their pain. But in such an experience and environment there would likely also be several additional factors that may tend to inhibit or block their later access to their memory. Related to the abuse, their awareness may be decreased and their ability to focus clouded, and their internal processing mechanisms may be so undeveloped, confused and conflicted that they end up feeling overwhelmed.

If the person who is abusing them is an important person in their life, such as a parent or parent figure (e.g., an older sibling, a teacher or a clergy member), they may be so confused, yet so dependent upon the person for caregiving and nurturing, that *to survive* they process the components of their inner and outer life experience by inhibiting their memory of the traumatic effects. At the same time, in a strange way, the child or adult may even idealize the abuser, who instead of acting in the child's best interest, has betrayed them.[241, 242, 687, 691]

Promoting and Reinforcing a Memory

By contrast, if the person expresses their experience in a *safe* environment, and if that experience is *validated*, they will likely be more able to process and remember it. If other factors are favorable, such as whether it is useful to remember the experience, if they have memories of similar or associated experiences, and they have awareness and expression of more than one component of their inner life, then it's more likely that the memory will be encoded and stored in their *conscious* awareness.

In addition, if they are able to focus their awareness on the experience, without overwhelming internal conflicts, if the experience was meaningful, and if they are able to process all of this with conscious awareness, then the likelihood of remembering the event will be even higher.

Often, though, abuse survivors remember only fragments of the experience, and/or are unaware that they were abused. Sooner or later they will need to have a safe environment in which to talk about their experiences. In that safe environment when they make a conscious effort to remember what happened, such as occurs in a program of recovery, they will likely be able to remember more accurately.

4

WOUNDING AND MEMORY

Child abuse is the single most common cause of mental illness.

W e can now go deeper into how mistreatment and abuse may negatively influence the process of memory. Growing up in a troubled, unhealthy or dysfunctional family and society, a person may be so stressed, mistreated or abused that their Real Self becomes wounded.* This wounding comes about in a sequence of events that, while different in its details for each person, is similar as a process. I describe some of these similarities as follows.

How the True Self Gets Wounded

Like most psychological wounding, this process is largely unconscious. The following summary is derived from several sources, including object relations psychology, self psychology, and the recovery literature.[122a, 245, 437, 687-689, 691, 706a] These dynamics are an integral part of trauma psychology.

---

* Other terms for the *Real Self* include *True Self,* our *True Identity, Existential Self, Heart, Soul,* and *Child Within.*[345, 437, 687-689, 691] This is opposed to the *false self,* also called the *ego* or co-dependent self, which is an assistant or kind of "sidekick" to the True Self that can help us negotiate our family and our world. (I use the term ego here in a more simple and expanded way from its conventional understandings, wherein it was previously viewed, perhaps with some confusion, as both True Self and false self.)

31

Wounding

1. Previously wounded themselves, the child's parents feel inadequate, bad and unfulfilled.

2. They project those charged feelings onto others, especially onto their spouse and their vulnerable children. They may also exhibit and project grandiosity (e.g., "I always know what's best for you!"—when they don't). They look outside of themselves to feel whole.

3. In a need to stabilize the parents and to survive, the child denies that the parents are inadequate and mistreating. With the unhealthy boundaries that it has learned from its parents and others, the child internalizes (takes in, introjects, accepts) the parents' projected inadequacy and shame. A common fantasy is that, "If I'm really good and perfect, they will love me and they won't reject or abandon me." The child idealizes the parents.

This dynamic of the child idealizing the parents can be illustrated in the following case history, as told by Chuck, who was a 48-year-old health-care professional.

> I've felt empty and sad for as long as I can remember, but I never really knew that I had been abused. I tried individual psychotherapy for a few months and a self-help group for nine months at age 32, which resulted in my beginning to awaken to some of my feelings and potential. It was not until age 42, after attending several Adult Children of Dysfunctional Families meetings, that although I didn't want to and even resisted, I began to remember having been mentally and emotionally abused as a child. The memories didn't come back suddenly or all at once, but trickled into my awareness, little by little over several years.
>
> During that time I found a birthday card that I had made at age eight for my father: I had written "You are Superman, You're so super," and I drew a color picture in crayons of Superman . . . which I gradually realized was a clue to my having idealized him, even though he was almost never there for me as a father. And when he was there, he often abused me. The abuse was often subtle to me, and included especially teasing, shaming, threatening and making vague demands. My father was a rageaholic and compulsive gambler and my mother was a meddler and controller. Looking back, I can see that both of them were wounded too. After so many years of trying all kinds of self-improvement techniques, it was only after I began to remember having been abused that I began to focus on what and how I could heal that old poisonous stuff inside that I'd been carrying around all of these years.

4. The child's vulnerable True Self is wounded so often, that to protect that self it defensively submerges ("splits off") deep within the unconscious part of its psyche. *The child goes into hiding* (Figure 4.1).

The "Child in hiding" represents what may appear at first to be a way that helps us to survive. Its down side is that going into hiding and staying there keeps us alienated from the power of knowing and being our True Self.

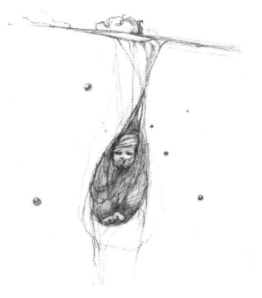

Suzette Billedeaux

Figure 4.1. The Child Goes into Hiding

By our True Self going into hiding we become alienated from our present experience in a number of ways—and from our past experiences by traumatically forgetting much of what actually happened to us. We become alienated from our internal experience—which includes our emotional responses to abuse of fear, shame, grief and anger. We also become alienated from our perception of what is occurring externally with others: "Daddy's not drunk. He was so tired he fell asleep on the lawn."

The establishment of the false self in these ways includes some aspects of traumatic forgetting that are accompanied by the behaviors and responses that allow us to stabilize the family and avoid abuse. Denial is often part of traumatic forgetting and is primarily a cognitive and emotional screen which reinterprets reality and substitutes a false reality according to the demands of the abuser(s) and emotional and physical survival.[202] As a type of traumatic memory distortion it characteristically involves a censoring of some aspects of experience, such as the emotional pain of the abuse, but it also may involve the forgetting of some experiences, or the substitution of an idealized past for the truth.[156] I discuss denial further in Chapters 10, 12 and 16.

When the True Self is in hiding—which it does to try *to survive* an otherwise unbearable life experience—it is unable to encode its impactful memories in a conscious and currently useful way. Yet, paradoxically it somehow stores these memories in its unconscious mind as "old tapes," unfinished business, stored painful energy or ungrieved grief, much of which the object relations psychologists call "object representations."[706a]

5. When we are not allowed to express our grief in a healthy way, our True Self will try to find its own way out and express its painful experiences, like an enclosed abscess that is waiting to drain. But without expressing our pain, this stored, toxic energy may then manifest in our life as a physical, mental, emotional or spiritual disorder, or more usually as a combination of these. Another term for this repeated attempt to express its trauma and grief is *repetition compulsion.*

6. The True Self takes in whatever else it is told — both verbally and nonverbally — about itself and about others, and stores it in its unconscious (mostly) and its conscious mind (sometimes and to some degree).

7. What it takes in are messages from major and impactful relationships, primarily parents, but these may include siblings, grandparents, clergy members, and other authority and parent figures. The experiential representations of these relationships in our unconscious memory that continue to affect us are called "objects" or "object representations" by the object relations theorists. These messages and representations are laden with feelings, and tend to occur in "part-objects" (e.g., good parent, bad parent, aggressive child, shy child and so on). The more self-destructive messages tend to be deposited in the false self. This has also been termed the "internal saboteur" by object relations theorists and is also described as the internalized or introjected, rejecting or otherwise mistreating parent.[706a]

8. Hurting, confused, and feeling unable to run our own life, we eventually turn that function over to our false self.

9. A tension builds. The True Self is always striving to come alive and to evolve. At the same time, the "negative ego" (the destructive part of the false self) attacks the True Self, thus forcing it to stay submerged, keeping self-esteem low. Also, the child's grieving of its losses and traumas is not supported. Because of all of the above, the child's development is disordered and its boundaries become unhealthy. This resulting "psychopathology" or "lesion" has been called a "schizoid compromise" (Guntrip), "multiplicity of repressed egos" (Fairbairn), and a "splitting off of the true self" (Winnicott). The outcome can be a developmental delay, arrest or failure.[706a]

10. Some results include traumatic forgetting, chronic emptiness, fear, sadness and confusion, and often periodic explosions of self-destructive and other destructive behavior—both impulsive and compulsive—that allow some release of the tension and a glimpse of the True Self.

11. The consequences of the continued emptiness and/or repeated destructive behavior keep the True Self stifled or submerged. Not living from and as their Real Self—with a full awareness of their experiences—and with no safe people to talk to about them, often dissociated and numb, in order to survive they traumatically forget, repress or otherwise shut out most of their painful experiences. The person maintains a low sense of self-esteem, remains unhappy, yet wishes and seeks fulfillment. Compulsions and addictions (repetition compulsions) can provide temporary fulfillment, but lead to more suffering and, ultimately, block fulfillment and serenity.

Recovery

12. Recovery and growth are discovering and gently unearthing the True Self (Child Within) so that it can exist and express itself in a healthy way, day to day (Figure 4.1). It also means restructuring the false self or ego to become a more flexible assistant ("positive ego") to the True Self. Some other results: aliveness, creativity and growth.

13. Such self-discovery and recovery are usually best accomplished gradually and in the presence of safe, compassionate, skilled and supportive people. Recovery is a cyclical process, and while it has its moments of joy and liberating self-discovery, it is also common to experience periods in which confusion, symptoms and suffering intensify. Participation in supportive recovery groups teaches us how to deal with

these cycles as we experience how others deal with their emotions and symptoms and with their joy, growth and accomplishments in the recovery process. With commitment to and active participation in recovery, this healing process may take from three to five years or more.[687-689, 691]

14. By listening, sharing and reflecting in a safe environment, we begin to remember what happened. We begin to reconstruct the fragments of our memory that were previously buried deep within our unconscious mind. This crucial and healing kind of remembering involves a process that evolves slowly over time.[326, 691]

Internal and External Influences

Given the above dynamics in the process of wounding that may result in traumatic forgetting, we can now look at some of the influences on some of the components of remembering that I described in Chapter 2 and 3, and begin to differentiate those that are either *inside* or *outside* of the experiencer. These components include the event itself, our attention to and awareness of it, and our experience of the event. Other components include encoding and storage, rehearsal, retrieval and expression. Finally, there is the effect of psychoactive chemicals on our ability to remember an experience. As shown in Table 4.1, each of these may be influenced by factors or dynamics that are either internal or external in origin. And each may influence us to remember better or worse, more accurately or less accurately. The memory process is complex, and each of these and other factors may impinge on our ability to remember or not remember our ordinary experiences and our traumatic ones, and each may be important in the process of wounding and healing.

Recovery and Development

In recovery we also get a second chance to remember what happened and to retrace and complete the developmental tasks that we never got to finish before. We also learn that *no one else* any longer *determines our destiny*. Rather, by our own motivation and by setting healthy boundaries, *we* create it. By choosing recovery and risking to be real, we set the healthy boundaries that say, "I am in charge of my recovery and my life, and no one else on this Earth is."

Part of that claiming of our personal power may include, if we choose, letting go of our perhaps rigid and unhealthy boundaries or walls, and

Table 4.1. Internal and External Influences upon some Components in the Process of Remembering

INFLUENCES

Components	Internal	External
Event	Effect on the experiencer; Prior knowledge and experience	Kind & intensity of event; Triggers and reminders of prior knowledge and experience
Attention & Awareness	Focus on both as appropriate, i.e., how the experiencer is aware and focused	
Experience	Degree of awareness of self and inner life; Degree of emotional and physiological arousal	Hearing others' stories or suggestions; Degree of meaning, nourishment or toxicity
Encoding	All of the above and below, plus feeling safe to know and express the experience	Sense of safety versus bribes, threats or manipulations
Rehearsal	Above, plus ability to express, elaborate and process the experience	Degree of safety and validation
Retrieval	All of the above and below, plus needing to explore and express, and feeling safe to remember, know and express the experience	Certain and repeated questions
Expression	Above, plus meaning, wants, needs and feeling validated	Degree of safety and validation
Psychoactive Chemicals and other factors	*Norepinephrine* increases long-term memory (unless level very high); *Oxytocin* and *endorphins* tend to decrease it: *Corticosteroids* may decrease ordinary memory	*Alcohol* and *benzodiazepines* decrease long-term memory; *cannabis* decreases short-term memory; *Electroshock therapy* decreases all memory, as may *hypnosis*

letting in selected safe and supportive others to assist us in our recovery. These may include any one or more of a number of people in our life, such as a best friend, therapist, therapy group, self-help group, sponsor or any other safe and supportive person that we may choose. And it may also include our Higher Power.

Setting and maintaining healthy boundaries thus protects and maintains the integrity and well-being of our True Self in a healthy cycle of recovery and living, since it is the True Self that by its own internal resources sets the boundaries, which then allows it to stay out of hiding,

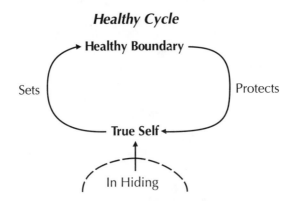

Figure 4.2. The Protective and Nourishing Cycle of Self-Generated Boundaries, which allow the True Self (Child Within) to come out of hiding and eventually stay out.

as shown in Figure 4.2. When we come out of hiding, in a safe environment, we can then begin to remember more and more of what happened.[691]

This process of recovery is not easy, especially as our awareness of our wounds increases. It takes courage, patience with the ups and downs that are normal to the process, persistence, and a dedication to healing our True Self, over a long period of time. While learning to set healthy boundaries and limits is crucial in this process, so is learning both cognitively and experientially about what happened.

5

THE FORGOTTEN DIFFERENCE:

Do you remember how many 1's and One's are printed on a dollar bill? If you cannot, does it prove that you have never seen, handled or spent one? This simple question is about ordinary memory. Traumatic memory is far deeper and much more complex.[518a]

Ordinary Memory versus Traumatic Memory

One of the claims of the "false memory syndrome" advocates is that "Experiments and studies on memory show that false memories are easily implanted, even in normal people." What they do not mention or discuss is that there are important differences between ordinary and traumatic memory. In their attempts to disprove the prevalence and validity of traumatic forgetting, they portray them as the same. Their reasoning goes: since all memory is the same, and since one can "implant" a "forgotten" but false ordinary memory into up to one in five ordinary people like college students for an unknown amount of time, then that must also apply to all who remember past traumatic experiences after they have forgotten them for a long time. This reasoning is similar to: since apples and oranges are both fruits, then all apples must look and taste like oranges.

Most of the FMS advocates are not clinicians who work frequently and long-term with trauma victims. Those few who do appear not to have a full awareness of the dimensions and natural history of trauma. While they may have a few similarities, traumatic memory and ordinary memory are quite different. Traumatic forgetting and remembering are more complex than the simple studies, mostly on ordinary memory, that are used by FMS advocates.

Ordinary Memory

While there are numerous studies on and descriptions of ordinary memory,[7, 20, 28, 484, 289] none begins to demonstrate what happens more simply than a classical study by Hermann Ebbinghaus in 1885 about forgetting nonsense syllables and another more recent one by M.H. Erdelyi and J. Kleinbard about remembering meaningful pictures,[205] as shown in Figures 5.1 and 5.2. These show us that in ordinary memory our retention of the details of an experience drops rapidly over the first hour and then trails off much more slowly over the ensuing hours and days. By contrast, to remember the generalities and the details of a past experience follows a similar pattern in reverse, depending on our needs and motivations to remember them. Other studies have added more details and dynamics, as I described in the previous chapter.[20, 28, 487]

We know that some details of the memory in both ordinary and traumatic memory are often erroneous, but in traumatic forgetting what is most important is the memory of the *essence* of having lived through the traumatic experience — and not remembering all of the details accurately.[641, 693] For these and other reasons it is important to differentiate ordinary memory from traumatic memory, both within and outside of this debate about memory.

Ordinary vs. Traumatic Forgetting and Remembering

Other Terms

In the literature, ordinary memory has been called by other names, such as narrative memory, explicit (simple, clear, uncomplicated) memory and declarative (evident, manifest) memory. By contrast, traumatic memory has been called somatosensory memory, implicit (entangled or entwined) memory and iconic (symbolic, imagic, representational) memory,[662] as I summarize in Table 5.1.

Ease of Recall

Important ordinary memory tends to be easier to remember and understand than traumatic memory. This characteristic is illustrated in part by the findings in seven studies showing that from 16 to 64 percent of traumatized people could not remember their traumatic experience for a long time after it happened[84, 102, 115, 329, 417, 552, 699, 700] (described later in Chapter

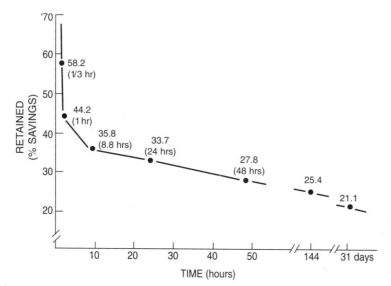

Figure 5.1. Ebbinghaus's Curve of Forgetting
(from Ebbinghaus [1885] 1964).

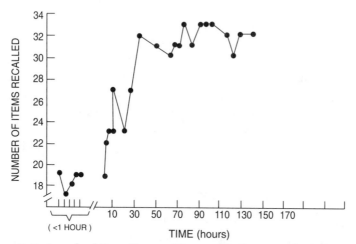

Figure 5.2. Level of Recall over Time with Repeated Testing
(Erdelyi and Kleinbard 1978, study 1).

8 on page 69). During traumatic experiences the person's awareness of internal and external reality tends to be confused, and they tend to have frequent personal boundary distortions, whereas these tend to be easier to sort out and differentiate in ordinary memory. The following history illustrates this aspect of traumatic memory.

> Jack was a 35-year-old businessman who had been physically, mentally and emotionally abused by his parents and older brother as a child. Over the past three years he has begun to remember episodes of his experiences of the abuse, although early in his process of remembering he had difficulty telling his own experiences from those of several of his family members. As he expressed his memories and pain, he had great difficulty differentiating his own pain from that which he presumed that his family members experienced. But over the course of the three years in group therapy and individual therapy he began to live from and as his true self. Learning to set healthy boundaries and limits, he was more able to own his memories and pain and keep others' pain separate from his experience.

While traumatic forgetting may occur in from 16 to 64 percent of people who experience child sexual abuse, by contrast, sometimes it is so hard to forget that the traumatic memories intrude involuntarily and repeatedly.[326]

Consciousness and Time

Ordinary memory tends to be more conscious, voluntary and flexible, while traumatic memory is usually more involuntary and unconscious, and it is often rigid. Ordinary memory tends to be more oriented in time, whereas traumatic memory is usually frozen outside of time in a kind of space that has been described as "primary process" or coming more from our unconscious mind. And even while it is frozen in time, when it surfaces unconsciously or when we consciously remember it we feel like it is happening right now, at this very moment, as opposed to having happened in the past.

Identity and Social Function

Because of the effects of trauma, especially the often overwhelming emotional pain, our True Self "goes into hiding" deep within the unconscious part of our psyche. This leaves the false self to try to run our life, as I described in the previous chapter. In traumatic memory we thus

Table 5.1. Some Differences Between Ordinary and Traumatic Memory

Characteristic	Ordinary Memory	Traumatic Memory
Other Terms to describe	Narrative, Explicit (simple, clear, uncomplicated), Declarative (evident, manifest, factual)	Somatosensory, Implicit (entangled, entwined), Iconic (symbolic, imagic, representational)
Ease of Recall	Easier	Frequently (at least 16 to 64%) more difficult
Internal and External Reality	Easier to differentiate	Confused, with frequent boundary distortions
Conscious and Voluntary	Yes	Usually Not
Flexibility	Yes	May be rigid
Relationship to Time	Yes	Usually frozen outside of time in a primary process space, yet often experienced as now
Identity	True or false self	False self runs life
Social Function	Yes; shared, etc.	Solitary, autistic*
Process	Shared, associated, assimilated & integrated	Intrusive and disruptive, dissociated, often forgotten
Feelings involved	Joyful or painful	Painful
Ease of Understanding	Easier	Non-verbal, often repeated somatized
State Dependent Learning	Sometimes to often	Usual
Evoked by Triggers	Often	More often, usual
Core Issues	Any	All-or-none, control, trust; shame, fear
Possibilities and Choices	Many to unlimited	All-or-none

* By *telling our story* of the trauma(s) and working through the associated pain, i.e., *grieving*, we can slowly transfer and transform our traumatic memory into a healthier kind of ordinary memory—something that we were not allowed to do before. This is one of the goals of memory work and recovery.

often experience a great confusion of identity—which contributes to even more dissonance, dissociation (separation) and isolation from the components of our inner life, which ordinarily should be integrated. By contrast, in ordinary memory we tend to live from either our True Self or our false self or a combination of the two.[693]

We use ordinary memory as an important part of our individual and social functioning. With it we tend to associate, share, assimilate and integrate the components of our inner life experience. But by the toxic nature of most unhealed trauma, the painful memory is dissociated and often forgotten, only later to intrude upon and disrupt our everyday life. "Autistic" and unable to tell safe people our experience of the trauma, and thereby not able to work through its pain, we are thus blocked from being able to grieve and heal around the trauma's painful effects.[326, 662]

Ease of Understanding and Feelings

But by telling our story of the trauma(s) and working through the associated pain, i.e., by grieving it, we can slowly transfer and transform our traumatic memory into a healthier kind of ordinary memory — something that we were not allowed to do before.[598] This process and transformation is one of the goals of memory work and the recovery process.

A serious part of the trauma of abuse usually includes invalidation of our pain by the perpetrator.[202] When our pain is invalidated and we are not allowed to express our experience of it, it will be retained within our unconscious mind and body, often reappearing as part of a repetition compulsion and painful emotional and somatic symptoms. In ordinary memory we are usually allowed to express our experience and are not invalidated, and can thus complete our psychological business around it.

In traumatic memory the associated feelings are mostly painful, whereas in ordinary memory they may be painful and/or joyful. We can explore this observation further by the concept of state-dependent learning.

State-Dependent Learning and Memory

Much of what we know about state-dependent learning applies to both ordinary and traumatic memory. We tend to remember better when we are in the same inner or experiential state that we were in when we first experienced or learned something. Rossi said "Sensation and perception are integrated with memory and learning in the limbic hypothalamic system . . .".[558a] While the "state" may mean any one or a combination of the components of our inner life, it most often refers to the kind and intensity of our feelings or emotions. Therefore, learning and remembering are dependent on our "state" at the time of the experience. If our internal state is different in the present from what it was during the original experience, then we may have difficulty remembering the experience or event.

Bower gives a dramatic example of state-dependent learning and memory.

> Sirhan Sirhan, who killed Bobby Kennedy in 1968, had absolutely no recollection of killing him. He murdered Kennedy in a highly agitated state, and under hypnosis, as Sirhan became more worked up and excited, he remembered progressively more, with the memories tumbling out while his excitement built to a crescendo leading up to the shooting. But in his ordinary waking state of consciousness he was amnestic of the experience.[68]

Both *victims* of trauma and their *perpetrators* may have state-dependent memory as a factor involved as part of their forgetting. Their memories acquired in one neuro-psycho-physiological state are accessible mainly in that state, but they are dissociated and less available for recall in an alternate state.[69, 70] It is as though the two states constitute different libraries into which a person places the material of their memory, and a given memory can be retrieved only by returning to that library or psychological state, in which the event was first stored.[68] The following case history also illustrates state-dependence.

> One week after prolonged and complicated surgery, Jackie urinated in her bed after struggling to call for help from the nurses. The feeling of the warmth of her urine on her body triggered a sense of panic. She suddenly felt like a small child again, and had great fear that her mother was going to come in and beat her. She then had a sequence of memory fragments of being physically abused as a child by her mother for many reasons, including having wet her bed. She had always struggled with low self-esteem and knew she had been hit as a child, but had never known or understood the severity of her abuse experiences until now.

In ordinary memory, state-dependence is often an important factor, but in traumatic amnesia, state-dependence is usual. This is why in simple interviewing and regular "talk therapy" the survivor and the perpetrator may not be able to remember their traumatic experiences or the events of abuse. For the perpetrator the act of abusing another may be a re-enactment of earlier trauma, partly or totally forgotten as soon as the state changes once again. Experiential therapies, which can assist a person to get into different states of consciousness, may be more helpful in the process of remembering and healing than talking alone.[680a] State-dependence also demonstrates why symptoms and mental disorders, which are often emotional and somatic memories of the original state, are indicative of abuse and often accompany the remembrance of trauma.

From these and several other studies we can see the importance of state-dependent learning on ordinary memory — and especially on traumatic memory.[68, 321, 559, 681]

Evoked by Triggers

In state-dependent memory, getting back into the original state can appear to be a catalyst to recalling an otherwise forgotten event or experience. But what kinds of triggers might help get us into our original state? Certain input into any one or more of our classical five senses may do so, including sights, sounds, tastes, smells and touches.[146, 326, 662-664] A sixth sense, whether we call it intuition, a hunch or a gut reaction, may also play a role in triggering our memory of an experience, as may a seventh sense — the kinesthetic or physical posture and positioning.[641]

This input may include any one or more of the following triggers or cues:

- Hearing another's story or observing another's struggle and recovery[688]
- Seeing a media presentation[688]
- Reading recovery oriented literature[688, 693]
- A certain taste, odor or smell[662-664]
- Being touched a certain way[229, 326, 384]
- Being in a safe relationship[641]
- Being in an intimate relationship[146, 688]
- Normal developmental milestones and events[146]
- Seeing a certain image or scene[641]
- Working a recovery program[465, 691, 692]

While ordinary memory is often evoked by triggers, traumatic memory is more often induced by these kinds of triggering experiences. One of the claims of the "false memory" advocates is that any outside experience, such as recovery books, TV programs, therapist suggestions and recovery groups, may bias or unduly influence a person's memories, and that unless they always remembered an experience without any such outside interactions, their memory is not valid.* But our knowledge of the experience of recovery and the process of healing tells us otherwise. Because traumatic forgetting is so common, insidious and complex, the amnestic survivor—once in a safe environment—usually needs the exposure to a variety of focuses to remember their traumatic experience. Remembering and accurately naming what happened is a crucial part of the healing process.[326, 688, 691] We cannot grieve and then let go of that which we have not firstly accurately named. The following history is an example.

> Jen was a 58-year-old divorced attorney and mother of three. She had a history of repeated bouts of back pain and eventually became chemically dependent on painkillers (opiates) and Valium. She suffered with back pain and chemical dependence for four more years, until she started her recovery. She also fit the American Psychiatric Association's Diagnostic and Statistical Manual (DSM) criteria for the diagnosis of post-traumatic stress disorder (PTSD). After abstaining from drugs for a few months in a Twelve-Step recovery program, she began working in a therapy group on her problems and issues from growing up in a dysfunctional family.
>
> After working for six months in group therapy, she remembered a traumatic event: 30 years ago she had found her husband in their bed with a family friend. Until now she had forgotten the experience since a few days after the event. Hearing a remark her daughter made about when the friend had visited the family over a holiday had triggered the beginning of the memory. Over the next year she used the memory to identify and grieve the pain of the original trauma, and to identify several other traumas. During this time her chronic back pain gradually lessened in its intensity and frequency.

Core Issues

An issue is any conflict, concern or potential problem, whether conscious or unconscious, that is incomplete for us—or needs action or change. A core issue is one that comes up repeatedly for many of us.[689, 691]

---

* Even if the abuse survivor always remembered the abusive experience, "false memory" advocates still tend to understand and demand only externally corroborating evidence, and do not usually understand or accept internal corroborating evidence —the After effects of the abuse,[694] as I describe in Chapter 15.

There are at least 15 core issues. These include:

- Control
- Trust
- Being real
- Feelings
- Low self-esteem
- Dependence

- Fear of abandonment
- All-or-none thinking and behaving
- High tolerance for inappropriate behavior
- Over-responsibility for others
- Neglecting one's own needs
- Grieving ungrieved losses
- Difficulty resolving conflict, giving love and receiving love

These core issues tend to emerge especially from several areas of our recovery and life: 1) *Relationships*—of any kind—with others, self and our Higher Power, 2) Doing *experiential recovery work*—throughout our healing, 3) *Feedback* given by our therapy group members, therapists, sponsors, friends and others, and 4) *Insight* from reading, listening, reflecting upon or working through conflict. Core issues can assist us in describing and framing some of the origins and dynamics of such concepts as our problems in living, day-to-day conflicts, "character defects" and our struggle with our attachment to our ego or false self.[688]

While any core issue may be associated with either kind of memory, certain ones tend to come up often in our memories of traumatic experiences. These include all-or-none thinking and behaving, needing to be in control, difficulty trusting, and the feelings of shame, fear and anger. The following case history illustrates some of these.

> Connie had just returned from seeing her critically ill mother in another town. For three days she had watched and interacted with her mother who was in a private room in the intensive care unit. Despite being heavily medicated, her mother was manipulating Connie and her brother at every visit. Although both Connie and her brother were in their 50s, they still felt the same feelings coming up as they did as children being raised by a chemically dependent, manipulative and hypochondriacal mother. They compared their feelings, and both validated each other's fear, anger and guilt.
>
> When Connie returned home she quickly realized that something was wrong when she became aware that she no longer trusted her fiancé. She watched herself pulling away and starting to create story lines of mistrust. A few days later she realized that in replaying her childhood trauma (mother helpless and drugged in a hospital, giving her a strong feeling of being abandoned once again), many of her core issues, including difficulty trusting, had returned.

Possibilities and Choices

We know that having the ability to anticipate possibilities and to make healthy choices as we live our life provides us with an advantage. In ordinary memory we tend to have these abilities, but in traumatic memory we tend to be frozen in an all-or-none stance. Our dilemma is that if we remember our painful experience without having the safety and support that we need to heal it, we will likely feel overwhelmed. It is often safer for us to dissociate from it and feel numb.[326, 641]

It is thus important for us to transform the experiential contents of our traumatic memory into that of ordinary memory, giving us the opportunity to see more possibilities and make healthier choices in our life.

Conclusion

From this introduction to some of the differences between these two kinds of memory, we can see that traumatic memory is far more insidious and complex than is ordinary memory. Traumatic memory is also commonly associated with post-traumatic stress disorder. Traumatic forgetting   constitutes several of its diagnostic criteria,[11] as I describe in Chapter 22 on pages 232-235. Some symptoms of PTSD represent the recurrent re-experiencing of dissociated states that accompanied the original trauma, as well as the avoidance of stimuli that could act as triggers.

Researchers are able to manipulate normal memory and implant false details into the minds of ordinary people under the non-traumatic conditions of simple laboratory experiments, such as having them view pictures of traffic accidents or hear close relatives repeatedly falsify stories of their becoming separated from their parents in a shopping mall.[417] However, it is hard to imagine that many thousands of therapists are implanting powerfully traumatic, state-dependent memories — with their accompanying painful symptoms — into hundreds of thousands of their patients or clients. Except under the circumstance of extremely abusive and inappropriate behavior by a helping professional, such as the forceful seduction of a patient long term,[604] or in other unusual circumstances,[390] they cannot induce PTSD into them.

In future research on traumatic memories, including a clinician with expertise in the long-term treatment of trauma survivors will be useful to help assure the clinical accuracy and credibility of the research project.

FMS advocates have made several other claims in their effort to defend themselves and others against appropriately examining their own past and present actions. I will discuss each of these claims in some detail in the following chapters.

6

Child abuse has been the most "repressed" idea in the history of psychology.

—James Cronin

A BRIEF HISTORY OF CHILD ABUSE

About 50,000 names are etched into the Vietnam War Memorial. If we made a memorial to children who have been sexually abused, it would be more than 1300 times the size of the Vietnam memorial. If we included other forms of child abuse it would be more than 7500 times its size. But these are not lives lost in military combat. These are souls lost in a betrayal and wounding that is so deep that most are unable to heal and reconnect with self, others and God without long-term recovery.

FMS advocates are not the only ones who have not fully been aware of the natural history of child abuse. Over the years there have been many. But with the integrity, courage and creativity of countless survivors and many helping professionals, we have made progress in the areas of prevention and recovery from child abuse, as I outline in Table 6.1 on page 53. The current backlash is but one of countless guises throughout history that reflect our society's denial and resistance to the reality of child abuse.

For centuries, women and children have been viewed and treated as property, although this was not universally so.[615, 616] Child abuse is a communicable and contagious disorder that has spread throughout societies over time. They—and "they" includes you, me, all of us—have been mistreated and abused in every conceivable way.[176] At times, societies have had more compassion for animals, as the Society for Prevention of Cruelty to Animals preceded the Society for Prevention of Cruelty to Children by several years (Table 6.1).[536a]

Historian Lloyd deMause has studied childhood and society for over 20 years, and points out that the history of humanity is founded upon the abuse of children.[176] He says:

> Psychohistorical study of the history of childhood has provided extensive evidence that childhood in the past was routinely filled with terror, neglect and abuse — both physical and emotional. Adequate parenting is a late historical achievement, and most countries in the world continue to severely abuse most children even today. Even in America, about half of all children are sexually molested, and the rates are even higher in non-Western nations. The traumatic effects of this widespread abuse is the source of the periodic wars and social violence that have been the hallmark of mankind until now.[176]

Child abuse has been our most powerful and successful ritual and secret, and deMause says that eradicating it is our most important social task today.[176]

While we can trace child abuse back to The Bible,[109] there has been horrendous abuse committed in nearly all times throughout our history.[65a, 500] Child sale and slavery for sexual purposes was common in Greek, Roman and other societies, and Stannard described the same phenomenon in later European societies.[615] Here I will focus on our progress and resistance over the past 100 years.

A Pivotal Denial

One of the most pivotal conflicts around denial of the truth in the history of child abuse happened at the end of the 19th century, when Sigmund Freud retracted his belief of the seduction-trauma theory. In the 1890s he had seen 18 adult patients (6 men and 12 women) who came to him with hysteria, and discovered that not only did they all have a history of having been sexually abused as children by their parents or other parent figures, but that when he listened to them and validated their experience, they improved.* His predecessors and colleagues had treated such kinds of histories as though the patients were making them up—as a fantasy—and they were so shocked at hearing Freud's findings that they threatened and shamed him not to publish them.** [187, 189, 237, 327, 435, 568]

Table 6.1 Landmarks in Child Abuse Prevention and Recovery

For	Against
1866 Society for Prevention of Cruelty to Animals founded	Children seen and treated as property for centuries
1874 Society for Prevention of Cruelty to Children founded	Religious fundamentalism comes and goes, but is always a factor
1896 Freud and Janet believe their patients' histories of abuse and they improve ("seduction-trauma theory")	**1897** Freud's retraction of this theory due to external & his own internal intrapsychic pressure: "They made up the abuse." Since then most psychoanalysts have not believed their patients' histories of abuse.
1940's Early descriptions of the grieving process and of post-traumatic stress disorder.	
1946 Caffey reports x-ray film findings of physical trauma inflicted on children	Continued resistance to recognizing much of our pain as "stuck grief" from the trauma.
1951-3 Silverman showed that this trauma was intentional	**20thC** The myth of "The Family" as always ideal and sacrosanct
1962 Kempe et al describe the battered-child syndrome	Resistance to these reports of trauma and laws against child abuse has been ongoing, and persists in numerous groups and individuals even today.
1973 Laws against child abuse enacted	
1977 First ACoA meetings	**1977 to present** – psychiatry, and to some extent other mental health professions, regress into a biological model to explain and treat human suffering.
1977-81 Information on Freud's retraction made public by several analysts	
1978 Alice Miller begins demystifying mental & emotional child abuse. Numerous books follow & expand this demystification.	**1981** Backlash against the messengers of the information. However, this time many of the public and helping professionals found out.
1983 Recovery movement expands. Many helping professionals enter their own program of recovery.	**1984** Victims of Child Abuse Laws (VOCAL) formed
1985 Increasing organizations (eg APSAC), information and education.	**1989** Anti-Recovery Movement backlash increases
1994 American Coalition for Abuse Awareness	**1992** FMS Foundation begins; media focuses here more than on real memories and recovery

But Freud did publish his findings as "The Aetiology of Hysteria," in which he said, ". . . at the bottom of every case of hysteria there are one or more occurrences of premature sexual experience, occurrences which belong to the earliest years of childhood . . . Children cannot find their way to acts of sexual aggression unless they have been seduced previously. The foundation for a neurosis would accordingly always be laid in childhood by adults. . . ." While he did not here address other forms of abuse, he addressed this sexual abuse of children by adults by concluding that ". . . we cure them of their hysteria by transforming their unconscious memories of the infantile scenes into conscious ones. . . . hysterical symptoms are derivatives of memories which are operating unconsciously." [237]

Freud and his colleagues Pierre Janet and Josef Breuer spoke early of the existence and importance of unconscious memories causing neurological and psychological symptoms and signs in many of their patients. Freud found that by carefully listening to his patients' stories and validating their experience, they improved. What would our collective state of mental health have been like if this message had not been taken hold of and developed by helping professionals and the public until today?

Instead, the opposite happened. Under the influence of pressure from his colleagues, his best friend Wilhelm Fliess, and his own internal conflicts, a year later Freud retracted his belief that the trauma of the abuse caused the symptoms, and substituted the Oedipal theory.*** As he wrote later in "An Autobiographical Study," "I was at last obliged to recognize that these scenes of seduction had never taken place, and that they were only fantasies which my patients had made up." [435] It was almost a century later that several psychoanalysts made all of this information public. [327, 435, 464, 567, 570]

From this early denial of the truth we have suffered the double trauma of the abuse itself and of countless psychoanalysts and other helping professionals treating us as though we were making it all up. "The abuse never took place," said Freud and many thousands of psychoanalytically oriented therapists who followed him, only the "desire for it" on the part of the child. Not only were our experiences invalidated, but they blamed

---

* Hysteria is a psychosomatic illness with neurological and psychological symptoms. It has been essentially replaced today by post-traumatic stress disorder. See Figure 22.2 on page 236.
** Some members of today's backlash are likewise threatening and shaming some therapists and authors who write about trauma psychology.

us for desiring to have sex with our abusers! Although ripples of this toxic legacy continue, over the last 15 years increasing numbers of helping professionals now believe most of their patients' and clients' stories and memories of having been abused. The majority of these abuse survivors who have persisted in their recoveries have shown a successful resolution of their symptoms and signs. A positive factor here is that many of these helping professionals also recognize that they themselves have been abused and are working to heal the effects.

Understanding the Memory

During most of the 20th century we paid little attention to the dynamics and nuances of our memory of the trauma, for several reasons. The psychology of memory was in its infancy for most of this time and has only recently begun reaching a moderate level of sophistication. Even so, there remains a schism between many academics who study ordinary memory in the laboratory and those academics and clinicians who observe and study traumatic memory in long-term psychotherapy and recovery.

The child abuse and recovery movements came into being mostly in the last quarter of this century, and only in the 1980s and 90s have some victims of abuse begun to speak the truth of their painful experiences. Some of these people have asked for financial compensation from their perpetrators—mostly to pay for their treatment—and this has created a major conflict for many of their abusers and co-abusers. To fight the accusations and thus preserve their "honor," some lawyers have teamed with selected memory researchers to help substantiate their denial. While this may be appropriate in a small number of cases, the great majority who assist with this defense appear to be only enabling the abuser's and co-abuser's

---

*** Freud's *theory* of the Oedipus complex—that every child somewhere between ages three and six sexually desires the opposite sex parent—thus makes it easy to blame the child for any incestuous act.[570] Disturbed by his own incestuous desires toward his daughter, his nurse's sexual abuse of him,[174] and by suspicions of his father's own incestuous wishes, Freud expressed enormous relief when he made this devastating change in his thinking and believing.[327] By contrast, De Mause cites evidence that Freud never doubted the "clear memories of incestuous attacks" in his patients. Rather, he says that it was Freud's *infantile* seduction theory that he retracted. Nonetheless, De Mause believes that most psychoanalysts who followed Freud have treated their patients' memories of sexual abuse as though they have made it up.[174] Also, we know today that the term "seduction" in no way conveys the brutality and pain with which children are so often sexually used.[187]

denial. A group that called themselves "VOCAL" (Victims of Child Abuse Laws) began in 1984,[703] and since 1992 the FMS Foundation and its advocates have expanded their claims and appear to be fueling this denial of the truth.[215, 216]

After Freud's retraction of the seduction-trauma theory, with few exceptions—such as psychoanalyst Sandor Ferenczi[221, 435]—we continued to deny the abuse. For most of the 20th century we also maintained the myth of "The Family" as being always ideal, private and sacrosanct, even in the face of the obvious abuse of millions of children and adults[401]. Religious fundamentalism helped us maintain this myth, with its all-or-none thinking and behaving and the frequent projecting of its own shadow stuff onto others—all helping to deny the truth of the abuse.[174, 704] Many fundamentalists often avoid any realistic discussions about healthy sexuality, and discourage bringing out the truth about the sexual abuse of children.[244]

X-Ray Film Findings

It was not until 1946—about halfway through the century—that physicians would dare to report even the most severe abuse, and this came as a *question* more than a realization. Radiologist J. Caffey's medical article described and then asked, "What mysterious happenstance could cause infants to have multiple fractures and chronic blood clots on their brains?"[108] At that time there were few with the courage to confront child abusers, but five years later another radiologist named F. Silverman showed that this trauma was from adults *beating* children, and a decade later, in 1962, he teamed with Kempe and others to write[594] a now classic description of the battered-child syndrome.[375] Why would it take these outrageous x-ray film findings—as examples of *extreme trauma*—for us to even begin to awaken to the reality of child abuse? One reason is that at that time we were so much more unaware of and in denial about the many manifestations of child abuse than we are now.

It took us another ten years to enact laws against child abuse and finally to name it as a crime in 1973. At that time the federal government created a system that eventually interacted with state and local governments to assist the victims and punish and treat the abusers. While we have made some progress in this direction, we have made many mistakes in trying to help the victims and even more mistakes in handling the abusers. A recent survey showed that only 11 percent of convicted accused pedophiles receive prison sentences, and fewer probably receive appropriate long term therapy (*Believe The Children* newsletter 1993). To assist offenders takes sophisticated training and genuine support from all of the appropriate agencies, and without these and a personal recovery program or an equivalent support system for the helping professionals who assist victims and abusers, they are at a high risk of burn-out from the high stress involved.[148, 446]

Two Steps Backward

Some researchers who studied sexuality and incest have also invalidated the experiences of survivors. For example, in the famous "Kinsey Report" and elsewhere, Kinsey, Pomeroy and Martin made numerous statements holding the victims once again responsible and exonerating the abusers. Some examples—

> It is difficult to understand why a child, except for its cultural conditioning, should be disturbed at having its genitals touched, or disturbed at seeing the genitalia of other persons, or disturbed at even more specific contacts.[382, 570]
>
> . . . the [sexual] experiences were repeated because the children had become interested in the sexual activity and had more or less actively sought repetitions of their experience.[382]
>
> Incest between adults and younger children can also prove to be a satisfying and enriching experience, although difficulties can certainly arise.[527]
>
> When we examine a cross-section of the population, as we did in the Kinsey Report . . . we find many beautiful and mutually satisfying relationships between fathers and daughters. These may be transient or ongoing, but they have no harmful effects.[527]

But when Russell and others examined victims' experience after the abuse, they found the opposite: ongoing pain resulting from having been sexually abused by parents or parent figures.[85, 86]

Another step backward has been the movement of modern psychiatry, and to some extent other mental health professions, from a previously psychodynamic and behavioral approach to helping people recover from trauma—into a mostly biological model. While there is some usefulness in exploring our biology in this manner, I and others see their overadherence to this model—by labeling people with diagnostic codes and then giving them mostly drugs to treat them—as a kind of professional regression.[73] We have found it helpful to describe the biological approach as *part* of only *one stage* of assisting people in their recovery, which I call Stages Zero and One, described on page 254.

The Offender System's Supports

Supported by the health insurance industry, the drug companies, mercenary and underground networks, and our dysfunctional media and political system, the helping professions continue to lean strongly toward the biological model. While biological psychiatry is an important part of trauma psychology, many biologically oriented psychiatrists do not use trauma psychology in their work. According to most health insurance companies, if therapy is required, they tend to limit it to only a few counseling or psychotherapy sessions. And we pay them our money to limit us in this way! To heal the wounds of child abuse, it usually takes working in many sessions over a prolonged period of time. And it is being shown now that doing so can ameliorate or prevent the severity and recurrence of many physical and mental disorders.[71, 73, 326, 689, 694]

Journalist and social ecologist Mike Males gives the following as examples of but two of the above—the media and our political system:

> . . . today's media devote far more coverage to side issues such as recovered memories than to the indisputable reality that millions of American children grow up in nightmarish conditions of rape, sexual violation and physical brutality inflicted by adults entrusted with their care.
> . . . politicians of both parties prefer to downplay child abuse. Few officials in Clinton's self-proclaimed "put children first" administration have sought to publicize the epidemic of sexual and violent abuses of children by adults.[428]

Nor have officials in previous times seriously addressed the identification and prevention of child abuse. From academia to business to politics, we continue to sweep the extent of child abuse under the rug of our many dysfunctions.[50]

In 1984 a group of accused abusers banded together to fight their accusers and the new laws on child abuse. They named themselves Victims of Child Abuse Laws (VOCAL), and while they are still in existence,[314, 487, 703] they appear to have paved the way for the formation of the FMS Foundation eight years later. Some members and board members joined both of these organizations. Both organizations are reported to have supported people who were later convicted of child molestation.[36, 157, 379a] Bass and Davis expect continued denial. They say:

> Both VOCAL and the FMS Foundation make some legitimate claims. False allegations have occurred, some investigators have asked leading questions, and therapists have, on occasion, misconstrued a client's history. But the extent of these problems has been greatly exaggerated by both groups, who then go on to draw distorted conclusions that they use to manipulate public opinion.
>
> Although particular organizations like VOCAL and the FMS Foundation may rise and fall, the backlash is likely to continue to evolve —and to find supporters—in other incarnations. Until we as a culture face the reality of sexual abuse, our collective denial will continue to feed—and need—such groups.[36]

In spite of all of the above resistance, we are now moving in a more positive direction. One of the indications is shown in the grass roots movement that involves personal recovery, which I describe later in this chapter.

With these and other factors feeding the offender system, trauma survivors and their therapists can get caught in a triangle, as shown in Figure 6.1 (I explain triangles briefly on page 179 and in more detail in *Boundaries and Relationships*). Many accused offenders and co-offenders are trying to threaten both survivors and their therapists in several ways, including by attacking the veracity of their memory and the usefulness of therapy and other recovery aids. Many of these contribute large amounts of money to legal and other actions that survivors and therapists cannot easily counter. By knowing more about the history of child abuse we can see that trying to silence the survivor by various means of intimidation is a frequent maneuver used over time by many in the offender system. But today the recovery movement has gained too much momentum to be squelched. Survivors and their assistants in recovery are using these threats to strengthen their recoveries and their relationships. By setting healthy boundaries, they can detriangle from these pressures and threats. By developing their spirituality they can strengthen their recovery in their search and evolution toward healing and wholeness. I describe the offender system further on page 215.

Maltreatment and Abuse

The current backlash regarding memory and abuse is mostly against allegations of sexual abuse. But according to recent national figures, sexual abuse accounts for only about 15 percent of all reported kinds of child abuse,[210, 483] as shown in Figure 6.2.

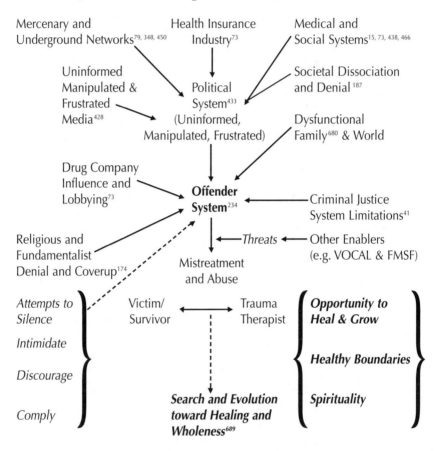

Figure 6.1. Factors that Feed the Offender System

In this survey, with 45 states reporting, child neglect accounted for 44 percent, physical abuse for 24 percent, emotional abuse for 6 percent, and other/unknown kinds of abuse for about 8 percent. An obvious error in this kind of typology arises from the fact that abuse victims are rarely ever mistreated in only one way. For example, children and adults who are physically abused are nearly always abused by a combination of other kinds of abuse. They are usually mentally, emotionally and spiritually abused, and sometimes they are sexually abused. Also, this figure appears

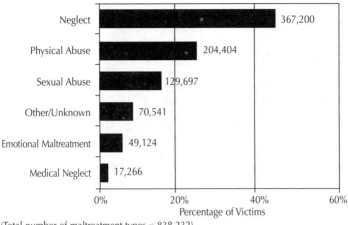

Neglect				367,200
Physical Abuse		204,404		
Sexual Abuse	129,697			
Other/Unknown	70,541			
Emotional Maltreatment	49,124			
Medical Neglect	17,266			
0%	20%	40%	60%	

Percentage of Victims

(Total number of maltreatment types = 838,232)

Figure 6.2. Type of Maltreatment (45 States Reporting).[483]

to markedly under-represent the amount of emotional abuse, which I and others estimate is the most common kind of maltreatment.[655, 656]

Being more vulnerable, younger children tend to be more often mistreated and abused, as shown in Figure 6.3. Of all the children reported as having been abused in any way, 40 percent were age five or younger. While physical abuse and neglect are about equal for both genders, girls are more often sexually abused than boys. Depending on the population studied and on the report, the percentage of boys who are sexually abused varies from three to 40 percent or more.[176, 225, 254, 255, 280, 401, 461] Boys tend to be underreported, may have more of a stigma against their talking about the abuse, may experience more shame and gender identity confusion, and have been studied only about one sixth as often as girls, and so we don't have as much information about them. This does not mean that girls do not feel intense shame or some gender identity confusion. All child sexual abuse, as well as other kinds of abuse, is painful.

Women are the perpetrators of the sexual abuse from four to 65 percent of the time, depending on the population studied and the dynamics of the abuse and its reporting.[3, 31, 64, 117, 254, 365, 374, 408, 439] For example, in day care settings, from 40 to 55 percent of the perpetrators are women.[374] Nonetheless, the stereotype of the sexual abuser is a man, and our society covers up for and underreports women as abusers. Abusive women tend to be more covert, subtle or seductive, and their abuse often takes the form of "caretaking" or "nurturing," and frequently occurs earlier, including in infancy.[305, 408] Just as we are only beginning to learn about the sexual abuse that is done to boys and men, we are also just beginning to

Age in Years

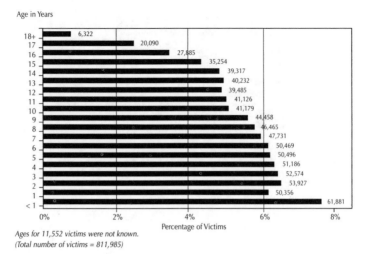

Ages for 11,552 victims were not known.
(Total number of victims = 811,985)

Figure 6.3. Percent of child victims by age (44 States reporting).[483]

learn about girls and women as abusers. See Appendix A on page 301 for further notes on children.

The Recovery Movement

The recovery movement includes the personal and professional work of all who are involved in recovery from trauma. Its knowledge and skills come from many sources, including psychology, Twelve-Step programs and the courage and dedication of many survivors of abuse, like Alice Miller, who demystified our prior knowledge of the psychology of trauma and spoke their own truth. I can't say exactly when it began, although following the first Adult Children of Alcoholics meetings in 1977, the adult child recovery movement began to expand from around 1983 until today. Probably hundreds of thousands of survivors of abuse have participated in it and have continued to heal. In recovery we discover that we are not bad, sick, crazy or stupid. We are just wounded, and we can now begin to heal.

When any new idea comes into our awareness, especially if it is useful and successful—as the recovery movement has been—there will be skeptics and challengers. Those skeptics who do their homework and perceptively examine the details and dynamics of the new idea can make a substantial contribution. But those who don't usually don't contribute much. I and others who work to assist people as they heal their traumas believe that most of these skeptics, also called backlashers, have neither done their homework nor been perceptive.[137, 155, 413, 497, 504, 507, 689] They don't seem to understand or get what the recovery movement is about. For example, FMSF board member advocate Frederick Crews wrote that "The Recovery Movement['s] . . . main intended audience is women who aren't at all sure that they were molested, and its purpose is to convince them of that fact and embolden them to act upon it." Numerous other critics have likewise missed the mark. In Table 6.1 on the next page, I have listed some of their misunderstandings, with the facts about each of these as I and others see them.

This table gives some examples of how some of the various guises of the backlash may misunderstand the process and movement of recovery. The recovery movement comes out of both *grass roots*, i.e., trauma survivors in recovery, and all our *accumulated knowledge* about the human condition and trauma psychology that is now being demystified by many writers and helping professionals.[326, 464, 688, 691] Many in the backlash, including those in academia, criticize the grass roots nature of this movement. The fields involving the treatment and prevention of child abuse and its effects—whether these effects may manifest in children or adults — are beginning to join with those in the recovery movement who had their origins in addictions and co-addictions recovery.

Critics misunderstand when they believe that the recovery movement and approach is separate and different from other approaches, when it is actually inclusive and expansive. They may mistakenly believe that its focus is negative, narcissistic, predominantly Twelve-Step oriented and that it blames and attacks parents and is therefore irresponsible. The reality is that its focus is constructive, promotes healthy self-caring, uses the Twelve Steps as one of many useful aids, and it names the truth of what happened for the recovering person, who uses it to heal, which is taking responsibility for their own recovery.

The critics may also erroneously believe that there is no scientific proof for the recovery approach—when they limit themselves to using mostly the scientific method. But we know that using the scientific method alone to study the many dimensions of the human condition is insufficient (see page 94 and following). Possible unconscious issues for some critics may include a threat of lost patients or clients and attention, financial loss, all-or-none thinking and behaving, needing to be in control and fearing their own wounds. (See Table 6.2).

If this "false memory" debate stimulates appropriate research and

Table 6.2. Some Misunderstandings of the Recovery Approach, with Facts Clarifying Each

	Misunderstandings	Facts
View of Recovery Movement & Approach	Separate and different	Inclusive and expansive
Focus	Negative	Constructive
	Narcissistic	Healthy Self-caring
	Predominantly Twelve Step	Twelve Step is one of many aids
	Blames and attacks parents	Names truth, facilitating grieving and healing
	Irresponsible	Responsible
Evidence for Its Truth	No scientific proof	Scientific method alone is insufficient
Possible **Unconscious Issues**	Threat of lost patients and attention	(probably true)
	Threat of financial loss	Financial advantage
	All-or-none	Both/and
	Needing to be in control	Sharing
	Fear of own wounds	Most recovery workers are in their own recovery

encourages therapists to provide more helpful therapy, then it will be useful. But if it makes some therapists reluctant to assist survivors for fear of being harassed or sued, or if it pressures some survivors to doubt the validity of their memories, remain silent or recant, then the debate becomes destructive. If it draws attention away from the real social problem of child abuse and perpetuates the myth that women believe anything anyone tells them, then it is even more damaging.[389]

We are dealing today with a social conflict that is broader than child abuse or "false memory," which is why there is such a strong reaction against the recovery movement at the corporate/think-tank/academia/media interface. Even though we have made some progress over the last century and much progress over the past 15 years, there are still many people, including some helping professionals and academics, who take an adversarial stance to this progress, especially as it applies to our memory of the abuse. I will examine some of their claims in the next few chapters.

7

HOW COMMON IS TRAUMATIC FORGETTING?

Abusers and co-abusers have been denying their actions and inactions for millennia. But with the recent progress of the recovery movement coinciding with that of increased child abuse awareness, identification and prevention, it has been getting uncomfortable for the perpetrators and their accomplices.

The False Memory Defense

With the tide shifting toward increasing awareness of the dynamics and nuances of sexual abuse, sexual harassment and dysfunctional families, abusers may have sensed that denying the abuse and attacking the victim would not be enough. Might a more subtle and sophisticated resistance stop the increasing numbers of adult survivors of childhood abuse who were confronting and sometimes suing their abusers?

Enter the "false memory" defense. Abusers and co-abusers deny the accusations and their lawyer hires a "memory researcher" and/or a convincing academic or clinician to provide testimony documenting the next subtle version of denial after such examples as Freud's Oedipal theory and Kinsey's distorted interpretations.

No matter whether the FMS Foundation folds or lasts for a long time, progressively increasing numbers of abusers and co-abusers in denial may be using an FMS kind of defense to avoid taking responsibility for having abused one or more people. And some academics and clinicians are still willing to speak out, write and testify on their behalf, all of which promote the continuation of the abuse of innocent children, adolescents and adults today.

Because of all of the above, the FMS defense may be the most sophisticated guise of denial of abuse—denial to a level finely honed[240]—that we have yet seen, and it is possible that it will be exposed for what some believe it to be—a front for abusers and co-abusers who are unable to take responsibility for having mistreated their children.[216, 441] But groups like VOCAL and the FMSF may nonetheless last for a long time. Currently these groups have lasted for eight and three years respectively, and have a growing "membership." But the FMS Foundation does not publish or disclose answers to many important questions, including: How is its membership, currently said to be about x-thousand * "families," determined? What is a "family" here? Do they include any contact who wants help? Any helping professional who asks for their literature? Only dues-paying members? And what are their actual financial involvements? These kinds of questions are not clearly addressed in their literature.

Because the FMS lobby represents one of the most superficially sophisticated guises of and arguments from the backlash, it may be useful to review some of their most frequent claims and answer each of these with facts from clinical literature and practice. Olio has recently described some of these,[504] and I have compiled her information and added some to it in Table 7.1. Reviewing these claims and facts can be helpful to survivors of abuse, helping professionals and interested others.

Are Delayed Memories True or False?

The FMS advocates claim that most delayed memories of abuse are false.* However, from what we know to date, most are true. "False memory syndrome" is a term made up by the FMSF, which appears to support any alleged abuser who is in denial. There are no appropriate scientific studies or clinical trials to substantiate or to make a diagnosis of "false

---

* This number appears to constantly change, usually going up with each FMSF newsletter, and sometimes it decreases. If you have ever called or made contact with the FMSF, could they be counting *you* as a "family"?

memory syndrome." [19, 34, 110, 113, 137, 216, 329a, 441, 661, 664] Most writers who mention it in their journal articles are on the FMSF professional advisory board and are not frontline clinicians who assist survivors of trauma over their long period of recovery.[413, 453, 497]

While most clinicians who work with survivors of trauma note that nearly all of the delayed memories they observe have most of the characteristics and symptoms of being true, there may be some situations where these memories are untrue, and it is here where we can learn about our mistakes as clinicians, which I discuss on pages 175 and 227.

Prior Studies

About one hundred years ago Janet, Breuer, and Freud reported that dissociated, repressed, and delayed memory of the experience was common in the sexual abuse of children.[326, 435] In their study of another kind of trauma to adults—the trauma of combat and war—Kardiner and Spiegel[371] and more recently Egendorf and colleagues[195a] described similar findings for adults: associated with the traumatic shock of war was dissociation, denial, numbness and difficulty remembering the traumatic events.

Motivated by the grass roots movement of veterans' organizations and the feminist movement, in 1980 these and other studies convinced the American Psychiatric Association to recognize the seriousness of psychological trauma in contributing to mental illness and to include post-traumatic stress disorder (PTSD) in their diagnostic manual. Part of the diagnostic criteria for PTSD are *avoidant behaviors* related to the trauma, including delayed memories, which I discuss in Chapter 2. In 1983 Summit described the childhood sexual abuse accommodation syndrome, wherein delayed disclosures of the abuse are characteristic[629] (page 84).

---

* While the FMS Foundation newsletter continues to say that "some" delayed memories of childhood sexual abuse are false ("Some memories are true, some a mixture of fact and fantasy and some are false") their literature and behavior implies that most, if not all, are false. They tend to address only "false memories" and rarely mention true ones. They appear to have a repetitive bias in favor of "false memories." This is in spite of the fact that some of their Professional Advisory Board at times say otherwise (Ulric Neisser, Ph.D., says in a keynote address to their 1993 Valley Forge conference, ". . . there are such things as repressed memories." [FMSF newsletter 3 May 1993] and Elizabeth Loftus, Ph.D., reports that 19 percent of 100 recovering chemically dependent women that she and her colleagues studied had delayed memories of sexual abuse, as cited later in this chapter). Also, I asked a member of the FMSF staff for their estimate of how many delayed memories of child sexual abuse were true, and their reply was "probably well over half."

Table 7.1. Claims and Facts about "False Memories"
(compiled and modified from Olio 1993)[504]

Claim	Facts
Most delayed memories of child sexual abuse are false.	Nearly all appear to be true. "FMS" is a term coined by the FMS Foundation, which supports any accused sexual abuser who denies the accusation. There are no appropriate scientific studies or clinical trials or reports to substantiate their claims.
Currently there are about x-thousand documented cases of "FMS."	These are unscreened, accused abusers and family members who have contacted the FMSF for support. FMSF admits it has no way of knowing who is right.
FMS Foundation members are nice-looking, good people— which shows that they could not have abused anyone.[215, 441]	Child abuse, here specifically child sexual abuse cuts across all social, educational and economic levels. Over half of all dysfunctional families fit the otherwise "looking good" category. This is one of their weakest claims.
Some abuse cases are not true, including "over 300" retractors.	While some of these are likely true, they are small in number compared to the vast number of actual cases of child sexual abuse, and it is likely that some of the retractors were actually abused and are now re-repressing or forgetting.
Repression has never been "scientifically proven" and therefore doesn't exist.	Appropriate *basic* scientific studies would be difficult to conduct. Using careful clinical observation and interpretation and the experiences of countless abuse survivors validates repression as one useful clinical concept in describing the dynamics of traumatic forgetting.
There has been no independent corroboration of delayed memories.	Independent corroborations are too numerous and diverse to count. The proof is in the internal and external corroboration and the successful healing of hundreds of thousands of survivors.
Abuse memories are a simple explanation for people's problems and gives them someone to blame.	Memories are a helpful part of healing the effects of abuse. Expressing memories of trauma is about *naming* what happened, not blaming others for it. It takes great courage and self-responsibility to heal from abuse.
Suggestions from pushy therapists, hypnosis, and reading self-help books are the major cause of "all of these false memories."	While nearly all therapists work appropriately, with or without hypnosis, there may be a small yet undetermined number who may lead their patients inappropriately. Even so, therapists cannot induce a person to have disorders like PTSD and other findings, nor can reading a self-help book.
Experiments and studies on memory show that "false memories" are easily implanted even in normal people.	Traumatic memory and ordinary memory are quite different. Traumatic forgetting and remembering are more complex than the simple studies reported by FMS advocates.

With these prior observations and studies that show that dissociated, repressed and delayed memories of traumatic experiences not only exist, but appear to be common, we can now turn to more recent studies that may give us some more specific answers regarding just how often they may happen.

Recent Studies of Memory in Child Abuse

From 1987 to 1995 seven studies examined the memories of abuse victims. By interviews, surveys and long-term clinical observation, their authors studied 1,039 people, mostly women, regarding their memories of having been sexually abused in childhood.[84, 102, 118, 329, 417, 552, 699, 700] While they did not address other kinds of abuse, they found that from 16 to 64 percent, depending on the study, had delayed memories of having been sexually abused (Table 7.2).

While all seven of these studies are helpful, perhaps the strongest is that of researcher Linda M. Williams, where there was a prior documentation by medical records of the childhood sexual abuse of all 129 of the women she studied.[699, 700] When interviewed 17 years later 38 percent had forgotten the abuse, and another 10 percent reported having forgotten the abuse at some time in the past, for a total of 48 percent. Starting with written documentation of the abuse and interviewing the survivors years later is one way of obtaining information about our memory of abuse.

Critics have said that some of these women could have been abused before age three, when memory for any event is said to be rare by some authors, and these would not prove the existence of actual repression (see page 24 for a discussion of "infantile amnesia"). Also, some could have had "normal forgetting," and not true repression, or simply preferred not to talk about their painful experience which they "actually always remembered."[412, 527b] If we account for these potential errors, would they have changed the study's conclusion that traumatic forgetting is common?

Another way to obtain reliable information is for skilled and experienced clinicians to observe possible victims of abuse as they work in therapy in their process of recovery over a long period of time, which is what trauma therapists and researchers Judith Herman and Emily Schatzow did in 1987. They found that 15 of 53 women, or 28 percent, had delayed memories.[329] I and other clinicians find that even when they

Table 7.2. Studies of Memory in Childhood Sexual Abuse

Numbered Studied Study		Delayed Memories
129 Women	17 years ago all had documented child sexual abuse, and were now re-interviewed. 80/129 (62%) remembered, although 16% (13/80 women, 10% of total) of them had gotten at some time in past. (Linda Meyer Williams, 1994)	49 of them (38%) had forgotten the abuse. Add the 10% of the total of 129 who have forgotten having been abused at some time in the for- past, and the total with delayed memories is **48%**.
450 (93% women)	Briere & Conte (1993) asked 450 people who had been sexually abused, "Between your first forced sexual experience and age did you ever forget the experience?"	**59%** people answered Yes. Found more likely to be forgotten if abused at younger age, repeated 18, abuse, fear of death if told others of the abuse, associated physical injury, multiple abusers & greater current symptoms.
60 women	Cameron (1994) surveyed, interviewed and followed up 60 women over 6 years (1986-92) who were in therapy for various reasons, including having been sexually abused as children.	**42%** had completely forgotten and another 23% had partially forgotten having been sexually abused decades earlier.
228 women	Roesler & Wind (1994) surveyed 228 women who were survivors of childhood sexual abuse.	**28%** had repressed memories of the abuse.
53 women	Herman & Schatzow (1987) observed 53 women in weekly therapy groups for incest survivors for three months.	**64%** had partial to severe amnesia and 28% had severe amnesi- for having been sexually abused; 2 of 3 had corroborating evidence of their abuse from other sources.
19 (11 girls/8 boys)	Burgess et. al (1994) prospectively followed 19 children sexually abused by day-care Mean age 2½. Follow-up into teens.	Even with extra-familial abusers only, (3) **16%** totally forgot on staff. follow-up and (5) 26% partially forgot, for a total of **42%**.
100 women	Loftus et al (1993) studies 100 women in outpatient treatment for substance abuse in NYC.	**19%** had delayed memories of having been sexually abused as children. Authors state that there could have been more who were abused but repressed the memory and had not yet regained it.
Total 1,039	By interviews, surveys and clinical observations the authors studied 1039 people, mostly women, regarding their memories of having been sexually abused in childhood. They did not address other kinds of abuse.	**16%** to **64%** were found to have delayed memories (traumatic forgetting) of having been sexually abused or traumatized in other ways. (See also footnote on page 73.)

have always remembered it, most patients don't want to remember the abuse. Instead, they tend to minimize and often even deny its existence. This is why, in assisting people in their recovery, a gentle and supportive approach is most helpful, so that the person can feel safe enough to allow their True Self to come "out of hiding" to explore their experiences of having been mistreated. As therapists assist people in this way, they are able to observe many dynamics and patterns, including their memory of the abuse. This is what Herman and Schatzow did in their study. Critics have said that some subjects in this study had only strongly suspected that they had been sexually abused but could not remember clearly, although the authors did not indicate just how many, and that their therapists or others could have unduly influenced them.[412] Others tried to use the "childhood amnesia" claim to exclude abuse memories before age six in one subgroup, and to use inadequate external corroboration in another subgroup to discount this study.[527b] While this may be possible, it is interesting that all critics of these studies that I am aware of are members of the FMSF professional advisory board,[412, 497, 498, 527b] and no one outside of that board has so far criticized them in these ways.

Another way to obtain accurate information about our memories of traumatic experiences is to survey people who have a clinical history of having been abused. Trauma therapists and researchers John Briere and Jon Conte did so with 450 people, mostly women who had been sexually abused, and found that 59% answered "Yes" to the question "Between your first forced sexual experience and age 18, did you ever forget the experience?" (paraphrased). They found that these 59% were more likely to have forgotten the abuse if there were one or often a combination of any of the following findings: (1) if it happened at a younger age, (2) if it was repeated, (3) if they feared death if they were to tell others of it, (4) if there was associated physical injury, (5) if there were multiple abusers, and (6) if there were more current symptoms than average.[84] Some have criticized this study, saying that there could have been a sampling bias and that since all 450 people were in therapy, the abuse was not externally corroborated or their therapists could have unduly influenced them to answer "Yes" or could even have suggested "false memories."[412, 527b] While these criticisms are important and possible in any study, how might they have affected the results? They may have lowered the number who answered "Yes," although probably not even close to zero.

Social psychologist Catherine Cameron surveyed, interviewed and followed 60 women over six years, from 1986 through 1992. All had a history of having been sexually abused by one or more adults as children and all were in psychotherapy for a time during her contacts with them.[118] Of the 60, 21 (35 percent) had always remembered having been abused, 25 (35 percent) had completely forgotten for from 15 to 50 years until their memories returned, and another 14 (23 percent) had partially forgotten having been sexually abused as children decades earlier. The women volunteered to be surveyed and interviewed and were not chosen at random, and Cameron said that they should be viewed as more descriptive than generalizable.[118] However, she noted that the women were probably similar to others who were entering therapy during the mid-1980s, which was a full six years before the current backlash about memory began.

Child psychiatrist Thomas Roesler and researcher Tiffany W. Wind sent surveys to 755 adults who had a history of having been sexually abused before age 16 and had agreed to answer their questions.[552] Two-hundred eighty-six surveys were returned (37.9 percent), and men respondents were excluded, leaving 228 women for the study group. While the study addressed the demographics and parameters of why they kept the secret or disclosed it, it also reveals that 28.5 percent had repressed their memories of having been sexually abused as children.

Trauma researcher Ann Burgess and her colleagues prospectively studied and followed up 19 children who had been repeatedly sexually abused at a mean age of 2-1/2 years old by day-care staff, proven by external corroboration[107a] and internal corroboration on follow up evaluations.[102] On five- and ten-year follow-up, three (16%) had no verbal recall of their experience of having been sexually abused and an additional five (26 percent) had partially forgotten, for a total of 42%. This abuse was extrafamilial, which with appropriate expression and support has a better prognosis than the much more common intrafamilial sexual abuse, and may explain the somewhat lower figures for forgetting than are found in adult survivors. While these children were growing up in military families, they received no formal treatment and their follow-up is ongoing.[102] This is an example of an ideal format for a study on traumatic memory and the natural history of trauma, although the children and their families should receive formal treatment (see also page 25 for further discussion of this study).

As co-author of the seventh study, normal memory researcher

Elizabeth Loftus is one of the most vocal and adamant of the FMS advocates, is a member of FMSF's professional advisory board, and regularly tries to disprove the existence of "repression" of traumatic memories. But early in her 1993 review article, she continues to use the word "repression" and "repressed" to describe the memories. She asks, "How common are repressed memories of childhood abuse?"[417] and replies that "There is no absolute answer available," even after acknowledging the results of three of the other studies and her own that found 19 percent having delayed memories of having been sexually abused as children.[412, 416] There is something inconsistent about a purely research psychologist and FMSF board member who argues strongly against the reality of delayed memory while reporting in her own study that "only 19 percent claimed that they forgot the abuse for a period of time and later regained the memory. . . . of course, the data obtained from [this] the New York sample may include an underestimation factor because there could have been many more women in the sample who were sexually abused, repressed the memory, and had not yet regained it."[417] She sounded equally uncertain in her 1992 article.[420] This kind of ambivalence, inconsistency, mixed messages and other conflicting information may remind one of the crazy-making behavior of an unrecovered adult child of a dysfunctional family.*[91] Reading or hearing this kind of information can be confusing and sometimes invalidating to survivors of abuse.

From these seven studies and from countless hours of clinical work with abuse survivors over long periods of time, we know that delayed memories of abuse are common, real and require patience, skill and compassion to assist a person in their recovery from the wounds of having been abused. Already feeling confused and doubtful about their delayed memories, these above study results can help validate these survivors' experience as being real and having actually happened.**

While more such studies will be helpful, the current evidence is

---

* Confusing and mixed messages are a common pattern among other FMSF representatives. For example, Pamela Freyd, their executive director, says "A characteristic of the FMSF is the assiduous avoidance of any conflicting information"(Aug-Sept 1993 FMSF newsletter, p.5) Yet in my opinion her writing, mostly in the FMSF newsletter and interviews[111, 245] contains numerous confusing and mixed messages and conflicting information.
** At press time for this book I became aware of an eight report. Roe et al (1995) studied 52 women with a history of inpatient treatment as adults for the effects of childhood sexual abuse. Their mean age was 38 (range 21 to 55). 40 (78 percent) experienced amnesia for the abuse from 3.5 to 45 years duration, with a mean of 23 years.[551a]

convincing that delayed memories are common among victims of childhood abuse.

Further Exploration

Do these studies provide us with enough useful information? My answer is *Yes* and *No*.

"Yes" for therapists and survivors to rest assured that delayed memories of abuse are real and occur frequently, in the range of from 16 to 64 percent as shown in these studies. And *"No"* because to further explore the relationship between memory and abuse can only be helpful.

Is the design and conduct of these studies adequate? As is true of most research, each may have aspects that can be improved upon. While one is prospective[102] and two have long follow-up periods (Williams[699, 700] and Cameron[118]), by necessity, most of these studies are retrospective, since it would be cruel and unethical to design a prospective one to study child abuse of any kind.*

But further useful studies can be controlled to some extent, and there may be a more practical reason for our wanting more research on memory and trauma: the clinician wants more information to use to assist the patient or client, and from which to build skills that will help survivors as they heal. And for many reasons, the survivor will also likely be interested in the results.

FMS advocates Pope and Hudson suggest that future study design include (1) external corroboration of the abuse, (2) interviewers who were over five years old when abused, (3) an interview, followed by (4) a clarification interview.[527b] Except for the age limitation, these suggestions were met in the Burgess et. al. study,[102] and as discussed in Chapter 3, the childhood amnesia claim is not substantially documented for traumatic experiences. While Pope and Hudson's understanding of trauma psychology appears to be limited, some of their suggestions for the design of this kind of study may be useful.

---

* In the winter 1993 issue of *Paidika: The Journal of Paedophilia*, FMSF professional advisory board member Hollida Wakefield, M.A., said, "It would be nice if someone could get some kind of big research grant to do a longitudinal study of, let's say, a hundred twelve-year-old boys in relationships with loving paedophiles. Whoever was doing the study would have to follow them at five year intervals for twenty years." While pedophilia is against U.S. law and allowing such a study to proceed would be unethical for the researcher, after making such a recommendation Wakefield remains on the FMSF professional advisory board (FMSF newsletter, November 1, 1994).

8

DOES DENIAL MEAN "FALSE MEMORY SYNDROME"?

My therapist didn't give me my memory; my perpetrator did.

— Abuse Survivor

F MS advocates claim thousands of "documented cases" of "false memory syndrome." But how are these cases documented? Has a neutral or unbiased clinician with skills and experience in working long-term with trauma victims and their families carefully screened them? It appears not. Rather, these appear to be anecdotal stories told by people who contact the FMSF for information and support because one or more of their family members have said that they or another family member sexually abused them.

I asked their director, Pamela Freyd, just how the FMS Foundation "documents" a case or an occurrence of "false memory syndrome." She replied in writing, "When the Foundation states that we have documented a certain number of cases, it means that the report we received fits the pattern described in our literature, that the people calling have asked to have their case investigated and that we know how to get in contact with these people so that a further study can either substantiate or not what has been claimed."[246] While "the pattern described in our literature" is vague—they publish only a regular newsletter—in reading their material it usually means any time an adult child accuses a parent, parent figure or any other family member of having sexually abused them. While many of these adult children of FMSF members had delayed memories of having been abused, some have always remembered it.[632] Could this kind of "documentation" be a part of the "pseudoscience" that observers have pointed out about some of their methods?[34, 110, 216] Since at least 95 percent of child molesters initially deny their abusive behaviors,[67] how can untrained lay people like Pamela Freyd and her staff "document" a real or unreal "case" of "FMS," as appears to be the case with most of their communications, which usually occur over the telephone or by letter?[216, 536]

In reading most of the issues of the FMSF newsletter from 1992 to the present, I have yet to find a story of an abuser or co-abuser who admits abuse and makes amends to their victim. While there may be a small number of "documented cases" of FMS somewhere, as are claimed in the FMSF newsletters, that are actual false accusations, the majority appear to be abusers and co-abusers who are not able to face and take responsibility for having mistreated someone who is now trying to heal from the effects of that mistreatment.

We might thus simplify their claim as actually meaning: denial by the accused abuser is false memory syndrome. If most accused child sexual abusers and many co-abusers deny having mistreated their alleged victims, then a quick way to appear right and to take the heat off of themselves is to deny the abuse and attack the victim with a term like "FMS."*

Can a "False Memory" Happen?

Based on my knowledge of the literature and nearly 20 years of frontline clinical experience, my answer is "Yes, rarely." The exact way it may occur is difficult to generalize, since there are so many variables associated with the person, their family, their therapist and their environment.

Estimating the Incidence and Prevalence

If I were to make an educated guess based on my knowledge of the literature and on my experience, I would say that the incidence of untrue

---

* Another term that they have coined is "RMT" (recovered memory therapy[497]), wherein they oversimplify part of the process of recovery from having been abused (FMSF Newsletter, July 6, 1994). By using terms like this, they don't have to be specific or accurate about this complex and painful process of being abused, surviving and recovering from it. As part of this process, there is also ample evidence that remembering childhood trauma is a complex, multiply determined phenomenon that defies easy dichotomies or simple models.[576]

memories of abuse, which may also be called "false memory syndrome" if it were appropriately documented, could be illustrated in the following Venn diagram (Figure 8.1). Here I divide the "FMS" into two types. I call one the "true FMS" and the other the "false FMS." The diagram shows them in relation to a pool of all people who have been sexually abused. The most conservative current estimates are that about one in three or four girls has been sexually abused by age 18 and for boys the estimate is about one in four to ten,* [21, 151, 199, 224, 349, 569, 570, 647, 706, 709] which means that with a U.S. population of 250 million, we can estimate that there are about 50 to 80 million people living in this country who have been sexually abused at a young age.

For many reasons, including the dysfunctional family and societal dynamics described throughout this book, I estimate that only a small percentage of the 50 to 80 million survivors of sexual abuse are in or have successfully completed a recovery program. While this number is also unknown, it could be as high as four or five million people. Of these, I estimate that as many as 300,000 people have confronted their abuser or co-abusers, i.e., they have spoken of their experience to them in a serious way.

False Versus True "FMS"

In my best clinical opinion and that of several experts in the field of recovery from child sexual abuse, it is likely that 92 to 99 percent of survivors are telling the truth and thus have real memories of having been abused.[328, 507, 585, 641] If an estimated 300,000 people overall have disclosed what happened to them to their abusers, then of these there would be 270,000 to 297,000 with real memories, which we might also call false "FMS." The remainder who actually have untrue memories would then equal somewhere between 3,000 to 24,000; these would hypothetically represent true "FMS." However, I believe, as do others, that these numbers are closer to from 3,000 to 6,000—if they are that high.

Although the above is all "best guessing" based on our current

---

* With the assistance of Donna Terman, researcher David Finkelhor compiled the results of 19 studies on the prevalence of child sexual abuse. In these, over 18,000 women reported from 2 to 62 percent and over 5,000 men from 1 to 16 percent having the *awareness* of having been sexually abused as a child.[225] Based on the inherent difficulty in obtaining accurate information about child sexual abuse, these figures probably underestimate the actual percentages.

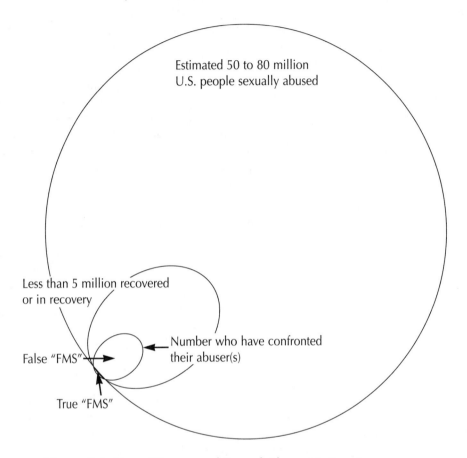

Figure 8.1. Venn Diagram of Sexual Abuse Victims in
Relationship to Recovery, Confrontation, and *true*
and *false* "FMS"

clinical knowledge, we can nonetheless ask, "What are the chances that
every alleged abuser who denies having abused, whether a member of
FMSF or not, falls into the category of true FMS?" What percentage of
FMSF members are actually abusers in denial? What if 92 to 99 percent of
FMSF members are simply in denial? If this percentage of their membership is in denial, or have otherwise traumatically forgotten, then who is
having the false memories?

The Experience of Clinicians and People in Recovery

From the experience of clinicians who work frequently with abused people and the experience of those abused people in recovery, we can make these and other clinically educated estimates. For example, Schwartz[585] writes of the "FMS": ". . . after working with over 1,000 survivors, we believe that this (false memory) is a rare occurrence of sexual abuse . . . Professional and public resistance to the recognition of sexual abuse has been so powerful that even in 1970 it was estimated by one psychiatric text that the incidence was one in a thousand, quite divergent from more recent figures of one in three for women. . . . In St. Louis there are 1,000 reports of sexual abuse of children each year."

Hearing other people's stories and hearing their issues may trigger memories, but this will almost never implant an untrue memory into our historical experience. Rather than making up stories or exaggerating them, what my colleagues and I observe instead in the patients and clients that we assist is a *strong tendency to minimize, deny and otherwise withhold* most anything from their inner life about their hurts, losses and traumas. This is especially true when it may involve their family of origin or other loved ones, where they usually have a strong sense of loyalty. It is only by gently supporting the expression of their experience, over time, including what they remember, that they are able to heal their wounds around the trauma.

The "Looking Good" Claim

While this claim may be used by any abuser and co-abuser, it is often touted by the FMSF and those with similar views. Pamela Freyd addressed the question, "How do we know we are not representing pedophiles?" Her answer: "We are a good-looking bunch of people: graying hair, well-dressed, healthy, smiling . . . Just about every person who has attended [our meetings] is someone you would want to count as a friend" (FMSF newsletter, February 29, 1992, p. 1). How does this kind of reasoning show that they could not have abused anyone?[710] (see also page 81).

Although this claim may at first appear to some to be logical, it is among their weakest. Child abuse cuts across and affects all ages and all social, educational and economic levels.[401, 483, 570] Our projected stereotype of the child abuser as being a sleazy old man in a trenchcoat waiting outside the schoolyard or in an alley somewhere has been replaced by any man and any woman—and even any child in the case of older children abusing younger ones. Any person can abuse children, adolescents or adults. There is no useful superficial stereotype, as I illustrate below. And most child sexual abuse occurs within families, and the minority occurs outside.

Age of Abuser and Co-abuser

Although an abuser or co-abuser may mistreat a child at any age, a 1991 study of 20,745 abusers[483] showed that they were most commonly between the ages of 16 and 45, as shown in Figure 8.2. By the time their abused children grow up and are able to gather the courage to heal their resulting wounds, which is most commonly after age 30, the abusers' ages will usually be 20 to 30 or more years older, in the age range of between 46 and 80, which I show as the dotted line on the right side of Figure 8.2. Thus, the claim by FMS advocates that they are "nice looking, gray-haired, and friendly people" is specious.*

Socio-Economic Level

In her study of 152 women with a history of having been incestuously sexually abused in their childhood, Russell found that there was no abuser stereotype regarding education or socio-economic class.[570] Her findings were that about a third (32 percent) of the perpetrators had upper-middle class occupations, a third (34 percent) had middle-class occupations and the other third (34 percent) had lower-class occupations. There was also no extraordinary racial or ethnic preponderance among the abusers beyond that of the general population.

Gender and Religiosity

While 7 percent of the abusers in Russell's study were girls and women and 93 percent were boys and men, others have found that 16 percent or more were women.[254, 365, 374, 392a, 408, 439] Russell did not directly study boys and men who had been sexually abused, although extrapo-

---

* Most FMSF members are over age 50 and a large percentage are retired or not employed, which gives them extra time to organize and write letters to authority figures and the media promoting "FMS" and attacking helping professionals, especially therapists who assist survivors of childhood sexual abuse.

lating from our knowledge of the abuser-victim cycle, all or nearly all of these perpetrators—whether men or women—likely were themselves abused in some way by other abusers in their past.[501, 651] I am unaware of anyone who has studied the co-abuser's history of sexual abuse or other trauma in any meaningful way.

Summit[629] and Russell[570] observed that abusers tended to be more religious than the general population. This may be associated with the observation in the previous chapter that religious fundamentalism, which can occur in any faith or denomination and not just those that may label themselves fundamentalist, can be a factor in protecting abusers, maintaining abuse and in denying the existence of the abuse.[174, 696] The way the Catholic

State annual reports frequently report information regarding perpetrators. Missouri's 1991 annual report, for example, provides summary data on the perpetrator's relationship to the child victim, gender, race/ethnicity, age and other characteristics present at the time of the incident. The chart below provides specific data with regard to age for 20,745 perpetrators found to have maltreated children in 1991.*

The chart below indicates that the age of perpetrators ranged from age 11 to over age 71. Nearly two-thirds (61 percent) of perpetrators were from 21 to 36 years of age.[483] See prior page for dotted line explanation.

Figure 8.2 Age of Perpetrators
Missouri Annual Report, 1991

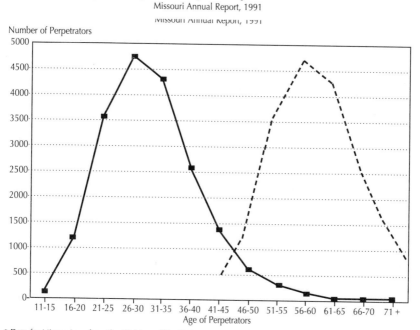

* Data for Missouri are from the Division of Family Services, *Child Abuse and Neglect in Missouri: Report for Calendar Year 1991*. Jefferson City: Department of Social Services. 1992, p.15.

Church has handled the countless accusations of child molestations by many of its priests is but one example.

The "Looking Good" Family

In a study of 75 child abusers matched with 75 controls, sexual abusers were found to self-report more positive views of themselves and their children and fewer family problems.[467] Over the past six years I have surveyed about 2,000 adult children of dysfunctional families, and about 60 percent identified their family of origin as having been in the "looking good" category. By this term I mean that the family "rule" is always to look good to outsiders, even though there may be sizeable dysfunction happening regularly on the inside. My survey showed that of the remaining 40 percent, about 25 percent of the 2,000 people identified their family as *not* looking good to outsiders, rather, they looked dysfunctional. About 10 percent of those surveyed had mixed features and 5 percent were uncertain.[695] For all of these reasons and more, the "looking good" claim as part of a defense against being accused of child maltreatment or abuse is not valid.

9

RETRACTORS AND OTHER "FALSE" ACCUSERS: SORTING OUT UNTRUE FROM TRUE MEMORY

Retraction is part of the natural history of child sexual abuse.

The existence of retractors is one of the legs of the three-legged stool upon which FMS lobbyists seat themselves in their claim that "FMS" is common. While not infallible, it is probably the strongest of the three. The other two legs are the denial of accused abusers and a few studies on ordinary memory plus a handful of questionable anecdotal reports.

FMS advocates may rightly say that some alleged abuse cases are not true, possibly including "over 300" retractors who have contacted the newsletter "The Retractor" or the FMSF. As I noted above, while some of these retractions are likely to be accurate, they are small in number compared with the vast number of actual cases of child sexual abuse, and it is likely that some of the retractors were actually sexually abused and that many were abused in other ways and have re-activated their traumatic forgetting.

How can we determine which of these retractors or recanters were sexually abused and are now reversing their story for some reason, such as pressure from their family, and which may actually have had untrue memories? My sense is that superficial observation, giving them surveys or other simple ways will not be very helpful in answering this question, and that even hearing their stories in some depth may still not give us accurate answers for many retractors. Sorting this out will not be easy. It will require using our clinical expertise and creativity, perhaps beyond the ways that we have used them to date. While other researchers and I will continue to explore this question, some of the following may be useful to consider.

Surviving the Abuse

Clinical experience shows that sexual abuse produces characteristic patterns of symptoms and signs, often including those of PTSD. There are other clinical findings that allow us to look at the dynamics of retraction. Well before this delayed memory controversy arose, in 1983 trauma therapist Roland Summit described some of the patterns and dynamics of children and adults who were sexually abused in their childhood, and called it the *child sexual abuse accommodation syndrome* (CSAAS). This syndrome describes the victim's responses that help them to accommodate the abuse and all its ramifications, and thus to survive. I summarize some of the essential features of the CSAAS in Table 9.1.[629]

The pre-conditions to the occurrence of the sexual abuse are (1) secrecy and (2) a power differential between the abuser and victim, relating to the helplessness of the victim. While these two characteristics feed on and promote one another, they also bring about three more consequences of the abuse: (3) entrapment and accommodation, (4) delayed, conflicted and unconvincing disclosure and (5) retraction. Each of these tends to interact upon and promote all of the others.

The Process of Retraction

In his description of the process of retraction, in what might perhaps be a worst-case scenario with a father as abuser and daughter as victim, Summit says:[629]

> Whatever a child says about sexual abuse, she is likely to reverse it. Beneath the anger of impulsive disclosure remains the ambivalence of guilt and the martyred obligation to preserve the family. In the chaotic aftermath of disclosure, the child discovers that the bedrock fears and threats underlying the secrecy are true. Her father abandons her and calls her a liar. Her mother does not believe her or decompensates into hysteria and rage. The family is fragmented, and all the children are placed in custody. The father is threatened with disgrace and imprisonment. The girl is blamed for causing the whole mess, and everyone

seems to treat her like a freak. She is interrogated about all the tawdry details and encouraged to incriminate her father, yet the father remains unchallenged, remaining at home in the security of the family. She is held in custody with no apparent hope of returning home if the dependency petition is sustained.

The message from the mother is very clear, often explicit. "Why do you insist on telling those awful stories about your father? If you send him to prison, we won't be a family anymore. We'll end up on welfare with no place to stay. Is that what you want to do to us?"

Once again, the child bears the responsibility of either preserving or destroying the family. The role reversal continues with the "bad" choice being to tell the truth and the "good" choice being to capitulate and restore a lie for the sake of the family.

Unless there is special support for the child and immediate intervention to force responsibility on the father, the girl will follow the "normal" course and retract her complaint. The girl "admits" she made up the story.

This simple lie carries more credibility than the most explicit claims of incestuous entrapment. It confirms adult expectations that children cannot be trusted. It restores the precarious equilibrium of the family. The children learn not to complain. The adults learn not to listen. And the authorities learn not to believe rebellious children who try to use their sexual power to destroy well-meaning parents.

In expanding its clinical dimensions, it can be useful to call this pattern and response the *adult* child sexual abuse accommodation syndrome. Knowing about this frequently observed CSAAS pattern in abused children can be useful in their healing process when they become adults. Note that the fourth characteristic—delayed disclosure—is also an important and integral part of the victim's entrapment (Table 9.1). Rather than being rare, it is common for the victim to forget about and/or not to talk about the abuse—often for many years.

Retractors Who Were Not Sexually Abused

By contrast, in any group of retractors there will likely be those who were not sexually abused. These may indeed have been somehow talked into or otherwise influenced into believing that they were sexually abused or abused in some other way by one or more people. And as I describe in Chapter 18, the person who so influenced them may have been a therapist, another helping professional, friend or another person—or more

Table 9.1. The Child Sexual Abuse Accommodation Syndrome: Characteristics and Manifestations (compiled from Summit[629])

Characteristic	Manifestations
Secrecy	Abuse happens in isolation — in bizarre contrast to the intruder's usual behavior. The child is confused and afraid to disclose even in the absence of a clear perception of wrongdoing or any spoken demand for secrecy. Abuser may say, "Don't tell anyone, or something bad will happen." If the child does tell, which is uncommon, most other adults discount, don't believe, or attack or blame the child. If the child doesn't tell and adults find out later, they attack and blame the child for not telling.
Helplessness	The child is (1) dependent on the adults for their survival and is thus generally helpless to resist or complain. Add (2) the threats by the abuser and often co-abuser of rejection, abandonment or harm to (3) the average age of the victim of less than five to age seven for initiation of the abuse, plus (4) the ways other adults in the helping professions and criminal justice system often react, and one can begin to understand some of the child's helplessness.
Entrapment and **Accommodation**	Feeling that there is no other way out, the child tries to survive by any one, or more usually a combination, of defenses and ways to accommodate the continuing abuse, from dissociation to domestic martyrdom to delinquency. Girls often handle their rage by "acting in" and boys by "acting out." Overwhelmed, utterly frustrated and blaming themselves, the child complies with being repeatedly abused. For many reasons, as discussed throughout this book, the child may dissociate so far from all of this pain that they forget a part or all of it.
Delayed, Conflicted or Unconvincing **Disclosure**	This major target of FMS advocates, discussed earlier in this chapter, was described by Summit in 1983 in part as the tension in the triangle between the abuser, victim and co-abuser. (Here, co-abusers may also include helping professionals of all kinds.) When a victim tries to tell the truth, they get invalidation, blame or attack. (I discuss triangles elsewhere[691] and Summit does briefly.[629])
Retraction	To lessen the tension and restore a semblance of peace in the family, the victim reverses speaking about having been abused and says that "It never happened." They may blame the "mistake" on something outside the family, such as a therapist, therapy group, self-help book, movie or some therapeutic technique such as hypnosis.

likely some combination of these.

While we are just beginning to understand some of the dynamics and differences between these two kinds of retractors, there may be some possibilities in helping sort out just which of them were sexually abused from those with untrue stories or "memories" (Table 9.2).

Those retractors with untrue stories, or true FMS, may tend to have any combination of strong doubts about their memories, a pushy or inappropriately suggestive therapist, a dependent personality, a need for secondary gain and/or other outside influences that are strong. They may not fit at all, or only slightly fit or identify with having the characteristics of the adult child sexual abuse accommodation syndrome.

Table 9.2. Some Possibilities in Sorting Out Which Retractors Were Sexually Abused from Those with Actual Untrue Memories*

Characteristics	True Memory	Untrue Memory
Symptoms and signs of sexual abuse	Present	None
Identification of adult child sexual abuse accommodation syndrome	Moderate to strong	Slight
Doubts about their memories	Mild to moderate to strong, and varying or wavering	Strong and persistent
Pushiness of therapist	None to mild	Strong and often persistent
Suggestibility	Little	Often much
Dependent personality	Minimal	May be present
Secondary gain	Little	Often much
Other outside influence	May vary	May be strong
Other terms	Sexual abuse accommodation syndrome, perpetrator empathy syndrome, false "FMS"	A false memory
Other observations and findings suggestive of true & untrue memory	See pattern for each from Table 9.3 on page 92	

* It is likely that most retractors were mistreated or abused in addition to or in other ways than sexual abuse.

Retractors Who Were Sexually Abused

By contrast, those with the adult child sexual abuse accommodation syndrome (which may also be called perpetrator empathy syndrome[399] or "false FMS") may tend to have mild to moderate doubts about their memories, which I have described throughout this book as being characteristic of many if not most abuse victims with delayed memories. If they have a therapist, the therapist will not be pushy or make inappropriate suggestions about the memories, and other outside influences may vary. But if the victim or an expert and experienced clinician were to carefully and experientially examine the retracting person's story over a long period of time, such as would likely happen during a program of recovery, they may see that there was a moderate to strong identification with the sexual abuse accommodation syndrome present.

People who are trying to navigate the experiential territory of early recovery often waver between acceptance and disbelief. Confusing and painful symptoms usually become more severe as the person becomes more aware of the abuse and its aftereffects that they are experiencing. All of these can become a kind of swirl that may drive retraction. With its accompanying mental, emotional and sometimes physical abuse, having been sexually abused is an awful idea to face, and when accompanied by increasingly painful and problematic symptoms, it is not surprising that some people withdraw their accusations.[156]

I don't want to invalidate the experience, confusion and pain of anyone, including any retractor who was not sexually abused. Even so, it may be helpful to ask some questions about their experiences. For example, what motivated them to go to a therapist or look into their past in the first place? If they were not sexually abused, were they abused in some other way? The chances are high that they were. If they were sexually abused, could they have identified the wrong person as their abuser?

Some FMS advocates, like Loftus, suggest that people go into psychotherapy with mild depression or a simple eating disorder and come out with a false memory.[388] This is another example of their often simplistic thinking. People who have been abused in any or a combination of their life areas—physical, sexual, mental, emotional or spiritual—may develop nearly any disorder as a part of or related to the aftereffects of their unexpressed and unhealed traumatic experiences. They frequently have post-traumatic stress disorder (PTSD) or another high-risk disorder, as I indicate in Chapter 15.

This book is about our memory of all kinds of abuse, not just childhood sexual abuse. Accompanying child sexual abuse there are nearly always other kinds of abuse, including physical, mental, emotional and spiritual abuse. And sexual abuse is commonly not overt. It is frequently covert, subtle or hidden. Covert sexual abuse symptoms range from telling dirty jokes to a child to flirting to making sexually suggestive remarks to being preoccupied with any aspects of a child's sexuality—and any other kind of inappropriate sexually-oriented behavior.

Retractors Who Grew Up in a Dysfunctional Family

Since from 80 to 95 percent of families in the U.S. have been described as being dysfunctional in some way and since most people with symptoms enough to come for therapy grew up in a dysfunctional family,[573, 687] it is likely that most true retractors grew up in dysfunctional families. Would it be useful for them to explore this possibility, and whether it has had any effect on their adult life? Could it have had an effect on remembering having been sexually abused and then reversing that memory? Would it be helpful for them to explore these questions and the residual effect of having been "misled" about the possibility of having been sexually abused? A problem is that many of these retractors develop a kind of "therapy phobia," and a fear of going near any kind of therapeutic inner work.

> One example is of a woman who described her therapist as being "controlling", so much so that she says that he kept asking her whether she could have been sexually abused by her father so often that she finally relented and said "Yes," and by then it was hard for her to change her mind for a long time. When she finally did change her mind and retracted, she stopped seeing the therapist and went back to her family of origin, apologizing to them.
>
> When I asked her if her "controlling" therapist reminded her of anyone from her past, she said "Yes, my father, who was always dominating and controlling; I'd never thought of that connection!" I asked her if she'd thought of finding another therapist to talk to and try to heal this trauma from the first one, and she replied, "No, I'm never going near another therapist!" I spoke with this woman only briefly, and she was not a patient of mine.

In addition to being "therapist phobic," there may be another explanation for those retractors who were sexually abused. Nearly 100 years ago Pierre Janet, an early pioneer in the field of trauma and recovery, noted that trauma victims are phobic of the *memory* of the trauma.[662] They may feel fear and repugnance when confronted with the traumatic memories, and it may not be just therapy or a therapist that they fear.

To date the FMSF reports "over 300" such "retractors" or "recanters" who have surfaced in the newsletter "The Retractor" and in the FMSF's search for them. These are nearly all women with a history of once believing they had been sexually abused, and later identifying themselves to the editor of the newsletter or the FMSF. Lawrence has suggested that many of these retractors may be so overwhelmed by being separated from their ties with their family of origin that they are compelled to "change their mind" and apologize to their family. She suggests the term perpetrator empathy syndrome to describe their dynamics, symptoms and signs.[399]

Anecdotal accounts of several retractors are given as examples in *True Stories of False Memories* by Eleanor Goldstein and Kevin Farmer. Most of these women appeared to have grown up in dysfunctional families and environments, and many had been sexually abused.[278, 648] Several had experienced clear and often outrageous boundary violations with their therapists and many were also heavily medicated or addicted to medications, which could have clouded their minds and made them even more vulnerable. One can understand how, with external and internal pressure from some of their family members, they would eventually decide that their memories were not true, even though some of them may have retracted by mistake.

Even as adults, people from dysfunctional families frequently have not completed their childhood development. Not having completely individuated and separated from their parents, they tend to retain many of their unsatisfied childhood needs for love and approval from their parents, even when these relationships continue to be dysfunctional and abusive. Confronting one's parents and severing relationships with them may exacerbate these childhood needs, and the social effects of disclosure often embarrass and disrupt the family. The trauma survivor may have to face the shame brought on by public knowledge of their abuse experience. In company with symptoms, these needs, fears and social disruptions may also cause retractions.[156]

Some of these retractors are suing their therapists. We do not know how many of them had real memories of abuse and re-repressed or dissociated them as they retracted. We don't know how many were sexually abused but accused the wrong person. We also do not know how many were not sexually abused by a family member or other close person, but fell prey to some outside influence or influences as FMS advocates suggest. If these and related questions could be researched by expert clinicians in the field of trauma recovery, we would know more about how to assist people with these painful situations and dilemmas.

Until then, we can use the information that we have right now, as I describe throughout this book and continue in Tables 9.2 and 9.3. If a person has a high risk disorder present (as listed in Table 16.1 on page 151), they are at a higher risk of having been abused as a child, adolescent or adult. In such a case it is the job of the helping professional to gently search for any causal factors, including what possible kinds of abuse may have happened. Just as we screen for other disorders like hypertension and cancer, as a competent helping professional we screen for a history of abuse. But screening for these and other medical conditions is easier than it is for sexual and other kinds of abuse.

Other Findings Suggestive of True and Untrue Memory

As we work with the patient or client, we look for other findings that may be suggestive of abuse. We notice whether certain of these findings are present or absent, as described by Frederickson,[233] which I summarize in Table 9.3. We can review these observations about traumatic memories and, over time, notice them when they may appear. When a cluster of several of these are present, they provide evidence that the memory is true. This clinical process takes time, and cannot be rushed. The person needs to feel safe and supported so that they can begin to open to exploring and finding out what happened in their past. Recovery aids, as I describe in *A Gift to Myself* and *Co-dependence: Healing the Human Condition*, can be helpful in this process of remembering and naming what happened.

Some have said that it was uncomfortable to read this chapter. It was also uncomfortable for me while I was writing it. For the true retractors, erroneously remembering such an untruth brought pain into their own life and that of their family. For the abused retractors, speaking the truth of having been molested had probably initially lessened their pain, because *most of the pain comes from keeping it inside*. But now, by retracting, they have to swallow that pain and go back to the prison of silence and pretending. Both kinds of retractors hurt, and they may have been bounced around from their usually dysfunctional family to a legal and helping system that may also have been dysfunctional. Yet I believe that we can learn from them if we can ask the right questions and if they can be real with us in answering them over time.

Table 9.3. Observations and Findings Suggestive of True and Untrue Traumatic Memory (compiled and modified from Fredrickson[233])

Observation	True Memory	Untrue Memory
High Risk Disorder(s) present	Yes	No
Attractions, fears or avoidances unexplained by known history	May Be Present	Absent
Indications of emerging memories (e.g., dreams, images, flashbacks or somatic sensations)	May Be Present	Absent
Evidence of Dissociation	Often Present	Absent
Time Loss	Often Present	Absent to Slight
Supplying inconsequential detail in abuse history	May Be Present	Absent
Story matches depth of pain and symptoms throughout life	Usual	May Be Present
Tends to avoid sympathy and support	May Be Present	May Be Absent
Knows or senses how a perpetrator will act	May Be Present	Absent
Corroborating data present (e.g., medical, witness, photos)	Usually Absent, but Helpful if Present[329]	Absent
High ambivalence about abuse, memories	May Be Present	Absent to Present
Evidence of florid imagination, psychosis or pathological lying (but dissociation may resemble and person may be misdiagnosed)	Usually Absent	May Be Present

10

TRAUMATIC FORGETTING: REPRESSION, DISSOCIATION AND DENIAL

To avoid taking responsibility for their hurtful behavior, abusers and co-abusers may try to use several other excuses, reasons or claims as they attempt to invalidate their victims' experiences. These include claims that (1) Repression doesn't exist, (2) There has been no independent proof of the truth of delayed memories, (3) These memories are only a simplified explanation for people's problems, (4) Something outside the person, like a pushy therapist, caused the "false memories," and (5) Experiments show that "false memories" are easily implanted even in normal people. In this chapter and the next two I will address their first claim.

"Repression Doesn't Exist"

In her long article attacking the reality of delayed or repressed memories, normal memory researcher Elizabeth Loftus, who is a regular expert witness hired by people accused of being child molesters, cites two memory critics who support her claim.[417] The first is George Ganaway, who while saying that he is neutral on this topic, appears to be not only a "false memory" advocate, but is also on the FMSF's professional advisory board. He is one of the few clinicians on their board who works with adults who were traumatized as children, and while he bases his attack of delayed

memories on his clinical experience and knowledge of some of the literature, he appears to be strongly biased against the truth of how abuse causes its aftereffects.[261] The other is David Holmes, a psychology researcher
and FMSF board member who, similar to Loftus, has done most of his
experiments on ordinary memory.[340]

There are few others who deny the existence of repression as a psychological defense against emotional pain.[453] Indeed, Holmes' view was
included in Singer's 1990 compendium of articles entitled *Repression and
Dissociation* not because what he said is necessarily true, but as Singer
notes, to add some controversy to the otherwise general acceptance of
the existence of repression and dissociation.[602] Loftus could have chosen
to study and cite any of these other 18 articles describing some of the history and dynamics of these defense mechanisms against pain, but
focused only on the one by Holmes.[340, 417]

My and others' understandings of amnesia or forgetting is that there
are two general types—ordinary and traumatic, as I describe in Chapter
5. In their research and arguments, Loftus, Holmes and others, and to
some extent Ganaway, appear to have tried to mix apples and oranges.
They have attempted to prove the non-existence of repression by studying ordinary memory and forgetting, while not focusing on the traumatic kind. They have then tried to inappropriately transfer their findings and
conclusions that ordinary memory can be modified by various influences
onto a different kind of remembering and forgetting: the traumatic. It can
be disturbing that these people, who are also teaching and influencing
some of our helping professionals-to-be, do not appear to understand the
difference between these two basic kinds of memory. This is unfortunate,
since otherwise some of their work has merit and they have each made
contributions to their fields of research psychology. But while they deny
the existence of repression, they still use the word frequently.*

---

* For example, after denying that repression exists, Loftus uses the word repeatedly, especially in describing her own study, thus giving it legitimacy, in which she and her colleagues
found that 19% of their 100 outpatients studied had "repressed" or forgot memories of having been sexually abused.[268, 417] She also acknowledges its existence in her other writings.[420]
The same for Holmes, who says, "...although there is no evidence for repression, it should
not be concluded that there is not selectivity in perception and recall. Indeed, there is good
evidence that transient and enduring factors such as cognitive sets, emotional states, and the
availability of labels can influence what we perceive, store and recall."[340] A rose is still a rose.

Methods for Determining What is True

How can we know for sure what is correct or true about something? What methods can we use to help us determine what is true? Scientist and author Ken Wilber describes three levels of methods to do so, according to what realm the "something" is in that we are measuring or testing.[37, 697, 697a]

The first realm is the physical. The most useful and accurate method for determining what is true about one or more physical entities is the scientific method. This involves measurement through one or more of our five senses and applying the appropriate mathematical testing formulas.**

The next realm is that of the mind, exemplified by the study of psychology. Observation (phenomenology) and interpretation (hermeneutics) are the most useful and accurate methods for determining what is true about one or more of its aspects. Using the scientific method alone to study the mind will produce erroneous results, what philosopher Gilbert Ryle[570a] and Wilber[697a] call a *category error* or mistake.*** To determine what is true about the mind requires going beyond the scientific method into observation and interpretation.

The final realm is that of the spiritual. The most useful and accurate method for determining what is correct or true about the spiritual realm of human existence is to apply the approach of *ontology*, the study of

---

** Expanding from this simple notion is the realization that there is no single scientific method, only problems such as observation, validation, emergence, causality, falsifiability, error, bias and such. Methodologies within individual sciences attempt to solve these problems. Also, most scientists do not formally use "the scientific method." Each scientist has their own way of working, and many simply fly by the seat of their pants, imaginatively and creatively, and use techniques, materials, procedures and instruments passed down from other scientists. Kekule, who discovered the structure of the benzene ring, did so by having a dream about snakes with their tails in their mouth![156] Recently some have criticized aspects of the scientific method as it is being attempted to be applied to psychotherapy and memory by author and FMS advocate Robyn Dawes and others. They conclude: "In theory, the scientific method is a fine tool, but in practice it is an imperfect instrument."[195] (An unnamed writer states on page 2 of the November 1994 FMSF newsletter that "The scientific method is irrelevant not just when it comes to believing Freudian theories but all sorts of theories." Some FMS advocates use "science" and "the scientific method" when it may support their claims and reject it when it does not.)

*** It is true that some methods are particular to individual sciences and not directly transferable, even from physics to biology, let alone to psychology. The problem has been that some have been so transferred. What seems to be the fundamental problem, as Medawar said, is that a "crude science" has been [mis-]applied to the incredibly complex problems of the social sciences.[456] This appears to be an example of what Ryle and Wilber[697a] refer to as producing category errors.[456]

consciousness or being. And the most sophisticated measuring device in the spiritual realm is experience. That experience may be direct or shared.****

People who have been in Twelve-Step self-help groups, other support groups or therapy groups are especially familiar with the shared experience to validate many aspects of their lives. Direct experience is what we have every second of every day, in relationship with ourselves, with others and with the universe.

To try to measure the spiritual with either of the two prior methods alone is again to make a category error. Such measurement and testing is not valid and will not work in the spiritual realm of our human existence. Table 10.1 summarizes these principles.

Table 10.1 Methods for Determining What is True

Area to be Tested	Tested by	Brief Description
Physical or Biological	Scientific Method	Measurement through one or more of the five senses, with or without a control group; Application of appropriate formulae*
Mind	Observation and Interpretation	Phenomenology and Hermeneutics
Spirit	Experience	Direct or shared experience

* See accompanying footnotes in the text

**** Many researchers do not view the realm of spirituality as being a legitimate area of inquiry or ontology as an important, separate but expanded method of measurement and description. However, numerous respected scientists, including Heisenberg, Schroedinger, deBroglie, Jeans, Planck, Pauli, Eddington, Einstein and Crick have used and validated their existence and importance.[153, 697] Others, such as Stanislav Grof, Robert Turner, Jean Shinoda Bolen, Larry Dossey, Francis Lu, Bruce Greyson, Kenneth Ring, Ian Stevenson, Michael Sabom, Leonard Laskow and Bonnie Greenwell are approaching the spiritual more directly.

Studying Memory

Ordinary memory can be effectively studied by using the scientific method and by observation and interpretation. It can be studied both inside and outside the clinical setting—during the course of therapy and in the laboratory. But to study traumatic memory and forgetting we expand our methods, not only to observation and interpretation but also to that of ontology, the study of consciousness and experience. The study of autobiographical memory and recovery is a helpful beginning here. It would also be unethical to try to conduct experiments involving traumatic memory on people in the laboratory—for obvious reasons.

The most convincing "proof" of the existence of any of these three defenses against emotional pain—repression, dissociation and denial—is to have personally experienced it and recovered from the hurt, loss or trauma that caused it. Perhaps the next most convincing is to observe this process unfold in others, which is part of what depth- and recovery-oriented psychotherapists do. (Some may have also gone through it themselves and realized a kind of personal ontology unfold.) But to attempt to prove their existence in the laboratory by the scientific method alone is like trying to study the universe with a pair of binoculars. Even though we may thereby be able to frame a belief system about it, the universe is too far reaching and complex for this limited method. Traumatic memory appears to be similar.

It is also difficult to communicate these personal and collective experiences as "proof" of the existence of recovered traumatic memories in the face of a wave of sensationalized articles and pseudoscientific arguments in the popular press and some professional journals supporting the FMS hypothesis. Unless one has undergone psychotherapy and recovery for problems related to childhood abuse, or, unless one has read the relevant professional literature and is at the same time experienced in conducting psychotherapy with abuse survivors where these symptoms and processes of traumatic memory are observable, it is all too easy to give credence to one or more claims of FMS advocates.

Lacking these experiences, the controversy for most has been just another battle of words and "experts." While an extensive body of research demonstrating the validity of repression, dissociation and denial and recovered memory exists, psychotherapists have been put on the defensive by the suddenness and force of the FMSF attack. Asking

Table 10.2. Dimensions of Repression Selected to Indicate Each Author's Working Definition of the Term [601]

Author	Generality		Definition		Differentiation		Mechanism			Awareness	
	Specific Defense	Class of Related Defenses	Theoretical	Operational	Dissociation	Suppression	Defense	Neutral*	Coping	Conscious	Unconscious
Blatt	•						•				•
Bonano and Singer		•		•			•		•		•
Bower	•		•	•	•	•		•		•	•
Bowers [b]	•		•		•			•			•
Davis		•		•			•		•		•
Edelson	•						•				•
Erdelyi	•				•		•				•
Holmes	•					•	•				•
Horowitz et al.	•		•		•	•	•			•	•
Kihlston and Hoyt	•		•			•	•				•
Lewis	•						•				•
Luborsky, Crits-Christoph and Alexander							•				•
Schwartz		•		•			•		•		•
Shevrin	•	•	•					•		•	•
Spiegel [b]	•		•		•		•			•	•
Vaillant	•			•		•	•		•		•
Weinberger	•	•					•			•	•

* Authors conceptualizing repression as a neutral mechanism characterize it as motivated, but they do not address whether the motivation or outcome is adaptive or maladaptive.

[b] These authors, who address dissociation rather than repression in their chapters, tend to adopt a traditional view of repression. Table from ref. 601.

psychotherapists to prove the existence of repressed memories and the falsity of the FMS claims to the general public is a little like asking a chemist to prove in the media that if you add an acid to a base a salt results from the chemical reaction. While chemists could conceivably pull everyone into the laboratory and show them, psychotherapists can hardly admit individuals into therapy sessions, let alone masses of people and reporters. FMS advocates have merely demonstrated the adage that an offensive attack can sometimes be the best defense.

Repression

Since a trauma induces and activates numerous components of our inner life as well as our biochemistry and physiology, what results is usually a painful experience. If we are developmentally healthy and have a healthy and safe support system in which to work through the trauma, we will be able to grieve and heal. But if we are not developmentally healthy, usually due to having grown up in a dysfunctional family and society that block healthy development, and if we have no healthy, safe and supportive environment, then it is unlikely that we will be able to work through the trauma to completion. Rather, all of the charged material—physical, mental, emotional and spiritual—can be repressed and will remain stuck inside of us like an abscess, until it can be worked through and let go.

As countless people have observed, this charged energy is then stored somewhere inside of us. That somewhere has been called the unconscious, the part of us about which we are unaware. In their definitions of repression, 25 modern clinicians and researchers, including Holmes, say that the repressed experience and memory of the traumatic event is stored in our unconscious, as is shown in the far right column in Table 10.2. And countless others, from Freud and Janet to Klein and Kohut, have made similar statements. Nearly all of these recognize and validate the existence of repressed memories in human experience. By definition, the human unconscious is a place or repository wherein we store cognitive information and emotional energy that relate to our past traumatic experiences that we have not yet consciously processed and healed to completion, and about which we are not fully aware. In a clinically useful understanding of repression, we are unaware of this material and it is lost for an indefinite period from our consciousness and our memory.

When this trauma-associated charged energy is so stored, we are unaware that it is there. No matter what term or concept we may attach to it, we "forget." We have lost the memory, the awareness of it, and are amnestic. But how is this charged energy and information transferred to our unconscious? Many clinicians who work long term with trauma survivors believe that traumatic forgetting comes about through mechanisms

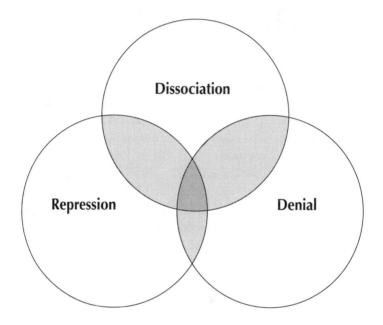

Figure 10.1. Venn Diagram of Psychological Defenses Associated with Traumatic Forgetting

such as dissociation, repression and denial, which I define in Table 10.3. Traumatic forgetting thus may proceed through any one or a combination of these defenses against pain (Figure 10.1). Dissociation, repression and denial may involve any of our physical, sexual, mental, emotional or spiritual experiences.

Freud's original 18 patients appear to have lost their memories of having been abused, and when they first consulted him they had been trying to expel their charged energy from the traumatic experiences unconsciously, in part through their psychosomatic illness—perhaps

Table 10.3. Definitions of Psychological Defenses Associated with Traumatic Forgetting

Mechanism	Definition
Dissociation	As a defense against emotional pain, dissociation is a separation from and loss of awareness of our experience of the present moment, including our beliefs, thoughts, feelings, decisions, choices, wants, needs, memories, sensations, intuitions and other life experiences. We may also separate from experiencing our inner life reactions to external events with full awareness. Dissociation is a process of separation and unintegration that functions in parallel on a time continuum.[69] This means that while we may be in part aware of some of our inner life components, we keep them separated and they are thus not integrated into our experience, memory and life for now. Dissociation may be acute or longer lasting and may be ordinary and benign, as in daydreaming, or extraordinary and used to defend against the pain of a traumatic event. Its degree may be mild, moderate or extreme and, like repression and denial, it may be associated with the loss of conscious memory for part or all of our inner life components around the event, even though a sizeable memory may remain in our unconscious mind and in our body.[229, 663]
Repression	Similar and related to dissociation and denial, repression is an automatic psychological defense against unbearable emotional pain wherein we forget a painful experience and store it in our unconscious mind. It is usually longer lasting and sometimes "deeper" ("vertical" in repression and "horizontal" in dissociation).[119, 336]
Denial	A complex defense that involves not recognizing and thus avoiding our awareness of the reality of a traumatic experience. While considered a "normal" defense at times because it may allow a graded acceptance of a hurt, loss or trauma, denial is maladaptive if it interferes with rational or appropriate action to address or heal the hurt, loss or trauma.[343, 396]

because no other way was permitted by their family and social environment.[237] It was by listening to them explore their pain and tell their
stories and by believing them that he assisted them in their healing. As
they remembered progressively more about the abuse and had a safe
person validate its reality, they brought the experience from their
unconscious, where it was stored because it was not otherwise safe to
bring it out, into their conscious awareness. Over time, they remembered
the traumatic event experientially by expressing it, and by beginning to
work through their projections (transferences) onto others, and their
symptoms improved. Less publicized until recently, Janet assisted his
patients in a similar way, as did Ferenczi and others.[435, 530, 659, 662]

Freud neither discovered nor invented the idea of repression, but
learned about and expanded it through his clinical experience, from
Herbart's work in 1806 and 1824[396] and from Janet.[530] Since then his colleagues and numerous others have studied it in progressively more
detail[601, 602] (Table 10.2). They have found that repression is not a single
or isolated event, but that it is an active, dynamic and creative process.
In this sense it is like dissociation and denial, and although these three
defenses can be helpful in our survival of traumatic events in an otherwise unsafe environment, they can also be maladaptive, especially later
in life after we are free of the more immediate threats of the traumas.[343]

Stored Painful Energy

The stored painful energy that traumatic forgetting helps us keep at bay
is like a jack-in-the-box that keeps popping up unless we keep our hand
on the cover.[343, 601] It is the unprocessed and unhealed stored painful energy that thus leads to several detrimental and painful results and only one
useful one: survival, as shown in Figure 12.1 on page 125. A key to our
healing is in increasing our awareness of the experience of our True Self
from moment to moment and remembering what happened, experientially and cognitively, to and for us in the traumatic events. To accomplish
these, we need a safe and supportive environment and plenty of time.

But growing up in an unsafe and unsupportive environment, whether
in a dysfunctional family of origin and/or society of origin, not only do
we not get the opportunity to process and heal from the traumatic events
in our lives, but we usually get the opposite, and are blocked from doing
so and often re-traumatized. In a dependent position like that of a child,

the only way to survive all of this painful experience is to separate cognitively and experientially from the trauma and the pain and pretend that
it is not happening and/or that it did not happen.

After observing this phenomenon in countless people, we can call it
traumatic forgetting, amnesia or any of a number of other terms such as:
"selective inattention,"[628] "thought stopping,"[182] "cognitive avoidance,"[468]
or any of Freud's many terms for it, like "effortless and regular avoidance
of the memory," "exclusion from thought activity," "not thinking of the
unbearable idea," "keeping something out of consciousness," "splitting-
off," or "dissociation" (which he often used synonymously with repression).[205] Whatever name we may give to traumatic forgetting, it can be
helpful to understand it by these three descriptive clinical names that we
have given to our innate human capacity to avoid overwhelming psychological and emotional pain: repression, dissociation and denial.

11

DISSOCIATION

In contrast to repression, dissociation and denial are at times a part of healthy psychological functioning. For example, denial plays a useful role early in the grieving process, and dissociation is a healthy function in several areas of life, including daydreaming, creativity states, hypnosis, highway hypnosis, guided imagery, meditation, prayer, some out-of-body experiences and mystical experience. It also becomes a useful survival mechanism for defending against the pain of mistreatment as a child and abuse or trauma at any age, as shown in Figure 11.1.

People who have experienced abuse or trauma frequently report "I went numb," "I just wasn't there" or "I left my body." To dissociate means to separate. Dissociation has been defined as a "...psycho-physiological process whereby information—incoming, stored or outgoing—is actively deflected from integration with its usual or expected associations."[114]

But what was an adaptive and useful skill in defending against the pain of childhood abuse may continue into adulthood as a maladaptive habit. There are two general ways that dissociation may be maladaptive. First, the adult pain-dissociator who has left the abusive environment of home and neighborhood may now live in a safe environment, yet they may continue to dissociate inappropriately, thus hampering their interactions and their relationships. Or second, they may remain in their abusive environment or move into another one, and while their ability to dissociate may still be useful, it may block their ability to access their inner life accurately and appropriately. In either of these the person may age regress frequently, which can also rob them of their ability to feel in charge of their life and to enjoy it.[688, 691] Age regression is a dissociative state, and many of the principles for its healing (see Chapter 5) apply for many of the other varieties of dissociation.

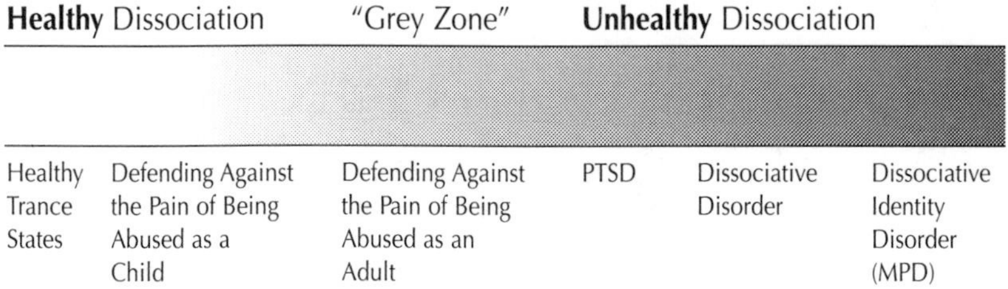

Healthy Dissociation		"Grey Zone"		**Unhealthy** Dissociation	
Healthy Trance States	Defending Against the Pain of Being Abused as a Child	Defending Against the Pain of Being Abused as an Adult	PTSD	Dissociative Disorder	Dissociative Identity Disorder (MPD)

Figure 11.1. A Spectrum of Dissociation

While a child is usually unable to escape an abusive environment unless they have an effective advocate, an adult who has awakened to being in an abusive situation may be able to muster up the courage not only to leave it, but also to heal their wounds from the past abuse that drew them into the abusive relationship. The wounding itself may manifest in any number of ways—from the characteristics of adult children of dysfunctional families that are familiar to many in the recovery movement to many, if not most mental disorders, including PTSD and dissociative orders. In any of these disorders, the recovering person can learn to recognize their dissociations and to use them more creatively and constructively.

Dissociation thus tends to be a more creative, active and fluid defense against pain than repression and denial. It may last from a short while to a long duration, and as is true for the other two defenses, there may be an associated loss of memory, also for a variable time, as shown in Table 11.1.

When I dissociate in a healthy way, I may focus my awareness on only one or two areas of my experience. Or I may shift, and scan many areas. Dissociation is thus a great facility and skill through which I may explore and experience parts of my life. Nemiah says that unhealthy dissociation

Table 11.1. Some Differences Among Dissociation, Repression and Denial

Characteristic	Dissociation	Repression	Denial
Usefulness	More creative	More limited	More limited
Activity	Action and result	More a result	More a result
Movement	More fluid	Less fluid	Less fluid
"Direction"	"Horizontal" (split awareness)	"Vertical" (repressed)	
Time	May be shorter lasting	Longer lived	Varies
Defensive Attitude	Varies; may be mild to moderate	Varies; may be mild to moderate	Common, may be marked
"Normality"	May be normal	Usually not	May be normal
Loss of Memory	Often	Yes	Yes*
Response to Therapy	Varies	May be more more difficult	Varies**

* The person who is in denial may have some degree of awareness of having experienced or committed the trauma, although that is usually defended against to a moderate to a high degree.
** With appropriate therapeutic intervention, caring and support, the person may lessen their denial over time.

can be differentiated from the healthy kind by (1) a significant alteration in a person's sense of identity, as seen in fugue states, dissociative identity disorder (i.e., MPD),[488] as well as in the common numbed dissociation of the True Self when we let our false self run our life and by (2) a partial or complete loss of memory.[488] Others agree.[610]

As mentioned above, I may also dissociate to defend against emotional pain. For example, dissociating is a protective and useful survival defense for growing up in an unhealthy family. It allows me to separate from my awareness of my inner life, especially my painful feelings and thoughts when I am being mistreated or abused. So here it serves a useful purpose. But after I grow up and leave that family, to dissociate frequently from all pain may no longer be necessary or particularly useful, especially if I am now around safe people.

Beginning to Heal Unhealthy Dissociation

In recovery, as we heal in the company of those safe people, we can begin to recognize when we are dissociating. If we are in group or individual therapy, the others can mirror what they see and hear. Our group can also describe what is coming up for them from their inner lives as we tell our story and describe how we are feeling.

Whether alone or with a safe person, we can experiment with deliberately trying to dissociate. Bringing what was formerly unconscious into our conscious awareness can be empowering.[272] As we dissociate—that is, alter our state of consciousness in this way—we can practice increasing or decreasing the intensity of our experience. We can thereby gain more awareness and control over what once may have felt out of control for us.

Identifying which people or situations may trigger the experiences of dissociation is also useful. Then we can begin to set healthy boundaries and limits around them so that they will not continue to hurt us.[691]

In all my years of practice I have never seen a person with a dissociative disorder who grew up in a healthy family. These dissociative disorders, along with PTSD and anxiety disorder, appear to be mostly disorders of fear. Each of these people grew up in a dysfunctional family and thus remains an adult child of it. The dysfunctional family repeatedly shamed and threatened the child, leaving that child in a continuous state of post-traumatic fear that manifested as either hyperstimulation or a feeling of numbness, or an alternating of the two.

Models of Dissociation

While healthy dissociation allows us to explore and locate stored material, with unhealed traumatic experiences it may become the unhealthy kind. Dissociating can bring about a divided, separated or parallel access to our awareness. Several areas of our inner life may appear to exist independently, and yet they are related, such as when we defend against the pain of a traumatic experience. Here at least three associated areas of our inner life may be seriously affected: our identity (is this me or someone else who is being abused?), our knowledge of the event (cognition and content, including any details) and our feelings (more often painful , but sometimes this pain may be mixed with pleasurable ones—and thus we may feel confusion). These experiences may become so separated, split off or dissociated from our awareness that we end up with: (1) no conscious memory of the experience, (2) memory of only parts of it, or (3) a vacillating confusion about our experience.

Trauma therapist Bennet Braun has added two additional dimensions, behavior and sensation, to make the BASK model of dissociation,[69, 140] to which I add identity, imagery and memory, as noted above, to spell the pnemonic BASKIM. These are illustrated as follows. (Figure 11.2)

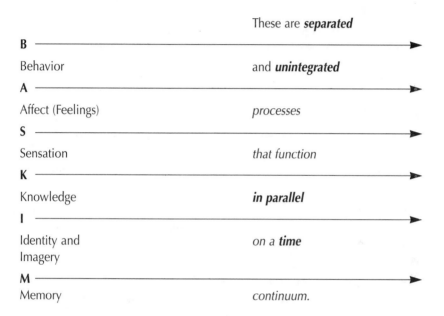

These are **separated**

B ──────────────────────────────────►
Behavior   and **unintegrated**

A ──────────────────────────────────►
Affect (Feelings)   *processes*

S ──────────────────────────────────►
Sensation   *that function*

K ──────────────────────────────────►
Knowledge   **in parallel**

I ──────────────────────────────────►
Identity and   *on a* **time**
Imagery

M ──────────────────────────────────►
Memory   *continuum.*

Figure 11.2. BASKIM Model of Dissociation
(expanded from Braun[67])

With no healthy models to teach us otherwise and no safe people or places to share and process our inner experiences, and because they are often so painful or confusing, we may split off any of these components of our experience deep within the unconscious part of our psyche. This is similar to what I have referred to in Chapter 5 as "The Child or True Self going into hiding."

This dissociation, separation or splitting off of one or more of these components may come about in any pattern or sequence. A common pattern is when a person cognitively remembers aspects of a traumatic experience and dissociates from their associated feelings, sensations or images for a long duration, as the following history illustrates.

> At age 30 Susan came for counseling because she had recently felt a repulsion for her five-year-old son and had begun to reject him physically and emotionally. After several counseling sessions she began to remember that her mother had treated her the same way when she was five, although more severely. It was at this age when she had realized that her mother was very disturbed. While she had always cognitively remembered that she had been sexually abused by a baby sitter at age six and by her grandfather at age nine, she had forgotten her emotions that were attached to the experience of being molested. While talking about it with her therapist, her painful feelings gradually returned. She then remembered telling her mother immediately after being molested by her grandfather (her mother's father), and her mother's dissociating and completely ignoring her. At that time she realized that her mother was molested as a child by him also. When she was 30 she told her aunt, who believed her and validated her experience. After expressing her story and her pain she was able to grieve the trauma that she had not been able to before. Her feeling of repulsion for her son disappeared.

Susan's experience is an example of a frequent pattern of the dissociation experience after trauma that is not allowed to be processed. It shows how even in those who have always remembered trauma they may still have ungrieved pain to experience and work through. While she was able to resolve her present complaint in 15 therapy sessions, she continues to work on residual associated pain and core issues, and her ability to function as an individual, wife and mother continues to improve.

Janet's Model of Memory and Dissociation

In the late 1800s and early 1900s the French neurologist Pierre Janet was a pioneer in the field of trauma and recovery.[361, 362] He coined the terms *dissociation* (déagrégation) and *subconscious*, where memories are automatically stored.[530, 659, 662] He was the first to articulate the clinical principles of the dissociative disorders, and was also the first to systematically explore and treat the underlying associated traumatic memories.[530] While he inspired Freud in his early work on the etiology of hysteria, which demonstrated trauma as the cause, Janet's findings became overshadowed by the denial of the abuse facilitated by Freud's oedipal theory.[187, 327, 435, 464] His work was mostly ignored until 1970, when Ellenberger credited him in *The Discovery of the Unconscious.*[197] For most of the 20th century, psychoanalysis—the study of repressed wishes and instincts—and descriptive psychiatry and psychology were used to deny the findings that trauma, often forgotten or minimized by the patient, caused or was a major factor in the "psychopathology" or "mental illness" with which they presented.[662] Janet's work has more recently been revived and applied to our growing understanding of the effects of trauma.[326, 530, 532, 659, 662]

Janet viewed memory as the central organizing apparatus of the mind and that which sorts and integrates the many parts of our experience of our inner and outer life. He saw healthy psychological functioning as the proper operation of the system of remembering.[665] He was also the first to differentiate ordinary memory from traumatic memory.

He did not usually address healthy kinds of dissociation, but focused more on the unhealthy kind. He said that the cardinal feature of this dissociation was amnesia—partial or complete loss of memory for events in the dissociated state.[530] Unintegrated, emotionally charged traumatic experiences lead to dissociation and the formation of traumatic memories, which Janet called "subconscious fixed ideas," or *idées fixes.* These influence our current inner life and relationships, and are usually accessible under hypnosis. The dissociated traumatic memories may return subtly or overtly and be manifested by any of a variety of physical sensations (somatic memories), images or nightmares, behavioral re-enactments, and other symptoms and signs.[662]

Other Models

In 1922 Wells described five kinds of dissociation: *Type 1*—dissociation from our awareness of an ordinarily consciously controlled process, such as speech, sensation and movement; *Type 2*—dissociation from the control of the main personality of a bodily process like digestion, heart action and elimination; *Type 3*—dissociation of a group of ideas from the main mass or stream of controlled associations, like automatic writing and dream productions; *Type 4*—dissociation of a system of ideas which displace consciousness in its control of the organism, like fugues, sleep walking and multiple personality; and *Type 5*—dissociation of one of several ideas which the main consciousness is aware of but fails to recognize and hence misunderstands, mislabels and projects.[462, 682] Calof says that "Type 5 dissociation accounts for 'scrambled' memory phenomena such as flashbacks and abreactions, where an individual projects unmetabolized traumatic content onto their on-going experience, as when a traumatized veteran drops to the ground defensively when a car backfires." [112, 114]

A few decades later, Spiegel defined dissociation as ". . . analogous to working in one directory of a computer without being able to access the main menu indicating the presence of other directories and without path commands enabling the directory to find information needed from another directory. The presence of the material in one directory makes the computer act as though the other material does not exist." [610] Hilgard has also spoken of dissociation as having a "horizontal" rather than "vertical" (as in repression) depiction of the relation between our conscious and unconscious awareness. He sees repression as existing when material is more deeply buried and harder to access, and dissociation as a series of available but unused aspects of consciousness that are closer to the surface. [337, 610]

In hypnosis, two or more of these inner life components, such as those shown in the BASKIM model or those in Figure 3.3 on page 109, may be activated and brought out during the session, and the hypnotized person may or may not remember the experience afterwards. [610] Van der Kolk and van der Hart said, "Repression reflects a vertically layered model of the mind: what is repressed is pushed downwards, into the unconscious. The subject no longer has access to it. Only symbolic, indirect indications would point to its assumed existence. Dissociation reflects a horizontally layered model of mind: when a subject does not remember a trauma, its 'memory' is contained in an alternate stream of consciousness, which may be subconscious or dominate consciousness, e.g., during traumatic re-enactments."

Areas of Dissociation

We may dissociate our awareness and experience in any of several areas of our life—the physical, mental, emotional and spiritual. The following are some examples.

Physical — Out-of-body experience, psychogenic or hysterical anesthesia or paralysis, some acute drug intoxication, physical self-harm, violence to another, overeating and purging.

Mental — Separating or distancing from one or more inner life components, such as our beliefs, thoughts and feelings; fantasizing, intellectualizing.

Emotional — Separating from feelings, whether painful or joyful, "numbing out," smiling or laughing at pain, "poker face" or a mask.

Spiritual — All of the above, as exemplified by age regression; plus feeling separated from others and the God of our understanding.

We may dissociate in any one or more of these areas in a healthy or an unhealthy way. We may also dissociate as individuals or collectively. Individuals may dissociate frequently, e.g., when they mean "*I* get angry" they say "*You* get angry" or "*One* gets angry." An example of collective dissociation is calling something by another name, such as when we call homelessness "displaced person status," or when we call fear "anxiety" and sadness or grief "depression." [689]

Other Manifestations

We can summarize the following manifestations or dimensions of dissociation, as shown in Figure 11.3 below. On the plus side, it is a healthy skill and a survival aid. On the minus side, it splits our inner life experience, is associated with age-regression and panic attacks, and can leave us feeling numb with a loss of our awareness, memory and identity. But as we heal, we can also see it as an opportunity. This opportunity includes its advantages of being once again a healthy skill. We now use it to help us heal.

Figure 11.3. Some Manifestations of Dissociation

Advantages to Dissociation

When we dissociate, we alter our state of consciousness. The person who can move spontaneously from one state of consciousness to another can have several advantages. One is that in recovery they may eventually be able to access their unconscious feelings and other inner life material more easily. And they can go in and out of therapeutic trance more easily. While fear is often still a block for some, they may be able to make more constructive use of experiential techniques in their recovery.

Spiritual Advantages

People who can dissociate consciously may also eventually be able to more easily experience a loving relationship with their Higher Power. For example, many people have had near-death experiences (NDEs) in which they seemed to leave their body and enter a realm of light and peace where they met beings who told them it was not yet their time to die. I have observed that people who are aware of having come from dysfunctional families may report experiencing a more loving NDE than do people who are not aware that their family is dysfunctional. In their study of 128 people, 74 of whom had NDEs, Ring and Rosing discovered some of these connections.[549a] Their report is striking.

> We begin by postulating that a history of child abuse and trauma plays a central etiological role in promoting sensitivity to NDEs. Our assumption, which reflects a now increasingly widespread understanding of some of the consequences of childhood abuse and trauma, is that growing up under such conditions would tend to simulate the development of a dissociative response style as a means of psychological defense. Children who are exposed either to the threat or the actuality of physical violence, sexual abuse or other severe traumata, will be strongly motivated selectively to "tune out" those aspects of their physical and social world that are likely to harm them by splitting themselves off from the sources of these threats, that is, by other, nonsensory realities where, by virtue of their dissociated state, they can feel safe regardless of what is happening to the body. In this way . . . dissociation would be predicted to allow, in turn, relatively easy access to alternate, nonordinary realities.
>
> When, in later life, such persons undergo the trauma of a near-death incident, they are thus more likely than others, because of their prior familiarity with nonordinary realities, to be able to "flip" into that state of consciousness, which, like a special lens, affords a direct glimpse of the NDE.

What we are suggesting, then, is that such persons are what we might call psychological sensitives with low stress thresholds, and that it is their traumatic childhoods that have helped to make them so. From our point of view, however, these individuals — our NDErs — are the unwitting beneficiaries of a kind of compensatory gift in return for the wounds they have incurred in growing up: that through the exigencies of their difficult childhoods they also come to develop an extended range of human perception beyond normally recognized limits. Thus, they may experience directly what the rest of us with unexceptional childhoods may only wonder at.[549a]

In 1970 Josephine Hilgard found a variation on this theme—a somewhat different connection between dissociation and trauma. She observed that more severe punishment in childhood was associated with hypnotizability, and she suggested "a possible tie between punishment and hypnotic involvement might come by way of dissociation . . . ."[336, 610] Some "expert" witnesses who have testified on behalf of accused child molesters have tried to use the abuse survivor's easy hypnotizability as a way to try to invalidate the authenticity of their memories of having been abused. Knowing the above information would tend to negate this kind of a defense.

A Course in Miracles defines dissociation as being caught up in or stuck between two worlds: God's and the ego's (the *Course* uses the term *ego* similar to what we call the *false self*). In this kind of expanded view, it says, "Dissociation is a distorted process of thinking whereby two systems of belief [i.e., God's world and the ego's world] which cannot coexist cannot be maintained." This observation emphasizes the usefulness of spirituality in recovery.[145] Since the dissociator in recovery can perhaps know God more easily, we are here transforming the curse of being wounded in this way into a gift.

As we advance in recovery we can make many important observations and have many empowering experiences. One of these is the discovery that, once we know in our hearts just what our destructive defenses and pains are, we can ask our Higher Power to transform or to remove them. The *Course* says, for example, "Defenses, like everything you made, must be gently turned to your own good, translated by the Holy Spirit from means of self-destruction to means of preservation and release."[145] I recommend the *Course* only toward the end of or after completing a full recovery program for healing the effects of trauma.[688, 689, 691, 692]

"I didn't do it."
—Father James
Porter in prison
for molesting at
least 28 children.

12

DENIAL

*Denial is much
more complex
than this.*

Denial is a complex defense that involves not recognizing and thus avoiding our awareness of the reality of a traumatic experience. While it is a "normal" defense at times—when it *assists* us in having a graded acceptance of a hurt, loss or trauma—denial is *maladaptive* if it interferes with our rational or appropriate action to address or heal the hurt, loss or trauma. Here, either alone or in combination with repression and/or dissociation, denial prevents us from normal, healthy grieving.

While there is generally a loss of memory in relation to the trauma, the person who is in denial may still have some degree of awareness of what the problem is. However, even that bit of awareness may be so strongly defended against that most of the time they cannot or will not remember.

The Dynamics of Denial

Our early understanding of denial was limited to the simpler definitions that came from a few psychoanalysts.[236, 396, 657] In the 1970s, evolving from the clinical observation and experience of workers in the addictions field, we began to understand some of the more complex dynamics of denial.[30, 55, 675] To the observer who knows what the abuse, trauma or problem actually is, such as alcoholic drinking, it can look like the person is *lying, minimizing* or just *covering up.* But in reality they are caught in a complex web of thinking and believing that protects them from facing and dealing directly with their trauma or problem. As addictions therapists and authors LeClair Bissell, John Wallace and I have described, denial may be due to any one or, more usually, a combination of factors.[30, 55, 675] It may be useful to illustrate these factors by describing some of their dynamics as they may occur in the perpetrator or abuser and co-abuser—as well as in the victim or survivor, which I show in Table 12.1.

In the process of denial, either the abuser or victim may be *consciously lying* to some degree, usually due to *fear* of the consequences of telling the truth. While the *abuser* may not want to take responsibility for their actions, the *co-abuser* may not want to take responsibility for their *in*actions, i.e., they let the abuse go on without stopping it. They may fear that to try to stop the abuse that they would lose everything. The *victim* may have other fears, such as the fear of physical harm, abandonment, death, betraying the abuser or confronting the co-abuser.

While classical denial is usually a factor in most who deny, a drug-induced *memory blackout* occurs in most alcoholics and sometimes in benzodiazepine (Valium-type drugs) intoxication or addiction. From 75 to 90 percent of alcoholics have experienced from several to numerous memory blackouts, during which they cannot remember what happened while they were drinking (for example, where they parked their car, an embarrassing joke they told their boss' wife, or having sex with someone).[667] An alcohol or other sedative-induced memory blackout may last for about an hour to as long as several days, but the person does not "pass out." Rather, they are amnestic of the events during the blackout, but without any loss of consciousness. Observers are usually not able to recognize that the person is in a blackout. But later, when their inappropriate or other behavior is exposed, the person or another may be able to identify what happened as being a memory blackout.[685] Since there is a higher than average incidence of alcoholism and other chemical dependence among physical and sexual abusers, it is crucial to screen for this illness in these situations. In the victim, unless they are drinking or using other sedative drugs, this type of memory blackout is unlikely. In heavy drinkers or users of legal or illegal drugs, other toxic effects may play a role in their ability to think, process information and remember.

Euphoric recall means remembering the good times or aspects of an experience and not the unpleasant ones. This may be a common factor in victims and may occur in abusers and co-abusers. The fact that *no one points out* what is really happening or intervenes is another factor that is common in both. This may be related to *denial by others*, such as family, friends, clergy, teachers and helping professionals. Their own pain, confusion and lack of knowledge may compel them not to look for the abuse or to believe it. *Wishful thinking* means that the person wishes that the associated pain and confusion were not present.

Most people don't know much about the existence and dynamics of child and spousal abuse, and so another factor in denial is *ignorance about the problem.* Having been abused in their past themselves, but not wanting to face it, the abuser/co-abuser may know no other way to handle the pain of their conflict but to deny the existence of the abuse.

There is usually a *social stigma* associated with any abuse. This generates strong feelings of both shame and guilt in all affected people. These are usually also associated with a *fear of the unknown.* The person may also fear some specific consequences, like being blamed, judged or not believed. The complex *thinking quandary* has been described by Wallace as an unusual difficulty in understanding the full dynamics and consequences of their behavior and experience.[675] The abuser or co-abuser knows that something is wrong, but cannot link their behavior to their drinking, drug using or other experience. They often try to find any other available "reason" or excuse—other than their abusive behavior—to explain what is not working in their life, but they cannot clearly connect it with their abusive or neglecting behavior—which they are also not able to recognize as being abusive or neglectful.

Especially in sexual abuse, and sometimes in other kinds of abuse, the abuser makes *threats of harm* to the victim or to others if the victim were to tell or actually tells of the event(s).[202, 629, 631] Finally, there may be *other dynamics of "the secret,"* such as the abuse of power, triangles and betrayal, which I have described in *Boundaries and Relationships.*[691] Several or all of these factors may be present in this complex web of denial, as I summarize in Table 12.1.

Memory may be altered in two ways in classical denial (1) The perception of experience in the present is altered. Via its habits of denial, the false self may adopt and encode a desensitized, alienated interpretation of reality. But even so, the submerged True Self retains the capacity to eventually re-interpret these memories, since the true but altered perception appears to be somehow stored in memory, with screening from

Table 12.1. Factors in the Complexity of Denial as Illustrated in the Abuser and the Victim

Factor	Abuser	Victim
1) Conscious **lying**	Some degree possible	Some degree possible
	—Both due to fear of consequences—	
2) Classical **denial**[236]	Likely	Likely
3) Memory **blackout**[667]	Occur in 75 to 90% of alcoholics and less often with other sedative drugs	Not a likely factor, unless drinking or using
4) Other **Toxic effects** on thinking and memory	Occurs in heavy drinkers or drug users	Not a likely factor, unless drinking or using
5) **Euphoric recall** (remembering only the good aspects)	Possible	Probable
6) **No one points out** or intervenes	Usual	Usual
7) Denial by **others** (family, friends, teachers, helping professionals)	Their own pain, confusion and lack of knowledge may compel them not to look for the abuse or believe it	
8) **Wishful thinking**	Both usually wish that the pain and confusion were not present	
9) **Ignorance** about the problem	Abused themselves, they may know no other way	Usual. Also often idealize the abuser
10) **Stigma** (shame and guilt) related to the abuse	Present	Present
11) **Fear** of the unknown[55]	Present	Present
12) Complex **thinking quandary**[675]	Usually present	Usually present
13) **Threat** of harm	The abuser usually threatens harm if the victim tells of the abuse	
14) Other **dynamics** of "the secret"	Usually Present	Usually present
	(e.g., the abuse is often enacted in private)	

* Factors 1 through 11 are from Bissell 1975,[55] 12 is from Wallace 1977[675] and the remainder from my observations.

the denial of the false self acting as a barrier to the true memory. (2) As a conditioned habit of misperception, denial not only may encode the distorted perceptions of the false self into memory, but often continues to screen any uncomfortable or painful memory thrown up by the True Self as time passes. It also continues to screen experience in adult life according to the conditioning it has received. One example of this is the inability of some people to perceive when they are being abused in adult relationships. As we become aware in our recovery of the nature of the false self and its mechanisms of denial, our memories are progressively freed of distortion, and our memories and perceptions of reality in the present become clearer.[156]

Denial by the Accused

The accused abuser and co-abuser usually deny that the abuse happened, and any of the above mechanisms may be operative. While we do not know as much about the trauma psychology of the abuser as we do about that of the survivor, there are a few pioneering therapists in this country who specialize in treating offenders. Duncan Bowen is one of these, and he has treated more than 2,000 offenders over the past seven years.[67] In commenting on denial by these abusers, he says:

There are different degrees of denial, or if you wish disclosure. First, there is denial to the public or others. Second, there is denial to one's self. Many abusers or offenders deny any abuse to others for many reasons. Most commonly it is the abuser's word against the victim's, and especially so in a situation where there is no physical evidence against them. Most abusers fight accusations with the technicalities of their case.

When a *court-ordered* or otherwise coerced abuser has been referred for treatment, about 80 percent are in denial at the first interview with the therapist. Anywhere during the treatment process, from intake evaluation to completion, which can be years, an abuser can move in and out of denial.

I have often seen abusers come out of denial in therapy but remain in denial to the public or their family. I have had many clients move out of denial to themselves in group therapy. When this occurs there is a constructive and freeing shift in their verbalizations, emotions and ways they approach their issues. Shortly after this, the person may move toward honesty in therapy with others. Just because an abuser is in denial doesn't mean that they will always stay there.

A client remained in denial of his charges throughout his treatment, which lasted about 1½ years. On the day of his last visit his estranged children, whom he had not spoken to in years because they accused him of sexual abuse, called him. Due to that phone call and reconciliation with his children, he came out of denial and stated he had abused them years before. Because of his acknowledging what happened, all family members were able to heal more and to reunite the family.

From Bowen's extensive clinical experience and from that of others,[31, 67, 202, 203, 680] we can see that denial by the accused abuser is usual, complex, and may vary over time according to different circumstances.

Other Defenses Against the Pain

While they may occur less commonly as part of the dynamics of traumatic forgetting than do dissociation, repression and denial, a person may unconsciously mobilize any one or more additional defenses against their mental and emotional pain. These may include the defenses of splitting, displacement, suppression, rationalization, intellectualization, projection, projective identification, somatization and others.[326, 641] Indeed, psychiatrist George Vaillant says that almost any of the defenses against pain may be involved.[658]

Splitting

Splitting occurs when the psyche unconsciously divides itself or part of itself into two or more components, similar to what people do in the core issue of all-or-none thinking and behaving.[85, 687] As a child, the 1958 Miss America, Marilyn Van Derbur, was repeatedly sexually abused by her father, and she traumatically forgot it until she was 24 years old. But on remembering the abuse, she eventually recounted that she had "...lost all memory of what was happening as it was happening."[641] To do this, she had split herself into a happy "day child" and a terrified "night child," so that she could survive and function better during the day. The "day child" didn't know what was happening to the "night child."[641] She described her experience as follows.

> In order to survive, I split into a day child, who giggled and smiled, and a night child, who lay awake in a fetal position, only to be pried apart by my father. Until I was 24, the day child had no conscious knowledge of the night child. During the day, no embarrassing or angry glances ever passed between my father and me . . . because I had no

conscious knowledge of what he was doing to me.[167]
But the more degraded the night child became, the more the day child needed to excel . . . from skiing on the University of Colorado's ski team, to being a debutante, to graduating with Phi Beta Kappa Honors, to being named Miss America.
I believed I was the happiest person who ever lived. I truly believed that.

As Terr describes it, splitting is a defense that is occasionally used by young children who endure long or repeated traumas.[641] Terr said that splitting also may occur ". . . when children project their own qualities onto imaginary companions or superheros, as many normal children do. No memory loss is inherent in splitting. But any defense can be used to effect forgetting, splitting included."

Splitting may also be involved in projection onto others—some people being "all good" and others "all bad." In an effort not to lose their adult children and grandchildren, some accused abusers and co-abusers may split so that their accusing child is "all good" and is simply the victim of an "all bad" therapist, technique, group or book. By contrast, a recovering patient may for a time idealize a therapist or someone else as being "all good" and their accused abuser and/or co-abuser as "all bad." Some retractors may have started out in this kind of stance and then reversed their split, so that now the therapist is "all bad" and their formerly accused abusers are "all good."

Displacement

Displacement is a defense against emotional pain that helps parts of the memory of it disappear by diverting attention to something that doesn't hurt as much, like focusing more on losing a casual friendship than the recent death of a parent. Displacement often combines with splitting in childhood. Terr notes that "When [some of these] defenses work against memory, they don't necessarily block out all of the memory. They sometimes go to work on only one bit—the most painful or conflicted part of the story."[641] But with traumatic forgetting, the entire story can also be lost for a long time, as has occurred with countless survivors of abuse.

Projection

Another kind of displacement is called *transference*. A person transfers, displaces or *projects* unhealed emotionally charged material from

their past onto others in their present relationships. Projection and transference are so common that most of us use them to some degree every
day.[658, 689, 691] *Projective identification* is a more complicated form of projection wherein one person projects their unwanted, unowned and usually forgotten pain onto another, and that other person then
unconsciously acts that pain out for them.[691] For example, if I don't want
to own and express my anger, I may unconsciously collude with you to
do it for me, which you then do—also unconsciously. Projective identification could be happening when abusers, in denial, project their own
"badness" onto their victim, who then unconsciously acts it out for them
—such as in some retractors and in many others. In fact, the backlash
may be in part a collective attempt at a reenactment of projective identification, with the now "innocent" abusers and co-abusers patronizingly
admonishing their "bad" accusing adult children and their "bad" therapists. The difference is that today most of these adult children and most
therapists are not acting out this projected "badness" for them.

Some Results and Consequences of Traumatic Forgetting

The results and consequences of traumatic forgetting and not healing
the trauma are legion.[43, 85, 86, 88, 92, 130, 138, 176, 186, 256, 270, 352, 501, 629, 663] They are devastating. After a single acute hurt, loss or trauma, if the victim has a *safe
environment* in which to express and process their pain, within a few
weeks or months of doing this it will usually be worked through. Severe
trauma or a bigger loss may take longer, as will repeated single traumas.
But if the person is somehow unable to process and grieve their loss or
trauma, whether it be due to an unsafe environment, untrained, inexperienced or unrecovered helping professionals, and/or a lack of knowledge or experience—a sequence of painful consequences will usually
begin to develop, some of which I show in Figure 12.1.

By the process of traumatic forgetting and/or the inability or lack of
opportunity to grieve the traumas, a chain of events ensues. When we
experience a traumatic event, the entire metabolism of our being is shak-
en, including that which is involved in the physical, mental, emotional
and spiritual. This experience results in an accumulation of stored,
painful energy—energy that to heal must be expressed, grieved and
processed. If this healthy grieving process does not happen, several
painful consequences occur.

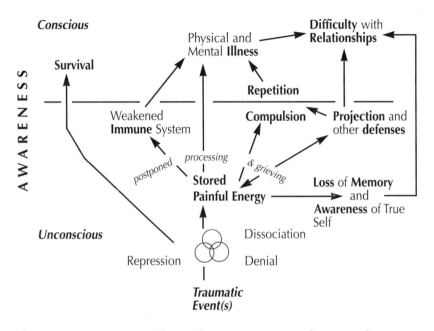

Figure 12.1. Some **Results** and **Consequences** of **Traumatic Forgetting** (Dissociation, Repression and Denial)

On a physical level, our immune system is weakened,[512] and we thereby become more vulnerable to all sorts of illness. On a mental and emotional level we may, in varying degrees, lose our awareness of our True Self.[122a, 345, 687, 691] This loss of awareness may be associated with a loss of memory for all or parts of the traumatic experiences, both of which may then lead to a difficulty with relationships.

Like an abscess that lies undrained under the skin, this energy tries to express itself and heal. These attempts at expression and healing may take almost any form on any one or a combination of our physical, mental, emotional and spiritual realms, and psychoanalysts call them the repetition compulsion. They may take the form of illness, difficulties in relationships or making the same mistake over and over, like the person who marries three active alcoholics in a row (see also pages 159-161).

When we experience all of this pain, we want to get rid of it. But we may be unaware of parts or even all of what is happening, and so one of our only ways of trying to dump it may be to try to give it to someone else, i.e., by projection. And as do other consequences, projection causes us even more difficulty in our relationships. We may also project some of our unfinished business onto the God of our understanding, which can also interfere with that relationship and our spirituality.

Conclusion

These are some examples of the downside of traumatic forgetting and not expressing our experience. But there is an upside. Stuffing our pain in whatever way we may have done it helped us to survive. And knowing what we do now, as we awaken to our past and present experiences more and more, we can begin to heal our resulting psychic injuries.

Trauma psychologists and researchers have observed that offenders and co-offenders deny different aspects of their behavior, including denial of: 1) the facts and the behaviors themselves, 2) the impact and seriousness of the abuse, 3) their responsibility for offending or co-offending, 4) their need for treatment, and 5) their awareness of any of the above.

Denial can range across a continuum, from total denial to dropping it, with subsequent advanced owning of their behavior.

Bruce Laflen and William Sturm, who assist sex offenders in recovery, see their denial as a narcissistically based coping mechanism that the offender and family use to maintain homeostasis within themself, their family and their community.[391a] They see four *stages* in recovery from their developmentally based wounds regarding the denial that covers their wounds and pain. These include: 1) denial of their behavior, 2) minimization of their behavior and need for treatment, 3) denial of responsibility for their behaviors, and 4) full admission of their behaviors, with acceptance of responsibility for and genuine guilt about having done them.[391a] This process is illustrated in Appendix F on page 319.

Since all three people involved—the abuser, co-abuser and the victim—may use any one or a combination of dissociation, repression, denial or other mechanisms, to defend themselves against feeling the pain of the abuse and dealing with it, and thus "forget" about it, they often look for ways to verify or corroborate that the abuse really happened. I will address these in the next three chapters.

13

VERIFYING AND
CORROBORATING
A MEMORY

Another claim by FMS advocates is that there has been "no independent corroboration of delayed memories." While this is a vague statement,
it may mean that they want a more neutral and objective person than the
survivor or their therapist, Twelve Step sponsor or close friend to verify
that the abuse happened. Or they may mean that they want an independent researcher to corroborate the delayed memories of a large group of
people. Of course, this latter request has already been answered by seven
such studies on a total of 1,039 people, mostly women, with a history of
having been sexually abused, in reports that were published from 1987
through 1995. These showed that from 16 to 64 percent of these 1,039
people were found to have experienced delayed memories of having
been abused,[84, 102, 118, 329, 417, 552, 699, 700] as I have described in Chapter 7 on pages
65 through 74.

These kinds of studies and their data verify and corroborate my clinical experience and that of countless other therapists who assist people
who are healing from the long term effects of trauma. But what about the
individual who wants to know if their memories of having been
mistreated or abused are true? Are there ways that they can verify their
experience? And what about their family and loved ones—especially the

accused abuser and co-abuser? In the absence of their own memories of abusing the alleged survivor—or witnessing or hearing the abuse*—how can they know that the accusations against them are true?

In most situations the abuser and co-abuser are unaware of their role, responsibility and involvement in causing the abuse, and unless there is strong external corroborating evidence to prove their involvement, they are unlikely to be able to open to that possibility. Such direct, external, circumstantial or "legal proof" of abuse may include: witness accounts, other victims' stories, diaries, letters, notes, photographs, medical records, or an admission by the abuser. While this kind of corroborating evidence may be useful to the victim, the accused and especially to the court, it is neither necessary nor required to convince the survivor or their therapist of the authenticity of the memory of the trauma, unless there is compelling evidence otherwise. Neither the survivor nor the therapist is a legal investigator. The focus of recovery should be on the healing process for the survivor and the focus of the therapy should be on assisting the person in that healing and in accomplishing their recovery goals.

More important than external corroboration in verifying the existence of any past trauma are its results or aftereffects, which we also call internal corroborating or verifying evidence.[641] These are the clinical conditions, symptoms, signs, dynamics and patterns that are experienced and observed over time, either in or outside of a program of recovery. In this chapter and the next one I will focus more on external ways of corroborating the existence of one or more traumatic experiences, and in Chapter 15 I will describe some important aspects of internal corroboration.

External Corroboration

Any victim of abuse who decides to talk about what happened may encounter a variety of responses, from positive to negative, that are validating or invalidating, depending on the listener and the circumstances surrounding the sharing encounter.

For those who decide to search for outside confirmation of the abuse

---

* At first glance it may be difficult to see just how an *abuser* could harm another person, especially a child, physically, sexually and to some extent mentally or emotionally, without knowing that they were doing so. As well, it may be hard to imagine how a *co-abuser* could witness, hear or otherwise know about the abuse of a child or anyone else in their family and not try to stop it. I address these questions in Chapter 16 on pages 170-174.

in a safe, focused and supportive setting, such as a therapy group where doing so is a major goal for several months, up to 65 percent may have one or more positive results. According to this study of 53 women out-patients by Herman and Schatzow,[329] 21 (40 percent) of them obtained corroborating evidence either from the perpetrators themselves, from other family members or from material evidence such as diaries or pho-tographs. Another 18 (34 percent) eventually discovered that another child, usually a sibling, had been abused by the same perpetrator, for a total of 65 percent who were able to find these kinds of external cor-roborating evidence. An additional five (9 percent) heard statements from other family members indicating a strong likelihood that they had also been abused. Six (11 percent) made no attempt to obtain corroborating evidence from these kinds of sources, and an additional three (6 percent) tried to find such evidence but couldn't, and their families denied the abuse.[329] *None* found documentation in past medical or other clinical records. These results may be unusually optimistic, and other similar studies may in the future help us in our understanding and approach to this painful question and process.

The accuracy of a traumatic memory is based on a combination of often complex and inter-related findings and experiences, including clin-ical symptoms and signs, a family history (that usually unfolds over time) and the gradual piecing together of the person's memory as it evolves, including any of their traumatic experiences that they can remember. If there are any questions, the person and their therapist can consider using any of the suggested findings in this book and elsewhere to try to clari-fy their condition and their memories.

In addition, and only if necessary to the recovery process, some sur-vivors and their therapists may wish to search further for other evidence that may corroborate their memories by exploring any of the following. While it is difficult to find verification in some types of abuse, such as sexual abuse—since it is nearly always perpetrated in private—and although using these may have disadvantages, exploring them may be helpful.

Witnesses

For a person to be a witness to an event, two things are required. Not only do they have to see or hear it, but they have to *know* what they are seeing or hearing. In fairly simple matters like a physical fight or a violent act such as murder, nearly everyone knows what they are witnessing. But to know what abuse is when one sees it usually requires a much higher degree of sophistication. And even if someone has some of this knowledge, witnessing some kinds of abuse in some situations may be so upsetting or traumatic for the observer that they actually dissociate from their own experience. Denial is also common.

In addition, a witness such as a family member or a friend of the family usually has varying ties with each member of the family. If they are closer to the abuser and co-abuser, they may allow their loyalty to them to prevent them from intervening in any way. If the victim is a child, we also know that children are still looked at today as being as much like property as being a person,[174, 176] and the witness may choose not to get involved in any way that might upset the family.

The *witness' memory* may be as influenced by the nature of the event(s) observed and their own reactions to it. We know that witnessing a traumatic event may be as traumatic for the observer as for the victim, and their own memory may thus be more of the traumatic type than the ordinary type of memory, as I differentiate in Chapter 5. So the witness' memory is subject to all of the contingencies as that of the victim, abuser and co-abuser (who is also sometimes a witness).

Some kinds of abuse are not often witnessed by another adult, such as physical, mental and emotional abuse by a single parent on their children. Others are rarely ever seen or heard, such as sexual abuse of a child. This kind of abuse is nearly always *enacted in private.* If there is a witness who is called upon weeks, months, years or decades later to corroborate the victims' story, that witness may feel guilty for not intervening at the time and may, as a result, choose not to tell the truth by denying having seen or heard what actually happened.

Sometimes a witness can tell only what they heard the victim tell them around the time of an abusive event. But even if they do, others, including a judge or a jury, may not accept their story as corroborating evidence. While this hearing was controversial, Anita Hill brought in four highly credible witnesses, and the Senate Judiciary Committee mostly rejected their statements.[442, 521, 690] In the trial of the two Menendez brothers—Lyle and Erik—who said they killed their abusive parents in a state of fear for their own lives, three witnesses testified to having heard them complain when they were children about having been sexually abused by their father. But not all witnesses have integrity. One of these three changed his story and apparently lied that he had not been told about the abuse. Much of the media have distorted the findings in these two trials, in comparison with what I observed in seeing its entirety live on Court TV.

Other Victims

Sometimes testimony may be available from other victims of the same abuser to help validate the memories and stories of a survivor. But for them to give such a testimony, they have to know exactly *what happened to them*, i.e., that they were mistreated or abused. We know that many abuse victims do not know that what happened to them was maltreatment or abuse. They often think that it was "normal." Or they may have dissociated from their experience and traumatically forgotten it.

Bill's story may be illustrative. He was a 52-year-old physician and described the following, slightly paraphrased.

> I grew up in a dysfunctional family where my father mentally and emotionally abused my mother and his three children, and he also covertly sexually abused us. I became aware of my own experience of having been abused nearly 10 years before my sister did. During that time when I tried to share parts of my story with her, she repeatedly tried to invalidate my experience and said that she had had no such abusive treatment by her "sweet daddy." Even so, I continued to see him periodically mentally, emotionally, financially and covertly sexually abuse her, her daughters and other family members. She began weekly psychotherapy about two years before he died, and about six weeks before he died she verbally exploded at him for always mistreating her, and she never spoke to him again. Our brother was slightly different. Although he never invalidated my experience, it took him about the same 10 years to discover the truth on his own. But our mother always validated my experience, and she corroborated it even more by telling me of how he also abused her.

This illustrates how four survivors can have different experiences, over time, of abuse by the same abuser. Had Bill asked his sister or brother to support him early in his recovery, they would not have been able to do so. Others may find such corroborating evidence in somewhat different ways, as shown in the following example.

> Joe was a 40-year-old man who had been sexually abused as a child by an uncle and his older brother. But he could not remember the

details and therefore doubted his memories. In his recovery and therapy he began to put some of the pieces of the puzzle of his experience
together. By talking to various family members over a six-year period,
he discovered that his uncle sexually abused at least one of his two sisters and that he had tried to abuse two of his cousins. Finding out this
information was helpful in his healing process.

But some victims stories may not be allowed in court proceedings and
other hearings.

Anita Hill's story was to have been strengthened by the testimony of
other women, such as that of Angela Wright, who said that Clarence
Thomas had also sexually harassed them. During the hearings the
Senate Judiciary Committee knew that Ms. Wright was waiting to testify, but they did not allow her to speak.[442, 521]

In the William Kennedy Smith rape trial, likewise several women told
the court of having been raped by Smith, but his lawyer convinced the
judge not to allow them to speak during the trial.

So the testimony of witnesses or other victims can turn out to be
complicated and at times may even backfire on the survivor, thus doubly
traumatizing them.

Letters and Diaries

Finding helpful information in letters and diaries may be as hard as
discovering reliable and validating witnesses or other survivors. But if
they contain useful information they can contribute more pieces to the
puzzle of our traumatic experience. The following history illustrates how
a letter was helpful.

Jo was a married mother of two, who as a child was sexually abused
by her father. She had just begun to remember the abuse and had started therapy to work through the associated pain. Both her father and her
mother denied the abuse, which caused Jo to begin to doubt her experience. She was about to drop out of therapy and try to forget about it
all when she found several letters that her father had written to her when
she was away at college. These letters talked about how much he and
her mother missed her but that he had missed her the most, especially
when she would pose for him and when they had their "special times"
in the guest house. She talked these over with her therapist and her husband, and realizing that these were more evidence of the abuse and that
they validated her experience, she decided to continue her recovery
work.

In our memories of abuse, questions and doubts tend to come up frequently. While searching for sources of corroborating information like this is often unproductive, sometimes it can be helpful, as it was for Jo.

Sometimes the information that we find can be confusing. In Jo's case above, she also found some very loving and caring words that were clearly separate from those of the abuse, and this made her feel that her father actually loved her as well. She and her therapist worked long and hard on her resulting ambivalence about all this, especially when she again talked of stopping her recovery work prematurely.

Photographs

Several people whom I have assisted in their recoveries have found it helpful to dig up their old childhood photos and arrange them chronologically in a scrapbook. Others have used old photos to assist their memories in other ways.

Milly was a 35-year-old married businesswoman who joined our therapy group a year ago to work on her relationship with her family and husband. She was six years abstinent from alcohol and drugs and had an up-and-down mood in group therapy, often getting into conflicts and arguments with other group members.

One day she asked to see my co-leader, who is a woman, for an individual therapy session, which extended into several sessions. Milly had felt stuck in group, and although she knew she had grown up in a dysfunctional family, didn't know what to do next to try to heal around it. My co-leader suggested that she be creative and look for any evidence of how the family treated her in the papers, cards and photos that she had saved. She brought in some old photos, and the co-leader suggested that she show them to the group for feedback. Milly flatly said "No" to this, but a week later brought them into the group with the stipulation that only the women in the group look at them, which they did.

They all told her that these indicated to them that she was being sexually abused. They were "kiddie porn" poses of Milly wherein her older brother had photographed her when she was from ages six to 11, and she had found them in the family photo album. Over the next few weeks she began to remember more details of her older brother having sexually abused her until she was age 14. She expressed her grief in a clear, strong way to the group, and she eventually joined an incest survivors self-help group in the community. In the subsequent two years she was much improved and decided to contact a lawyer to request that her brother pay for her psychotherapy. At first her brother denied the accusation, but when she threatened to file suit against him, he agreed to pay for her therapy.

The photos were a key to Milly's ability to accurately name her experience as sexual abuse, which was then a trigger for her ability to grieve her traumatic experiences within a safe space, such as the therapy group, and to some extent with her husband. To this day she remains alcohol- and drug-free and has an improved relationship with her husband, although she still experiences some tension with her brother and parents.

In the Menendez trial, old family photos played a role as evidence to show that the brothers Lyle and Erik had been sexually abused by their father and that their mother had been a co-abuser. These photos showed several frontal views of them as boys, nude from the waist down and one seemingly innocent one of Erik in his father's lap, both fully clothed—but with his father's hand on Erik's crotch. These photos were accepted as evidence by the judge, and the defense lawyers used them in their arguments that the boys had been sexually abused and were still suffering from that abuse.

While it is uncommon to find these kinds of old photos, it can be useful to spend some time looking at whatever is available. They can help our recall.

Medical Records

It is rare to find medical or other clinical records that would help document abuse. There are several reasons: (1) The parent, parent figure or others fear being exposed, and they keep the child or adult victim from being examined or evaluated. (2) Even if the victim gets there, the helping professional may not be trained or experienced in making a diagnosis of abuse, which is thus not recorded, and (3) the records may be cursory, lost or destroyed. This first reason is illustrated by the following example.

> Richard is a 50-year-old helping professional who remembers at least one time when his routine pediatric appointment was postponed because of a large bruise and welt across his shoulder when his mother had struck him with a belt and buckle. He was nine years old at the time. For years he had forgotten this incident, until he went to an acupuncture therapist and mentioned that his shoulder had always been numb, and over the next four sessions, as the therapist worked with him, the memory came back to him. He remembered that it happened when he was sitting on the basement steps and asked his mother if he could go outside, and his mother said "No" and hit him with the belt and buckle. His mother postponed his appointment with the pediatrician until the bruise healed.

Some FMS advocates have a naive notion that as soon as a survivor recovers memories of having been abused—or even if they always remembered, their therapist should get on the telephone and search out any prior records that might indicate abuse. They further suggest that they should immediately bring in the person's family to ask them for evidence of past abuse.[215, 453] Of course, a psychotherapist's doing this would be not only counterproductive to the person's recovery, but may be unethical and would likely cause the person to distrust the therapist.

Herman and Schatzow's study of 53 incest survivors who had memories of abuse showed that while 65 percent could find some external evidence for their experience, not a single one found it in medical or other clinical records.[329] This finding argues strongly against the usefulness of immediately calling past physicians or other helping professionals for such evidence, even if doing so were ethical and appropriate as part of psychotherapy.

In writing about the significance of medical findings in cases of suspected sexual abuse, pediatrician and researcher Joyce Adams ends her review article on the topic with these conclusions: "(1) The child's statement is the most important evidence of molestation," . . . and "(2) The medical examination will usually be normal or non-specific. Most kinds of touching leave no signs.[4] Other physician experts in this area agree.[66, 173]

Williams' study of 129 women who did have documented records of child sexual abuse and were re-interviewed 17 years later showed that 39 percent had completely forgotten the experience and another 10 percent had forgotten it in the past, as I described on page 69. This is the kind of near-prospective study that can be so useful in helping us sort out the truth of forgotten memories of abuse.

There is an additional way to externally verify and corroborate a memory, and that is through an admission by the abuser or co-abuser, which I address in the next chapter.

14

The absence of evidence is not evidence of absence.

—Steven J. Gould

ADMISSION BY THE ABUSER OR CO-ABUSER

Of all the ways of trying to confirm abuse, admission—sometimes called "confession"—by an abuser or co-abuser, is one of the most complex and difficult to deal with, for a number of reasons. If the abuse happened, the abuser and co-abuser may be so shocked to hear the subject brought up that they are not able to admit having done it, or for the co-abuser, that they knew about it and did not try to stop it. When and how the subject is broached by the survivor may also affect their reaction.

As I describe later in Chapter 17 on page 170, the abuser and co-abuser(s) are likely themselves to be unrecovered adult children of dysfunctional families. The abuser will probably have been abused in the same or a similar way that they abused the survivor.[501, 586, 651] Because their behavior is usually so heavily laden with shame, guilt, fear and confusion, they may also have shut the information out of their conscious awareness through some mechanism like dissociation, denial or repression. They may be unaware or only partially aware of their behavior.

Reasons for Keeping the Secret

In their survey of 228 women who had a history of having been sexually abused as children, Roesler and Wind found that they had several reasons for keeping the secret of the abuse,[552] as shown in Table 14.1. These included threats to their safety, shame and guilt, traumatic forgetting (here described as repression), a sense that it wouldn't help to tell, fear of the impact on the family or blame and punishment from others, and loyalty to the abuser. Summit observed similar reasons in this description of the child sexual abuse accommodation syndrome.[629]

Table 14.1. Reasons Provided for Keeping the Abuse Secret
(from Roessler & Wind 1994)

Reason	N	Percentage[a]
Fear for safety (threats)	76	33.3
Shame/guilt	75	32.9
Repression of memories	65	28.5
Would not help to tell	43	18.9
Fear impact on family (protect family member)	32	14.0
Fear blame or punishment (from people other than perpetrator)	22	9.6
Loyalty to perpetrator	8	3.5

a. Women could list more than one reason for keeping the abuse secret, so percentage exceeds 100%.

Reasons for Telling the Secret

In this same survey Roesler and Wind found that these 228 women eventually had more reasons to *tell* their secret. These reasons to disclose included: their wanting to heal, feeling safe in a relationship, having retrieved their memories of the abuse, wanting protection from abuse, noticing that keeping the secret interfered with their being intimate, someone asked the right question or disclosed to them their own abuse, they couldn't hold it in any longer, they wanted to protect another child, someone else discovered it, they were angry, their perpetrator died, they felt a safe distance from the perpetrator, or they realized that it was wrong not to tell.[552] The number and percentage for each of these reasons are shown in Table 14.2. Later in this chapter I expand on these reasons from the observations of other researchers.

Table 14.2. Reasons Provided for Disclosing the Abuse
(from Roesler & Wind 1994)

Reason	N	Percentage
Wanted to heal	43	19.2
Feeling safe in a relationship	32	14.3
Retrieved memories	29	12.9
Wanted protection from abuse	20	8.9
Secret interfered with intimacy	20	8.9
Someone asked the right question or disclosed their own abuse	19	8.5
Could not keep it a secret any longer ("blurted it out")	17	7.6
Wanted to protect another child	11	4.9
Someone discovered the abuse	10	4.4
"I was angry"	8	3.6
Perpetrator died	5	2.2
Felt physically safe (distance from perpetrator)	3	1.3
"I realized it was wrong"	2	0.9
Other	22	9.8
No reason given	4	1.8

Acknowledgment and Apology

Taking these findings into account, in my experience what the survivor is usually looking for when they confront the abuser is an acknowledgment that the abuse happened and an apology for having done it. For the co-abuser, the same is desired for having known about it, yet not having stopped it. If these people would simply so admit and apologize, I suspect that there would be a great relief for them and for their victim, and the healing process would be well under way for all concerned. But it takes great courage for the survivor to bring up the subject and for the accused to admit and apologize for what they did—or perhaps due to their own denial or traumatic forgetting, "didn't do."

Sometimes the survivor is also requesting financial compensation or payment for the therapy that they have undertaken or would like to pursue. This therapy is an aid for healing the painful after effects of the mistreatment, abuse or neglect. Ideally, paying as a gesture toward some compensation and apologizing would likely be much easier and less complicated than their not doing so, as they would likely end up with less long-term tension and grief within the family, as well as expensive attorney fees, should lawyers and the courts become involved.

Risks and Dangers

Even though the survivor may know that the abuser and co-abuser are unlikely to so admit and apologize—the chance being substantially less than 20 percent in my estimation—survivors commonly bring up the subject to assure themselves that they have done everything possible to try to heal from the abuse and their unhealed conflict with the abuser and co-abuser. Even though many survivors want to do this, I do not advise that they do so, especially in the first half or more of their recovery. If they are ever going to do it, they should have already done a lot of healing around the abuse and developed a healthy sense of their Real Self, with healthy personal boundaries, before attempting it.[578, 687, 691]

Because they have not usually been in recovery, and perhaps for other reasons, the most common responses from the abuser and co-abuser are to deny the abuse and to blame and attack the survivor. This reaction is seen in many variations in numerous people's stories and is exemplified in part in the FMS-oriented literature. Abusers often project their pain onto others as well, especially including any therapist or other recovery aid, and they may threaten to or actually sue the therapist.

Just as the original abuse and co-abuse was harmful, wounding and even soul-murdering[464, 590] to the victim, the confrontation is in some ways similarly disruptive for all involved—except that now the process is starting in reverse, and is beginning to heal. The survivor is taking a monumental risk in trying to speak their truth, to ask for simple acknowledgment of the abuse at the least. Even though the survivor may desperately want to heal by doing so, they should be aware that their *chances of acknowledgment are small* and of an apology, even smaller.

After studying and for six years following up on 72 women who had been sexually abused as children, Cameron concluded that, "Findings on the reactions of both the accused (e.g., denial and attack) and the accuser (e.g., disappointment and disillusionment) strongly suggest that many confrontations, even those that are objectively positive, can be quite costly psychologically."[118]

If they know all of the above and still want to bring up the subject with or confront their abuser and/or co-abuser, in today's climate of FMS advocacy, media hype and hair-trigger litigation, there is a possibility that the therapist will be vulnerable to being sued. Because of this, it may be useful for the therapist to consider asking the person to read, discuss and sign an informed consent form similar to the following.

Informed Consent

I, _____(name)_____ , have been fully informed by my therapist, (__therapist name__), of the dangers and risks of confronting my abuser and/or co-abuser about my having been abused or neglected by them. These dangers and risks include my being invalidated, blamed, rejected, ridiculed, shamed, attacked or labeled as mentally ill, or the like, by the abusers or those close to them.

I realize that while there may be benefits to confrontation, this process will likely be very painful for me and for the accused, and that the accused may attack my therapist and recovery program in various ways, such as claiming that they unduly influenced me or biased me against them. I understand that the likelihood of the accused acknowledging their having mistreated, abused or neglected me is small.

I understand that (therapist name) has advised me not to confront my abuser and/or co-abuser now, and if I decide to go ahead with this confrontation that I am doing so entirely at my own risk, and I will hold my therapist harmless in this matter. I also understand that even if I decide to confront my abuser(s), my therapist will continue to see me in psychotherapy and support my recovery work just as they have in the past.

Signed _____(name)_____ (date)*

Witness _____

Asking a person to read and talk about these kinds of issues may be more useful as "grist for the mill" of their healing process than it could be as a legal document alone. Having to anticipate these risks and dangers allows them to face them and work through them, rather than be shocked and doubly traumatized later. When introduced at an appropriate time, reading and discussing this kind of information can be helpful in assisting the person in their recovery work and in their decision making.

---

* This is a very specific kind of informed consent, and is not intended to be an example of a general informed consent, which psychologist T.F. Nagy begins to outline on page 303.

Advantages

In a study of 80 recovering people, Schatzow and Herman observed the following advantages of telling the truth of the secret of their abuse:[578]

- Letting go or unburdening the guilt, shame and sense of responsibility
- Encouraging free communications within the family
- Helping others at risk of abuse
- Taking a step toward renegotiating relationships within the family
- Seizing the opportunity to heal relationships, including the mother-daughter bond.[578]

Cameron also found the following factors as favoring confrontation.

- Can put power in survivor's hands
- Often provides closure for unfinished business
- Helps to clarify relationships
- Helps to clean out damaging emotions
- Can begin to resolve the troubling question of forgiveness.[118]

These advantages are the ideal, but they tend not to come about in most cases. However, they do offer the survivor some possibilities to consider as they prepare to tell one or more of their family members the truth about having been abused, should they decide to do so.

Even though the chances of having a favorable outcome from confronting the abuser is small, sometimes benefits do result. But when they occur, the results are more often mixed and complex, as is shown in the following case history.

> Paula is a 66-year-old married woman, now retired, and mother of two daughters. The older of them, Cathy, is married with two children. Cathy came to her three years ago asking her for support in confronting her father, Jack, to whom her mother was still married, for having sexually abused her. Paula was shocked and extremely upset, but remained open to hearing her daughter's pain. She agreed to go to a therapist with Cathy, and there they aired many of their feelings. They both agreed to invite Jack to come to a session where Cathy would confront him and ask for acknowledgment that he did abuse her. While he reluctantly met with them, he denied the abuse.
>
> Paula's feelings of anger at Jack and her compassion for Cathy, combined with shock from the confrontation, upset Jack for the next several weeks. When they met alone later, he finally admitted to Cathy that

he had sexually abused her, and he told her that he was sorry. But he would not admit it in Paula's or anyone else's presence and refused to go back to the therapist with them. Over the next few years he became a quiet crusader against sexual abusers, although he never spoke again of having been one himself.

Cathy had tried to talk with her younger sister to explore whether she had also been abused by their father or whether she had known anything about Cathy's abuse. Her sister strongly denied both and refused to talk about it, blaming Cathy for even considering it. Their relationship remained tense for several years since then, and her sister was recently hospitalized for a "nervous breakdown."

In therapy, Paula worked on her relationships with her family and on her own wounds from having grown up in a dysfunctional family. She talked a lot about her guilt from not having known about the sexual abuse, and often wondered if Jack had also abused her younger daughter.

This is an example of a "good" outcome, and it shows a few of the advantages of telling "the secret." Once the secret is out, the dynamics within the family change.[691] The most remarkable dynamic that changed in Paula's story was that she and Cathy healed their relationship and became much closer. After her father admitted to the abuse and apologized to her in private, Cathy was much relieved and was able to get on with her life more constructively. And when the secret came out, their younger sister could apparently no longer deny her own psychic injury and was now in an internal crisis of her own. Whether her father actually sexually abused Cathy's younger sister or not, the telling of the secret and the other changes in the family's dynamics could have been a trigger for her sister's own current crisis.

But every person and every family is different. At the same time, there are similarities. How one person's speaking their own truth turns out may be both different from and similar to another's. But other than knowing that our chances for a good outcome around unsafe people are small, the results are not predictable for any individual person or family.

Cameron found the following factors as *discouraging* confrontation:[118]

- Having a lack of information
- Feeling emotionally unready
- Feeling protective of others
- Having a realistic pessimism—having no hope for other than a negative outcome.

To which I add:
- Being too early in the recovery process.

Cameron found that the survivor has no control over the offender's [and co-offender's] responses and little chance of attaining even one of the goals listed above under the beginning of "Advantages" on page 141. Clear, recognizable goals depend on the survivor's behavior, and not on any of the others involved. Confrontation is a declaration from a survivor, not a petition to an abuser. To have the best chance of a favorable outcome, the survivor needs clear and realistic goals, confidence and preparation.[118] In her six-year follow-up of these 72 women, Cameron found that disclosure occurred by letter [preferably unmailed and read in therapy first], telephone, through a lawyer, face-to-face or by a combination of these.[118] In her observations:

> The decision to confront was not lightly made, and some women had been in therapy for years before feeling ready. For survivors who had risked much to take a stand, it often seemed at first that they had gained little. They felt invalidated by their abuser's refusal to hear them, undermined by his outright denial, or confused by his claims of misunderstanding. Statements such as "You need therapy for your memory, not for incest!" proved especially devastating to participants who had worked their way out of amnesia. Even those who had never forgotten might briefly doubt their own clear memories.
>
> While therapists should never push clients into premature confrontation, they may need to protectively caution a formerly amnesic client who wants to confront too soon. This is especially important if she feels suicidal, and if her new memories are interspersed with doubts. These characteristics can make her extraordinarily vulnerable to the power of the abuser. If, in addition, she has idealized him in order to forget, she may suffer severe disillusionment. Premature confrontation can be a manageable setback in many cases, but it can be highly dangerous in others.[118]

Getting Ready to Tell

Knowing the above, the therapist and the survivor can now approach the issue of whether, when and how to disclose with more creativity and flexibility. While each case is unique, the following may be useful in offering some structure and strength to the process of telling the family about our experience.[578]

1) The work of disclosure has a better chance of a healing outcome if it is done in the later stage of recovery, i.e., toward the end of Stage Two recovery (see Table 24.1 on page 255).

2) Just getting ready or preparing to tell may take from six months to three years in my experience working in an outpatient setting, depending on how far along the person is in recovery when they express the wish to tell.

3) Some landmarks or criteria for being ready to disclose may include the following:

   a) The survivor experientially knows their True Self and is living from and as it.[122a, 687]

   b) The survivor has healthy boundaries, and demonstrates that they have stable self-care and self-protection.[691]

   c) The survivor has reasonable access to their own memories of the abuse, and is able to express the details of the abuse in therapy and to another safe person outside of therapy and can bear the associated pain without dissociating, "acting in" or "acting out."[578]

   d) They understand clearly that the responsibility for the abuse lies not with them but with the perpetrator, and the responsibility for their not being protected lies with the co-abuser.

   e) They rely on a strong support system in addition to the therapist (e.g., a therapy group, a self-help group, a sponsor and/or safe close friend)

   f) They have enough "ego strength", which I call self-strength, to be able to withstand the active denial, invalidation, blaming and rejection that may occur when they tell of the abuse.[578]

4) They have grieved most of their ungrieved hurts, losses or traumas from the abuse and from other mistreatment, abuse and neglect.[598, 687]

During this time they may need to "borrow" the ability to observe and the strength of others such as their therapist, group, sponsor or trusted friends who are also well into recovery. As they begin to learn about boundaries and limits, they may need assistance in negotiating and setting them with family and others who continue to mistreat or abuse them.[691] As they work through their painful memories, they may find it useful to limit or reduce phone calls or visits to those who behave abusively or who feel toxic to them.[578] Or when there is contact, they may decide to observe their family dynamics and to acquire information that would help with their memories of the abuse.[688]

Schatzow and Herman suggest that the survivor first consider telling their most trusted or safest family member of the abuse and if successful, graduating to each of the next safest, finally ending with the perpetrator if appropriate and safe.[578] Building from telling the most to the least receptive family members, information and experience gained with one family member is processed and incorporated for use with the next. The survivor asks each family member for what they want and need, such as first just to listen and not take sides or actions or offer advice. It is usually best not to confront the abuser until alliances have been built with other family members, although they may not be willing to become allies.[578]

Should they decide to confront their abuser, the survivor should (1) have a clear and detailed agenda for the disclosure session, (2) feel capable of taking charge of the agenda within the session, (3) have anticipated the possible outcomes of the disclosure, (4) be ready to accept a painful outcome, and (5) be ready to stop or end it if it does not go well.[49, 150, 578] They may wish to use a neutral therapist or ask their own therapist to mediate the session. Before the session, they and their therapist may find it useful to read Schatzow and Herman's article on the process of disclosure[578] and Cameron's on confrontation.[118]

After each disclosure, they can process their experience with their therapist and other safe people. They may have to grieve some more during this time, especially if they were invalidated, blamed or shamed for speaking their truth. It is more likely that the family members will react in this way or with confusion or ambivalence than with validation and support. But how the others react to the disclosure is not the responsibility of the survivor. Maintaining healthy boundaries[691] and using a strong support system will help the recovering person as they heal.

Some people, including many retractors, may have rushed into a confrontation—perhaps too soon in their healing process—without the above careful and patient preparation. When they tried it, they were traumatized again and may have decided that the only way for them to survive was to go back into hiding, to dissociate the memory once again, and re-align with their abuser and co-abuser. Some may also project their anger and blame onto the therapist or another recovery aid.

Confrontation in Therapy

Whether the therapist has a "duty" to the accused abuser, regardless of the therapist being present or not in a confrontational meeting with the accuser and accused, is now being tested in some courts.[344, 581, 596, 597] Before participating in such a meeting where a survivor discloses to their accused abuser, both the therapist and the survivor may benefit from legal counsel with an attorney who specializes in this area. I discuss these issues further in Chapters 19 and 20.

As an option, the survivor can confront, express and heal in therapy, without bringing in the accused, by using other methods such as writing an unmailed letter to the abuser or co-abuser, using role-play or family sculpture, and working through transference (conflicts that come up) with the therapist and other group members.[122a, 691] Working the 12 Steps of recovery may also be helpful. These all provide the advantage of a safe way to do inner work and healing without the exposure to unsafe or toxic people who might re-open the recovering person's wounds.[688] Even if the survivor does decide to disclose to family members, these aids will likely be helpful in their overall recovery and in preparing for a more formal disclosure as described above.

Confronting and Corroborating in Court

Trying to confront and corroborate the truth of abuse through the legal or court system is as risky as confronting the abuser and co-abuser directly, probably even more so. It is likely to cost many thousands of dollars and may expose the recovering person to the numerous abuses of the legal and court processes as they are. While it is sometimes helpful,[154] the legal system and the courts are often a toxic environment. Looking back, many people wish that they had never filed a suit.

There are statutes of limitations in most states, and often true and helpful evidence for the survivor is not allowed into the court proceedings. Other toxic consequences such as "gag orders"—wherein the survivor is no longer allowed to talk about the abuser or to warn others—may occur.[226]

Conclusion

While any of the above external corroborating evidence from this and the previous chapter may be useful in their process of recovery, and while it is sometimes helpful in a court situation, it is neither necessary nor required to convince the survivor or the therapist of the authenticity of the trauma, unless there is compelling evidence otherwise. External evidence is most useful when the survivor initiates the search for it, or if there is confrontational or legal involvement. The therapist is a clinical assistant and explorer, not a legal investigator. The focus of the therapy should be on assisting the person in their healing and on accomplishing their goals of recovery.

As the recovering person and their therapist explore what is happening now and what happened in the past, they can begin to observe certain findings that *internally* corroborate and verify that the abuse did happen.

15

INTERNAL VERIFICATION AND CORROBORATION OF TRAUMATIC MEMORY

Symptoms are a form of remembering without awareness.

—M.H. Erdelyi, 1990

In clinical work with abuse survivors the most important kind of verification and corroboration of a traumatic memory is the internal kind.[641] But outside of clinical work most people, including family members and even some helping professionals—especially lawyers, judges and law enforcement worker—understand only the external kind. External corroboration that abuse happened includes: witnesses, others who were also abused, photographs, letters, notes, diaries, clinical records, scars, confessions by the abuser and other statements or evidence. While some survivors of sexual abuse are able to find such external evidence,[329] many cannot do so.[641]

In my own and others' clinical experience, internal verification is usually accomplished by observing and demonstrating over time a combination of four or more of the following clinical findings: (ACAA Working Group 1994).[694]

- The presence of a high risk disorder or illness
- Post-traumatic stress disorder
- Age regression and other re-living of the trauma
- Repetitions and repetition compulsions
- Characteristics of the memories themselves
- Other patterns, dynamics and connections

149

Observing these findings cannot be accomplished in a short time. Their identification usually occurs in a progressive and cumulative fashion over the long course of the recovery and healing process. If any external corroborating evidence is also present, there may be fewer of these internal factors required to corroborate the existence of the abuse. Sometimes the discovery of internal corroboration leads to finding external corroboration, and vice versa.[641] These criteria are based on my own clinical observations and those of numerous others who work long term in assisting survivors of trauma, and will help us explore and define this important area.* More clinical research will help us sort out their nuances and usefulness.

High Risk Disorders

The presence of a disorder that has a strong association with childhood or other past trauma is one kind of evidence that can add to the internal verification of a memory of a person's traumatic experience. As summarized in Table 15.1, several disorders or conditions show a high percentage of trauma histories. For example, in *psychiatric inpatients,* 50 to 60 percent were found to have been abused as children; for *psychiatric outpatients* the findings were in a somewhat wider range, from 40 to 70 percent (see these and following references in Table 15.1). Nearly all people with *dissociative identity disorder* have been severely and chronically abused as children (DID is also called multiple personality disorder, which I and others prefer to call multiple personality response or reaction).

While some FMS advocates disagree,[527a] people with *eating disorders* have a higher likelihood of having been abused as children than the general population, as do those with *chemical dependence* (alcoholism and other drug dependence). These two categories fit under the category of addictions, and we know that people with other kinds of addiction, such as *sexual addiction,* also have a high incidence of having been abused as children.[122] People with *depressive disorders,* including *major depression* and *suicide attempts,* have a high incidence of having been abused as children, adolescents or adults.

---

*The DSM diagnostic criteria are formulated in a similar way, i.e., by the consensus of a group of experts on the particular disorder in question.

Table 15.1. High Risk Disorders that are Associated with Child Abuse, with Example Evidence.

Disorder or Situation	Frequency Found	Example Authors
Psychiatric inpatients	50 to 60% abused as children; 20 to 50% with a dissociative disorder	Jacobson & Richardson 1987 Chu & Dill 1990 • Swett & Halpert 1993 • Emslie & Rosenfield 1983 • Lobel 1992 Brown & Anderson 1991 Husain & Chapel 1983 • Swett et al 1990 • Carmen et al 1984 Beck & van der Kolk 1987
Psychiatric outpatients	40 to 70% abused as children	Jacobson 1989 • Bryer et al 1987 Swett et al 1990 • Brier & Zaidi 1989, Surrey et al 1990 • Coons 1990
Dissociative Identity Disorder ("MPD")	Nearly all have severe, chronic child abuse	Bliss 1980 • Coons et al 1988 Putnam et al 1986 • Coons 1986
Eating Disorders	Likelihood of higher abuse history than general population	Schechter et al 1987 • Goldfarb 1987 Gleaves & Eberow 1993 Coons et al 1989 • Hall et al 1989 Felitti 1991 & 1993
Chemical Dependence (Alcoholism and other drug dependence)	Likelihood of higher abuse history than general population	Root 1989 • Wallen & Berman 1992 Ladwig & Anderson 1989 Young 1990, • Edwall et al 1989 Herman & Schatzow 1987
Depression, Major Depression and Suicide Attempts	High incidence among those with these disorders and a history of child abuse	Herman 1992 • Kaufman 1991 Roberts & Hawton 1980 Lowenstein 1990 • Walker et al 1988 • Bryer et al 1987
Somatization Disorder	Likely abused as children	Stone 1990 • Lobel 1992 Ogata et al 1990 • Bryer et al 1987 • Morrison 1989 • Herman 1992
Borderline Personality Disorder	Majority have severe, chronic child abuse	Bryer et al 1987 • Herman et al 1989 Gross et al 1980-81 • Westen et al 1990
Psychosis	44% self admit child abuse history	Goff et al 1991
Abused and Neglected Children		Cameron 1994 Reilly & Pedigo 1994
PTSD	Trauma history in nearly 100%	McLeer et al 1988, 1992 Greenwood 1990
General Disorders		Briere & Runtz 1987, 88 Cole & Putnam 1992 Kendall-Tac-Kett & Simon 1988 Putnam & Trickett 1993 Herman et al 1986
Sexual Dysfunction	Common	Breier et al 1988 • Herman et al 1986
Self-destructive Behaviors		Green 1978 • van der Kolk et al 1991 de Young 1982
Violent Behaviors	(Including sadomasochistic behaviors)	Lewis 1992 • Walsh & Rosen 1988
Prostitution	About 80% sexually abused as children	James & Myerding 1977 Ross et al 1990 • Pines 1983
Pedophilia	About 65% sexually abused as children, nearly 100% traumatized in some way	Carnes 1993 • Schwartz 1993, Tyler 1993

Herman and others describe the high likelihood of those with *somatization disorder* and *borderline personality disorder* to have been abused as children, often severely and chronically. *Post-traumatic stress disorder* is another condition with a nearly universal finding of a trauma history, and which I discuss further below. Goff et al report that about half of a group of *psychotic patients* were able to give a history of having been abused as children.[275] *General psychiatric disorders* have also been found to be associated with a history of childhood trauma that is higher than that of the general population, as have *self-destructive behaviors* and *violent behavior*. *Sexual dysfunction* often results from having been sexually abused as a child. Finally, there are two conditions that many people don't want to deal with: *prostitution* (about 80 percent were sexually abused as children) and *pedophilia* (about 65 percent were sexually abused as children and nearly 100% traumatized in some way).

Therapist and author John Briere suggests that if mental health workers addressed childhood trauma appropriately, the DSM-4 would be able to be reduced in size and most diagnostic categories would be included under a heading of childhood trauma, while the remainder would be biological effects, adult trauma, and the diffuse effects of racism, sexism and other social phenomena.[82] For something like this to happen our entire "mental health" system, which is currently not working well, would itself have to undergo drastic internal changes.

Other Medical Disorders

Until recently, studies involving the after effects of childhood abuse have focused on the mental health-related after effects of abuse. Increasingly, however, researchers have been attempting to determine what effect a history of childhood abuse may have on adult survivors' physical health.[18, 545a] While these may be harder to prove in their association with abuse, they can at times provide additional evidence of the occurrence of childhood mistreatment.

The results of these investigations have been striking. During the past decade a large number of physical ailments have been identified in the medical literature, such as gastrointestinal, respiratory, gynecological and neurological problems that may indicate a history of abuse. In some cases, the chronic pain endured by some survivors may be the result of injuries sustained during a childhood assault. In others, medical conditions that appear to have no organic cause may be an indication of an unresolved abuse history.*[320]

In a study of 131 patients with a history of having been sexually abused, coming for a complete medical evaluation and compared with 100 random controls, physician and researcher Vincent Felitti found that the abuse survivors had more medical problems,[218] including depression (P < .001), 50 pounds overweight (P < .001), gastrointestinal disorders (P < .01), headaches (P < .05) and augmentation mammoplasty (breast implants) (P < .05), as illustrated in Figure 15.1.

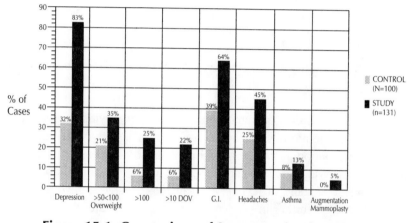

Figure 15.1. Comparison of Symptoms in Abused and Control Groups
(from Felitti 1991[218]) DOV = doctor office visits per year

In a second controlled study of 100 significantly overweight women, Felitti found statistically significant differences from 100 always-slender women. Those overweight had more often been sexually abused as

---

* All too often, however, health care professionals do not ask about a history of abuse and survivors do not mention it. When this happens, a series of diagnostic mis-steps are set in motion, resulting in additional visits to physicians' offices, treatments that do not work and frustration on the part of providers and patients alike—that never seems to end or stop costing us money. One analysis, for example, of the cost of health services provided to adult survivors of child sexual abuse notes that survivors visit physicians' offices far more often than those who haven't been abused.[8, 218] According to these data, the costs associated with such additional office visits alone are estimated at $2.8 billion annually. Just as occurs with addictions, it costs us a lot of money *not* to treat and prevent child abuse.[8]

children (P = < .001), abused in other ways (P = < .01), had one or more alcoholic parents (P = < .001), lost a parent (P = < .001), alcohol or drug abuse (P = < .05), current marital dysfunction (P = .001) and chronic depression (P = < .001) or chronic anxiety (P = <.05). Psychologist James Jacobs likewise found that survivors of child sexual abuse have more problems and complications during pregnancy and childbirth.[355] These results may represent only the tip of the iceberg in many medical disorders.[162, 190, 542, 613]

Health care professionals can be trained to recognize the symptoms of a history of abuse, treat patients with a full knowledge of its after effects, and make referrals to mental health professionals when necessary. Without such training, health-care professionals will continue to misdiagnose physical ailments related to childhood trauma—at cost to individuals and the health-care system that none of us can justify or afford.[545a&b]

These high risk disorders and conditions are in varying degrees suggestive but alone are not usually diagnostic of a history of having been abused in childhood. I summarize them and list some references that substantiate their association with an abuse and trauma history in Table 15.1. In the overall scheme of recovery, I call these "Stage Zero disorders", which I describe further in Chapter 24 on page 254. After the particular Stage Zero disorder is stabilized for from six months to three years or longer in a specific Stage One full recovery program, the person may become more able to open to their memories of the abuse and trauma. To do so with awareness, they usually need to feel some degree of safety, which is what Stage Two recovery can help provide.[641, 688, 691]

Post-Traumatic Stress Disorder

Post-Traumatic Stress Disorder (PTSD) is a Stage Zero disorder that spans all three of the stages of recovery, although it tends to have more clinical relevance for most people in Stage Two recovery, wherein the afflicted person addresses and heals their injuries from having been abused during their childhood and adolescence. It extends well beyond being only a high risk Stage Zero disorder and in this sense is also a separate and distinct category in the process of internal verification. Thus, if PTSD is present, I don't use it twice, i.e., as constituting two criteria. I use its presence only once in these criteria for helping with internal corroboration.

PTSD and dissociative identity disorder are perhaps the two from Table 15.1 that nearly always have an association of a history of damaging trauma in childhood, adolescence or adulthood, and many of the others have nearly as high an association. A person who is recovering memories of traumatic experiences may have more than one of these high risk disorders, and PTSD tends to be the most common and pervasive of all of them. In other words, a person with any of these high risk disorders is likely also to have some degree of post-traumatic stress disorder.

PTSD is a physical and psychological disorder that is nearly always associated with a history of trauma and painful memories, conscious or unconscious, of the experience.[11] Except in unusual circumstances, such as the rare war veteran seeking to gain an inappropriate legal or financial advantage, PTSD is not and usually cannot be faked.[390] Its range of symptoms and signs are too protean and diverse to be fabricated easily, and they are often subtle.

The diagnostic criteria for PTSD include avoidance symptoms and signs and a disruption in the process of remembering the traumatic experience. Like a hand in a glove, the combination of such memories with the other symptoms and signs of PTSD support the validity of one another. The presence of PTSD tends to strongly support the authenticity of the memories of the traumatic experience(s). In a recent court case (*Crook v Murphy* 1994), the presence of PTSD with no other explanation for its cause but the history of sexual abuse was ruled by the Court to be a legitimate form of corroboration of Lynn Crook's delayed memories of having been sexually abused by her parents.[718] I describe this case further on page 203.

Age Regression and Other Re-living of the Trauma

Age regression and other re-living of traumas, such as having an abreaction or a flashback, are themselves kinds of intrusive memories of traumatic experiences that are trying to surface into our awareness so that we can heal around them.

From a personal perspective, age regression happens when we suddenly feel upset, confused and scared, like a helpless little child. There may be no apparent cause for it, and it may last a few minutes or longer. It can feel as though one minute we are an adult, feeling okay, and in a matter

**Figure 15.2. Age Regression as Shown by
Artist Carol Neiman, 1987**

of seconds we feel like an out-of-control and helpless little person.[691] Figure 15.2 shows a drawing that represents the artist's rendition of part of this experience.

We can start to heal ourselves around such an age regression when one happens by beginning to observe our inner life and what is happening around us. As we heal from the wounds of our unhealed traumas, we can discover that while it is painful and debilitating, age regression is actually a healing gift in disguise. For one thing, it can teach us about our memories. This is because the genesis of age regression and its recurrence throughout childhood, adolescence and adulthood nearly always mean the same thing. Our boundaries are being invaded, they are about to be invaded or this particular experience that I am having right this minute is somehow reminding me of a past traumatic experience when my boundaries were invaded.

Age regression can arise under many and various circumstances, such as when someone yells at us or shames us in some way. These may include such otherwise trivial things as a comment about our weight or a mistake we may have made. There is therefore usually a *trigger* that initiates the rapid sequence of age regression. This trigger may be any of a number of possibilities, including any mistreatment or abandonment by anyone, any negative message from anyone, any form of invalidation or anything that reminds us of any of the above.

We can age regress at any time, in any place and for any reason. Immediately after the triggering event, we may suddenly feel the following in rapid sequence: fear, hurt, shame, guilt, anger, confusion or disorientation. We may end up feeling dysfunctional and out of control, almost as if we want to scream. But our True Self feels too weak even for that, so it may want just to go back into hiding.

When age regression continues to wound us repeatedly, with no healing around it, we may remain paralyzed, confused and dysfunctional, and our True Self stays in hiding. When we recognize it and heal it, age regression can be a useful opportunity in our healing and well-being. To heal it we recognize it, work through it and learn from it. To do all of this can take many months and more often several years in a full recovery program.

Healing Age Regression

The first step in healing age regression is to recognize it when it happens. This is a kind of self-diagnosis. Visiting our family of origin is often an opportune time to self-diagnose age regression because we tend to get mistreated, mentally or emotionally abandoned or invalidated there so frequently.[688] When it happens, I might say to myself something like, "Hey, I'm age regressing now," or "I just age regressed." This is a great moment, because when we name it, we can do something about it.

We can then begin to take some slow deep breaths. And then begin to walk around the room. (The point is not to be still, since that may contribute to perpetuating our feeling of immobilization and helplessness.) Then begin to look at various objects in the room. Walk into another room and do the same.

We can also pick up our keys and begin to play with them. Keys are symbolic of freedom. They open doors and start car engines. An accompanying practice in preventing and managing the sometimes crippling effects of age regression is, when convenient, to always have a way out of our family member's house or any other potentially toxic environment if the going gets too difficult. We can bring our car with us, stay in a motel or have some other way to get out should we need to.

Processing the Experience

As soon as possible, talk about it with a safe person. It can be helpful to bring a safe person with us when we visit—or when an unsafe person visits us. If there is no one to talk with, we can call a friend or write down what happened and how it felt, and then talk it over with a safe person later. Even later we can talk about it some more. This is a great healing opportunity and it can be most helpful to talk it over with our therapy group, therapist or other safe people.

It is helpful eventually to work through what happened and how it felt during the age regression in a deeper and experiential way. Some techniques to facilitate this process of working through include telling our story, anger bat work, writing and reading (to a safe person) an unmailed letter, family sculpture, Gestalt techniques and the like.[688]

Then consider the levels of meaning that the age regression may have for us. For example:

Level 1 - I was mistreated in the past.
    2 - I am being mistreated now.
    3 - I don't want to be mistreated anymore.
    4 - I'm going to set firm boundaries and limits in this relationship.[691]
    5 - I'm going to take a break from or possibly even leave this relationship if the mistreatment continues.
    6 - I can get free of this unnecessary pain and suffering.
    7 - I am thus growing from my awareness of this age regression.
    8 - By using it, I am healing the effects of my traumatic experiences.

At about Level 5, people sometimes may feel as if they are being mistreated without looking at their role in the mistreatment. Or perhaps they may be also mistreating their partner, such as intruding on their partner's boundaries without realizing it. They may not realize how their words or behavior may be invading their partner's boundaries in a sometimes subtle way.

We recognize these triggers and other triggering events as they come up for us. By doing so, we can then avoid situations where we may anticipate they will happen. Finally, we can use all of the above constructively. We can now begin to recognize and heal any future age regressions, avoid or minimize contact with people who do triggering behaviors, protect our True Self, stop blaming ourselves and bring the unconscious in our life more into our full awareness.

Further Meanings

When approached in a conscious, self-caring way, age regressions can be healing since they get us in touch with our past unhealed injuries. We heal ourselves in this way in a safe environment. If we are continually exposed to mistreatment, we can heal an age regression in a safe place such as our therapy group, a similar support group or in individual counseling. For some people, age regressions may be associated with panic attacks, and the above steps can be helpful in handling some panic attacks.

Age regression is a sudden decompensation that is triggered by a hurt that is nearly always due to an actual or a possible boundary invasion in a traumatic experience.[691] It occurs commonly among adult children of unhealthy families and in people with post-traumatic stress disorder (PTSD).

Age Regression and Memory

Age regression, abreactions and flashbacks, themselves primitive kinds of memories, can eventually help us bring our traumatic memories more into our conscious awareness. The presence of these phenomena are common in PTSD and they provide another kind of strong evidence of having had a traumatic experience, since it is difficult to feign them. The trigger of the age regression may or may not be associated with the memory itself or the traumatic experience. When age regressions, abreactions or flashbacks are experienced or observed, they help validate the reality of the traumatic experience that is now being manifested in the memory.

Repetitions and Repetition Compulsions

Repetitions and repetition compulsions are when we make the same mistake over and over or continue the same behavior that is detrimental to self or others. They tend to be behavioral and experiential re-enactments of the original traumas. For example, in the California case of Eileen Franklin, who had traumatically forgotten her witnessing of her own father, George Franklin, having raped and brutally murdered her best friend when she and her friend were eight years old, she showed at least three kinds of repetition compulsions. The first was shortly after the crime, which she had forgotten immediately, when she began pulling her hair out on one side of her head, thus creating a big, bleeding bald spot near the crown.[231] As Terr[641] describes it, "Most likely, young Eileen unconsciously set out to duplicate the horrible wound that she had seen on Susan Nason's head. This behavioral re-enactment provided internal confirmation for me of the truth of Eileen's memory. Even though the traumatic event Eileen behaviorally repeated was, at the time, entirely repressed in her mind, her re-enactment demonstrated that the murder memories still lived and carried an influence."

Eileen's second repetition was that later, after leaving high school without graduating, she was veering toward promiscuity and tried prostitution for six weeks.[231] Since her father had also raped her several times at a young age and she had also forgotten that, she was probably re-enacting these old traumatic memories. Having been traumatized by this forced sex in childhood, prostitution may have given her a chance to control sex, choose it and even be paid for it.[641] Her third repetition compulsion was that of being the neighborhood volunteer "safety lady" when she was in her 20s. She felt the need to deliver home any stray child that she found in her neighborhood.[641] If someone had done that for her best friend Susan Nason, she would probably still be alive.

Table 15.2. Examples of Repetitions and Repetition Compulsions

Self or other destructive behavior

Addictions and some other high risk disorders*

Obsessive behaviors

Other strange, unusual or associated behavior

Certain professions** or careers

Some hobbies

Anniversary reactions

Projections

Core issues

Frequent separations from one's inner life, e.g., dissociation, splitting, projection, projective identification and the like.

---

* As mentioned for PTSD, I would not use these as a criterion twice.
** Likewise, if prostitution is used as a high risk condition, I would not use it again here.

Eileen Franklin's delayed memories of two decades were so clearly verified by both internal and external corroborating evidence—that were also consistent between one another—that her memories alone were enough for the jury of his peers in the state of California to find George Franklin guilty of first-degree murder of Susan Nason. But even with this kind of overwhelming evidence, "false memory syndrome" advocates, some of them on the professional advisory board of the FMS Foundation, still try to invalidate Eileen's traumatic memories.*[413, 417, 497]

I list several other kinds of repetitions in Table 15.2. These re-enactments, or reliving and re-expressing of the traumatic experiences, are usually unconscious, and they provide more internal evidence that the person's memories are correct. When we heal our pain around an original trauma, through the work of recovery, which includes memory work, we usually don't have to repeat it anymore.

Characteristics of the Memories Themselves

Certain characteristics of the memories themselves also provide internal verification and corroboration. I have described these throughout this book (see especially Tables 5.1, 9.2 and 9.3 and pages 41, 88, 91 and 217), and others have described them elsewhere.[146, 233] Many of these kinds of characteristics cannot be easily feigned, and their presence offers more evidence that the person's memories are authentic. For example, part of Eileen Franklin's memory of the murder of her best friend when she was eight years old was associated with a horrible sound that kept coming to her memory as *two* sounds. Five years after her first recovered memory of this event, she said:

> One of the things that I knew when I had my memory was the sound when the rock came down [on Susan's head]. That sound is the closest thing I've ever known to driving me nuts. I would lie awake at night and hear that sound. When I was examined by a psychiatrist prior to the trial I was asked to describe that sound, and as with other things with my abuse, there are some things where I can't even say the words, because it makes it too real, because it hurts too bad . . . . I heard that sound [as

---

* With the assistance of FMS advocates, after several appeals by George Franklin, a high court *dismissed* the charges against him on April 4, 1995, based on two minor legal technicalities that had nothing to do with Eileen's memories. Prosecutors have 90 days to appeal. He may have to stand trial for a second murder, based on evidence from police data and Eileen's memories.[642]

occurring] twice. The first time I ever gave a statement, which was anonymous over the telephone, I heard the sound twice. When I got on the witness stand, I heard the sound twice, and when I went to the psychiatrist.

Twenty years after Susan's death, for the first time, the pathologist who did the autopsy when her body was discovered, without knowing me, without having heard my testimony or my statement, re-examined all of his evidence, and he said [in summary], "This girl died by being hit twice."[231]

Here, this part of her memory correlated with objective external evidence to provide an important bit of internal corroboration that strengthened the likelihood that her traumatic memory was accurate in its essence. The external evidence found by the police complemented and verified the internal.

Other Patterns, Dynamics and Connections

Other observations and experiences, including patterns, dynamics and connections, may also provide internal verification of a traumatic memory. Examples may include *intrusive voices, dreams, somatic memories, certain behaviors* or *statements* and the *aftereffects* of the recovery process.

Art work and *responses* to other kinds of experiential therapies may also provide this kind of evidence. For example,

I worked with a 39-year-old woman with PTSD who often drew pictures in art therapy of children with bleeding genitals. For over a year she denied any meaning in her drawings, apparently oblivious of their actual content. When her sister told her later that their maternal grandmother had sexually abused her, she began to remember their grandmother inserting inappropriate objects into her vagina and anus when she was a child. She had not been prompted to remember in this way by her prior therapist or other influences, and she eventually began to use her art work to help her remember these traumatic experiences.

In a controlled study of 109 alleged child sexual abuse victims, the presence of genitalia spontaneously drawn on a child's human figure drawing was positively associated with alleged sexual abuse, but not associated with child rearing practices (e.g., bathing, nudity, etc.) or medical history (e.g., enuresis).[334]

Another example is from the case of the 1958 Miss America, Marilyn Van Derbur, who was sexually abused by her father throughout her childhood. In interviews she frequently made potentially corroborating statements such as, "I hated dolls because you can do anything you want to a doll and the doll has no power."[641] Repeating statements like this is also a form of repetition.

In addition to the many effects of the abuse mentioned above and elsewhere,[85, 86, 88, 92, 130, 138, 176, 186, 256, 352, 501, 629, 663] some of the after effects of the recovery process can also provide evidence that the abuse happened. As we observe a person work through and express their abuse-related emotional pain and core issues over time, we and they may notice that their symptoms and signs improve. While we know that these may worsen for a while as they become progressively more aware of their feelings and issues, there is generally a trend of overall improvement over time. When this improvement occurs in close association with the gradual uncovering and expressing of the person's painful current and past experiences, this association or connection provides additional evidence that the person's experiences actually happened.

In the field of medicine there is a 50-year-old precedent for this association that is called a "therapeutic trial." For example, if a person has symptoms or signs of an infection, but the type of infectious organism has not yet been found, physicians may institute a therapeutic trial of the antibiotic drug treatment that would be most appropriate and specific for that organism *were it the causative agent.* If after such a trial the person's symptoms and signs sufficiently improve, physicians may conclude with a reasonable degree of medical certainty that the person's illness was caused by an infection with the specific organism addressed.

While this approach is not infallible—nor are most treatments in medicine—the therapeutic trial is a tried-and-true modality of treatment. Some of the most common conditions where a therapeutic trial is used include debilitating fevers of unknown origin, certain kinds of meningitis, tuberculosis and other systemic infections. As an example, if tuberculosis is still suspected after an appropriate medical evaluation, a favorable response to a therapeutic trial of anti-tuberculous medication would provide strong evidence that the person's symptoms and signs were due to tuberculosis.

* * *

As is true for all of the above kinds of evidence, no one of these alone is proof of the veracity of a traumatic memory. But taken together, in a cluster of at least four or more of these criteria, they may provide strong internally corroborating evidence that the essence of the traumatic memory is real and that the trauma actually happened. Noticing these kinds of patterns, dynamics and connections usually requires clinical experience and sophistication, plus an openness to listen to and observe what our patients or clients tell us and show us. These kinds of observations can provide more internal evidence that a traumatic memory is real.

Documenting the Verification

One of the most appropriate ways for the clinician to help establish the validity of a traumatic memory is to keep detailed and accurate records over time. To assist with such record keeping, I have included a one-page sheet that will allow the therapist to keep a summary of their documentation of the memories of their patient's or client's traumatic experiences (Table 15.3). This kind of chart is meant to supplement and not take the place of complete clinical records.

Conclusion

While external verification has in the past been more often sought and used in a court of law, knowing the kinds of internal verification that clinicians and survivors use can help to substantiate the authenticity of a traumatic memory. We look not just for external evidence of the existence of the abuse itself (what happened) or who did it, but we also look inside of what the person says and does. We look not just at the person's content, but also at their context and process, and here our work may be similar to that of an archaeologist. Context is a fundamental principle in archaeology, in that those artifacts that are discovered (external evidence) are best understood if they are studied in their relationship to nearby findings and to the level in which they are found (internal evidence).[78]

For the clinician and the survivor, this internal information and evidence is more useful in the healing process. If any external validation is found, then that is also useful. But while it may be desirable to the survivor and to others, it is not always necessary in the process of memory work and healing. To recognize these kinds of verification is not easy. Many are subtle, and it takes clinical sophistication and experience to identify them. These categories of internal verification can also be used in assessing *abusers* and *co-abusers*, including all of the above criteria plus their strong denial, other dissociations, double messages, and criticism and

Table 15.3 Summary of the Documentation of Traumatic Memories

External **Verification**   Date Recorded

Witnesses

Photographs

Diaries, Journals or Letters

Medical or Clinical Records

Other Person(s) Abused

Confession by Abuser

Other Statements or Evidence

Internal **Verification**

High Risk Disorder Present

Post-traumatic Stress Disorder

Age Regression, Abreactions and Flashbacks

Repetitions and Repetition Compulsions

Characteristics of the Memories

Other Dynamics, Patterns, Observations and After effects

Write in the main features of each of the above, with the page number or other reference from the clinical record or elsewhere. Where possible, include the date when the observation was made and also when you recorded it on this summary page.

aggression.[202] Clinical observers such as Gene Abel,[1] Robert Emrick,[202, 203] Mark Schwartz, Mary Jo Barrett,[31] Duncan Bowen[67] (see pages 121 and 170) and others have begun to describe some of these findings and dynamics in abusers. Co-abusers have been studied less often.[31, 583, 680]

*How smooth must
be the language,
when one can
make right look
like wrong, and
wrong like right.*

—Blackhawk[202]

16

PROJECTING THE PAIN

Another claim by FMS lobbyists is that memories of abuse are a "simple explanation for people's problems, giving them someone to blame for their problems." They have at least three of their own simple explanations for other people's problems to choose from, which I summarize in Table 16.1.

All three of these explanations attack and blame the therapist as being somehow incompetent or sick. They see the therapist as being either naive or acting out personal unfinished business, and not acting in the best interest of the patient or the family. While these factors may be true in rare situations, it is unlikely that, among the hundreds of thousands of people with traumatic forgetting who later remember their abuse and use therapy or another recovery aid to heal, these explanations are the reason for their painful memories.

Regarding the accusing adult child's role, the first theory in the table is the most forgiving of them, i.e., that they are just trying to be "good children," and do their "best," but they get caught in the web of a "bad therapist." The other two theories also label the accusing adult child as being either sick or immature, making them more vulnerable to the ways of the "bad therapist." While a number of colleagues and I believe that this kind of scenario is rare, it may be a possible explanation for some cases where no abuse was committed by the accused person or persons.

About his own and others' theories, George Ganaway, a psychiatrist on the FMS Foundation's professional advisory board, said this:

Unfortunately, people often tend to interpret what they read according to their own preconceived belief or hypothesis they wish to confirm (I'm sure I'm no exception to this). But I was presenting just one example of an alternative psychodynamic explanation for pseudomemory in a particular patient [see the third example in Table 16.1]. Every patient is unique and brings a complex set of defensive operations designed to resist either [the] patient or therapist developing a conscious awareness of the true underlying conflicts, which may range from conflicts over fears of loss of the needed other, loss of the other's love or approval, fear of physical harm or humiliation, fear of one's own conscience or fear of fragmentation of the ego (disintegration anxiety) if unconscious sexual and/or aggressive wishes and fantasies are gratified. The result usually is a compromise that allows for the wish to remain unconscious while still being partially gratified through the symptoms. In this particular case the symptom of a pseudomemory that is validated and reinforced by others (such as a therapist or support group) may mask the true wishes and fears by offering the patient a simplistic explanation for complex, mixed, often unacceptable feelings toward the needed other person or persons . . . . I do not mean to convey by the particular illustration [in Table 16.1] that I think this is the "correct" way of explaining most or all allegedly false allegations of abuse. I think each case must be evaluated on its own, allowing plenty of time to understand the psychodynamic defensive operations unique to that individual as played out in the transference.[260]

Here Ganaway is being more concise, flexible, and if a particular case did involve a pseudomemory, for the most part clinically appropriate in my opinion. Each case should be evaluated on its own, allowing plenty of time for the hurting person to heal in their own way and in their own time. A problem is that Ganaway and other FMS advocates appear to view most memories of sexual abuse, whether delayed or always remembered, as being untrue unless there is clear external evidence to verify it.

Who Has the False Memory?

How is it possible that hundreds of thousands to perhaps several million people who say they remember being abused all have "false memories" and fit into one or more of the above proposed explanations? Is that possible? Or could there be yet another explanation?

My suggestion is that not only may it be true for the accuser, but either the abuser or co-abuser or both may also be suffering from their own traumatic experiences in which traumatic forgetting by any one or a

Table 16.1 FMS Advocates' Proposed Explanations for Delayed Memory of Abuse (from references 215, 260, 261, 265, 267, 710)

Explanation	Background and Proposed Dynamics	Conclusion
The "Good Achiever" theory	The family is so close, stable and happy, and the children behave and perform so well that they are used to doing their "best"—no matter what they attempt. They enter therapy for ordinary problems and become the best patients who give the therapist exactly what they want.	The therapist believes that sexual abuse is the cause of every problem in their setting. These grown children then do their "best" for the therapist and remember the most bizarre stories. (FMSF newsletter 1992)[215, 246, 710]
The "Projection"	A woman expresses her anger against a man (her father) for sexually abusing her, when she is actually projecting onto him her own unacceptable sexual desires for him (this is a repeat of Freud's notion when he retracted his original observation of his trauma/seduction theory). She then builds an entire fantasy of abuse around the projected fantasy of sexual desire.	She enters therapy with a woman therapist who may have been sexually abused herself and who wants to punish men. The therapist uses her patient to act out, in a triangle with the man, the therapist's morbid hostility. The man is innocent. (Gardner)[265, 710]
The "Adolescent"	The accuser has not separated emotionally from her parents, and while wanting to break away, she feels strong guilt for doing it, fears independence and is angry at her parents and unconsciously blames them for keeping her tied to them. This conflict from her early childhood leaves her with an intolerable but unconscious, hostile dependence on her parents. While she has been an achiever, she has also had a low self-esteem and constantly needs approval. Through transference she may displace her dependence onto her therapist, who may then become an unconditionally idealized substitute mother-parent figure, all-accepting, approving, possibly offering her a mechanism by which she finally separates from her parents.	Rather than helping the accuser understand and work through her unconscious conflicts, the therapist permits the formation of "a new symptom...the belief that her parents committed such heinous crimes [i.e., the abuse] that the previously puzzling and unacceptable...anger toward them is now logically explained and totally justified." Her new belief about what they allegedly "did" to her gives her an excuse to cut the cord and emotionally separate from her parents. However, she is now enmeshed in a dependent relationship with her therapist and may become stuck there long term. (Ganaway)[260, 261, 710]

combination of dissociation, repression and denial are a factor. The literature of trauma psychology indicates that abusers nearly always have a history of having grown up in a troubled, unhealthy or dysfunctional family of origin.[1, 39, 57, 126, 202, 250, 294, 304, 385, 482, 501]

As I described in the process of wounding in Chapter 4, page 32, the parent or parent figure is previously wounded from having grown up in a dysfunctional family and world. As a result, they feel that they are inadequate and bad at their core, yet they have a toxic store of unfinished business inside. Because there is no safe place to express it, the parent or parent figure then regularly or periodically tries to express their pain, but ends up discharging it in the form of abusing self or others, including their children or others in or outside of the family. The abusers and co-abusers are thus themselves survivors of various kinds of abuse, but they do not usually consciously know it—or are they usually doing anything to heal from it.

Duncan Bowen, who specializes in treating sex offenders and whom I quoted in Chapter 13, said:

> The more adamant that an alleged abuser is that he/she is innocent, the more this individual denies having "any" problems in life. I see countless offenders who deny the alleged abuse, have no current problems in life, have experienced no past trauma and consider themselves as "normal."
>
> In treating offenders I have found that their memories are not very good in regards to their own sexual traumas in the initial phase of therapy. Nearly all (95 percent) deny having been sexually abused as children. Through the course of recovery, memories of trauma usually surface and the abuser is better able to understand the victim to victimizer path they had taken.[67]

While most wounded people do not physically or sexually abuse others—rather, they tend to mentally, emotionally or spiritually abuse themselves instead—some do. Their own past trauma may have been so hurtful that rather than face it, they also separate from it through the process of traumatic forgetting. Dissociated from much of the knowledge and pain in their inner life, their True Self splits off deep within the unconscious parts of its psyche, a process that I have called "the Child goes into hiding" (page 33). To survive, their false self takes over, although that false self is not competent and is not programmed to run the persons' life successfully. Unless they enter a program of recovery, this process of numbness and abusing others often continues throughout their childhood and adult life.

When the people who they have abused speak up about their experience, the accused person is still metaphorically asleep. Their whole method of avoiding pain has been based on a system of defenses that has allowed them to function in their day-to-day life, even though they have all the while continued to abuse others.

When a person abuses another, they usually experience an associated guilt and shame for having done it and fear being confronted and exposed. When the confrontation and exposure finally happens, they are shocked. If they have shut out their own double experience of abuse— once abused and then again of abusing another—years or even decades later, they too may not remember it.

The co-abuser may have had a similar process going on with them, and even if they knew about some or even all of the abuse when it was happening, they may, consciously or unconsciously, also prefer to block it out of their mind and forget it.[367] And if they knew it at the time, they may have feared losing their child or children if they spoke up about it. To confront the fact that their mate, upon whom they have been financially and emotionally dependent for all of these years, was abusing their own child, who they as a parent were supposed to protect, would be too overwhelming to even think about, much less believe. And so they join with the abuser and take the easier way out in the short term, although confronting their actions, inactions and pain would have likely made it easier for them in the long run.

When an accusation of child abuse is made, depending on their relationship to the accused, the co-abuser has several questions to consider —consciously or unconsciously. These questions may produce some painful feelings, such as fear, guilt, shame, hurt, anger and confusion. The first question is: *Is the accusation true?* If it is true, that implicates me in child neglect. If it is true, *why didn't I protect my child? If it is true, how should I respond now?* If the child is still vulnerable, *how should I protect them? Should I leave the accused person now?* Later, I may have to face up to my own unhealed pain form the past, from my own childhood. If the authorities find out, *will I lose my child (or my children)?* If I leave, *how will I survive financially? How will I handle the humiliation if others find out?*

Later in life, when an adult child accuses—perhaps decades after the abuse—many of the same questions and painful feelings may arise. With these, the co-abuser may feel so overwhelmed with pain that they dissociate, repress or deny it in order to survive and not lose the relationship with the accused. This is similar to what the abuse survivor often does.

Projection

Both of the accused—abuser and co-abuser—are thus caught in an intolerable situation. Unable to make sense of their predicament, they do what any other wounded and unrecovered person would do: they try to get rid of their pain. They try to express it in various ways, including by trying to give it to someone else.[691]

They try to project it outside of themselves. They may do so by trying to invalidate, blame or otherwise attack their accusers and their accuser's supporters. When they were abused as children, they were also likely invalidated, and so they are just continuing the cycle of abuse and invalidation of the expressed experience of their own spouse and children. These behaviors will also be related to their own personality structure and prior ways of coping with their painful experiences. Given this background, it is not surprising that those who are accused of abuse and co-abuse act the way that they do, especially when a survivor confronts them.

A Way Out

Alienated from one or more of their children, who frequently will not allow them to see their grandchildren now, they may remain shocked, hurting, angry and confused for months to years. Some may have given money to organizations like the FMSF, and after years of not getting their children and grandchildren back, may be interested in exploring other possibilities. Is there a way out of this intolerable and seemingly no-win situation? My sense is that there is, although to do what it takes to heal around it would take great courage.

I believe that most accused abusers and co-abusers and their adult child accusers occupy or function in separate but parallel universes, similar to the dynamic shown in the BASKIM model of dissociation on page 109. The difference is that if they are in a recovery program, the adult child accusers are well along in their own healing process, in contrast to most of the accused.

This idea can be shown in a simplified form in Table 16.2, where most accused abusers would be doing one or a combination of items 1 through 4 at the bottom of the table. Early on, they may be trying to avoid the pain of the shock of the accusation and of healing their own prior injury. Eventually they may try to project their pain onto others, as I discuss above, and then to cope with and eventually handle their pain. Many of the FMSF members that I spoke with at one of their conferences seemed also to be trying to make some sense out of and find some *meaning in* their conflict and pain. While their own *memories of* what happened may still be absent to some degree or even be unconscious, for some of them at this later point (dynamic number 4), their memories may be surfacing, just as the memories of their accusers' did in the early stages of recovery.

Table 16.2. Memory and Healing in the Accusers and the Accused: Evolution of the Process *(reading from bottom to top)*

Memory of What Happened	Psychological Dynamics	Evolution
Fully Present, Conscious	7) Healing their own wounds and/or their part in the wounding of their own children.	Most Adult Children Accusers, Survivors in Recovery
↑	6) Facing the pain experientially and cognitively with progressively more awareness.	
	5) Beginning to face experiencing the pain of healing their own wounds and/or their part in the wounding of their children.	
Surfacing	4) Trying to make some sense and meaning out of their conflict and pain.	
↑	3) Trying to cope with and eventually *handle* their pain.	Most Accused Abusers
	2) Trying to project their pain onto others, e.g., their accuser, the accuser's therapist or someone or something else.	
Absent, Unconscious	1) Avoiding their part in the wounding of their children and the pain of healing their own wounds.	

By contrast, most of their accusing *adult children* will likely be working somewhere in the area of items 5 through 7 at the top of Table 16.2. They are usually in some stage of *recovery*. As is shown in the upper left corner of this table, it is their memories of what happened about which they are now much more fully aware that are, on the surface, the topic of this "false memory" debate. But I believe that underlying all of this is a much greater and deeper phenomenon: *our society's preference not to deal with the ravages of child abuse* in all its multiple and protean manifestations. Here we have these two groups, separated (i.e., collectively dissociated) and functioning in the two parallel universes of recovery and non-recovery, of parallel increasing awareness and numbness.

If the *accused* people had the courage and would dare to take a risk and explore their own inner life by feeling and confronting their pain in a safe environment, such as recovery offers, they might begin to heal. We are just at the beginning of helping offenders, when they allow us to help. But the belief prevails among many helping professionals and others that most abusers are hopelessly resistant to healing on a deep level. And it would take great dedication and compassion from a therapist to work with them long term. There are some therapists who do this work well, and anyone interested in locating them can find them through agencies and organizations such as the Family Violence and Sexual Assault Institute in Tyler, Texas, at 903-595-6600 and The Association for the Treatment of Sexual Abusers in Lake Oswego, Oregon at 503-643-1023.

Conclusion

Most memories of abuse are neither a simple explanation for people's problems, nor do they give the person someone to blame. Most people with painful memories of having been mistreated or abused would rather not have them, and if they blame anyone they tend to repeatedly blame themselves.

Yet our memories are a helpful and even crucial part of healing our wounds. Expressing our traumatic memories is about *naming* what happened in our experience and *grieving* it, and not about blaming others for it. It takes great courage to heal from having been abused—and it may take even more to heal from abusing another person.

17

THE COMPETENT HELPING PROFESSIONAL AND THE TROUBLED HELPING PROFESSIONAL

Another claim by the FMS advocates is that suggestions from "pushy therapists, group therapy and self-help groups, hypnosis and related aids, and reading self-help books are the major cause of all of these 'false memories.'" While this may be yet another erroneous claim, since these healing aids are usually not that powerful, it may be useful to explore the role of the troubled helping professional. A small number of therapists may at times mislead their patients and clients regarding their memories and their recovery.

While the majority of helping professionals—and here especially the majority of psychotherapists—are ethical, skillful and assist their patients or clients appropriately, some, probably a small percentage, may not do so. We have known about incompetent and impaired therapists for a long time (Physician: heal thyself), but only recently have professional organizations and societies and licensing boards been involved in helping us in an effective way. In 1973 the first program for troubled physicians was started in Arizona, and now every state has a similar one to assist those in need.[303] Other helping professionals, such as dentists, pharmacists and nurses, have followed. Still others, such as social workers, psychologists and counselors, have formed programs in some states, with varying levels of effectiveness. Clergy, lawyers, judges and law enforcement workers are still in need of establishing effective programs for their own impaired professionals in some locations.

There are problems in assisting impaired professionals. For instance, psychotherapists may be a part of any of several of the above professions, including physicians, nurses, social workers, psychologists, counselors and some clergy, which makes them hard to locate or address as a group. If one exists, how should the troubled-professionals program for each address a complaint or problem involving a therapist who is harming the patient or client by inappropriate suggestions of traumatic memory? (Even so, some competent and some less competent therapists and counselors are not licensed and may have no professional society affiliation.) Finally, how can one know and prove that malpractice has occurred in relation to memories of trauma?

These are not easy questions to answer, and I will not attempt to do so completely here. That will be for professional organizations, licensing boards and the courts to do. But I will explore some possible answers and directions, and offer some guidelines.

Assisting a Troubled or Accused Professional

How then should a troubled-professionals program address a complaint or problem involving a therapist who is so inappropriate in assisting with traumatic memory work that the patient or client is harmed in some way? Most troubled-professional programs have a protocol by which they evaluate a referred member, and up until recently most have focused on screening for the most common problems, such as chemical dependence and DSM diagnosable major psychiatric illnesses.[303] But the success of these programs varies with the expertise of their personnel, their rules and financial backing. And their experience and effectiveness in some areas may be incomplete. For example, one area that is still not well-addressed by most of them is the helping professional who has sex with a patient or client.

Few organizations have the experience or means for assisting a professional who has been accused of being inappropriate in helping with memory work. They will likely have to develop a new protocol and/or refer the professional to a therapist with expertise in traumatic memory work for an evaluation and recommendations for rehabilitation, if required.

I believe that a small percentage of helping professionals may mislead their patients or clients, and from that misleading, untrue memories and at times inappropriate actions by the professional or the person may occur. These caregivers may be: (1) naive, untrained or unskilled, (2) wounded themselves in some way and thus projecting their unfinished business onto their patients and clients, or (3) unethical or even sociopathic. Or a combination of these. But how can we identify them, and if we do, how can we help them to be better helping professionals?

For the naïve, untrained or unskilled, remedial training and long-term supervision would be helpful. For the wounded and projecting therapists, working their own program of recovery would be appropriate, with or without additional training and supervision. But for the unethical or sociopathic helping professional, the most helpful course of assistance is more difficult, and some end up losing their licenses to practice.

The above discussion assumes that the professional has been turned in or guided to receiving assistance by a competent troubled-professionals program or state board of examiners, and that they get a fair and compassionate evaluation and recommendations by someone with expertise in the area of their problem or difficulty. But hurt and angry accused family members and possibly misled and/or mismanaged patients may not know of the above recourse—and they may choose to sue the therapist. In today's climate, such lawsuits appear to be initiated by accused parents and often by "recanting" patients or clients. Just how often this is happening is difficult to determine, as there are no accurate numbers available. One helping professional estimates that 4,000 suits are currently filed in the United States against professionals concerning memories of abuse.[518] Another says that this figure may be conservative. Of "retractors," i.e., patients or clients who have talked about reversing their memories of having been abused, as many as one third may have sued their therapist.[485] Perhaps the majority of these suits involve alleged malpractice, while a smaller number are other kinds of civil suits.

Proving Malpractice

How can one know and prove malpractice that is related to the assisting of a patient or client with memories of trauma? The laws governing malpractice are different in each state. Therefore, it is essential to consult with an attorney who specializes in this area for precise information in each jurisdiction. However, the following general principles may be useful.

Malpractice is just another name for professional negligence. It has been broadly defined as a breach of the standard of care, i.e., doing something, or failing to do something, which is normally done by other health care providers in like circumstances. This threshold principle is generally established by the testimony of one or more experts in the field. The opinion of the expert is said to be with a "reasonable degree of certainty." It means that something is more likely so, than not.[444] To prove negligence, four findings must be present: (1) a legal duty of care, (2) a breach of that duty, (3) resulting injury, and (4) that the breach caused the injury.[596, 597]

The injury may be mental, physical or financial. However, it is possible to prove malpractice without the alleged wrong doer being held responsible for any damages. Once negligence has been established, it must be proven that the negligence was a proximate cause of an injury. There may be more than one cause for an injury or loss. A person need not prove that the malpractice was the only cause. The person need only prove that it was a contributing proximate cause.[444]

Of course, the burden of proving the malpractice and consequent damage is on the person who makes the allegation. This burden must be met by a "preponderance of the evidence." Like a "reasonable degree of certainty," this also means that it is more likely so than not. The traditional example used by the legal profession is that the burden of proof is met if the scale of justice tips, even ever so slightly, in one's favor. It is not met if the scale remains evenly balanced or tips the other way.[444]

Here are some potentially negligent acts that may occur around assisting in the healing of trauma:

• Telling a patient/client that they were abused without having sufficient evidence for doing so, or telling them too early in the course of therapy, which may frighten them into abruptly stopping the therapy and leaving them without a support.

• Telling them to separate from or confront their abuser if the abuser is a close family member (unless there is current, active abuse of self or others, or it is otherwise deemed appropriate by the therapist).

• Forcing a patient/client to stay in a hospital until they have remembered enough of the details of their abuse.

- Publicly defaming the alleged abusers.

Examples of potential damages to the patient or client may include:

- Painful alienation from family or other loved one that was clearly damaging to the patient *or* was directly associated with a demonstrable and marked decrease in their functioning *in the absence* of clinical indications to separate from the family.
- Financial damage: fees for prolonged psychotherapy or for hospitalization that were clearly not indicated.

A problem is that over the course of healing from past traumas of a physical, sexual, mental, emotional or spiritual nature, when viewed by a third party from outside the context of the therapeutic process, especially by someone who is unfamiliar with it, some of the above or other observations may appear to be happening, although in fact they are not. For example, the need to regress before progress occurs ("no pain, no gain") is well known to therapists and most people in recovery. As the person identifies pain, and as they feel it and begin to express and grieve it, they may appear to an outsider to be "getting worse," when in fact they are only working through unhealed conflicts and are appropriately grieving.

If that outsider is not also in recovery (or has not *been* in effective recovery), and especially if they are currently accused of abuse or co-abuse, they may combine the shock of being accused with seeing the accuser as now "worse," and conclude that it was caused by a "bad therapist."

Avoiding a Triangle

Such a lawsuit or threat of one by the accused abuser may immediately disrupt the recovering person's confidence in themselves and in their therapist. If all of this interferes with the natural flow of the therapy toward healing, the patient or client and the therapist may blame the suit on some "conflict" or "problem" between them. The suing family member has now "triangled in" the recovering abuse survivor and their therapist, and the prior conflict that was between abuser and survivor may now transfer to survivor and therapist, as is shown in Figure 17-1. I describe the dynamics of triangles in *Boundaries and Relationships*.[691]

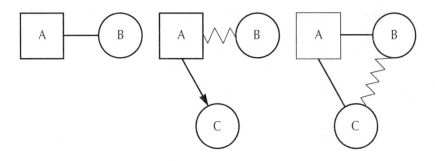

Figure 17.1. Common Dynamics in the Foundation of a Triangle
(from Kerr and Bowen 1988)[380a]

The left diagram in Figure 17.1 shows a "calm" relationship (e.g., abuser and survivor) in which neither person is sufficiently uncomfortable to triangle-in a third person, place or thing. The center illustrates the occurrence of conflict and unbearable pain. The more uncomfortable person, **A**, triangles a third person, **C** (the therapist). The right diagram shows that as a result a substantial amount of the conflict and pain has transferred mostly out of the original twosome and into the relationship between **B** and **C**.[380a, 691]

The way for a helping professional to avoid becoming entangled in such a triangle is to have healthy personal and clinical boundaries, practice competent and compassionate psychotherapy, and be aware of potential clinical and political pitfalls. And if a triangle develops, we can be aware of it and if necessary get assistance, such as through supervision and/or professional consultation. Triangles are inevitable in our life outside the clinical setting. But they can sometimes be avoided, and once they have become obvious, can usually be minimized. They are easier to avoid in the clinical setting, unless a third party tries to enter or does enter. In that case the following may be useful.

The healthy variation of a triangle is a healthy three-way relationship, also called by family therapist Thomas Fogarty and others a "threesome."[691] A threesome is the interaction of three healthy two-way relationships and has several important characteristics that help to differentiate it from a triangle, as shown in Table 17.1. However, in the therapeutic relationship the therapist is bound by the guidelines and practices of a contractual agreement, which include strict confidentiality

Table 17.1. Triangle and Threesome: Some Differentiating Characteristics

	Threesome	Triangle
Condition	Healthy	Unhealthy
Definition	Three healthy two-way relationships interacting	An unhealthy three-way relationship
Awareness of our Inner Life by Each Member	High awareness	Low to absent awareness
Consciousness of Each Member	Mostly True Self	Mostly false self
System	Open	Closed
Spontaneity	Mostly present	Usually absent
Movement	Flexible	Fixed, rigid or reciprocal
Interaction	Closeness	Fusion
Boundaries	Healthy	Unhealthy

about the existence of the relationship with the patient or client and all that goes on within it, plus an allegiance to assist and support them as they work to accomplish their goals. Thus, the only way to keep a healthy three-way relationship here is to honor the therapeutic contract and to maintain healthy boundaries with others outside of the twosome, unless the patient or client has given written permission to do otherwise.

The notion expressed by some FMS advocates[453] that the therapist should begin an immediate investigation of any questionable memory of abuse by calling past helping professionals and schools for their records and bringing family members into the therapy session to ask for evidence of the abuse, would not only destroy the needed trust between the therapist and the person, but it would also threaten and possibly violate the therapeutic contract. (Of course, Herman and Schatzow found in their study of 53 survivors of sexual abuse who searched for external evidence for the abuse that not a single one found any in past medical or clinical records.[329]) The only time that a therapist can legally go outside the contract is if they believe that the patient is a real danger to their own life or that of another. Remembering one or more experiences of having been abused does not fulfill this single exception.

However, if the patient wants to look for external corroboration of their memory or if they want to confront their abuser, then it would be appropriate for the therapist to assist them in their search in any way that would not violate their therapeutic contract. If they are seriously considering confronting an abuser, it may be useful for the patient to consult an attorney who has expertise in this area.

18

SOME GUIDELINES
FOR ASSISTING
WITH MEMORIES
OF TRAUMA

While there are no simple or easy answers to preventing lawsuits related to this difficult and complex area of memory and abuse, there are some guidelines that we can consider. The following may be a useful start.

These guidelines are for therapists with appropriate clinical training and experience in psychotherapy and who have a basic working knowledge of memory and abuse. These are clinical suggestions only, not legal suggestions, and are not meant to be used in or out of court for any legal purposes. They are based on my own clinical experience and that of some of my colleagues.[94-97, 146-149, 326, 513, 571]

1) As usual, after the intake evaluation, establish rapport, safety and an ongoing clinical working relationship. Screen for and manage any active Stage Zero disorders (addictions and other disorders), self-harming or toxic or destructive relationships. Memory work is best done in a Stage Two recovery program, after these disorders are stabilized in a Stage One full recovery program (see page 254).[326, 687, 688, 691]

2) Let the person or group go at their own pace. Allow enough time for them to integrate what they have heard, expressed and experienced.

3) Do not assume, lead or suggest anything about the content of the past trauma.[571] Don't assume that everyone with X disorder was sexually abused. Give the patient a chance to consider other possibilities for their symptoms and signs other than childhood trauma, and document that you have done that in their clinical record. At the same time, screen for abuse, especially in high risk situations.

4) Avoid phrases like "You were abused" or "You were sexually abused."

5) When appropriate, it can be helpful to ask questions like these: "Have you ever wondered if you might have been abused? or . . . sexually abused? or ____ abused?" Or "Do you think that what happened to you was child abuse?" or "Do you think you were abused?" Be aware of the laws in your state. For example, in Texas a licensed professional counselor is not allowed by law to take an abuse history.[518]

6) Some contra-indications to "uncovering" or experientially oriented psychotherapy include:

- Acute physical illness, active psychosis, marked personality disorder or very low self strength ("ego strength").
- Person lives in an unsafe environment (physically, mentally, emotionally or spiritually).
- Person is actively grieving a current loss, e.g., separation, divorce or death, or is undergoing a current crisis (although in some cases expressive methods may be helpful).
- Person is not committed to longer term recovery work.
- Person doesn't have an adequate ongoing support system.
- Transference or countertransference issues that might interfere.[571]

These are not hard-and-fast rules, however. For example, at times uncovering and expressive therapy can be useful in helping a person realize the advantages of moving out of an unsafe environment and finding an ongoing support system.

7) Sexual abuse appears to be the most delicate and difficult for families to heal around, especially when a parent is the abuser. The abusive family is usually enmeshed and often highly dysfunctional, and when the "secret" is exposed there is usually shock, confusion and either defensiveness and/or ambivalence among the accused parents and other members. Family loyalty becomes divided, and tension can be high.

8) In people with memories of sexual abuse, it is helpful to ask if there

blackouts. If the abuser was intoxicated and in a memory blackout and the co-abuser was asleep, gone or in denial, there may indeed be no memory of the abuse by either of them.

9) Take a family religious history. Overt and covert sexual abuse may be more common in strict religious and fundamentalist families.[174, 176, 570, 704] Some core issues for fundamentalists may include: all-or-none thinking and behaving, conflicted feelings, especially fear, shame and anger—and projecting these and other unfinished business onto others, needing to be in control and difficulty being real.

10) Enmeshment and boundary invasions are common in these and other dysfunctional families.[691] Anticipate ambivalence, confusion, fear, shame and guilt in the survivor. If they have named the abuse, talk about recanting is common.

11) Be careful when suggesting that the person not be in contact with their family of origin. If you do make such a suggestion, or if the person decides to do so on their own, document your reasons (e.g., active abuse of self or children, or fear of it) in the record. Do not defame the character of any family member; this can be balanced against assisting the person as they name the truth of their experience and what happened for them in their family.

12) Do not suggest that the person sue their abuser. If they bring it up, do not encourage them to sue, but work with them around their associated feelings, wants, needs, fantasies and other inner-life material.

13) Likewise, do not suggest that the person confront their abuser either. If they bring it up, also work with them around their associated feelings, wants, needs, fantasies and other inner-life material. If they want to confront their abuser, suggest that they read Chapter 14 of this book or Schatzow and Herman's[578] and Cameron's[118] articles. If they decide to confront their alleged abuser, refer them to an attorney who works in this area for assistance in the decision and the confrontation.

14) Document all appropriate material, events and progress in the person's clinical record.

15) Obtain clinical supervision, especially in difficult situations, and document it in the person's clinical record. Be open to possible countertransference issues with your patients or clients. Also, watch out for projective identification dynamics between you and them.[691]

16) Don't try to do "too much, too fast."[689] Let the person work and move at their own pace. Be wary of charismatic teachers who may tell you differently.

17) Avoid using intravenous short-acting barbiturates such as sodium amytal unless necessitated by a crisis or recommended by expert consul-

tants and documented in the clinical record. Know that while this aid may be helpful, using it may be risky should there be any later legal involvement (see Appendix D for further discussion).

18) Be aware that using formal hypnosis alone is risky and not admissible in court in some states. In some states any use of hypnosis may invalidate the entire memory and may cast doubt on the process of therapy if brought into court. While hypnosis is not a guaranteed way to the truth, it may be helpful at times as part of a full recovery program to assist in processing and healing the results and the memories of the trauma. Use hypnosis only if you have well-documented and recognized training. Obtain informed consent before using hypnosis,[513] and be aware of other guidelines (as described in Appendices B & D).

19) Disbelief, doubt and denial by the recovering person are frequent, and if necessary, after a thorough search up to 65% may find some kind of corroborating evidence for sexual abuse.[329] This kind of legal proof may include witnesses, others who were also abused, diaries, letters, notes, photos, medical records or admission by the abuser. While this kind of corroborating evidence may be useful to the person and in court, it is neither necessary or required to convince the survivor or their therapist of the authenticity of the memory of the trauma, unless there is compelling evidence otherwise. The therapist is not a legal investigator. The focus of the therapy should be on assisting the person in their healing and accomplishing their goals. Over time, internal corroboration (Chapter 15) may be more useful in the healing process than external corroboration. But this is not an all-or-none issue. At appropriate times both may be useful.

20) In that regard, it can be helpful to make a treatment or recovery plan, in which the person describes their problems, goals (what they want to happen) and objectives (how they plan to reach those goals), and keep a copy in their clinical record.[688, 692]

21) When group therapy is appropriate, refer to a group that is at the same level or focus of treatment as the person (for instance, don't refer someone to an incest group who has not yet retrieved memories of incest).[513]

22) Maintain healthy boundaries with the person and their family. Avoid seeing two members of the same family separately in ongoing therapy unless there are compelling reasons, and avoid any dual relationships (boundary and trust issues can hamper the therapeutic relationship here).

23) If you are not well acquainted with complex or advanced dissociative disorders and you have an especially difficult patient, obtain a consultation or make a referral to a therapist who is. Consider joining a peer support or study group.

24) If the person has a spontaneous flashback or abreaction, after assisting them in working through it, help them then get grounded. This may include making a plan to handle any such future experiences in a constructive way and learning how to self-soothe or to close them down.[622]

25) If the person uses any of a number of experiential aids to assist in their processing of the memories, such as art therapy, sand tray work or writing an unmailed letter, pace the session so as to provide enough time for them to process that experience and to become grounded before each session ends.

26) Memory work is usually most helpful when done in a middle phase of recovery, after the person has developed some strengths and support systems. This first phase may take from several months to several years to develop.* This is another reason why it is important not to rush the process (even though others, such as "managed care" companies may try to do so).

27) Process is equally as important as content if not more. While details of the content of the memory may be helpful, helping the person clarify the essence of the memory, their perspective and how they have understood it is necessary and usually more helpful.

28) If the person has spontaneous delayed memories of any satanic cult or ritual abuse, alien abduction experiences or abuse that they sense may have been in a past life, consider obtaining a consultation from a well-respected therapist who has expertise in that area.

29) Avoid ever invalidating any of the person's inner life or experiences.

30) Don't "walk on eggshells" around this issue. Continue to give the good clinical care that you have always given and document it.

31) We can be creative in our methods of documenting our therapy sessions, from keeping complete notes, audiotaping some sessions if appropriate, to using aids such as Bruhn's *Early Memories Procedure.*

32) The literature and a vast clinical experience shows that from 16 to 64 percent of sexually abused people forget the abuse and may remember it later. This remembering and naming the abuse for what it was and how it affected them is a crucial part of their process of recovery.

---

* I call the first phase *Stage One* recovery and the middle phase *Stage Two,* as I explain in Chapter 24 on page 254.

An Example

The following is an example of a patient I assisted.

Doreen was a 40-year-old journalist and mother of three children. She had worked for nearly a year in group and individual therapy and the self-help group of Overeaters Anonymous on issues of low self-esteem and a difficult marriage. In group therapy she raised the question of whether she might have been sexually abused as a child. She spoke of several possible symptoms and experiences that had led her to consider this possibility, including a long-standing aversion to having sex, recurrent pelvic pain, a history of frequent periods of dissociation during her twenties, painful but vague memories of being left alone with an uncle and a babysitter, and other symptoms. At this time she had no strong external corroborating evidence that she was sexually abused by anyone, although she showed some of the possibilities for internal corroboration (see Chapter 15, page 149). She also had a diagnosis of PTSD and had experienced frequent age regressions, although it was too early to tell whether there were any other criteria present for internal corroboration.

The therapy group and the two group leaders supported her exploration of this possibility, and other members shared some of their own similar questions about their lives. There were no suggestions made that she was or was not abused, and the leaders said that her symptoms and experience could be due to other causes as well, and they encouraged her to continue talking and exploring.

While there are many ways to record what happened in this group therapy session in the clinical record, I wrote the following progress note.

"Worked on her concern about whether she may have been sexually abused as a child. Group and leaders told her that the symptoms she described could be due to sexual abuse or other causes, and encouraged her to share more with us as she progresses in her recovery process. No suggestions were made by anyone that she was abused sexually."

Before this recent threat upon therapists I would have done the same things in therapy, but would not have documented what my co-leader, the group and I did regarding "suggestibility" in quite this detail.

The Two Sides of Suggestibility

Critics of the validity of traumatic memory have claimed that therapists often misuse their position of authority by making suggestions that result in convincing their patients or clients that they were abused when they were not. There may be times when that happens, and to avoid the unnecessary pain for all people concerned—the patient, their family, the accused abuser and the therapist—we need to know more about how this process comes about.

Everyone is suggestible to some degree about all kinds of things. People who are hurting emotionally are vulnerable to those from whom they seek assistance, whether friend, family or a helping professional, and they are at times susceptible to some of their influences. Our knowledge of just how any of these people may make suggestions about abuse is incomplete, and we need to know more. As one of the strongest critics of memories of abuse and the recovery movement, Yapko has "suggested" a list of some suggestions that he believes may be a factor in erroneously convincing a person that they were abused.[712] Most of Yapko's examples, reproduced in Appendix E, suggest perhaps his own lack of knowledge and experience about trauma psychology and recovery. Few therapists actually make such suggestions. But it may be useful for everyone to know what he, as one critic who had input from the FMS Foundation and board members like Loftus, believes that therapists frequently do with their patients and clients. I show some of these in Appendix E at the end of this book.

From what we know about suggestions and ordinary and traumatic memory, it is much easier to make suggestions and induce or "implant" untrue *ordinary* memories than it is for traumatic memories. About this observation therapist David Calof[112] said:

> The false memory ideologues who suggest that there is an epidemic of false memories of sexual abuse caused by suggestion and mass suggestion have an antiquated, comic book understanding of hypnotic suggestion. They assume, for example, that a subject will uncritically accept suggestions that are antithetical to a subject's self-image by the sheer power of the operator. They posit that there is some kind of state that can be induced (even accidentally) in which a person is uncritically suggestible to the operator's suggestions even when they are inimical to the subject's own wishes and desires. This Mandrake the Magician notion of hypnosis and suggestion is now antiquated. Just because a state of suggestibility exists does not guarantee that suggestions will be accepted. Milton Erickson, M.D., the most masterful hypnotist of our time, realized there are no universally effective suggestions. He taught that for a subject to accept a suggestion, it had to be "framed in a way that appeals to their individual wishes and desires while taking into account how they learn," or it would not be accepted.[112]

Like anyone else, FMS advocates can make contradictory statements. In his 1990 book *Trancework* Yapko said, "If a [therapist's] communication is not consistent with what a person believes to be true, it is not likely to go far. . . . Information contradictory to what the person believes to be true is defended against through a variety of means in order to preserve the original belief (p.126-7). . . . Cognitive dissonance as a basic human process leads to the conclusion that suggestions must be consistent with a person's self image in order to be successfully integrated" (p. 132).[714] These statements are essentially the opposite of what Yapko says in his more recent "false memory" oriented writings.[113, 712]

Commenting on this issue and on these statements, Calof[113] said:

> If I tell you something that isn't true about yourself and you deny it and I insist it is true, how much rapport will I have with you? If you insist you weren't abused and I insist you were, how understood will you feel? Will you feel a great rapport and willingness to be led or will you feel resistance to me and my ideas? In light of all of this why would a person who had not been abused integrate suggestions that they had been? Why would they make up something they'd rather not believe?
>
> One cannot induce numerous complex, durable false memories of abuse; break powerful, positive, long-term loving family bonds; cause complex amnesia for years of benign memories; cause self-injuriousness and self-destructiveness; create terrifying ego-alien body states, bizarre behavior, horrific pain, sorrow, terror, humiliation and shame that an actual abuse survivor would feel, merely by reading some words in a book describing abuse or being asked if one had ever been abused, when one had not.
>
> We need to look at cases in which there is alleged false memories of abuse not in terms of whether we believe the accuser and not in terms of whether we can believe that atrocities happen regularly in American families. We need to evaluate them in terms of whether the alleged perpetrator has the signs and symptoms of a sex offender and whether the alleged victim has the signs and symptoms of an abuse victim. If we are to critically examine the psychology of the alleged victim, we must also do so for the alleged perpetrator or our inquiry will not enlighten us as to what is occurring in these ever so conflicted families.[113]

These are the observations and opinions of a respected and experienced trauma therapist. They reflect how difficult it may be to instill or "implant" untrue traumatic memories into a person who experienced no actual trauma.* They also reflect the importance of critically examining the psychology of the alleged perpetrator, as well as that of the alleged victim.

For example, in the California case of George Franklin, described further on pages 161 and 218, Franklin denied having raped and murdered his daughter Eileen's best friend Susan Nason when she was eight years old, 20 years before Eileen recovered her memories of it. Yet among numerous bits of external corroborating evidence found was that Franklin kept an extensive collection of child pornography, and he had bragged to his colleagues at the fire department where he worked about having picked up and raped many young girls who were hitchhiking in the 1960s and 70s.[642] While there were other bits of internal corroboration in George Frankin, three of them included that he didn't act like an innocent person would have when he interacted with Eileen and others just before the trial, and that he had written to women in lonely hearts clubs, met them, and asked them if he could sleep with their daughters and photograph their daughters nude.[642] He was also reported to have often said a slogan of some pedophiles, "Sex by eight, before it's too late."[231] While it takes skilled and experienced observation over a long duration to find bits of internal corroboration in survivors of abuse, it appears to be more difficult to do so in *abusers*, as Bowen describes on pages 121 and 170.

We need to know more about all of these dynamics. Until we do, given our current climate of minimization and denial about the incidence and after effects of child abuse, and the tendency of accused abusers and co-abusers to project their own pain onto others, especially onto therapists and child protection workers, we need to be aware of and anticipate their attacks. We also need to be aware and compassionate about any alleged abuser who is erroneously accused. A delicate balance.

Conclusion

Accused abusers and co-abusers often project their pain onto targets other than helping professionals. These may include therapy groups and self-help groups, hypnosis, guided imagery, "regressive techniques," self-help books, the recovery movement and even the New Age. I have

---

* I discuss legal aspects of suggestibility in Appendix D on page 311 and in a footnote on page 314.

briefly addressed some of these in the guidelines above and elsewhere in this book, and give an example of a potentially important malpractice suit in the next chapter.

We know that most people who come in with histories of trauma are also diagnosable with PTSD, a dissociative disorder, an eating disorder, chemical dependence, borderline personality disorder or other disorders that reflect a high risk of having been abused in some way. It is difficult to conceive how any of these targets of the accused abusers and co-abusers could have caused any of these serious disorders in the accuser. Therapists are not that powerful. It is also extremely rare for a person to "fake" one of these disorders, including combat-induced PTSD.[390]

How easily can we see the pain of people who are guilty of abuse but who are now shocked and hurt at being confronted? It is easier to see the pain of an accused person who is clearly not guilty of abuse. But how can we prove that the alleged abuse did indeed happen? And how can we prove that there was no abuse? This book and other sources[88, 137, 149, 154, 326] may offer some assistance as we begin to answer some of these questions.

19

A MEMORY-BASED SUIT AGAINST THERAPISTS
by a Family Member

The following account is of a widely reported case,[106, 107, 134, 159-161, 163, 537, 640] and may contain information that is useful to everyone concerned, and especially to therapists.

Holly Anne Ramona was 19 years old when in August of 1989 she saw Napa Valley psychiatrist Barry Grundland for bulimia. That summer she agonized daily over her weight and she began binging and purging, and she was depressed. Dr. Grundland was also a psychiatric consultant to the winery where Holly's father, Gary Ramona, held a high-paying executive job, and had seen members of the Ramona family for various issues, including marital discord. At that time Grundland suggested that Holly get a referral for multidisciplinary treatment at the University of California at Irvine where she was a sophomore in college. Her mother, Stephanie Ramona, helped her find a therapist, and that September she began treatment with Marche Isabella, a licensed marriage, family and child counselor (MFCC) who specialized in eating disorders.[159-161, 351, 539, 540]

For the first few months Isabella helped Holly focus on her eating habits, body image, phobias and family dynamics in weekly individual and group psychotherapy for people with eating disorders. Holly's life had felt chaotic, and she had noticed two personalities in her father that

193

paralleled the two images of their family—happy and good on the surface and a lot of fighting underneath, during which he was often manipulative and cruel.[159-161, 539, 540] Her parents were frequently on the verge of separation and divorce. In November 1989, Stephanie Ramona was seriously considering separation. She was already seeing Dr. Grundland for her husband's not having had sex with her for four years.[540]

Holly worked about twice weekly in therapy with Isabella for 4 ½ months before Holly remembered having been molested as a child by her father. In January 1990 she told Isabella that over the Christmas holidays her father had looked at her in a way that had felt sexual. "He looked at me as though he should be looking at my mother." It was a "steady gaze . . . . This was something different. It started to bring something back."[537] In February, in part responding to her mother's question, "Do you remember when your father used to come into your room at night?" Holly began to experience fragments of memory of having been molested when she was five to eight years old—a hand on her stomach, a flurry of bed sheets, physical weight upon her and a hand over her mouth[159-161] —and actual rape.[351, 539, 540] Later, her memories of the abuse extended up to age 16, at which time she started her menstrual periods. Stephanie began to wonder if this may have been why Gary Ramona had often wanted her to leave him alone with the children.[540] Holly had also started to have a weight problem at around age nine. She had always felt uncomfortable hugging her father and from age five she had felt protective of her two younger sisters, Kelli (two years younger) and Shawna (six years younger). Holly was her father's favorite, and her mother and sisters often went through her to get favors for them, as though Holly were a surrogate wife. With all of these memories surfacing, she began to express anger at her father.

During that time Holly's grades dropped and her life became progressively more dysfunctional. By early March of 1990 she was hospitalized. She had already asked Isabella once before this for a sodium amytal interview to help her clarify her memories of the abuse, thinking she must be crazy, and wanting her painful memories out all at once. She didn't want to experience so much pain that was associated with her memories. After hearing another patient tell of her amytal interview in the hospital, she asked again. She felt guilty and very fearful, thought she might be crazy, and wanted to know more about what really happened. "I've got to be sure I've used every avenue before I confront him."

Isabella discouraged her from using the amytal procedure, but Holly persisted, and Isabella then asked Dr. Richard Rose, chief of psychiatry at the hospital, who after careful consideration performed the amytal interview.[351, 539] Although she said that she felt safe and had no fear during the procedure, she said almost the same thing under amytal that she had said previously. Dr. Grundland had wanted Holly and Isabella to fly up to Napa, where Grundland could confront Gary in their presence, stating that he had reason to believe that Gary could be violent, and mentioned a murder occurring in a similar situation in Napa. The confrontation needed to be done in a controlled manner, Grundland said.[351] According to Rose's chart notes, that day Holly identified her father as her molester. The next day, on March 15, 1990, with her mother present, Holly asked her father to acknowledge that the abuse happened. Almost walking out immediately when he saw Holly, Stephanie and Isabella in the room, her father stayed and listened and then denied that he had done anything of the kind. Later, several people evaluated Gary Ramona clinically, including Albert Kastle, a Ph.D. clinical psychologist, who determined that he had narcissistic personality disorder and PTSD.[351] There was no mention of alcoholism, although family members said that when he drank he consumed a full bottle of wine in an evening.[351] Stephanie had filed for divorce about a week before that confrontation took place.[540]

During the first few days after hearing of Holly's memories, Stephanie Ramona had tried many ways and many times to sort out the facts and to decide whom she should believe. She finally made a list of all the points in favor of believing each. She ended with 28 reasons for believing Holly and two for Gary (these were that "he was Holly's father" and "a father wouldn't rape a daughter").[351, 540]

Holly continued in therapy after leaving the hospital. In December 1990 she initiated a $50,000 lawsuit in Napa against her father, in part to protect her younger sisters and because she thought that a court order might be the only way she could get her father to listen and to get treatment. Gary Ramona countered with a $10 million lawsuit, also in Napa, against Isabella, Rose, the Western Medical Center, where Holly had been hospitalized, and against Stephanie and his former employer. In an unfortunate delay,[351] Holly's lawyer had her lawsuit against her father refiled in Los Angeles County.[351] In Napa there were numerous small-town enmeshments and potential conflicts of interest, including that Gary Ramona had given the judge gifts of wine in the past and that the judge's ex-wife was a therapist.[351, 605]

From 1990 until now (March 1995) Holly's symptoms have improved remarkably, and she has also completed an undergraduate and master's degree. In my opinion and that of others,[640] her improvement provides additional internal verification of her memories and are indicative that she received appropriate and adequate treatment by Isabella, Rose and the hospital staff.

The Verdict

This was the first time that a non-patient had filed a lawsuit against a relative's therapist for "implanting false memories" of having been sexually abused. The trial took 35 days (7 weeks). A jury of eight women and four men, after 16 hours of deliberation, voted 10-to-2 in finding these degrees of negligence: 5 percent negligence against Gary Ramona, 40 percent against Isabella, 10 percent against Rose, 5 percent against the hospital, and the remaining 40 percent against others, including Grundland, Stephanie Ramona and the chief executive officers of the winery where Ramona had worked. After spending a reported $2.5 million to sue these people, Gary Ramona was awarded $500,000 damages for lost earnings and received nothing for mental distress.[106, 107, 161, 351]

This strange, inappropriate and unfair verdict came about in part from a number of strange, inappropriate and unfair circumstances, some of which I have described above and including the following. Besides his own conflicts of interest, the judge asked the jury to answer questions that appeared to completely ignore whether or not Gary Ramona had sexually abused his daughter:

> 1) Were any of the defendants negligent in providing health care to Holly by implanting or reinforcing false memories that plaintiff had molested her as a child?
>
> Answer—Yes (see above %, and information below).
>
> 2) Did any of the defendants cause plaintiff to be personally confrontive with the accusation that he had molested Holly Ramona or affirmatively act in the events leading to that confrontation with the knowledge that the confrontation would occur?
>
> Answer—Yes (see above %).
>
> 3) Has plaintiff suffered damages that were caused by the negligence of any defendant?
>
> Answer—Yes.

4) What amount of damage [to Gary Ramona was there] from other mental and emotional distress?

Answer—None.

Questions 5-8 inclusive, What damages were done to Gary Ramona in loss of earnings?

Answer—$500,000 for lost past and future earnings.

Observations

If at all, the two cases should have been tried in reverse. It should have first been determined whether Gary Ramona had sexually abused his daughter. If the answer was yes, then Ramona would have had no claim against the therapists and others that he would like to have blamed, since they simply helped Holly as she remembered the truth. (If Gary is found guilty in the trial of the lawsuit filed by Holly, will that exonerate those found guilty?) If the answer was no—and obtained in a fair trial with an unbiased judge and jury—then Ramona's first trial would have been logical and appropriate to follow. But our civilization is not as advanced as we might think it is. Similar to the Scopes monkey trial that tried to disprove evolution, there are several aspects of this trial that demonstrate how painful it is for us as a society to face the consequences of child abuse and the emotions involved in trauma psychology.

In the trial, Gary's lawyer was described by several observers as being condescending and theatrical, and he used every excuse that he could find to make Holly's memories unbelievable.[159-161, 351, 640] One was that Holly had a catheterization of her bladder when she had recurrent urinary tract infections as a child, and Gary's lawyer suggested that this was the experience she was remembering. That was indeed a possibility—which Isabella had explored in their first session. But why would a young girl have recurrent "unexplained" urinary tract infections? That information could also be seen in the reverse—that genital trauma could have caused these repeated infections, just as it often does in adult women. Holly also had a gynecological examination that showed that her hymen had been broken equally, all around, which suggests that she had been penetrated.[539, 540] There was no history or diagnosis of another trauma or an accident.[4] This evidence was discounted by the jury and the Court.[539]

Holly's sister Kelli has so far had no memories of such experiences. But her younger sister Shawna, about whom Holly had always been most protective, did. She remembered being in bed with Gary and his mother, and Gary's taking off his towel in front of her in the bathroom.[539] While these memories are not strong external corroboration, they may provide a cue and process through which Shawna may be able to remember more in the future, should she feel safe enough to do so. This information was kept out of the trial. A "suspicion of child abuse" report was filed on behalf of Kelli and Shawna in April 1991. That case was "investigated and closed," since Gary Ramona was no longer living in their home.[351, 540]

After the verdict, Gary Ramona* told the media and others that he had been exonerated from the accusation, and FMS advocates began to hail the results of this trial as proof that they are right about false memories (FMSF newsletter, June & August 94). But *the jury made no such finding.* The jury foreman said that for the first 10 of their 16 hours of deliberation, they debated whether Holly's memories were true, although they had apparently not been specifically asked to do so. Their answer: There is a possibility that he did molest her. But "it was difficult for us to agree that this could happen to one person over many years and for her to completely suppress it." The foreman said that the finding was "not that they implanted false memories, but that they [the defendants] were negligent in not challenging her memories." They were "too quick" to believe her. "We didn't . . . declare him innocent. We didn't find that he suffered a lot."[537]

A psychiatrist, Robert Gerner, testified for Gary Ramona that psychological tests given to Holly by a psychologist "proved" that she had not been sexually abused. Was he trying to mislead the jury? On cross examination Gerner conceded that the original report of the psychological examination was "invalid" and that psychological tests neither prove or disprove that a person was sexually molested. He also admitted to having a patient orally copulate him in his office, and he had agreed to a confidential out-of-court settlement. The California Medical Board is reviewing his case.[161] This information calls into question the validity of his testimony.

It was clear that Isabella, Rose and the others were not heard and judged by a jury of their peers. These 12 were not therapists, and none

---

* I tried to reach Gary Ramona several times and he did not respond to my request for an interview regarding his side of the story.[538]

of them was known to be in recovery, so they probably would not have known much about the recovery process. Even if the jury had been peers, how many would have had expertise in trauma psychology and recovery? The jury selection process was supposed to have screened out anyone who had a personal or family history of sexual abuse. But it was later revealed that three of them did have a family history of sexual abuse, and two of these voted strongly against the therapists.[351] One of these two had even refused to deliberate, since she had already made up her mind at the start of the trial.[351] And what about any of the jury who were abused as children and were not yet aware of it?

Holly still has her lawsuit against her father upcoming in late January of 1995 and said, "I needed to say what had happened, because otherwise I'm afraid I would have died."[537] Even though there was no clear external corroborating evidence, Holly said, "I have no doubts I was abused by my father." Psychiatrist and traumatic-memory author and expert Lenore Terr was a witness for the therapists, and noted several bits of internally corroborating evidence, including Holly's continual fear of her father, repulsion at the idea of having sex with men her age and repulsion at eating a whole banana or pickle. There were others, including her surrogate wife role, her having bulimia, PTSD, the nature of her memories and what triggered them and her successful recovery while under the care of the therapists whom Gary Ramona accused and she remains well even until today for (a total of four years).

Terr said, "I have no reason to doubt any of her memories, because they are borne out by her symptoms and signs."[640] There was more internal corroboration, including that Holly was paralyzed with fear at the thought of contact with men. Her body contracted during physical examinations, making such exams impossible. She could not utter sexually related language. She feared being stared at, apparently because she had felt uncomfortable with her father's looks at her. She was afraid of men with sharp teeth like her father's to the point of being uncomfortable watching movie star Tom Cruise, whose teeth resembled her father's. She avoided foods that reminded her of oral sex, including white sauces and mayonnaise. A theme of her games from childhood on was trying to destroy a villainous man, and throughout her adolescence she played games where she and her sisters were to find out each other's hidden secrets. She had constant and repetitive ailments in her lower abdominal regions that might simulate the pain of rape.[163] She had never touched herself sexually.[640]

The defendants named above and their attorneys were united before, during and after the trial. They appeared on a TV talk show about a week after the trial to tell their story, since the media had either provided little information or had slanted it. A therapist and FMS advocate, Michael Yapko, was the invited antagonist, and without apparently knowing much about her story, he expressed many assumptions about how the defendants "implanted false memories" into Holly's mind. By the end of the program, however, Holly and the others had provided him with enough information so that he was beginning to show some indication of changing his view.[713] He illustrates how many people make up their minds before knowing the essential facts.

What can we learn from this trial and its results? Months before this verdict I wrote the guidelines for therapists in assisting with their patients' memories of abuse, and on reviewing them now, I would not change them (see the previous chapter). Overall, the vast majority of survivors and their therapists are doing well in their work. If either of us questions a memory or has any concerns about it, we can document that in the person's record. But I think it could be invalidating and a real disservice to question our patients aggressively to try to "prove" that an abuse experience really occurred or did not occur. In my clinical experience and that of numerous others, it is rare for a person to make up a story of having been sexually abused as a child. When they do, we can be observant and record what we see and hear, and begin to differentiate the true from the untrue. We can also use aids like Bruhn's *Earliest Memories Procedure*[94, 95] and appropriate information such as that outlined in Tables 9.1 and 9.2 on pages 87 and 92 and throughout this book to assist us in more carefully documenting our work with people's traumatic memories.

Family members may sue their adult child's therapist in the hope that the court will punish the therapist and the "real facts" will be heard by their child in the authoritative setting of the court. They hope that their child will come to understand that they have been misled by the therapist and that a reconciliation with the family will occur.[596] The alternative of complaining about a therapist to the state board of professional examiners (or quality assurance) may require permission given by the patient or client (the adult child) to release their records, and may not produce the above desired results of recantation and reconciliation. Taking their complaints to the courts, the accused parent(s) must get by the questions: Does a therapist owe a "duty of care" to a third party? And under what conditions and on what grounds can a therapist be held accountable to a third party for their actions?[596, 597]

More Questions

But other questions may follow. Is it the therapist's obligation to protect a third party from the choices and decisions of their patient? When there is the serious threat of physical harm, such as suicide or homicide, by the patient to self or another, then the therapist has a legal obligation to inform the proper authorities. However, in other cases, including those involving the effects of trauma and associated memories of the traumatic experience, it appears that it is substantially beyond the range of a therapist's duties. Therapists are bound by ethics and the law to keep a strict confidence in their relationship with their patient or client. If a high court were to rule that a therapist must also protect all third parties from the choices and decisions of their patient, it would substantially and severely damage the therapist-patient bond, a bond that is crucial to the patient's ability to trust the therapist and the process of recovery. There would now always be a third party disrupting the safety and sanctity of the therapeutic setting. By what ways can we, as survivors and therapists, protect ourselves from this heinous attack?

This decision by a trial court was at the lower level of our court system, and it demonstrated all of the problems indicated above. While there is still no clear precedent set at this time, this conflict will re-surface, either at a higher court level or through more tests at this lower level. Its only legal advantage for accused abusers was that one lower court judge has said it is okay for a third party to sue in this circumstance.

While the large majority of abuse memories and accusations appear to be true, a small but unknown number may be untrue. To determine the truth or untruth of an individual situation will likely require more sophistication than our current court system demonstrates. The lawyers involved will need to learn more about trauma psychology and traumatic memories, and therapists more about the law.

When the trial ended, the malpractice insurance companies of the defendants had two months to file an appeal, but finally declined. If they were to have appealed and won, it might have helped slow the offender system of denial and projection onto therapists (and survivors), and thus save themselves a lot of money in the long run. If Holly wins her case and her father is found guilty, that appeal would have had more strength. Trials similar to this one are in process, so these malpractice insurance companies may be waiting, in hope that they will have different results.

A problem is that many malpractice insurance company attorneys are now litigating the sensationalism and not the reality of the effects of child abuse. They tend not to be as knowledgeable about trauma psychology, including traumatic memories and offender psychology and behavior, as they might be. They habitually treat these cases as though they were regular medical malpractice, which they are used to defending. These attorneys also work for the malpractice insurance companies and not the therapists, and rather than fully defending them, they will try to follow the company requests and save them money. Some malpractice insurance companies tell their attorneys not to spend too much time doing research on their cases. Could this be a hidden conflict of interest? Therapists and other helping professionals can ask for better coverage and service, and in some cases may have to hire their own attorneys.

FMS advocates often try to shame or threaten therapists or make them feel guilty for not involving the family in trying to determine whether the remembered sexual abuse really occurred. But the result of the Gary Ramona case pushes therapists away from involvement with any third party so that they will not take a chance at owing them a "duty of care." The therapist is now outwardly in a double bind:[37] pressure by FMS advocates, inappropriately, to bring the alleged abuser and co-abuser into their private and confidential relationship with their patient or client, and also pressure to avoid ever being involved with them in any way so as not to expose themselves to a "duty of care."

On December 12, 1994, trial court Judge Burton Bach of Pomona, Ca., dismissed Holly's suit against her father.[540] This appears to be another attempt to invalidate and silence an abuse survivor by one trial court judge who is part of a dysfunctional legal and criminal justice system. Holly's lawyers plan to appeal this decision and expect the trial to occur in 1996. Gary is likely to appeal if he loses. So far, the lawyers and judges appear to be the only ones who are benefiting from this ongoing case. (Holly's lawyers are working *pro bono*.)

20

TWO SIMILAR
LAWSUITS WITH
OPPOSITE RESULTS

The following are two traumatic forgetting-based, legal case histories
that are similar in their essence and several details, but which had essentially opposite outcomes in their verdicts.

After 45 years of traumatic forgetting, Lynn Crook remembered having been sexually abused by her parents. Two years ago she filed a civil
suit against them. Her parents joined the FMS Foundation, were supported by them, and have been ever since.[157] Two of her sisters told the
court that their father had sexually abused them also. Her other two sisters denied any abuse and opposed Lynn's suit. After a grueling trial of
four weeks, on March 4, 1994 Judge Dennis D. Yule of a Superior Court
in a town in Washington state wrote that he believed Lynn's allegations
and awarded her $149,600 in damages.[718]

In spite of two FMS Foundation professional advisory board members
(Elizabeth Loftus and Richard Ofshe) testifying on behalf of her parents,
Judge Yule ruled on the total convincing evidence of the case, which
included: (1) the credible nature of her memories, (2) her having PTSD
with a lack of other causes, and (3) that two of her sisters gave a history of having been sexually abused by their father. The Court concluded
that "...repression of child sex abuse memories and retrieval years later
of [these] memories is a valid hypothesis accepted by a substantial seg-
ment of the mental health community."[718]

203

The Court made several observations about FMS Foundation board member Richard Ofshe, including that ". . . the Court found his credibility to be limited by his stridency." Ofshe's opinions and judgments" . . . detract from his credibilities as a thoughtful and reasoned expert."[718] Ofshe claimed that a single hypnosis session that Lynn experienced (after several months of therapy and the recovery of about 25 abuse memories) had implanted "false memories" into Ms. Crook—one of Ofshe's and other FMS lobbyist's party lines. The Court found that there was ". . . simply not sufficient evidence . . . [for any] suggestion, influence, or pressure surrounding the plaintiff that would explain her formulation of false memories."[718] The single hypnosis session was only to try to help Lynn remember some happy times in her childhood, and it was not successful.[157] This may illustrate how thorough Ofshe's research may have been in this case.

The Court further found that Ofshe was ". . . engaging in the same exercise for which he criticizes therapists dealing with repressed memory. Just as he accuses them of resolving at the outset defining repressed memories of abuse and then constructing them, he has resolved at the outset to find a macabre scheme of memories progressing toward satanic cult ritual and then creates them. Or Ofshe [also] equates recovered memories of early childhood sexual abuse with the recovery of past life traumas or memories of abduction of space aliens. He explains that he is the only one who has such a progression to satanic cults because he is perhaps 'the only one who studied the record [of the evidence] to the depth that I have studied it.'"[718]

It appears to more sophisticated observers that while Ofshe may be preoccupied and perhaps even obsessed with what he thinks therapists do, including frequently "implanting false memories," and with satanic rituals and space aliens, he himself may be trying to project these from his own mind onto abuse survivors and their therapists. This is similar to what some other FMS advocates frequently do.* One might also wonder whether the Court's paucity of comments about Loftus' testimony was related to the degree of Ofshe's stridency and divergence from the facts in the case, all of which made Loftus' testimony appear to be conservative, when in fact it was not.[416] Lynn Crook's attorney, Barbara Jo Levy, asked Loftus such focused, sophisticated and penetrating questions that Loftus' testimony exposed numerous contradictions in her claims about her own and others' scientific studies, and about some of her own beliefs. After reading her depositions and court testimony and others,' I began to notice a pattern.

Levels of Statements about Memory

Reading the verbatim transcripts of depositions and court testimony in lawsuits can sometimes be a rich source of information. When I began to read some of them, I noticed that a pattern emerged in the statements of some expert witnesses for the defense of accused child molesters and abusers. When I compared their statements made *under oath* with some of their others, such as quotes made to the media and in their academic writings, I observed a difference that was sometimes remarkable.

As an example of this pattern and these differences, I will cite some of the statements made by Loftus about her "lost in a mall" study of implanting "false memories" in different contexts. Here I observed five of these contexts, including statements made: (1) to the media or in some public speeches, etc., (2) in "scientific" or academically oriented writings or talks, (3) in answers when under oath, (4) when related to the most probable beliefs that underlie the above, and (5) when they speak from their hearts about their own personal and authentic experiences (see Table 20.1).

While I have noticed inconsistencies throughout Loftus' writings about memory and trauma, these differences became clearer when I saw them in her statements about her "lost in a mall" study that she made under these different contexts. The first was what she wrote in several professional journals[268, 412, 417] as well as what she said in some of her talks to professional

---

* Some FMS lobbyists also try to inappropriately construct a strange kind of "guilt by association" for traumatic forgetting by mentioning how "incredible" memories of Satanism, space alien abductions and past lives are. For example, in an interview Pamela Freyd says, "In false memory syndrome we recognize a constellation of emotions, behaviors, and responses to the environment that are remarkably similar from one patient to another and derived from an imagined event, e.g., false memory abuse, alien abduction, past lives."[111] And in the July 6, 1994 FMSF newsletter she says "Will the FMS phenomenon find its place in history as the Recovered Memory Mistake? Therapy for space alien abduction! Therapy for past lives!" (see also FMSF newsletter July 21, 1992, page 3 and other issues) Are these statements reminiscent of the inappropriate suggestions they claim that many therapists regularly make? What might they be trying to prove? They are the ones who make these associations with memories of child abuse, not the abuse survivors or their therapists. Could this be simply a tactic of distraction, even more extreme than trying to compare apples with balloons? Could one usually have nothing to do with the other? In response, FMS advocates may reply that their initial membership survey showed that 15% of accusers had "ritual abuse" as part of their memories (FMSF newsletter May 21, 1992, p.3), or that in subsequent surveys they found X-percent of Y symptom or memory. These surveys were done by Ralph Underwager, Hollida Wakefield and Pamela Freyd of the FMSF and were funded by the FMSF, and were not conducted by independent and objective observers who are well grounded in trauma psychology.

audiences and to the media, an example of which follows:

> Loftus and Coan (in press) provide evidence that entire events can be suggested in an experimental setting. Five subjects, all friends and relatives of our research group, were led to believe they had been lost in a shopping mall at the age of five. [We viewed this kind of remembering of being lost in a mall as being] . . . a moderately* traumatic event.[268]

Beside the immediate potential conflict of interest, dual roles or inappropriate boundaries in involving friends and relatives in a scientific study, which also makes everyone involved less objective, Loftus and her co-authors are leading us to believe that this was a valid scientific study wherein all five subjects were convinced that they had been lost in a mall at age five. They are also publishing this same study in professional journals, one each in 1993 and 1994, and as part of Loftus' 1994 book, the latter of which imply that Loftus continues to believe in the scientific validity of the initial study. In fact, in that book *The Myth of Repressed Memory* she said "These five cases offered proof. . . that it is possible to create false memories for childhood events."[413] Nowhere in any of these writings does she say that this study is not scientifically valid. But under oath some truth comes out, as she says in the verbatim transcript of her deposition on January 24, 1994 and her court testimony on February 17, 1994 as she testifies against Lynn Crook and in favor of Lynn's parents, who were found to be guilty of having sexually abusing her as a child. Barbara Jo Levy is the questioner.[416]

> *Question* . . . you . . . completed [another] eight subjects [in the "lost in a mall" study]?
>
> *Answer.* Right. (p.1621)
>
> Q. . . . and only one . . . had . . . the false memory implanted?
>
> A. [Yes.] [That is, in only one subject out of eight, or 12.5 percent.]
>
> Q. And the five case histories are not a scientific study, are they, Dr. Loftus?
>
> A. Well, it's not an experiment. Let's put it that way. (p.1622)

Without informing the readers of her above referenced articles, Loftus has thus dropped the first group of five as not constituting a scientifically valid study.

> Q. . . . Can you tell me why you started over?

---

* In her 1993 article, Loftus described being lost in a mall as being mildly traumatic.[417]

Table 20.1. Levels of Statements that May be Made about Emotionally Charged Experiences and Issues

(reading from top to bottom, from the most indirect to the most direct)

Level	Description
1) Media, Public Speeches, etc.	Although the person may make statements that appear to be direct, they often make generalizations based on their beliefs and their partially finished or unfinished business (level 5 below) that they would not usually make on the other levels.
2) "Scientific" or Academically Oriented Writing or Talks	These statements tend to follow a structure and pattern prescribed by the customs in the literature in which they appear. These are usually the most indirect and conservative.
3) Answers Under Oath	These are beginning to become somewhat more direct, although they tend to be related to the sophistication and focus of the questioner. They are usually limited to depositions and court appearances, the transcripts from which may be a rich source of deeper and more accurate information about the person who is making the statements.
4) Beliefs Underlying the Above	Here the statements are even more direct because they are approaching the core of the person's experiences and biases, upon which their beliefs are likely based.
5) Experiences from their Heart	These are the most direct. When a person speaks from their heart, their authentic experience, they tend to be the most direct. People in recovery tend to be able to speak and write in this way more easily than those who are not.

A. The chief investigator [the student she was apparently supervising] left the project and . . . paperwork in somewhat of a disrepair . . .

Q. So . . . you have totally thrown out the first part of the study? . . . are you using those first six [additional] subjects or not?

A. . . . . No, not the first six [either] (p. 60 deposition)

Even though her testimony is confusing, she says under oath that these first five subjects (a number, or "N," of five who were friends and relatives of the researchers, in a study left in "disrepair,") do not constitute a valid scientific study, nor do the next six subjects appear to be, for a total of her first 11 subjects.[416]

The truth of the next two levels (4 and 5), as shown in Table 21.1, in anyone is usually more difficult to discover, but transcripts can sometimes be helpful here, too.

Q. [Dr. Loftus] you were sexually abused as a child; correct?

A. Yes.

Q. And you always had the memory of being sexually abused?

A. Right.

Q. Is there any independent corroboration of that abuse?

A. No.*

Q. Could anyone ever convince you that you were not sexually abused?

A. Well, I sort of doubt it, but it's not impossible. (p.51d)

Q. The fact that there is no [external] corroboration of memories does not mean the memories are false?

A. Right. [i.e., she is agreeing that true memories of abuse do not need external corroboration to prove their veracity].[416]

In another deposition taken in California in 1993, she was asked if she had ever been sexually abused as a child, and she said "Yes."[418]

Q. Did you repress memories of your childhood sexual abuse?

A. No.

Q. May I ask what age you were at the time of the abuse?

A. Probably five or six.

Q. Was it one occurrence or multiple occurrences?

A. Possibly a number of them. It's hard to know. I remember one in particular.

About her experience of this memory, she wrote, "The memory flew out of me, out of the blackness of the past, hitting me full force . . . . I was abused when I was six years old . . . After that, there is only blackness with not a pinhole of light. Howard [her abuser] is simply gone, vanished, sucked away. My memory took him and destroyed him."[413a] Might

---

* While she says there was no independent corroboration, on Seattle television (KOMO) she agreed that when she was abused she had people to talk to and who listened to her, which can be considered to be one kind of corroboration. Most abuse survivors did not have that, as Summit[629] and others have described (pages 84-87). This is another inconsistency in her supposedly factual statements.

this indicate that she traumatically forgot? Yet she says she always remembered this abusive experience, but doesn't say that she forgot perhaps a substantial portion of Howard's total abuse. Confusing? Yes. Trauma alone dissociates and confuses memory, and trying to block it with guilt, shame and threats of harm can drive it into the victim's unconscious.[629]

Q. And no one was a witness to that episode, is that correct?[416]

A. Correct.

Q. And no one could ever convince you that that episode of abuse did not occur, is that correct?

A. Well, I'm not sure of that. I believe it happened, but I have no idea if the details of my memory are accurate. (p.1629) [She again tries to focus more on the details than the essence of her own traumatic memory.]

She says she believes she was sexually abused but is uncertain about the details in her memory, a finding upon which she and others use to try to attack the veracity of abuse survivors' memories.

Q. And it's your opinion that it's at least possible for someone to experience a painful memory or a painful event . . . and if asked about it, they won't remember it?[416]

A. That's possible. (p. 1642)

Q. [Are] *accused* people motivated to *deny* they have been abused as a child? [my italics]

A. I think that would be a motivation; yes.

Q. And so denials of abuse are not evidence that a victim's memories are not authentic, isn't that correct?

A. Right. (pp. 97-98d)

Q. Have you conducted an experiment to show whether people who read books regarding sexual abuse start having false memories of sexual abuse?

A. No. (p. 40d) [Nor has anyone else.]

Q. You've never had a client or patient for a therapy?

A. Right.

Q. You've never diagnosed anyone with a mental disorder, is that correct?

A. Not formally, no. (p. 1624)

Q. [Are] all the [legal testimony] cases that you are working on . . . on the side of there being a suggestive or false memory, whether it's for the plaintiff or the defendant? . . .

A. Yes. (p. 20d) [nearly all are for people accused of child molestation.]
Q. . . .you charge $350 an hour for everything? [including travel time]
A. I do; yes.[416]

While there is more, this information is helpful in our beginning to understand what is actually occurring "between the lines" of some of her writings and talks. We can learn a lot about anyone, including FMS advocates and their views on memory and trauma, by their statements from all five of these levels shown in Table 20.1. Reading this testimony made under oath can be useful. (Attorneys and others interested can search out more such information given under oath by contacting the *American Prosecutors Research Institute* at 703-739-0321 [99 Canal Ctr Plaza, #510, Alexandria, VA 22314]). Finding authentic information in levels four and especially level five will likely be difficult.

A Similar Lawsuit That Was Lost

Lynn Crook's case is but one example of the attempted intimidation and invalidation of abuse survivors by the backlash nationwide, including many accused abusers and co-abusers, and FMS Foundation board members claiming to act as "experts." While some of them may have some expertise in such isolated areas as general psychology, psychiatry, sociology, jurisprudence and ordinary memory, most are not qualified to offer expert testimony in cases involving traumatic memory. Many of us who are experts in the field of trauma psychology are puzzled and dismayed as to why they are repeatedly allowed to pose as experts in an area where they have not demonstrated clinical or scientific expertise. Because of their testimony of disinformation like the above and an often naïve and dysfunctional court system, many—perhaps most—abuse survivors lose their cases. The following history is but one example.

> After over a decade of traumatic forgetting, at age 28 Kathy O'Connor remembered that her father sexually abused her as a child. While at first she doubted the truth of her memories, she came to believe them with an unshakable conviction, and eventually filed a civil suit against her father for personal damages of two million dollars. Her father was said to be a violent alcoholic who physically and emotionally abused his children, and was said to have sexually abused two of his ex-wife's sisters when he was in his 20s, and Kathy's older sister had memories of him sexually abusing her.[63, 494] When her father was about age 25, Kathy's mother had found him in bed with her 15-year-old sister more than once.[494]

Kathy was diagnosed as having PTSD and borderline personality disorder, had been harmfully involved with alcohol and other drugs, and had been promiscuous in high school and college. Her current two therapists believed her memories of having been sexually abused by her father, and a past therapist suspected sexual abuse but never suggested it. She recalled these memories when she was not in therapy.

In spite of the strong external and internal corroborating evidence in support of the accuracy of her memories—similar to those in Lynn Crook's case, after seven days of court time and only two hours of deliberation, a six-person jury found her father to be innocent. His attorney got about $130,000 in legal fees and she got nothing. While she was stunned at the verdict, she was glad that she sued him and got her secret out in the open. She also felt sad for him. Later, one juror said that none of the jury believed that Kathy was lying, but that her memories "lacked a certain precision,"[63] although he was not "precise" about just what the lack was.

Juries and judges usually have inherent deficiencies. A jury is a group of from six to 12 people who come from the general population, of which about 95% has been estimated to have grown up in an unhealthy, troubled or dysfunctional family and a troubled world.[573, 687] Most judges and members of juries will thus be unrecovered adult children of a dysfunctional family and world, and will bring to their work many of their own core issues (see page 48), which will likely be activated by the contents and dynamics of the trial proceedings. The members of a jury usually argue with and pressure one another until there is finally a majority rule by the more forceful over the less forceful. Several people usually try to persuade others to view the "truth" of the case in the way that they see it. Since difficulty handling conflict is a common core issue for most people, a number of the jurors finally gives in to the others.

While the legal profession believes that the jury system is the most accurate way to arrive at the truth, given the above state of most judges and juries, that belief will tend not to be true in many cases, as it appears to have been in the case of Kathy O'Connor. Just as in our families of origin, as we went along with others' opinions, demands and manipulations to survive, we may continue to do the same today in most group situations that we may find ourselves in, including being on a jury. Another problem is jury selection. Lawyers can pick juries to be biased in their client's direction,[5] as happened in the William Kennedy Smith trial and appears to have happened in the Gary Ramona case.

Could Kathy's father have actually abused her and the three other girls and young women, but does not remember it because he had an alcoholic blackout or repressed it himself? When asked by *The Washington Post*, he responded to this question vehemently: ". . . absolutely impossible . . . It is out of the question. None of it happened."[63] Of course, this kind of response, by "protesting too much," may itself be a kind of internal corroborating evidence that can come from the offender or co-offender.

David O'Connor told me that he grew up in a normal, happy but strict Catholic family and that he was not abused. His father's father was alcoholic and his parents were teetotalers. He told me that he wasn't an alcoholic,[493] although he was arrested in 1973 for drunk driving,[63, 494] his daughter Karen testified that he was a violent drunk who beat her,[494] and Kathy and his ex-wife had complained about his drinking. He told me that his cardiologist who had examined him yearly since 1974 also said he "wasn't alcoholic." He admitted to having an affair while married for one year with his wife's "16-year-old" sister, but not with her other sister, as was claimed. He said that he took and passed two polygraph tests, but these were not allowed into court.[493] At the end of our interview he added that *The Washington Post* articles had made Kathy look too good, because she had been a "prostitute and a drug addict"[493]—which he probably didn't know added to the internal corroborating evidence that she had been sexually abused.

Her father's "expert" witness was Dr. Paul McHugh, chief of psychiatry at Johns Hopkins School of Medicine and a long time, active board member of the FMS Foundation. As Kathy testified, at the end of a 60-minute evaluation McHugh tried to talk her out of going ahead with the lawsuit by attempting to make her feel guilty and afraid, and she had to terminate his persistence in that part of their conversation.[494] He did not review one page of her extensive clinical records.[668] After seeing Kathy for that one brief session only, McHugh told the jury that her "psychiatric problems" made her "susceptible to hallucinations," which in his opinion was what her "dreamlike" memories were. Instead of the reverse, which is backed scientifically by numerous studies, he said "that her [memories] were a symptom of her illness, rather than a cause." But her own psychiatrist who had been assisting her long term refuted McHugh's opinion by saying that "She wasn't the kind of [patient] for whom the distinction between fantasy and fact are blurred."[63, 668]

I have heard McHugh speak on the topic of "false memories" several times recently, and he usually talks the same party line: There is no such thing as multiple personality disorder. Therapists and others are on a "witch hunt" to find sexual abuse—or to criticize him.* Many accusers are mentally ill. Their memories are simply "hallucinations." When an abuse memory surfaces, all therapists should immediately go outside the therapeutic relationship and look for external verification. (McHugh avoids any mention of internal corroboration of abuse and appears to focus only on external corroboration.[453] In McHugh's 1983 book on psychiatry, which is nearly all from a biological perspective, he never mentions childhood trauma as a cause of mental or emotional problems.) And despite the notoriety and shortcomings of the polygraph, he pushes accused perpetrators to take a polygraph or lie detector test, which is not usually admissible in courts of law.**[453]

While it is helpful, in this case external corroborating evidence (the three other women saying they each had been sexually abused also) was apparently not taken seriously by the jury or by Dr. McHugh. Being a psychiatrist of such high position, McHugh should have known that Kathy's father was an active alcoholic during the time of the alleged abuse, and therefore should have known that her father could have had alcoholic memory blackouts and thus not remember having abused these

---

* Some FMS advocates, including McHugh[453] and Richard Gardner,[591] use the term "witch hunt" to mean that therapists and prosecutors are seeking out innocent people when they accuse them of child sexual abuse. Psychiatrist Jean Shinoda Bolen describes the hunting and killing, usually by burning, of about nine million women over a 300 year period of our history.[62, 364] Those labeled as "witches" included any woman who spoke openly of her own healing or was a healer herself. Perhaps the most famous was Joan of Arc, who at age 19 in 1431 was publically burned at the stake. Her "offense": wearing men's clothes, having short hair and being a magician and a "heretic." She was a healer. Could it be that some FMS proponents have it backwards? Might *they* be hunting and attacking people, mostly women, who speak openly about healing from sexual abuse and who assist others as they heal? Part of their healing is naming the abuser and expressing the truth about what happened.

** The FMS Foundation listed as one of its goals to "Provide financial assistance to families who need help in paying for polygraph tests, counseling, or legal services" (FMSF Flyer, July 1992). While it is likely that they will not make public who or how much they finance their members (e.g., did they or anyone else finance Gary Ramona or other cases?), it is reported that Peter Freyd, the father accused by his daughter Jennifer of sexually abusing her and co-founder of the FMSF, took a polygraph test, which found that he was "not deceptive."[315] Just as many other people similarly accused, he cites this result as "proof" that he is not lying. But most courts of law view polygraph tests as being too unreliable to use as evidence, since many known criminals pass them.[636] Indeed, polygraph expert Robert Brisentine Jr., who tested Peter, said, "A polygraph can only determine what the individual has on the conscious level. It is not necessarily based on fact. It's based on the perception of the person taking the exam."[315]

four women. Others have written of McHugh's misadventures,[40, 128a] and he continues to testify essentially exclusively for accused perpetrators and speak out aggressively against real delayed memories.[453]

The "False Expert Syndrome"

Even though nearly all FMS advocates are not experienced in working long term with recovery from trauma, and most are not clinicians, they continue to use intimidating and at times bullying tactics to try to silence the voices of abuse survivors. In my and others' opinions, some come across with a histrionic style (e.g., McHugh, Ofshe, Loftus), while others are more subdued but no less angry in their tone (e.g., Ganaway, Gardner, Lief). While these and others in the backlash may be otherwise well-meaning people, they tend to become zealots, each in their own way, when they talk or write about memory and sexual abuse.

This memory debate is the most polarized and public issue that has come up in the field of mental health and recovery in decades. But from it there may come several related problems and opportunities. As workers in the legal system learn from clinicians and vice versa, and as we all learn more about the disinformation of the FMS advocates and how to deal with it, we will be able to use the legal system more effectively. In the meantime, we can speak out in favor of the truth in all kinds of abuse, and inform our lawmakers of our wishes. And if they don't change the laws and the system, we can vote them out of office and vote for those who will make appropriate changes.

Lawyers who specialize in trial advocacy, i.e., who prosecute or sue for damages, can learn the party line and styles of various "experts," many of whom make a large portion of their incomes by testifying in favor of people accused of molesting children. Defense lawyers tend to use them to try to attack the credibility of the accuser, portraying them to the judge and jury as a troubled person with a faulty memory.[341] While some of their testimony may be appraise and accurate, I believe that much or perhaps most of it is not. Some lawyers are compiling profiles on some of them, and interested people may inquire about such information from the American Coalition for Abuse Awareness and the American Prosecutors Research Institute, both in the Washington, D.C. area, and The Family Violence and Sexual Assault Institute in Tyler, Texas, and various trial and legal information resources. To disallow testimony, judges can react only to the evidence that is presented to them. It is the responsibility of attorneys and their aides to search out and present to judges that a proposed "expert" is not qualified to talk about traumatic memory.

The FMS Foundation is encouraging its members to file formal complaints with their professional state licensing boards against targeted therapists. While it would be poor practice for therapists to try to do so, I am unaware of any state board that has any admonition or law against "implanting false memories," and it would be difficult for them to prove such an occurrence even if it did. With the well-organized and angry desperation of some accused offenders and co-offenders, we are likely to see more of these and similar kinds of harassment and attacks on targeted therapists and to an extent, on therapists in general. Some attorneys have defended several therapists who are being sued by families or patients for "implanting false memories" into them or their family members and are familiar with this specialized area of the law.

The Offender System

As Emrick, Fredrickson and others have described, the offender mentality is usually characterized by boundary invasions and distortions, family secrets, defensiveness, manipulation, projection and attack.[202, 234] When their abusive behavior is uncovered and exposed to anyone outside of their offender system, they tend to resort to the same intra- and interpersonal behaviors that they enacted when they committed their original abusive and co-abusive acts. Now out in the open, they may also try to hide behind all sorts of things, from religion (often with a fundamentalist bent) to the "looking good" claim (see page 79) to attempting to enact laws so they can see their grandchildren.

Like some survivors, Lynn Crook also worked as a counselor at a sexual assault agency, where she became familiar with over 200 cases of sexual abuse. There she observed that:

> When offender behavior is exposed—and initially it is often exposed within the system—the offender first denies in some form. Then he goes to other members of the system saying, "She's crazy, menopausal, wrong, confused, always had problems, and now—the memories were implanted by her therapist." Then comes the next level of denial within the family system: "We were a perfect family, she had a happy childhood, we sent her to college, he never beat her, we don't remember

anything like that, if that had happened Mom would have known, she never said anything as a child, he was too busy with work and golf, etc." Then if the accuser goes public (published writings, legal system) the offender, with any consensus he has established within the family, continues this same behavior.[157]

Other Legal Cases

I have looked for over a year for a bona fide case of "false memory syndrome" that appeared within or outside of the legal system. While some have written their stories that were not clinically verifiable,[278] so far I have found only one, which Terr describes in Chapter 5 of *Unchained Memories*, and that was of a young girl influenced by her mother.[641] The FMSF invited me to visit their office so they could show me some of their "documented" cases, but when I asked twice to meet with one of their staff, they did not respond. I am still open to hearing convincing cases, which I think must exist. Whether it is a "syndrome"—or goes by some other name—awaits the clinical demonstration in the peer-reviewed trauma literature of a pattern that is replicated in many people by several different clinician observers over time. Although there is also already a literature on abusers,[1, 3, 31, 39, 57, 64, 67, 117, 126, 202, 203, 250, 254, 294, 303, 304, 365, 374, 385, 391a, 429, 439, 483, 501, 529, 587a] we need to know more about them as well. It will thus be useful to similarly document the forgetting or denial process in the abuser and co-abuser, which may be a hundred times more common, whether it might be called the "false innocence belief syndrome"[543] or some other name. Abuse and its perpetrators and co-perpetrators have many dimensions and have been described in many places. We will learn more about trauma psychology as we observe them from other perspectives and as they may risk being real with us.

I wonder if there is a way that clinicians who know trauma psychology well, and who assist recovering people long-term can begin to meet with some FMS advocates to begin a sharing of concerns from both sides? How might that meeting come about? Could we begin to define some mutual goals? To do so would likely require great humility from all involved.

21

THE BABY
AND THE
BATHWATER

Still another claim by FMS advocates is that "Experiments and studies on memory show that 'false memories' are easily implanted, even in normal people." I began discussing this claim in Chapter 5 on Ordinary versus Traumatic Memory, and continue it here.

A characteristic of both ordinary and traumatic memory is that there are often details around some of the external aspects of the remembered experience that are erroneous. Researchers on ordinary and traumatic memory observe that these kinds of errors are common.[420, 641, 705] But do these mistaken details make all memories invalid and "false?" My sense and that of others[328, 329, 502-507, 641, 661, 662] is that they do not, and that this tends to be especially so for traumatic memories. With few exceptions, it is the essence or core of a traumatic memory that is true. That essence is the characteristic of the memory that makes it believable and valid, and not the small details.

FMS advocates try to use this claim as part of their "false memory" defense. Like throwing out the baby with the bath water, they say that this finding of errors in the details is strong evidence that "false memories" are common and easily implanted in both normal people and in trauma victims. In doing so, they tend to cite two kinds of reports: anecdotal and experimental. From these, they usually then speculate without having a firm clinical basis.[507, 508]

Anecdotal Reports

It is understandable that researchers and others who are unfamiliar with the natural history and nuances of trauma would confuse traumatic experiences with those that are only mildly to moderately stressful. But for them to arbitrarily label a study as "traumatic" and cite it as "evidence" that real traumatic memories can be changed, and then expect that helping professionals and the general public will accept their pronouncements as "authoritative," may illustrate some of their own erroneous thinking and behavior. For example, Loftus[417] cites eight reports of "memory distortion" under a heading in large type, "Can Real Traumatic Memories be Changed?" and which I summarize in Table 21.1. Yet of these cited reports, only the first two are severely traumatic (the cases of George Franklin and Paul Ingram), and that trauma was inflicted on the *victims* of the abuse. The next two (about Jack Hamilton and Elliot Thorpe) appear to be stressful or possibly traumatic experiences. And these first four are each only anecdotal reports. Of the remaining five examples, Loftus offers no evidence of theirs being anywhere near the kind of traumatic intensity of Eileen Franklin's experience or that of Paul Ingram's family, whom he confessed to have abused—*or* of the kind that trauma therapists treat.

Eileen Franklin's Traumatic Memories

Loftus and others have tried to invalidate Eileen Franklin's traumatic memories by pointing out that some of the details had been published in the local newspapers after the murder, when Eileen was eight years old, but which came to her awareness about two decades later while recovering her memory. They said this led Eileen to change some of the details of her story.*

---

*The critics seldom speak of what actually happened in these newspaper stories, which reported many inaccuracies about the murder. FMS proponent Harry MacLean says "she simply could have been repeating what she had been told or read," (Terr book review FMSF newsletter, September 1994) as he continues to believe that she made this all up and that George was an innocent victim of her "false memories." Anyone who had used these newspaper stories to make up all or parts of their memories would have included the inaccuracies, which Eileen Franklin never did.[231] She also remembered details that fit perfectly with

Table 21.1. Evidence Cited as Proving That "False Memories" Are Common and Easily Implanted Even in Trauma Victims

(compiled from references 268, 397, 413, 417, 420, 497, 506, 519, 641, 705)

Type of Evidence	**Examples Cited**
Anecdotal	• The California case of Eileen Franklin who remembered seeing her father, George, murder her 8-year-old friend after repressing it for decades. Based on the strength of her memories, correlated with the findings of the murder, George was convicted in court. FMS advocates say that because Eileen changed some details of her memory over time, this was simply a "false memory."[413, 417, 497, 641] • The Washington case of Paul Ingram who was convicted on six counts of sexually abusing his two daughters. Even though Ingram confessed immediately after being accused and his wife, daughters and one son verified the abuse, FMS advocates argue that "false memories" were implanted into Ingram by authority figures.[417, 497] The judge on the case and trauma therapists Olio and Cornell rebuke these speculations.[506, 519] • Baseball pitcher Jack Hamilton misremembers some details about the game in which he hit and wounded a batter with a pitch.[420] • General Elliot Thorpe years later misremembers some details of his experience of the bombing of Pearl Harbor.[417] • Piaget's memory of his "attempted kidnapping" when he was two years old was implanted by his nanny, who later confessed that she made up the story.[417, 641]
Experimental	• In two retrospective studies, about one third to 40% of people made errors in remembering details of their experience of hearing of the 1986 explosion of the space shuttle Challenger.[641, 705] • Hypnosis can implant false memories, such as a person's having heard loud noises at night.[397] • After viewing a videotape of a girl lying about an assault, 4- to 7-year-old children were led to believe that they saw a man hit the girl when he did not.[417] • Five people had easily implanted memories of their being lost in a mall as a child (see Loftus' own testimony about this study in the previous chapter).[268, 413, 417]

We know that aspects of traumatic memories usually change as the person remembers more and more about them over time, so that this characteristic alone is not enough to prove or disprove the validity or falsehood of a memory.[641] Nor is the fact that details about an experience are not entirely accurate.

In fact, under the painful and often overwhelming circumstances of a traumatic experience, when the person is usually in a dissociated state, often age-regressed and trying just to survive the whole thing, it is expected that they will not usually be attending to most of the trivial details around them. But sometimes people do notice and remember some of these details accurately, and they may come out in their memory spontaneously, as Eileen Franklin's did and as shown in Table 9.3 on page 92. So it is no surprise that in anecdotes like those of Jack Hamilton and Elliot Thorpe there were some details that they did not remember correctly. But what is important is that they did not forget the essence of what happened in their experience: Jack Hamilton remembered that he injured a player with his pitched ball, and Elliot Thorpe remembered the painful experience of being in Pearl Harbor when it was bombed.

The Paul Ingram Case

Another FMSF board member, social science researcher Richard Ofshe, has tried to invalidate the traumatic memories of the wife, two daughters and son of Paul Ingram, a law enforcement officer and strict religious man who was convicted of sexually abusing his daughters.[497, 498] While Ingram initially confessed to the offense, Ofshe argued that because he was later in a trance from a relaxation technique when questioned by authority figures, he was thus inadvertently "hypnotized," which to Ofshe automatically "proves" a pseudomemory.** But no such technique was used on Ingram, and Ofshe makes several other erroneous assumptions and conclusions.[497] Even though Ingram was not in therapy, Ofshe still attributes his actions to psychotherapy and accuses therapists of ". . . influencing their clients to find 'memories' that the therapists believe to

the physical findings of the murder that were not published.[231, 641] George's appeals to be released from prison continue to be denied, despite FMS advocates' support.

**At the same time, Ofshe wrote in his report, "I have no opinion if the daughters were raped here." This statement is not congruous with his "pseudomemory" belief and his other statements about the case.[495]

be buried in the client's unconscious."[497, 506-508]

After hearing Ofshe's testimony in the Ingram trial, Superior Court Judge Robert Peterson found five problems with Ofshe and his behavior.[519] First, Ofshe was not a clinician. Second, "...he's not an expert in sex abuse or with matters with regard to victims of sex abuse." Third, he found Ofshe's behavior to be "odd." Ofshe attempted an "experiment" on Paul Ingram wherein he tried to "implant" a "false memory" into him, and according to the Court this experiment was not appropriate and was poorly timed. Fourth, he found the "relaxation technique" mentioned in the previous paragraph, which Ofshe appeared to summarize from reading a dry record, to be "strange." Finally, two weeks after Ingram pled guilty to six counts of sexually abusing his daughters, Ofshe called Ingram and for an hour and a half tried to convince him to recant. Judge Peterson expressed "great cause for concern" and found that Ofshe was "considerably less qualified" than the other three expert witnesses on the case.[519]

Ofshe's is but another example of an anecdotal "analysis" where someone attempts to generalize about dissociated traumatic memory. Unfortunately, the general public can be misled just because an idea is in print and written by someone with "credentials" like Ofshe, who is a professor of sociology at Cal Berkeley, or like Loftus, who is a professor of psychology at the University of Washington. Many people — including those in the media, some helping professionals, judges and the general public — automatically assume that what these "experts" say is true. Both Ofshe and Loftus are on the FMS Foundation's professional advisory board, and yet neither is a clinician nor a trauma psychologist. They are not experts in these kinds of cases. Both have also written a book expressing their assumptions about "repression" and attacking the frequent observation of traumatic forgetting and the therapists who assist trauma survivors. Both still appear to believe that Paul Ingram, George Franklin and others found guilty of sexual abuse or murder were innocent, including those in the Lynn Crook case[413, 417, 497, 498] (see page 203).

A criticism of the Ingram case was that his wife, daughters and one son described some "satanic rituals" that were associated with the abuse. Because of their difficulty finding concrete and believable external corroborating evidence for satanic ritual abuse (SRA), most law enforcement and criminal justice workers, including Ken Lanning, who compiles investigations of these kinds of cases for the FBI, do not believe it when anyone mentions anything that could be associated with SRA. In fact, it is almost the "kiss of death" for the prosecution in any abuse case where anything of the kind is described. Even so, Lanning said about the Ingram case, "It is clear that there was some truth to what he [Ingram] had to say [in his confessions] and [that there was] some fabrication, and it depends on where one draws the line . . ."[395a] Paul Ingram's was the first nationally publicized abuse case in which someone was convicted of a crime in which SRA was a part of the evidence, and he was the most publicized perpetrator to admit to having repressed memories himself.

The young actor River Phoenix died of heroin and cocaine overdose in 1993. His parents belonged to a cult called "The Children of God" since he was a baby, and the cult openly believed in regularly using children for sexual purposes. What was not reported in the popular press was that young River lost his virginity to an adult as a four-year-old. The cult has been investigated in the U.S., Australia, France, Spain and Argentina, and while some children have been rescued, its activities continue across the world, as skeptics and backlashers continue to claim that there is "no real evidence" for cult abuse of children other than tainted reports of hypnotized patients.[79, 348, 409, 450, 698] Jonestown, the Manson family, the Branch Davidians and the Solar Temple tragedy are but the tip of the iceberg. Many cult abuse survivors quickly learn that their stories will not be believed, and they remain painfully silent.*[214]

Loftus also cites the Swiss psychologist Jean Piaget's story that he was almost kidnapped when he was two years old, and that his nanny had rescued him. Until Piaget was 15 years old he had a clear memory of this event. His nanny then took her story back, saying that she had initially wanted to impress the wealthy Piaget family with it. What Piaget does not tell us, and what Loftus does not address,[417] is whether he ever manifested any physical or psychological symptoms because of his imagined abduction. The child psychiatrist Lenore Terr doubts that he did.[641] As I described in Chapter 15 on *Internal Verification*, people with traumatic memories usually have associated symptoms and signs.

These five anecdotal reports constitute the basis of the peer reviewed, published "scientific validation" of the "false memory" lobbyists. The next comes from experiments that were conducted mostly on ordinary memory.

---

* FMSF director Pamela Freyd calls the recovery movement "cult-like," although she says "they have no charismatic leader."[216] Could she be projecting?

Experimental Observations

In the two retrospective studies of people's recollections about their experience of hearing about the 1986 explosion of the space shuttle Challenger, it was found that 30 to about 40 percent made some errors in remembering the details of their experience.[705] What was not talked about much in these reports was that from nearly 60 to 70 percent of these people did not make significant errors about details. And all of them remembered the main events, the essence of their experience.

The topic that inspired these and other studies was the exploration by memory researchers of so-called "flashbulb" memories, coined by Brown and Kulik in 1977 after their study of people's memories of November 22, 1963, when President John F. Kennedy was assassinated.[705] The 12-year retention of vivid memory of their experience on this day lent credibility to the claim of this kind of remarkable memory. With memory research still in its infancy, it seemed unusual then, as it does now, for people to recall events so vividly over those many years.[705] But the flashbulb metaphor has remained controversial even to this day and as expected, FMS advocates use the finding of errors about usually trivial details that occur in less than half of people's "flashbulb" memories to try to discredit and invalidate the reality of traumatic forgetting.

The remaining three studies that Loftus cites (at the bottom of Table 21.1) do not appear to be about people's traumatic memories. But they do show how suggestible (i.e., how a person responds to communication) people can be in certain situations, such as when under hypnosis or when influenced by forceful or enthusiastic people. Loftus also frequently quotes the "lost in a mall" study of five people to try to disprove the role of traumatic forgetting in the natural history of trauma, although she may have little success in doing so on people who know what she said under oath (summarized in the previous chapter) and that this was not a study about traumatic memory.[417] Terr said, "Experiments on college students do not simulate clinical instances of trauma. And they have little to do with childhood trauma."[641] In a debate with Loftus in 1994, Calof said:

> While bearing little relevance to child abuse, the findings in the "lost in a mall" experiment suggest that if Dr. Loftus could so easily implant a benign memory in a child, using a relative or a trusted caregiver, we then have to consider what effect tyrannical, abusive parents could have

in distorting a powerless child's true memories of abuse over the years ("There, there, dear, you just had a bad dream. How can you say that about your father?") Any child, to preserve the idealization of their parents and the illusion of affiliation, safety, protection and security, would rather trade off their perceptions and accept the interpretations of the tyrannical authority than to embrace their true perceptions and lose that idealization in the process.[116a]

Calof observes that Loftus' research studies neither natural ordinary memory nor traumatic memory. She conducts mostly contrived scenarios in the laboratory only, using mock courtrooms, films, videotapes, slides and other unnatural imaging devices.[116a] This can be viewed as being a distorted kind of "guided imagery"—which she regularly attacks when it is done by a therapist—only she is manipulating the scenario. In therapeutic guided imagery it is the inner life of the patient that determines most of their experience. Loftus focuses more on the details, such as whether laboratory subjects remember a stolen candy bar as a *Snickers* or a *Butterfinger*, and not on the essence of an experience, such as that on videotape they saw a person steal something in a store.

As "expert" witnesses for the defense of people accused of being pedophiles, Loftus, Ofshe and other non-clinicians exploit these experimental results to support a shaky "If not *all* true, then *not at all* true" stance.[116a] To learn the natural history of traumatic memory we need to study clinical populations of survivors, offenders and co-offenders. Yet Loftus and others say they don't need to do such studies, relying on analyses from their court cases where they are paid to help prove that people accused of child molestation are innocent.[116a]

Finally, Loftus and Kaufman add to the confusion by writing statements that appear to contradict their prior remarks, e.g., that ". . . traumatic memories take many forms: Sometimes they persist as flashbulbs, sometimes they are repressed, and sometimes they are repressed but return." The latter two are rare statements for an FMS advocate to make, admitting that sometimes traumatic forgetting is valid, but without making any suggestions as to how to sort out just *when* it is not valid. They continue, "In *all* cases [my italics], the memories appear to contain at least some elements of errors."[420] This does not appear to be the case in all reports, since some people do remember even the most pertinent details of an experience correctly, as demonstrated in the Challenger studies and others.[641, 705]

The "Videotape" Analogy

Even with a videotape record of some traumatic events, there are still controversies in the way people interpret them. For example, in the Los Angeles trial of Rodney King in which two policemen were convicted of brutality, and the trial of Reginald Denny, in which two L.A. rioters were likewise convicted, there was much controversy within and outside the court as to how to interpret these videotapes. Numerous witnesses and bits of evidence were submitted by both sides. So even if we had a videotape version of an abuse experience that was in our memory, given the nature of the human psyche and the criminal justice and court systems, there would still likely be disagreement among accuser, abuser, co-abusers and others. Ultimately, each person's experience is their own, and each can use the recovery process to help mobilize their memories and heal their wounds. It takes great courage and persistence to do so.

In cases of overt abuse a videotape would likely be useful, although in covert abuse, given the awareness and experience of the average observer, it might not be as useful.

The Essence of the Memory

Memories are not always easy to sort out. In some situations minor errors do not affect the whole of the memory and its validity. In the healing process it is the essence of the memory that is important, not unimportant details. But in the court, opposing lawyers naturally bring in memory "experts" and use every other way possible to try to discredit the memory of the accuser, including focusing on irrelevant details that may be difficult for the accuser to verify.

Among any group of memories of abuse there may be a combination of truth and falsity, accurate and inaccurate information. Terr describes these as fitting into four categories:[641]

1. True memory of the essence of the abuse and true memory of the associated details.
2. True memory of the essence of the abuse and a mixture of true and untrue memories of the associated details.
3. Untrue memory of the essence and one or more true memories of the associated details (here abuse may have occurred, although it may not have been exactly the kind that was remembered, as may happen among some "retractors").
4. Untrue memory of both the essence and the details.[641]

This latter kind of memory appears to be the great exception among people who remember abusive experiences,[329] even though FMS advocates and other critics by their words, attitude and behavior may try to convince us that they are the rule.[215, 264-266, 413, 453, 497, 498, 712] Indeed, some members of the FMSF's professional advisory board have been criticized and rejected by the courts for their erroneous testimonies in this direction when attempting to be sworn in as "expert" defense witnesses on behalf of accused perpetrators.[519, 572, 620, 635, 645, 718]

The Accused

From the perspective of the accused abuser, how will they be feeling and functioning after being accused? We know that nearly all abusers have some degree of post-traumatic stress disorder and are themselves prone to dissociation and traumatic forgetting.[586] Rather than simply trying to "win" their case, how can their lawyer or their therapist best help them to heal their wounds? It appears to be much more difficult to heal the wounds around being an abuser, who nearly always will have a history of having been abused in some way, although they may not be aware of it. For the co-abuser, unless they have a complicating factor like a personality disorder, active addiction or another debilitating psychiatric disorder, the difficulty of their healing is often in between that of the accuser and the accused. In their research and writings the FMS advocates almost never address these issues. I describe these and other dynamics in the accused further throughout this book, especially in Chapters 6 and 16 and at the end of Chapter 17.

After Effects

In many situations of reported abuse there may be no way of knowing for sure that the abuse actually happened. But a well trained and experienced therapist can recognize the after effects and consequences of abuse, which is a part of internal corroboration, that the person has manifested and continues to manifest. Given time over their recovery, the survivor of the abuse can also recognize these effects (see Chapter 15).

When 14 of the more than 100 adults who were sexually abused as children by the Catholic priest James Porter spoke of their abuse in court, they did not describe the abuse itself in detail. What they said was how they had been affected by the abuse—the after effects and consequences of Porter's repeated molestation when they were children. Now as adults they were suffering from such painful experiences as addictions, low self-esteem, confusion, ruined relationships, hearing intrusive voices, depression and more.[227, 528] After decades of traumatic forgetting, some of them were now just beginning to heal through recovery. The memory critics do not tend to address these kind of crucial issues in their research and writings; they focus more on the details than the essence of a memory and the after effects of the trauma.

How Hard Is It to "Implant a False Memory"

Of the nine examples given in Table 21.1. of Loftus' attempt to prove that "false memories" are common and easily implanted even in trauma victims, only four may have some validity. These include the story of Piaget and the first three studies cited in the experimental section. But these last three are simple experiments conducted on people apparently without post-traumatic stress disorder or traumatic forgetting. (Terr and others have commented that there is no evidence that Piaget had PTSD, nor was there any other internal corroborating evidence that would go along with his story—so that an aware therapist today would not be easily convinced of its veracity.)[112, 116a, 641] To prevent these kinds of errors, it would be more constructive to have a memory researcher collaborate with a trauma therapist in future explorations of the nature of memory and abuse.

Except in very unusual and extreme circumstances, such as those described by Smyth,[604] a therapist cannot "implant" a serious disorder like PTSD or another dissociative disorder into their patient or client. But what may happen is that an untrained, inexperienced, unhealed or unethical helping professional misleads a vulnerable patient or client who already has a serious disorder into believing that they had certain experiences that they did not have. This may be what happened with some of the "retractors" described in Chapter 9.

> Loftus cites a publicized story of a father who was accused by his 26-year-old daughter of incest after she recently remembered her repressed experience of the abuse. He hired a woman who was a private investigator to visit his daughter's therapist, complaining that she had nightmares and insomnia, and apparently wearing a wire. On the third visit the therapist told her that she was an incest survivor. When the pseudopatient said she didn't remember any trauma, the therapist told

her that ". . . many people . . . go through this when the memory starts to surface" and recommended that she attend incest survivor groups and read *The Courage to Heal*.*[417, 471]

As therapists we need to know our own limits and obtain a consultation or make a referral when we have doubts about what is happening with our patients or clients. We need to know our own history and heal our own wounds and not diagnose everyone who comes to us with our own diagnosis. At the same time, we need to have a high index of suspicion for a history of child abuse in the people we see, and to screen for it. If a physician did not screen for breast cancer (which afflicts an estimated one in every nine women) or for prostate cancer or for high blood pressure, and the patient developed it in the next year, we would call that malpractice. With a prevalence in the general population of at least one in three to five for child sexual abuse alone, we cannot not screen for that, even if a national lobby group tries to intimidate us into not doing so.

Neglecting Abused Children and Adults

In this book I have used nine claims of FMS advocates as starting points for discussing some of the important aspects about memory and abuse. They have made other claims as they try to defend themselves and refute the reality of abuse and traumatic forgetting. One of the most confusing examples of these follows.

The FMSF regularly makes qualifying statements such as this: ". . . we do not deny that child sexual abuse exists to any extent that is greater than previously suspected, that it is a terrible thing and that every effort should be made to see that it is stopped." (FMSF newsletter July 21, 1992) But at the same time they continue to devote essentially all of their energy, efforts and literature to support and enable essentially all of their thousands of accused members, without any clinical screening, who deny having sexually abused a child. They remain a lay advocacy group and a special interest lobby which appears to use a "professional advisory board" the guise of "science" as ways to support the denial of many

---

* In 1994 two retractors filed a lawsuit against the authors of *The Courage to Heal* for "implanting false memories" of child sexual abuse into them via the book when they read it. Both were dismissed at the trial court level in September 1994, and the First Amendment of the United States Constitution (freedom of speech) remained intact.[587b]

accused child abusers, most specifically people who sexually abuse children.*

For abusers and co-abusers, their recovery is difficult even with the best recovery program, and even with that, the abuse frequently continues. Without participating in a full- and long-term program of recovery, a perpetrator usually continues to abuse innocent children. Therapist Mark Schwartz writes, "In our perpetrators' program, many individuals who had previously acknowledged their perpetrations have begun carrying around 'false memory' articles to fuel their denial, resulting in more perpetrations."[585]

The FMSF says that real abuse is bad and that those abusers should be punished, and then usually proceeds to invalidate survivors and attack their therapists. They never seem to address "real abuse" or what to do about it. The FMS Foundation staff and its professional advisory board

---

* Technically a *tax-exempt*, non-profit organization i.e., a 501(c) 3 corporation as the FMSF, cannot formally lobby in the U.S. political process. But they can do it *indirectly*, such as by influencing the media and courts, by the actions of its individual members and board members, and by activities of its independent subsidiaries. A recent example is a project of many state and regional FMSF offshoots, headed by attorney R. Christopher Barden of Plymouth, MN and the Illinois FMS Society, wherein they are asking for money to support Barden's work on the passage of a proposed "Mental Health Consumer Protection Act." This act would: (1) require full disclosure of all of the risks and hazards of psychotherapy to patients *before* therapy begins, (2) ban federal, state and private insurance funding for *any* psychotherapy procedures that do not meet stringent tests for safety and effectiveness, (3) permit third party (family) lawsuits against therapists who engage in willful and reckless acts such as "memory retrieval therapy," (4) criminalize fraudulent practices such as the willful or reckless induction of false accusations of abuse, (5) ban pseudoscience testimony from courtrooms including *any* psychotherapy procedure, method or process that has not been validated and accepted by a substantial majority of the scientific (not the psychotherapy) community, and (6) create a Model Licensing Act for psychotherapists requiring maintenance of detailed therapy records, acquisition of malpractice insurance, lengthy statutes of limitations for suits against therapists and other important changes." This legislation has been proposed in 25 states.[29, 181a, 519a]

However, many therapists already use informed consent, and it is the job of the state boards of professional examiners or quality assurance and the state professional societies to monitor and assist helping professionals. It is not the job of the federal government or of "scientists" to police helping professionals. Third-party lawsuits would allow perpetrators or anyone alarmed by someone else's therapy to sue therapists and invade the privacy of the patient/client-therapist relationship. As for banning "pseudoscience" from the courtroom, psychotherapy is not unscientific. Given the ethics involved in "experimenting" with human subjects, combined with our current base of knowledge, psychotherapy is as proven and effective as is possible today. It is backed by programs at accredited universities around the country and by criteria mandated by state boards of examiners and quality assurance. Psychotherapists are required to take approved continuing education credits each year. Regarding false accusation of abuse, if accusations that end up being untrue are prosecuted, then even the suspicion of abuse that is mandated by state law would *not* be reported.

simply do not address this major problem of child abuse, other than to deny the behavior and responsibility of any accused people who join their membership and many who do not join. They even allow membership to some perpetrators who have been found guilty in court.[157, 718] If they would clarify and focus their goals and actions, ideally with the assistance of independent trauma therapists, they might begin to help rather than hinder in the prevention and treatment of child sexual abuse.

Many of these abusers have post-traumatic stress disorder, as do many co-abusers and survivors of abuse. It is the relationship of PTSD to memory and abuse that I will describe in the next two chapters.

(cont.)

Mandated reporters would be afraid to report abuse and the state system for reporting child abuse that—even now with the current regulations—is underreported, would be destroyed. Finally, model licensing acts are already in effect nationwide. Most therapists in all states are already licensed, regulated and monitored by the state licensing boards that monitor various forms of therapy.[519a] Barden and his colleagues neglected to include the importance of consultations, second opinions and supervision—practices which most therapists use regularly when appropriate. (Barden is now offering workshops for therapists to help them stay out of trouble in this area to which he appears to be contributing.)

As with most other professions, therapists continue to explore new areas of research and other frontiers, and thereby improve their knowledge and services.

Therapists who are concerned about preventing the above invasion of the therapist-patient/client relationship can call and write their professional associations and societies. Survivors who are concerned can monitor bills filed in their local newspapers and testify at public hearings—all of which would benefit from several survivors working together on such a project. Both therapists and survivors can call or write the ACAA (see Resources on page 373.) FMS advocates are extremely well organized and plan to force this and similar bills through the law-making process in each state. Since there are *many* more therapists and survivors than accused offenders, they can win if they are equally or better organized. Accused offenders have more money and free time. Therapists and survivors have more numbers and expertise.

As an example, the *Child Abuse Accountability Act (1994)* allows childhood sexual abuse survivors who successfully sue for resulting damages to garnish the federal pensions of their abusers. This law holds offenders responsible for the injuries they cause, as determined by a court of law. It has nothing to do with the reliability of memory.[535a]

This bill was nearly killed in the senate by FMS lobbyists. But as word of the backlash's lobbying spread, therapists, survivors and supporters joined together in a grassroots letter writing and phoning campaign to support the act; and they were successful with this support. The FMS lobbyists did not persuade a single senator to vote against the bill. Voted into law, this important act showed how survivors, therapists and supporters can express an effective voice in legal policy.[535a]

22

MEMORY AND
TRAUMATIC STRESS *Part One*

Trauma occurs when any act, event or experience harms or damages the physical, sexual, mental, emotional or spiritual integrity of our True Self. Simple upsetting or disrupting of it is not usually enough to cause actual damage, unless it is repeated over time and is of human origin. And if we are vulnerable, i.e., if our True Self is already wounded or damaged from prior trauma, then we may be more likely to develop additional or more severe symptoms and signs of post-traumatic stress from being exposed to one or more less traumatic events. The American Psychiatric Association has described a spectrum of psychosocial stressors that ranges from mild to severe.[11]

Some Limitations of Diagnostic Criteria

There are many different ways to define a traumatic experience. What is a trauma to one person may not be traumatic to another. Before recovery a person might define a trauma differently than they do after they have been in recovery for a while. During recovery our understanding of a trauma often changes.

The original DSM-3 committee defined a trauma as a "recognizable stressor that would evoke symptoms of significant distress in almost everyone." Seven years later they narrowed it down to any event that was "outside the range of usual human experience and that would be markedly distressing to almost anyone." (DSM-3R) Their major purpose for doing so may have been to distinguish unusual stress, with which people are unprepared to deal, from everyday stress.[169a] Unfortunately, in their most recent definition (DSM 4) they have focused mostly on the person's physical integrity wherein they react with intense fear, a definition that I, as do others view as being clinically limiting* (see item A in Table 22.1).

For example, in the DSM-3R definition (the second one cited above), how easily can we agree on the word *usual?* And how can we determine what "markedly distressing to almost anyone" means? Davidson and others have written about the importance of the subjective perception and appraisal in response to a traumatic event. Two people may respond differently to the same event. With this more accurate understanding we can begin to examine What Davidson calls the "specific details [that] need to be understood about each experience, including characteristics of the event itself and the perceptions, affects, and interpretations in the victim."[169a] I and many clinicians who assist trauma survivors prefer to focus more on items B, C, D, E, and especially F from the diagnostic criteria for PTSD (Table 22.1). Item F says that "the disturbance causes clinically significant distress or impairment in social, occupational or *other important areas* of functioning" [my emphasis].

The three main clusters of symptoms in PTSD include a *re-experiencing of the trauma* in various ways, a *persistent avoidance of stimuli* that are *associated* with the trauma and *persistent* symptoms of *increased arousal.* In addition to the trauma history, there is also usually a *numbing* of the person's awareness of their *inner life*, especially their feelings, and frequently some degree of *traumatic forgetting* (Figure 22.1).

Difficulty remembering aspects of traumatic experiences is so common

---

* What could be influencing the DSM working committees for each diagnostic category to limit them in this way? Could there be other groups, such as the health insurance industry, drug companies and the committee's peers in modern psychiatry, that emphasizes the biological and behavioral over trauma psychology, that consciously or unconsciously influence their decisions to narrow the diagnostic criteria to less than what is clinically useful? An example is their rejection of the DESNOS (Disorders of Extreme Stress Not Otherwise Specified) diagnostic category, which would have expanded the whole PTSD diagnostic category and made trauma psychology more credible, and thereby would have helped clinicians and patients alike.[326]

Table 22.1 Post traumatic Stress Disorder and Memory (309.81)[11]

A. The person has been exposed to a traumatic event [or events] in which both of the following have been present:

(1) the person has experienced, witnessed, or been confronted with an event or events that involve actual or threatened death or serious injury, or a threat to the physical integrity of oneself or others

(2) the person's response involved intense fear, helplessness, or horror.

B. The traumatic event is persistently **re-experienced** in at least one of the following ways:

(1) recurrent and **intrusive** distressing **recollections** of the event, including images, thoughts, or perceptions.   **Intrusive Memories**

(2) recurrent distressing **dreams** of the event.

(3) **acting or feeling as if the traumatic event were recurring** (includes a sense of reliving the experience, illusions, hallucinations, and dissociative flashback episodes, including those that occur upon awakening or when intoxicated)   **Unconscious Memories Abreactions & Flashbacks**

(4) **intense psychological distress** at exposure to internal or external cues that symbolize or resemble an aspect of the traumatic event   **Psychological Memories**

(5) **physiologic reactivity** upon exposure to internal or external cues that symbolize or resemble an aspect of the traumatic event   **Somatic Memories**

C. **Persistent avoidance of stimuli associated with the trauma** and numbing of general responsiveness (not present before the trauma), as indicated by at least three of the following: **Avoidance of the Memories**

(1) **efforts to avoid** thoughts, feelings, or conversations associated with the trauma

(2) **efforts to avoid** activities, places, or people that arouse recollections of the trauma

(3) **inability to recall** an important aspect of the trauma   **Traumatic Forgetting**

(4) markedly diminished interest or participation in significant activities

(5) feeling of **detachment** or **estrangement** from others

(6) **restricted** range of **affect** (e.g., unable to have loving feelings)

(7) sense of a foreshortened future (e.g., does not expect to have a career, marriage, children, or a normal life span)

D. **Persistent symptoms** of increased arousal (not present before the trauma), as indicated by at least two of the following:

(1) difficulty falling or staying asleep

(2) irritability or outbursts of anger

(3) difficulty concentrating

(4) hypervigilance   **Somatic**

(5) **exaggerated startle** response   **Memories**

E. Duration of the disturbance (symptoms in B, C, and D) is more than one month

F. The disturbance causes clinically significant distress or impairment in social, occupational, or other important areas of functioning.

Specify if:
     Acute: if duration of symptoms is less than three months
     Chronic: if duration of symptoms is three months or more
Specify if:
     With Delayed Onset: onset of symptoms at least six months after the stressor[11]

in PTSD that it is used in at least 10 of the approximately 20 diagnostic criteria of the DSM-4. Indeed, rather than being the exception after experiencing a trauma as skeptics claim, memory difficulties tend more often to be the rule, as many clinicians have described[326, 532, 641, 662, 663] and as I have shown throughout this book.

Figure 22.1. Major Components of Post-Traumatic Stress Disorder

An important part of healing from PTSD is in the process of remembering what happened in the traumatic experience. This remembering is not simply cognitive but is also experiential. As we heal, we experience it in our now clearer and richer inner life, which evolves during the recovery process.

Guises of PTSD

Like the diagnostic criteria for other disorders, those for PTSD are also a double-edged sword: while they are useful, they are also limiting at times. PTSD today presents itself in many guises, just as it has throughout history. In the late 1800s and early 1900s, during the time of Janet, Freud and their colleagues, it was called *hysteria* and was seen most often in young women.[326, 532] During the World Wars it was seen most often in young men, and was called *shell shock* or *combat neurosis*. And when people are taken hostage or kept and abused in *concentration camps*, what results is also PTSD (Figure 22.2).

Even though children have been physically and otherwise abused for millennia, we did not begin to recognize it until about 1962, when the *battered child syndrome* was described,[375] another guise of the disorder. (While not originally described as a psychological syndrome, it was instrumental in increasing our awareness of PTSD and is often associated with it.) Twelve to 15 years later, two more variations of PTSD were described: the *rape trauma syndrome*[99] in 1974 and the *battered woman syndrome*[562] in 1975-9. One of the more recently recognized guises is the *child sexual abuse accommodation syndrome*,[629] described by Summit in 1983 (page 84 and summarized in Table 9.1).

PTSD is also commonly seen among adult children of dysfunctional families and occurs often (e.g., with eating disorders and chemical dependence) to nearly always (e.g., with dissociative identity disorder—also known as multiple personality disorder) in people with the high risk disorders listed in Table 15.1 on page 151. While these guises may have various things in common, including their association with PTSD, people who are afflicted with any of them tend to be laden with fear, shame and guilt. Fear because of the terror of the unhealed original trauma. Shame because our political, social and helping professional systems are generally so unfamiliar with what to do to help survivors and abusers, and appear to be so fearful of facing their own wounds that they tend to project their own unhealed shame onto the victims of these many kinds of abuse. Rather than assist and help, they often hinder and re-wound. As but one example, just look at how our legal and court systems mistreat survivors of abuse.[478, 629-631] And guilt because we as survivors feel that we somehow caused the abuse, even though we did not. We share other commonalities as well, including core issues and disordered basic dynamics in relationships.[687, 691]

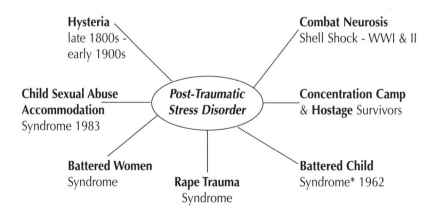

Figure 22.2. Guises of Post-Traumatic Stress Disorder from an Historical Perspective

Central to all of the above is that when we are traumatized and then naturally and appropriately try to express our resulting pain, in these dysfunctional systems we are repeatedly invalidated for doing so. Being invalidated not only blocks and often destroys our natural mechanisms for healing, but it frequently inflicts a double trauma on the victim of the mistreatment. Most all of the backlashes (whether individual or collective) against our genuine attempts to heal are thus just another kind of trauma—known as *retraumatization.*

Vulnerability Factors

Not every person with one or more traumatic experiences gets PTSD and it appears that not everyone is at equal risk for developing it. Risks for developing PTSD are associated with: (1) the nature of the traumatic experiences themselves, (2) preexisting vulnerability factors and (3) an interaction between these two.[169a] While our knowledge of these vulnerability factors is incomplete, some nine have been described so far, as shown in Table 22.2. In the presence of one or more of these factors, an event may assume greater traumatogenicity.[169a]

The intensity of the trauma, characteristics or kind of trauma and the person's subjective response to it, including their opportunity and ability to process and heal the traumatic experience, are all important in influencing the personal and clinical consequences that result from the trauma. To have been mistreated by our parents or another person who is supposed *to be protective of our welfare and well-being* is traumatic enough. But to heap on top of that trauma their *blocking of our ability to grieve* the traumatic experience and heal ourselves is equally as traumatic.

Diagnostic Criteria and Memory

While the DSM-4 diagnostic criteria for PTSD may have some of the above mentioned limitations, they are clear in their inclusion of problems involving memory,[11] as shown in Table 22.1. All five of the B criteria involve disordered memory in one way or another, including intrusive memories, unconscious memories, abreactions and flashbacks, psychological distress from the memories and various manifestations of somatic or body memories.

The first three of the C criteria involve avoidance of the memories, including *forgetting* them. While less specific, the remaining four of the

Table 22.2. Some Pretrauma Vulnerability Risk Factors for Developing PTSD (compiled from Davidson 1993[169a])

Factor	Comments
Childhood trauma	May result in wounding (see p.32), which lessens a healthy sense of self and possibly a loss of memory of the traumatic event.
Low self-esteem	With loss of a healthy sense of self, combined with psychologically traumatizing messages (see Table 26.1 on p.276) and other factors, the person is less able to form healthy coping skills and may blame themselves.
Introversion	May accompany the lost selfhood and result in an inability to express their pain, wants and needs and to set and maintain healthy boundaries.[691]
Extroversion	Can be a way of avoiding or covering up the pain of the traumatic experiences and lost selfhood.
High **neuroticism**	A term perhaps more clearly understood today as the various individual manifestations of lost self-hood.
Prior psychiatric disorder	In a vicious cycle, the lost selfhood may make the person vulnerable to high risk disorders (see Table 15.1 on p.151), which in turn may increase their exposure to more trauma.
Psychiatric illness in first-degree relatives	Wounded themselves, these relatives may negatively affect the child and adult through mistreatment and abuse, including repeated invalidation of the person's expressed experience.
High stress	Other high stresses or an accumulation of repeated ordinary stresses in a person with a low self-sense may be traumatizing.
Parental **poverty**	Additional stress, which aggravates an already low self-esteem.

C criteria may at times indicate or be associated with remembering or forgetting, as may the first four of the D criteria. The last of the D criteria, an exaggerated startle response, is a manifestation of various somatic memories that the person may experience. I have mentioned above some aspects of the psychological distress from the memories and will now describe abreactions, flashbacks and somatic memories.

Abreactions and Flashbacks

Abreactions and flashbacks are generally a more dramatic form of age regression, which I described in Chapter 15 on page 155. They are a kind of re-enacting and re-experiencing of the trauma from a perspective of the person's total being—including their physical, mental, emotional and spiritual aspects—and they represent a kind of memory that may be either specific or non-specific corroborating evidence of the veracity of a particular memory.

Clinically, I view an abreaction and a flashback as being essentially the same. They are an outpouring of previously unexpressed psychic pain and energy. This pain and energy may be accompanied by visual images, somatic states, action and other manifestations.[80] If the experiencing person has a safe and supportive environment, including people who accept their expression of pain and do not invalidate them, then they have a chance to heal their associated ungrieved grief from the past unhealed trauma.

> Pat was a 22-year-old college student who grew up in a troubled family. She had repeatedly experienced much discomfort and fear when she and her boyfriend had tried to be physically and sexually intimate but was never able to understand why. One weekend while visiting her mother, some of these feelings began to surface spontaneously and she began to cry. As she walked down the steps to the basement where her mother was working, an associated memory of having been sexually abused by her maternal grandfather came to her. (She had been abused in the basement at age nine, and walking down those same steps while having those feelings helped trigger the memories.) At that instant her terror and grief poured out, as she screamed and cried, telling her mother about it all.

What was so healing for Pat was that not only had she expressed her grief and told the truth of her experience, but her mother believed and

Figure 22.3. The Continuum of a Traumatic Event and Attempting to Heal It (from Whitfield 1993)[691]

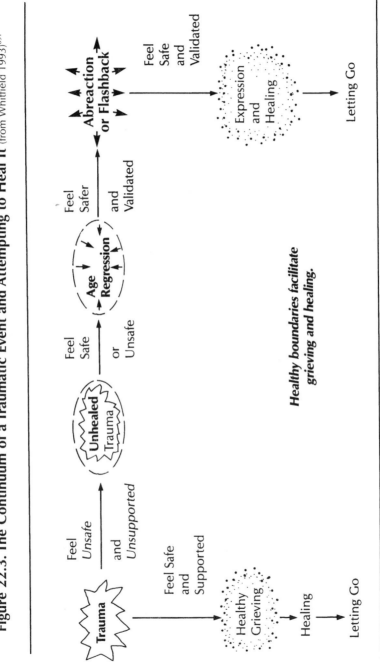

supported her. Her mother then helped her find a counselor to see and work further through her pain. Had she not believed and supported her, Pat would likely have been re-traumatized. This is an example of an abreaction. Through her own abilities and motivation, and with the help of her mother's support and many counseling sessions, Pat was able to sort out, own and begin to work through the pain of her past, ungrieved traumatic experience.

An abreaction is an extreme and dramatic kind of age regression. When recognized and supported in a safe setting during recovery, such an experience can be an important part of the healing process. In fact, I believe that an abreaction may be a natural continuation and extension of age regression, given a safe environment and validation of the person's experience as shown on the continuum of a traumatic experience (Figure 22.3).

When a hurt, loss or trauma happens to us, we have a natural tendency to heal it by the grieving process. Even though as children we already know how to grieve, we have to be supported and to feel safe to express the grief so that we can heal and then let go of its painful energy. To see our parents model their own healthy grief will support and further teach us this process. But if we feel unsupported, with no such healthy modeling, and if we feel unsafe in expressing our pain, we will store that unexpressed energy as an unhealed trauma. One manifestation of the trauma may be repeated age regression, and another and more dramatic manifestation may follow as an abreaction or a flashback, as we continue attempting to heal ourselves around the past traumatic experience.

A key to the orderly flow of this healing process is feeling safe, supported and validated by others, which includes these others not invading our experiences and our boundaries. Support for a child or an adult by healthy parents or others, by skilled therapists or by safe peers such as usually happens in a therapy group, provides a safe and nourishing "holding environment" where the wounded person can express the pain of their grief and thereby begin to heal. Self-help groups may be similarly helpful.

Some skeptics tend to misunderstand the role of group therapy and self-help groups and what goes on inside them. They often make such erroneous statements as Loftus made in the *Crook v. Murphy* case,[718] "Well, just, you know, she is in this group therapy and the memories seem to get more and more and more bizarre and wild." and [two of my colleagues, McHugh and Ganaway] ". . . really are worried that the ingredients in the stories that others tell in the group situation can influence the expansion or development of memories . . . and the pressure to produce memories. . . ."[416] In my 18 years of experience of personally co-leading at least four therapy groups a week, and in the greater experience of my colleagues, I have not observed or heard of such a "contamination" of anyone's memories in group therapy.

Traumatic stress that is kept inside is usually released little by little through expression and grieving—if the survivor feels safe and ideally has skilled guidance to do so—and in fits and starts over time. In Pat's case described above, over the next four years she continued to experience the pain that her offender grandfather had inflicted upon her for two years when she was between nine and 11 years old. But she also began to *express* and *grieve* this pain as well. She saw a counselor for 10 sessions, but had a hard time telling her about the details of her abuse experience. She stopped seeing the counselor a year ago and eventually, over a four-month period, composed the following "unmailed letter" to her grandfather. She then read it to me and to two trusted others, and without our suggestion, decided to mail it to him and to every other close family member. Her letter is as follows:

> I am writing this letter to you, Curtis Jackson Sr., to tell you how furious I am about the way you sexually abused me when I was nine and ten years old! I remember you laying down for a nap when Grandma went to the store. I, an innocent child (your own child's child!), lay next to you on the bed for an afternoon nap, but that's not all you had in mind. More than once you pulled up my shirt and touched and kissed my nipples before they ever had a chance to be the untouched breasts of a young woman. You also put your big nasty fingers down my pants and underpants and felt my vagina. You put your dirty finger inside my vaginal opening and rubbed it! What were you thinking? I can say that, as a child, I trusted you as my grandfather to take care of me. I did not know what it was that you were doing, only that I trusted you that this was something grandfathers did to their grandchildren. How many other children have you abused? How many were also related to you?
>
> Of course, I can't seem to forget about the tongue game you got me to play, sticking out my tongue so you could open-mouth kiss me. I remember your nasty, smokey breath. I also remember sitting in the den in the chair on your lap while you fingered me once again as we watched TV. You always said, and I quote you, "This is our little secret." Well, the secret is bullshit and it's out now. Copies of this letter have been mailed out to Sandra, Joe and Andy, Curt and Jackie, Susan, Martha, Jake, Sam and Barbara. My parents (Sam and Barbara), Andy, Sean and our St. Louis family all support me. This kind of abuse is extremely devastating to a person. When Mom confronted you about this in 1985 you "did not remember." You have got some problems and you need some help.
>
> You have humiliated me, degraded me, used me, lied to me, hurt me, deceived me, and, most importantly, destroyed my innocence! A

young woman's first kiss, first touch should be pure, and given by her boyfriend, not by the dirty old man who was too horny and confused to control himself. I was just a child! You took my innocence and I will never be able to get that back!

When I am in a relationship with my boyfriend, past or present, I have horrible memories of what you did to me. This has affected my sex life since it began. My first experience with sexuality was from my own grandfather, so I have naturally developed fears and uncomfortable feelings about my own sexuality. I don't want to see these flashbacks of your fondling me or kissing me when I'm laying next to the man I love, yet these memories return every time. It's just a matter of how easy it is to block it all out of my mind. This isn't fair to me, I deserved to keep my innocence! There is nothing you could ever do to make this up to me. I will get over the flashbacks and memories eventually, but not for many years. I will never be able to forget what you did to me. You took advantage of a child! What an evil thing to do! For your own pleasure! That is so selfish and sick! You are a child molester. You committed incest on your own granddaughter.

There is also someone else who you lied to and cheated. This wonderful, loving woman is your wife, my grandmother. How could you do this to her? She is the one you vowed in marriage to be with forever, to love and to trust. How could you risk losing your relationship with her by doing something sick to me? How will she feel when she finds out these terrible things you did to me? Did you think I'd keep your secret forever? I believe I need to speak out about this truth in order to heal. I also respect Grandma enough to tell her the truth after all these years. She is one of the last to know.

I want you to know that by sexually abusing me in 1977-78 you have shamed your family and your name. I no longer use the name Jackson as my middle name because it is your name. I wish to have no part of you in my life from this day on. You are no longer my grandfather, or my friend. Please try to get yourself some help, at least for Grandma's sake.

—Pat Wilson

I advise that survivors *not* mail this kind of letter until they are well into ongoing psychotherapy and recovery and have taken a lot of time to consider its consequences and their own personal goals. Pat's goals were to continue to cleanse herself of the toxic secret that her grandfather had inflicted upon her and coerced her to keep and that her mother and stepfather, once they found out, had later also influenced her to keep hidden. She is now 27 years old and is beginning to feel lighter and freer. Learning of the secret has distressed some of her family members in various ways, but Pat knows that she is not its cause—her grandfather's offending behavior is.

23

MEMORY AND TRAUMATIC STRESS *Part Two*

Somatic or Body Memories

The body stores and re-enacts traumatic memories in gross and subtle ways. While skeptics may doubt their existence and may even laugh at them, scientists are intensively studying the body's role in memory. They no longer believe that the brain is the only repository for feelings and memory, as the following statements illustrate:

> In the beginning of my work, I matter-of-factly presumed that emotions were in the head or brain. Now I would say they are expressed in the body and are part of the body. I can no longer make a strong distinction between the brain and the body.[384] **Candace Pert Ph.D**, former chief of brain biochemistry at the National Institute of Mental Health, currently visiting professor of neuroscience at Rutgers University

> Memory doesn't occur by itself in the brain; nor is it confined to a particular site in the brain. It depends on communication with everything that is happening in the body. Fifty billion neurons and trillions of synapses are our body's telephone lines.[384] **Marvin Mishkin, Ph.D**, chief, laboratory of neuropsychology, NIMH

> [The] body is an organ of memory as well as perception.[61] **Jean Shinoda Bolen, M.D.**, clinical professor of psychiatry, University of California School of Medicine, San Francisco

> The trauma is stored in somatic [body] memory and expressed as changes in the biological stress response. The body keeps the score.[663] **Bessel A. van der Kolk, M.D.**, professor of psychiatry Harvard Medical School and director of the Trauma Clinic, Massachusetts General Hospital in Boston

> Memory resides nowhere, and in every cell. Its about 2000 times more complicated than we ever imagined.[384] **Saul Schanberg Ph.D**, professor of pharmacology and biological psychiatry, Duke University

Despite this complexity, based on decades of front-line experience, therapists who have assisted trauma survivors in their long-term recovery have observed traumatic memories manifesting themselves in the body in numerous ways.[102, 151, 229, 326, 384, 472, 549, 641, 663, 678] Some of these may include:

- Aches and pains, such as chronic headaches, neck and back pain[185, 297]

- Chronic pelvic pain, including cystitis, premenstrual syndrome;[309] some chronic constipation[292]

- Dysphagia (difficulty swallowing), easy gagging[190] and temporomandibular joint pain

- Surface numbness of the skin, with or without deeper tissue pain[297]

- "Holding tight" in jaws, pelvis or anus to prevent unwanted entry

- Breath holding and shallow breathing, especially when touched[306]

- Stuttering

- Accident proneness

- Self-harm or -injury[179, 678]

- Panic attacks and other manifestation of hyperarousal[326]

- Some skin problems, including eczema[229, 306]

While these above manifestations are not always caused by unhealed traumatic experiences, their association occurs frequently enough to make it worthwhile to explore their possibility in a serious way, as the following two case histories illustrate.

> Jack was a 48-year-old businessman who had served nine years in a prison for people with mental disorders because he had physically harmed someone while he was having a psychotic episode. While there he observed the prison staff regularly mistreat and abuse the other inmates, and they abused him also—although for several years he had forgotten about his own abuse. On completing his prison sentence he

started a slow process of recovery in individual psychotherapy, attending self-help groups regularly and using bibliotherapy, plus low doses of major tranquilizers to manage his thought disorder.

During his recovery he began to have vague aches and pains in his chest, abdomen and thighs that on a medical evaluation were not attributed to any kind of rheumatic or arthritic disease. Within a few months he began to remember his having been abused by the prison staff, the first of his memories being triggered by his having slipped and fallen on the floor in his kitchen. Over time these memories became more defined. "I remember sliding nude around on the floor of a back room in the prison, being kicked and hit by about 15 of the staff, after they grabbed me out of the shower. The staff included the clerks, attendants and one registered nurse." He remembered several of the staff by name.

He eventually contacted the director of the prison, who promised him a fair evaluation of his complaint, although upon its completion none of the remaining staff could (or would) remember or verify such an incident, and the nurse said that Jack must have been hallucinating. In spite of this invalidation, it was an experience for which I observed several bits of internally corroborating evidence and one of external corroboration (a fellow inmate, now also released, reported witnessing this and numerous similar events). When he was able to express the pain to safe others and me, his aches and pains began to decrease in their frequency and intensity. After he wrote an unmailed letter to the director and the staff and did expressive therapy to release much of his hurt and anger, these body aches and pains stopped. These therapeutically successful after effects of the recovery process are also evidence that is internally corroborating.

Jack's history shows how, through their cognitive abilities, a person may have forgotten a traumatic experience, but their body somehow remembers it. It is as though the body is trying to do what the mind often does as it attempts to heal a trauma, through expressing it the only way that it currently knows how.

A second example shows how the process of therapy itself can be a trigger to an important but forgotten memory.

Robin was a 45-year-old woman who was referred to a massage therapist by her physician to help heal the effects of physical abuse when she was a child. She had a long history of chronic pain in the frontal area of her right thigh. During the second session she felt patchy numbness over her right thigh and moderate to severe burning with deep tissue massage. At first she asked her therapist to avoid touching that area. Over several sessions the therapist gradually approached the area and finally deep massage was done, while Robin was "breathing in" to the painful area. She then spontaneously remembered her mother striking her with a metal hanger several times in that area at the age of about eight. She also reported that she had seen an orthopedic surgeon at age 25 who had suggested surgery to cut a nerve to the area where the pain was located. With continued massage therapy and expression of her pain over the next four sessions, her previously chronic pain subsided.

Robin had never completely grieved her traumatic experiences of having been physically and emotionally abused as a child, and her physician and massage therapist appropriately reasoned that it was her body's expression of her stored but forgotten memory that was the cause of her chronic pain. Knowing that her orthopedic surgeon wanted to treat her by cutting the sensory nerves to her thigh, we can wonder how many pain syndromes have been mistreated in various ways because the helping professionals were not aware of the existence of such somatic memories. With the support of her physician, Robin's massage therapist referred her to a psychotherapist who assists trauma survivors to help her complete her healing.

Neurobiology and PTSD

Trauma may result in long-term changes in a person's behavior and their body's neurobiological systems, including memory loss and long-term abnormalities in their brain's neurotransmitter and neuropeptide systems,[76] as illustrated in Table 23.1.

The nervous system's neurotransmitters, or chemical messengers, that are importantly involved with stress and possibly with memory include: (1) the stimulants *norepinephrine* and *dopamine*, (2) the painkillers called *endogenous* (meaning "within the body") *opiates* (also called narcotics), and (3) the hormones *cortisol* and *ACTH*. In states of acute stress these tend to have an increase in their release or turnover, but in states of chronic stress their levels may increase and/or decrease.[76]

While the "anatomical location" of our memory systems remain a mystery, several areas are frequently cited, including the *cerebral cortex* (the large surface of the brain) and some of the deeper structures known as the *thalamus, hypothalamus, hippocampus* (or "cognitive map"[662, 663]), *amygdala* (involved with meaningful experiences and fear[663]), *locus coeruleus* and the *midbrain*. Each of these locations in the brain are postulated to be involved with the above neurochemical changes that are associated with hyperarousal, fear, paranoia, emotional blunting and encoding or alterations in memory,[76] as summarized in Table 23.1.

Table 23.1. Changes in Brain Neurotransmitter and Neurohormonal Systems with Stress, with their Effects on Memory. from Bremner et al[76]

Neurotransmitter	Acute stress	Chronic stress	Brain regions involved	PTSD symptoms
Norepinephrine	Increased turnover	Increased responsive-ness of LC neurons	Hipp, Hypo, LC, Cor, Amyg	Anxiety, fear, hypervigilance hyperarousal, irritability, encoding of traumatic memories
CRF-HPA axis				
Brain **CRF**	Increase	Increase/ decrease	Hipp, Hypo, Cor, LC,	Anxiety and fear, memory
Peripheral **ACTH**	Increase	Increase/ decrease	Amyg	alterations, hyperarousal
Peripheral **coritisol**	Increase	Increase/ decrease		
Dopamine	Increased release	Increase	PFC,NA	Hypervigilance, paranoia, alterations in memory
Endogenous **opiates**	Increase release	Decrease[a]	MB, Hipp	Analgesia, emotional blunting, encoding of traumatic memories

Legend: LC = locus coeruleus. Hipp = hippocampus. Hypo = hypothalamus. Cor = cerebral cortex. Amyg = amygdala. CRF = corticotropin-releasing factor. HPA = hypothalamic-pituitary-adrenal axis. ACTH = adrenocorticotropic hormone. PFC = prefrontal cortex. NA = nucleus accumbens. Stris = striatum. MB = midbrain. Decrease[a] in receptor binding measured by B_{max} (from Bremner '93.)

The Two Extremes of PTSD

While a wide variety of experiences may trigger a memory (whether ordinary or traumatic), traumatic ones may be precipitated by a norepinephrine increase and by physiological arousal, as was illustrated in the case of Sirhan Sirhan on page 45. Indeed, hyperarousal is one of two common extremes of experience that occur in PTSD, which I summarize in Table 22.2.

Inhibition

People with PTSD tend to vacillate between these two uncomfortable extremes of experience—*inhibition* and *hyperarousal.* In the inhibition state it is common for them to have a loss of memory for all or part of the traumatic event or events. They tend to have a constricted awareness of some or even many of their painful memories, and they often manifest frozen feelings, also called anhedonia. They also often have an inhibition of their ability to take appropriate action in a particular situation, especially if the situation is similar to their past traumatic experiences. They may feel and be isolated in their relationships. They may at times feel righteous indignation, vacillating with a feeling of helpless rage.

Table 23.2. The Two Extremes or All-or-None Aspect of PTSD

Awareness of Experience	Inhibited Experience	Hyperarousal
Memory	Forgetting	Hyperamnesia and hypervigilance
Awareness of Painful Memories	Constriction	Intrusion of painful memories
Feelings	Frozen feelings (anhedonia)	Hyper-reactivity—Floods of intense, overwhelming feelings
Action	Inhibition of action	Irritable, compulsive and impulsive action
Relationships	Isolation	Fearful clinging
Projection	Righteous indignation	Helpless rage[326]

Hyperarousal

By contrast, the trauma survivor with PTSD may also feel the opposite of being inhibited. In their over-stimulated state they may be hypervigilant. They may not only remember their traumatic experiences, but they may remember them more vividly and clearly, both cognitively and experientially, than they would an ordinary memory. Indeed, they frequently wish that the intrusive painful memories would stop. They may be hyper-reactive to all sorts of stimuli, with floods of intense and overwhelming feelings coming into their awareness. Rather than take appropriate action, they may often be compulsive and impulsive. And instead of a lonely isolation, fearing abandonment,[687, 691] they cling to their relationships. Herman describes these characteristics in some detail.[326]

Most people with PTSD are caught in a trap of flip-flopping between these two positions of this guise of the core issue called all-or-none thinking and behaving. But this is more like all-or-none *experiencing,* vacillating between feeling numb and feeling over-stimulated with the adrenaline rushes of fear. Stuck here, we may have little comfort—until we begin to use our memory to help us heal.

Using Memory in Healing PTSD

Remembering and accurately naming what happened in any traumatic experience is crucial to healing from its hurtful effects. We can estimate that somewhat more than half (with a range of 46 to 84 percent) of the people have always remembered on one level or another their abusive or traumatic experience of having been sexually abused, and that a little under half (with a range of from 16 to 64 percent) have had prolonged periods when they could not remember what happened. There are also those in a grey zone, who remember parts but not all of their experience that would be important in their process of healing.

But simple remembering to some extent is not always associated with accurately naming what happened. People are abused or mistreated—or experience other traumas—and for a number of reasons they frequently are not fully aware of the nature of their experience. To heal the detrimental effects usually requires a series of several actions, including stabilizing, awakening, remembering, naming what happened, grieving, working through core issues, making transformations and finally integrating all of these into our psyche and daily life. While I describe these

Table 23.3 Stages of Recovery from PTSD

(from my experience and others',[285, 396a, 687, 689, 691] as expanded from Herman[326])

	STAGES		
Condition	**One** (Whitfield's & Other's Stages)	**Two**	
	One (Herman's Stages)	**Two**	**Three**
Hysteria (Janet 1889)	Stabilization, symptom-oriented treatment	Exploration of traumatic memories	Personality reintegration and rehabilitation
Combat trauma (Scurfield 1985)	Trust, stress-management, education	Reexperiencing trauma	Integration of trauma
Complicated post-traumatic stress disorder (Brown and Fromm 1986)	Stabilization	Integration of memories	Development of self, drive integration
Multiple personality disorder integration (Putnam 1989)	Diagnosis, stabilization, communication, cooperation	Metabolism of trauma	Resolution, development of postresolution coping skills
Adult child syndrome (Whitfield 1987, 89, & 91, & others)	Stabilization and treatment of Stage Zero disorder	Awakening, remembering, naming, grieving, core issues, transformations, integration. Stage Three continues as spirituality (see next chapter)	
Traumatic disorders (Herman 1992)	Safety	Remembrance and mourning	Reconnection

in some more detail in the following chapters, it may be useful here to look at an overview of recovery from PTSD that Judith Herman compiled in her book *Trauma and Recovery*. Over the last century these stages and tasks of recovery have been described for various guises of PTSD, yet each has enough similarities for us to discern a pattern that has become progressively clearer over time,[326] as is shown in Table 23.3 above.

In four out of these six descriptions, remembering the traumatic experiences is an integral part of the recovery process, and in the other two remembering is implied as being a part of re-experiencing and "metabolizing" the trauma.

In the next chapters I will expand upon these stages and process of recovery and describe how remembering and accurately naming what happened fits into the sequence of healing. Bear in mind that this process of recovery cannot be rushed. It is most successful when the person is given as much time as they may need to heal themselves within the structure of an individualized recovery plan[692] that is supported by skilled assistants and that takes place in a safe environment.[641, 687, 688, 691]

The same concern about the external evidence that is necessary in the courtroom is not required in recovery and healing. Recovery is an internal process and experience that makes use of safe and supportive external aids.

24

RECOVERY

Recovery is the process of healing our wounds. As described in Chapter 4, the wounding is usually the result of mistreatment and abuse by the parents, parent figures and others projecting their own unfinished business onto the child. When the child tries to react by appropriately expressing pain, the adults invalidate and stifle it. When this pattern happens repeatedly, the pain begins to feel overwhelming. Not having been taught healthy skills to deal with pain, the child's Real Self then retreats deep into the unconscious part of its psyche, a movement that I call "The Child goes into hiding," as illustrated in Figure 4.1 on page 33.

While the person can usually survive and function fairly well through relying on their false self in their outer life, they do not tend to do that so well in their inner life. This is because the wounding has brought about a lost awareness and lost sense of self, which results in a low self-esteem, difficulty in maintaining intimate relationships, and frequently one or more kinds of repetition compulsion, such as addictions, compulsions, and self- or other-destructive behaviors. We can call this wounding by many names, including the *adult child syndrome* or condition.[285, 389a, 691]

The Stages of Recovery

This wounding is usually also associated with the presence of one or more medical or psychological conditions, which I call Stage Zero disorders.[688-692] A person's memory can be disordered in any of these stages.

Stage Zero

Stage Zero is manifested by the presence of an active illness or disorder, such as an addiction, compulsion or another disorder. This active illness may be acute, recurring or chronic. Without recovery, it may continue indefinitely. At Stage Zero, recovery has not yet started (Table 24.1).

While memories of past impactful experiences may occur here, the person often tries not to think about them, or they may unconsciously use the Stage Zero disorder to help them avoid working through the associated pain. These Stage Zero disorders may include one or more of those listed as high risk disorders that may be used as internal corroboration of the veracity of the abuse actually happening (see Table 15.1 on page 151). During the active phases of the disorder(s), the person usually doesn't feel safe enough to allow too many painful memories to surface. The disorder is also demanding and has a life of its own, and thus distracts from our being able to remember having been mistreated or abused.

Stage One

At Stage One, recovery begins. It involves participating in a full recovery program to assist in healing the Stage Zero disorder. (A partial recovery program may also help, although it will be less likely to be as successful as a full one.) Memories of past impactful experiences may begin surfacing more often here, and the person may or may not allow them to stay current enough in their conscious awareness to work through their associated emotional pain. The focus in Stage One recovery is on stabilization and healing around the specific Stage Zero disorder. Herman's description of Stage One recovery (Table 23.3) is similar to what I have described here and elsewhere.[688, 689, 691, 692]

Stage Two

Stage Two involves healing adult child or co-dependence issues that have resulted from the traumatic experiences and from not being allowed to process them when they happened. It is about healing the wounds that I described in Chapter 4. Once a person has a stable and solid Stage One recovery—one that has lasted for about a year or longer—it may be an opportune time to consider looking into these deeper issues.

Table 24.1. Recovery and Duration According to Stages

Recovery Stage	Condition	Focus of Recovery	Approximate Duration
3	Human/Spirituality	Spirituality	Ongoing
2	Adult Child	A C Specific Full Recovery Program	3-5 years
1	Stage Zero Disorder	Basic-Illness Specific Full Recovery Program	$\frac{1}{2}$ to 3 years
0	Active Illness	Addiction, Compulsion, Disorder ------------------ Woundedness	Indefinite

An adult child is anyone who grew up in an unhealthy, troubled or dysfunctional family. Many adult children may still be living in a similar unhealthy environment, whether at home, in one or more relationships, or at work.

It is in Stage Two recovery where deep healing occurs and where the most constructive memory work happens. In fact, memory work is crucial here, and if it does not happen, healing will usually be less successful. Herman sub-divides this stage into two stages, which she calls remembrance and mourning (her stage two) and reconnection (her stage three[326]). My understanding of Stage Three recovery (which would extend beyond Herman's stage three), is that it is about a more subtle and expansive experience of reconnecting that we can call spirituality.

Stage Three

Stage Three recovery is about spirituality and its incorporation into daily life. This is an ongoing process. Here, memory work usually continues, but on a different, expanded and more spiritual level.

*　　　　*　　　　*

A more simple and early kind of memory work is useful in Stage One recovery according to the disorder or condition from which one is recovering. For example, the recovering alcoholic may begin to remember more clearly the serious and painful consequences of their drinking. The person with migraine headaches may begin to remember associations with the onset of their pain as they learn to avoid factors and stresses that trigger a headache. And so on.

By Stage Two recovery, while these early memories may still be useful, the person is working on deeper areas of their life, such as the wounding that they experienced from growing up in a dysfunctional, troubled or unhealthy family and society of origin.

Jackie, a 46-year-old woman, completed her Stage Two healing and was beginning to realize her spiritual self with more experiential awareness. The following is a summary of her understanding of her recovery.

> When I was a kid I was numb from just trying to survive. Then when I was 20 I became more numb from alcohol, and that lasted for eight years. I stopped drinking for awhile and then started again, all the while being in and out of bad relationships. What you call Stage One [Jackie is here talking to me] took me nearly seven years to go through, because I kept relapsing on alcohol. I haven't had a drink since. Eventually I woke up to some of the pain that I was trying to numb as a child, just to survive. I got into your therapy group and I've been surprised I stayed there for over five years. There, and elsewhere, I learned how to be me. But to do that I had to feel all that old pain from my past that I didn't know how to handle all my life, until now. Going to some Twelve Step group meetings has also helped. They added a lot. Now I'm through with most of that work [Stage Two], although problems still come up. But now I can handle them better. Lately I've been learning how to pray and meditate, and for the first time feel like I have some spiritual feelings in my life. My life is going better now.

Relationship with Wounding and Memory

Figure 24.1 shows a simple diagram of the relationship among the wounding, its manifestations and memory. This wounding is manifested by the adult child syndrome or condition.[285, 389a, 691] Most people enter recovery by first wanting to lessen the symptoms of a Stage Zero disorder. Once that disorder is stable, they may sense that something is still missing in their life, that they are still hurting emotionally, and begin to explore what they may do about it. As they explore, both ordinary and traumatic memories usually begin to surface. The Stage Zero disorder represents the tip of the iceberg, with the bulk of the iceberg being the adult child syndrome and spiritual issues. Depending on genetic, familial

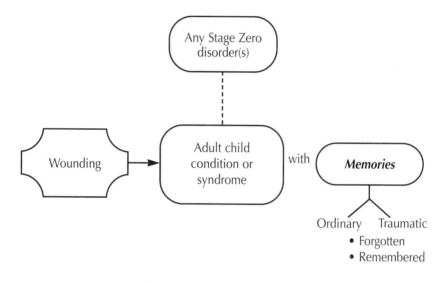

Figure 24.1. Interrelationships Among the Adult Child Syndrome, Stage Zero Disorders and Memory

and environmental factors, each person will likely manifest a different Stage Zero disorder or set of disorders.

A person who obtains specific treatment for the Stage Zero disorder is now in Stage One recovery, which usually takes a few months to a few years to stabilize, as shown above in Table 24.1. In Stage One, any addiction, compulsion or related disorder may be addressed. Once stabilized, the person may wish to address the underlying adult child syndrome. This Stage Two recovery usually takes from three to five years or longer in the best full recovery program. In Stage Three recovery the person is then eventually more able to address and realize a more fulfilling spirituality.

The Recovery Process: Peeling Away the Layers of Pain

One way to view the process of recovery is to compare it with peeling away the layers of an onion. Each layer is a manifestation and consequence of the false self and our attachment to it. And each layer surrounds, constricts and imprisons our True Self, the core of our being.

There are three layers to this onion. The first consists of the numbness, pain and confusion that are but a part of the many foggy manifestations of the second layer. Until we cut through this often nebulous first layer, we are still in Stage Zero recovery, which is no recovery at all.

The second layer that binds our True Self consists of addictions, compulsions and various other disorders. To penetrate any of these usually takes from many months to several years of working in a Stage One full

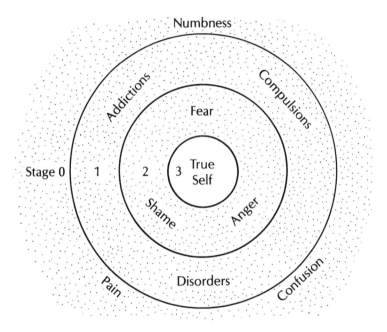

Figure 24.2. The Constricting Layers of Pain

recovery program.

Underneath this layer is the third and final layer: adult child wounding and one of its major manifestations, co-dependence. This layer contains a lot of fear, shame and anger, three of several painful feelings that we have to deal with in the long and exciting process of Stage Two recovery, as shown in Figure 24.2.

We can also call these three constructing layers manifestations and consequences of our attachment to our false self. Underneath all of these layers, at the core of our being, lies the goal of recovery and our true identity: our True Self.

We peel away these layers throughout the entire process of recovery. The work of peeling away each layer involves recognizing, addressing, experiencing and healing multiple problems and concerns, called "unfinished business." Remembering and naming what happened through memory work helps us complete this unfinished business. While I described some of the influences of and approaches to handling these three stages here and elsewhere, my focus in this book is on the relationship of memory and abuse. Finishing this business includes the following areas of recovery work: grieving, original pain work, working through core issues, doing "personality" work, completing developmental tasks and setting healthy boundaries. These kinds of recovery work interact and merge with one another. They are not necessarily distinct or separate areas of the healing process. Figure 24.3 shows a Venn diagram of their relationships.

Grieving

Unresolved grief festers like a deep wound that is surrounded by scar tissue, a pocket of vulnerability ever ready to break out anew.[598, 687] It stifles our aliveness, creativity and serenity. We need three elements in order to grieve our ungrieved hurts, losses and traumas:

1. Skills for undertaking the grief work.
2. Safe and supportive others to validate our experiences and assist us.
3. Enough time to complete the process.

An important part of grief work includes what can be called "original pain work."

Original Pain Work

"Original pain work" is a term that helps us describe and heal a particular acute and deep part of our ungrieved hurts. It greases the wheel of the grieving process and is an important part of the grief and memory work. Like grieving and recovery in general, this process cannot be forced or rushed, or our Child Within will likely go deeper into hiding.

While there are many approaches to facilitating original pain work, the following eight actions can help in this process and are examples of some of its components in an effective healing sequence.

Figure 24.3. Key Areas of Recovery Work: Venn Diagram of Their Inter-relationship

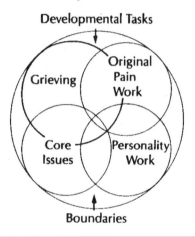

Personality work includes all work, plus working through transferences as they come up.

1. I tell my story of any current upset, as it may unfold, to safe and supportive people, for example in my therapy group or in individual therapy.

2. I cognitively and experientially connect my current upset, conflict and feelings around them to my past. To help with this process I ask myself, "What does any of this current experience remind me of?" and then begin to answer. By connecting my present experience with similar ones from my past, I can begin to remember in progressively more experiential and cognitive detail.

3. To facilitate this process, I may write about it in my journal or in an unmailed letter.[688] Or I may work through this conflict and its emotional pain by any of several other possible experiential techniques.

4. I bring in and read my unmailed letter (or describe whatever else I've done experientially) to my therapy group or therapist. I may also enact

parts of the resolution of my original pain with these safe people, such as by using further experiential techniques (for example, Gestalt or psychodrama techniques facilitated by my therapist).

5. In the company of these safe people, I then discharge the stored toxic energy associated with these memories until I feel as complete with it as I can for now.

6. Then I listen to feedback from the therapy group or therapist.

7. After listening to each person's feedback, I describe how my doing all of the above feels for me now.

8. I connect any future upsets and conflicts with what I have learned above.

Doing this original pain work can be an important stimulus to remembering what happened and grieving our ungrieved hurts, losses and traumas. However, by itself this original pain work is not sufficient to complete our grief work, which usually requires several years to complete.

Working through Core Recovery Issues

I describe an overview of core recovery issues in Chapter 5 on page 48 and some basic principles of working through core recovery issues in *A Gift to Myself*. These include the following.

Working Through a Problem, Conflict or Issue

1. Identify and name my specific upset, problem or conflict.
2. Reflect upon it from my powerful inner life.
3. Talk about it with safe people (i.e., tell that specific part of my story).
4. Ask for feedback from them.
5. Name the core issue.
6. Talk about it some more.
7. Ask for some more feedback.
8. Select an appropriate experiential technique.
9. Use that to work on my specific conflict and feelings at a deeper level.
10. Talk and/or write some more about it.
11. Meditate upon it or pray about it.
12. Consider how I might learn from it.
13. If I still feel incomplete, repeat any of the above.
14. Whenever I am ready, let it go.

Doing "Personality" Work

The terms "personality" and "character" should not be equated with an individual's identity. While we are each unique and individual beings, as represented by the many aspects of our True Self, I believe that nearly all of the unhealthy and destructive aspects of our personality are due to a combination of our being wounded and our attachment to our false self. Because these are so deep and unconscious, it takes some focused work with a specially trained and experienced therapist to help heal them. Doing "personality" work means healing the results of our prior wounding. Even when these are influenced or partially caused by constitutional or "genetic" factors, I have observed that it is most conducive to the healing process to approach them as nearly all being due to wounding.

Some Therapist and Group Tasks in "Personality" Work

Personality work is complex. It requires trust and surrender on the part of the recovering person and experience, skill, and compassion on the part of the therapist. This work is described in part elsewhere.[122a] A helping professional who wishes to learn it will require clinical supervision by one or more experienced therapists. While using this work is not to be taken lightly, the following brief description may be helpful in providing an overview and outline of part of this process.

1. The therapist—and in the case of group therapy, the group—empathically connects with the person. This connection is important throughout their ongoing relationship.

2. The therapist (and group—with the facilitation of the group therapists when needed) accompanies and guides the person while working through their unfinished business and associated memories.

3. The therapist recognizes the presence of: (a) transference (projecting emotionally charged material that was acquired in the past onto others in the present); (b) related core issues; and (c) any "stuckness" in developmental tasks, and assists the person in working through them. When we over-react—that is, react beyond what is appropriate for the situation or circumstances—this is one sign of the presence of transference. While transference can be dramatic in presentation, it is more often subtle. For example, transference occurs when we see and expect or experience the therapist or other as being an ideal parent while forgetting their human inadequacies; or when we attend to the therapist or other mostly to please them, while neglecting our own healthy needs.[691]

4. In such situations the therapist's constructive responses may include one or more of the following actions:

- Listening to and tolerating any projected material, while empathically connecting.
- Asking questions such as this (infrequently and only when appropriate): "Does this remind you of anything from your past?" This may facilitate recalling important memories.
- Aiding movement in any constructive way.
- Supporting the person's needs as appropriate.
- And (rarely or seldom) interpreting a particular and appropriate dynamic or connection.

In group therapy, if the group member appears to be transferring onto one group therapist, the group co-therapist steps in and works with and facilitates the group member's work through the conflicts and the transference.

5. By using constructive feedback, the therapist (and in a therapy group, the other group members) validates, mirrors and supports the person during the work.

6. The therapist and other group members, as appropriate, set healthy boundaries. These boundaries and limits, coupled with a therapist who does not talk too often or too much, help provide the person with a healthy amount of frustration that helps to fuel working through the unfinished business.[689]

7. The group and the therapist(s) provide the recovering person with new, safe and healthy interpersonal experiences that are part of the "grist for the mill" of recovery work.

Healing the person's wounds includes all of the work of recovery plus the specific tasks around working through transferences as they occur. For a therapist to be able to provide healthy and skilled work requires a training experience of appropriately supervised work assisting many people over several years, as well as having completed a substantial portion of their own recovery work.

Completing Developmental Tasks

The work of completing developmental tasks is exacting and requires a working knowledge of the stages, issues and tasks of healthy and unhealthy human development.[122a, 691] When appropriate, the therapist gently guides the person through these.

Setting Healthy Boundaries

Learning to set healthy boundaries and limits is a crucial part of recovery. Healthy boundaries protect and maintain the integrity and well-being of our True Self, as shown in Figure 4.2 on page 38. We cannot heal without them. Some people, including some in our family of origin and elsewhere, may try to invalidate our memories and our experience. In recovery we can learn to identify and set healthy boundaries and limits to protect the integrity and well-being of our True Self. I describe boundaries in some detail in *Boundaries and Relationships.*

Summary

Figure 24.4 graphically summarizes some of the components of the process of peeling away the layers of pain and unfinished business that surround and constrict our True Self. This illustration also shows how most of recovery is experiential, while some important parts of it are cognitive and behavioral.

Using Experiential Recovery and Treatment Aids

My best guess is that about 90 percent of adult child (Stage Two) recovery and memory work is experiential—in the realm of personal experience that occurs in and from our inner life. About 10 percent of healing and recovery is cognitive—in the realms of our intellect and mental understanding. Of course, much of the experiential can have cognitive dimensions, and vice versa. Nonetheless, recovery cannot proceed successfully only in our head. It must also be experienced in our heart, guts and bones—in the deepest fiber of our being. The behavioral part of recovery adds to and uses the experiential and the cognitive, and all three are components of our memory process.

While healing is most effective when we initiate, work through and thus create our own healing and recovery, we now have available a variety of experiential recovery and treatment aids to assist us in that creative process. When we experience, we are aware of and are in our powerful inner life. A goal in healing is to continue experiencing that inner life, which is a major part of our True Self. Eventually we learn that when our false self comes in and takes over, we just notice that, and then decide whether we need it right now. In Chapter 22 of *Co-dependence* I describe some ways of letting go of our attachment to our false self.[689]

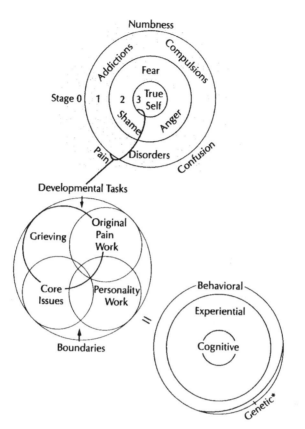

* Genetic Factors are more important in Stages Zero and One and less important in Stage Two recovery.

Figure 24.4. The Interaction of Key Areas of Recovery Work with their Cognitive, Experiential and Behavioral Components

We can begin to experience our inner life by choosing one or more experiential techniques that may facilitate our experiencing. These techniques tend to have some of the following characteristics in common.

- Being **real**—we tend to be our True Self when we are using an experiential technique, although at the beginning we may feel uncomfortable when doing so.
- Being **focused**—we are focused on one or more aspects of our inner life.
- **Structure**—there is a structure or form to the technique itself.
- **Safe**—to be most effective and healing, it is generally done in a safe and supportive environment.[688]

As our memories, feelings or anything else from our inner life come up at any time, we can share them with one or more appropriate and safe people and then work through them toward a healthy resolution. A person can ask their therapist any questions they might have about any of these.

Some Cautions

While experiential techniques usually help us in our healing, at times they can block our healing. Here are three potential blocks:

1. **Addiction to their "quick hit,"** "fix," or "rush." Some of the more dramatic or fast-acting experiential techniques can open us to our deep feelings, memories and other parts of our inner life so quickly or effectively that we believe that they are the only way we can open up and access them. As with any addiction, we may think there is no other way. This can limit our ability to open up to ourselves and our feelings spontaneously and in a number of other healthy ways.

2. **Diversion from living life authentically.** If we focus too much on the technique itself, we can become diverted from living our life naturally—from, through and as our True Self.

3. **Excluding less dramatic techniques** that are equally or even more healing. Some experiential techniques are more subtle and their healing works more slowly. For example, just being real and speaking from our heart can be as healing as the most dramatic, action-oriented family sculpture.

As we heal we can use experiential techniques constructively, while being aware if we become overly attached to their trappings and drama.

There are two more components to the process of recovery that are important in the relationship between memory and abuse: having our experience validated and setting healthy boundaries with those who invalidate us. I will describe these in Chapter 27.

In the next two chapters I offer some experiential exercises to assist with remembering some of our traumatic experiences.

25

REMEMBERING
WHAT HAPPENED

To name things accurately is personal power. When Anita Hill told us of her experience with her former boss Clarence Thomas, she helped us collectively to give an accurate name to a kind of covert sexual abuse that is called sexual harassment. She—and we—accurately named what happened to her. Even though she was invalidated by many people, including her abuser, a larger and still growing number of people validate her experience as having really happened.[442, 690] Since then, this ongoing event has given validation and permission to countless abuse victims to speak their truth and set healthy boundaries to stop the abuse.

Psychiatrist and author Jean Shinoda Bolen reminds us of the importance of accurately naming what happened.

> You might think it odd that I am writing about something that can only be known through personal experience. But what if women have been venturing unknowingly into sacred territory and been without words for the experience? Then what was felt deeply and never articulated, shared, or put into a context fades from conscious awareness. Without words or names for an experience, memory is hampered: it's a bit like not knowing how to access information that is stored in a computer, only much more complex because what is unconscious in us still affects our bodies, relationships, and dreams. Furthermore, only when

we have words that fit what we know deeply is it possible to contemplate the meaning of an experience.

To heal wounds that resulted from the abuse, it is not important that our abuser and co-abusers validate our experience. While having this happen would be helpful, we can heal our hurts around the trauma without it. We do so by risking to talk about our experience with safe people.

Whenever we are ready, we can begin to identify and name a lot of things. I list some of the these below (Table 25.1).

Table 25.1. The Power of Naming Things in Adult Child Recovery Wherein I Name . . .

Who I am	My Wants
	Needs
What happened	Similarities or sameness
	Differentness or uniqueness
How I was mistreated	Relationships
	Addictions, attachments
My ungrieved hurts, losses	or compulsions
and traumas	
	My Core issues
Any toxic secrets	Basic dynamics
	(including boundaries & limits)
Any chronic distress	Dreams
	Goals
My Beliefs	
Thoughts	
Feelings	What is wrong
Possibilities	
Choices	What I want to happen
Experiences	How I can make that happen

To **name** things accurately is **personal power**.[689]

Remembering the Abuse

In our experience of having been abused, the memories about what happened usually don't come easily, as the following history shows.

Jim was a 48-year-old man who at age 40 identified himself as having grown up in an unhealthy family. It took several more years of working on his pain, including journal writing, meditating, attending self-help meetings and group therapy, and reading recovery-oriented literature, before he was able to remember and name specific ways that he had been abused. Some of these included frequent abandonment, rejection, covert sexual abuse and regular shaming by his parents.

When Jim began his healing process, he was not aware of his experience of these mistreatments. While he always suspected that his family was kind of "crazy," he went for over 40 years believing that he was the problem and had no clear idea that he had been abused in these ways. During this time his memories came slowly and gradually, with no exposure to hypnosis, "pushy therapists" or any kind of "mind control."

During the first two years of his recovery his mother, who was herself beginning her own healing process, validated many of his experiences of having been abused. She said that they did really happen. She also apologized to Jim for any abuse that she inflicted on him. His father, a rageaholic, was unable to understand Jim's experiences and concerns, and not only denied having mistreated him in any way, but attacked Jim whenever he would try to communicate with him. Even though they all three knew that their family was dysfunctional, Jim's older brother, in some recovery himself, validated some of his experiences. But his younger brother could not validate him for several years, until a few months before their father died, when he awakened to the fact that he had abused him too.

Numb and unaware of how he had been mistreated as a child—and to some extent as an adult—Jim had no memories or conscious awareness of the abuse until age 40, when the memories and awareness gradually began to return. Regardless of the type of abuse, this is a common pattern in the healing process for many people. In my own practice of individual and group psychotherapy with about 400 people over nearly 20 years, this form of remembering experiences of having been abused is by far the most common type, occurring by my estimate in well over half of these people. Lenore Terr calls this kind of trauma or abuse "Type II," wherein a person is abused repeatedly over time, and says that it is usually associated with memories from childhood that are frequently delayed for many years—even for decades[638] (Table 25.2). The reasons for this phenomenon of memory delay are both simple and complex, as I discuss throughout this book.

By contrast, Terr observes that after a single unanticipated severe trauma, which she calls Type I, the event and experience is usually remembered by the person in some detail.[638] This kind of experience may occur in a child, adolescent or adult who has at least a safe and supportive family and

Table 25.2 Trauma, Memory of the Trauma, and other Dynamics after Single and Repeated Abuse

(compiled and modified from Terr 1991)

	Trauma	*Memory*	Other Dynamics
Single (Type I)	Unanticipated	Usually *remembered* in single, severe trauma in some detail since the event*	Tend to talk freely about it when supported. Often ask "Why me?" and other cognitive reappraisals such as "How could I have avoided it?"
In Between (Intermediate, "Crossover")	One or more traumas	May contain either or both variations in memory	Ongoing stress of first trauma pushes the person's dynamics toward those characteristics of repeated (type II) traumas. May find features of both I and II.
Repeated (Type II)	Repeated, moderate to severe trauma	Usually *forgotten*, lost from conscious memory	Massive attempts to protect the True Self: denial, repression dissociation, psychic numbing, identification with the aggressor (projective identification), aggression against self, "stuck grief" repetition compulsions, anger, rage, passivity, self-mutilation. Recurring fear, "walking on eggshells," no talk rule, difficulty trusting, avoidance of intimacy, boundary distortions, enmeshment and other core issues[691]

* Unless trauma occurred before about age 2 to 3 years, when it may be less likely to be clearly remembered cognitively. (Also see pages 24-26.)

community environment in which they can talk more freely about what happened. In Chapter 3, in the first two columns of Table 3.1 on page 22, I described some of these factors that tend to provoke or reinforce remembering.

But this opportunity to talk freely and be validated and supported may not be available in many, if not most families and communities, especially if (1) the type of abuse is so charged and fearful, (2) if the abuser threatens the person, or manipulates them not to tell, and (3) if the person's experience is invalidated by others when they may try to tell someone or talk about it in any way. In any one or more of these kinds of situations, even a single trauma may be forgotten or repressed for many years. Jane's story is an example.

> Jane, a 47-year-old woman, was sexually abused one time by her grandfather at age seven. Even though he had told her not to tell anyone, she tried to tell her parents about it. They told her she was mistaken, pointing out many mistakes she had made since birth. Her grandfather died shortly after that, and she forgot the entire experience.
>
> As an adult, she was diagnosed as having an anxiety disorder and she later became alcoholic, for which she eventually entered treatment around age 44. At that time she began to remember parts of the experience of having been sexually abused, and since then more associated memories have come into her awareness. It was only in a safe environment that she was able to talk about her memories of having been abused.

Jane's history illustrates how a single trauma may be forgotten for decades. Factors include the fact that she grew up in a dysfunctional family to begin with, that she was not allowed to talk about her experience, was invalidated and attacked by her parents, and an additional shock— her abuser died shortly after the abuse. Even though hers was a "single trauma," this pattern of remembering it is more compatible with either the Intermediate type or the Type II trauma, as shown in Table 25.2.

In the following section I describe three experiential exercises that can help in remembering mistreatment and abuse, as well as in healing our wounds.

Making a Genogram (Family Tree)

There are many ways to begin to remember what happened, as I describe in *A Gift to Myself*, which is a workbook and guide to help in

Starting with yourself, write the name and the age inside the circle and in it or next to it write any outstanding or memorable characteristics of that person. Use any of the following abbreviations:

Alcsm = Alcoholism	Co-dep = Co-dependent	In = Incest
CD = other Chemical Dependence	RA = Religious Addiction	Ca = Cancer
AC = Adult Child	SR = Strict Religious	MI = Mental Illness
CG = Compulsive gambler	ED = Eating Disorder	Su = Suicide
Wksm = Workaholism	DF = Dysfunctional Family	Rec = Recovering
Viol = Violence or physical abuse	ND = Nicotine Dependence	VA = Verbal Abuse
SA = Sexual Addiction	Rgsm = Rage-aholism	PI = Physical Illness

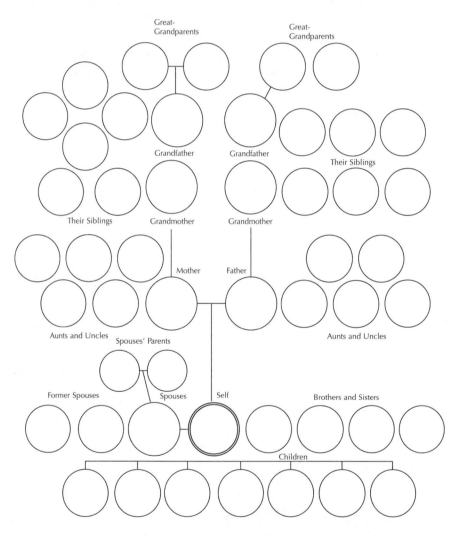

Figure 25.1. My Family Tree

healing the after effects of having been mistreated or abused.[688] One way is to make a genogram or family tree, showing all that you can remember or what others may tell you about your family of origin and extended family. To gather some of this information, you may need to do some careful detective work, interviewing one or more people who were in or close to your family.

If you would like to write out your genogram, you may use the blank family tree that I have provided on the previous page (Figure 25.1) Take as long as you need to fill this in. And when you write, remember that none of these kinds of experiential exercises are about blaming anyone. Rather, they are about naming the truth of what happened for you.

After completing your genogram, here are some ways to use the resulting information and insight:

1. Discovering who in my family may have been dysfunctional or troubled, and how or why they might have been so.
2. Seeing how they were then unable to be a healthy father, mother, brother, sister, aunt, uncle, grandmother, grandfather, step-relative, etc., to me.
3. Seeing how I didn't get my needs met as a child.
4. Beginning to see more clearly why my Child Within needed to go into hiding to survive.
5. Facilitating my grieving of the hurts, losses, or traumas that I experienced, but that I never got to grieve and complete.
6. As a part of my healing, sharing this information with trusted and safe others, such as my:
- Best friend (if they are not in denial about their experience and family)
- Counselor or therapist
- Self-help group (e.g., Adult Children or Co-dependents Anonymous)
- Therapy Group
- Sponsor (if in Adult Children or Co-dependents Anonymous)

Critics may say that these are "suggestions" or may "implant false memories" into our minds. As you do these experiential exercises and this recovery work, feel free to use any such criticism that you might read, hear or experience from anyone as "grist for the mill" of your healing process.

As we remember what happened to us, we can then begin to give an accurate name to any mistreatment or abuse that we may have experienced.

26

NAMING THE MISTREATMENT AND ABUSE

I define mistreatment and abuse as any action or behavior that hurts, threatens or attacks a person in any parts of their being, whether it may be physical, mental, emotional, spiritual or a combination of any of these. The abuse tends to bring about several results:

1) The victim's True Self tends to go into hiding.

2) The person is thereby not allowed to openly grieve the pain of the trauma.

3) The charged and unexpressed energy—that in a healthy family and community environment would ordinarily be expressed, validated and discharged—is instead stored deep within the person's unconscious mind and also in their body.

4) All of this results in physical, mental, emotional and spiritual consequences, from physical to mental and emotional disorders to difficulty having healthy relationships.

In *Healing the Child Within* and *A Gift to Myself* I name some of the specific ways that one person may abuse another, here reproduced in Table 26.1. As you look over this list of possible kinds of mistreatment, abuse or trauma, make a check mark next to or underline any that you can remember that may have happened to you. If you are uncertain that a specific kind of abuse happened to you, put a question mark next to it. If you are interested in exploring any of your memories further, consider talking about them with a safe person.

Table 26.1. Negative Rules and Negative Messages Commonly Heard in Dysfunctional Troubled Families

---

Negative Rules	Negative Messages
Don't express your feelings	Shame on you
Don't get angry	You're not good enough
Don't get upset	I wish I'd never had you
Don't cry	Your needs are not all right with me
Do as I say, not as I do	Hurry up and grow up
Be good, "nice," perfect	Be dependent
Avoid conflict (or avoid dealing with conflict)	Be a man
Don't think or talk; just follow directions	Act like a nice girl (or a lady)
Do well in school	You don't feel that way
Don't ask questions	Don't be like that
Don't betray the family	You're so stupid (or bad, etc.)
Don't discuss the family with outsiders; keep the family secret	You owe it to us
Be seen and not heard	Of course we love you!
No back-talk	I'm sacrificing myself for you
Don't contradict me	How can you do this to me?
Always look good	We won't love you if you . . .
I'm always right, you're always wrong	You're driving me crazy!
Always be in control	You'll never accomplish anything
Focus on the alcoholic's drinking (or troubled person's behavior)	You're so selfish
Drinking (or other troubled behavior) is not the cause of our problems	You'll be the death of me yet
Always maintain the status quo	That's not true
Everyone in the family must be an enabler	I promise (though breaks it)
	You make me sick
	We wanted a boy/girl
	You _____
	(fill in the blank)

When you finish this exercise, you may want to take a break of several days before going on to the next page.

Identifying and Remembering Painful Messages

There are also other kinds of mistreatment and abuse, including negative rules and messages that you might have heard growing up in your family and community. I list some of these in Table 26.2. You can do the same exercise with these kinds of abuse that you did with the naming exercise above. Then share what comes up for you with a safe person.

Table 26.2. Some Terms for Physical, Mental, Emotional and Spiritual Trauma That May Be Experienced by Children and Adults

Abandonment
Neglect
Abuse: Physical—spanking, beating, torture, sexual, other
        Mental—covert sexual (e.g., flirting, seducing)
        Emotional—(see below)
        Spiritual—(see below and text of reference 691)

Shaming	Limiting
Humiliating	Withdrawing/
Degrading	Withholding love
Inflicting guilt	Not taken seriously
Criticizing	Invalidating
Disgracing	Discrediting
Joking about	Misleading
Laughing at	Disapproving
Teasing	Making lights of or minimizing
Manipulating	your feelings, wants or needs
Deceiving	Breaking promises
Tricking	Raising hopes falsely
Betraying	Responding inconsistently or arbitrarily
Hurting	Making vague demands
Being cruel	Stifling
Belittling	Saying "you shouldn't . . . feel such and
Intimidating	such, e.g., anger"
Patronizing	Saying "If only . . . e.g., you were better
Threatening	or different" or
Inflicting fear	"You should . . . e.g., be better or
Overpowering or bullying	different"

If you would like to explore doing some more experiential exercises to help you remember what happened, consider looking at *A Gift to Myself* or a similar workbook and guide. These memories are often painful and may not be not easy to allow into your awareness. If the pain is too great, you may want to consider consulting a therapist who has expertise in assisting adults who were abused as children.

Getting Help from Safe Others

Sorting out all of our memories doesn't usually occur easily or spontaneously. When we are embroiled in our own conflict and pain, much

---

Table 26.3. Some Characteristics of Safe and Unsafe People

Safe	Unsafe
Listen to you	Don't listen
Hear you	Don't hear
Make eye contact	No eye contact
Accept the real you	Reject the real you
Validate the real you	Invalidate the real you
Nonjudgmental	Judgmental
Are real with you	False with you
Clear	Unclear
Boundaries appropriate and clear	Boundaries unclear, messages mixed
Direct	Indirect
No triangles	Triangle-in others
Supportive	Competitive
Loyal	Betray
Relationship authentic	Relationship feels contrived

---

of which may be unconscious to us, the truth about what was and is actually going on in parts of our inner life may not be readily available to us. This is why it can be useful to obtain assistance from safe and skilled others as we remember what happened and other dynamics in the process of our healing. While there are no hard and fast rules regarding just who will be the most likely to give us the most objective and accurate feedback about our memory work, the following may be useful.

The first principle is that the people from whom we may obtain assistance and feedback should be safe. We should be able to trust them to be real with us and to have most of the characteristics of safe people, as shown in Table 26.3. Safe people tend to listen to you and to hear you. They accept the real you and validate your experiences and whatever you may tell them about your inner life. They are clear and honest with you and nonjudgmental. Their boundaries are also appropriate and clear. They tend to be direct with you and not triangle others into conflicts that may develop between the two of you. Finally, they are supportive and loyal, and the relationship with them feels authentic.

By contrast, unsafe people may not really listen to you or hear what you are actually saying, although they may pretend to do so. They may or may not make eye contact with you. They often reject or invalidate the real you and your inner-life experience. They may be judgmental or false with you. They are often unclear in their communications. Their boundaries may be blurred and they may often send you mixed messages. They may be indirect with you, often triangling in another when they are in conflict with you. Rather than being supportive, they may be competitive and may even betray you. Overall, the relationship just feels contrived.

Not all of these characteristics are absolute. For example, some people who make eye contact, listen to you and are supportive may still be unsafe. And a safe person may be unclear and even appear to be judgmental at times. However, over time these characteristics and others may be helpful in differentiating who is safe from who is unsafe. Gradually your awareness, perception and intuition will become clearer.

27

MEMORY AND
VALIDATION

Validation is healing. It usually happens in a safe environment. Validation of our experience by others allows us to open ourselves to a painful memory, explore it and work through it.

Validation is manifested by any one or a combination of behaviors, from simple listening to being supportive to being loyal, as shown in Table 27.1 on page 283. When you tell me about a memory of an ordinary experience, I have numerous choices as to how I can relate. How I relate to you may make you feel heard and safe, unheard and unsafe, or somewhere in between.

But when you have a memory of a traumatic experience, how I respond to you takes on more importance, and how heard and safe you feel becomes crucial to how you process it. This is because if a person doesn't feel heard and safe, their True Self tends to go back into hiding and they tend to shut down in their motivation and ability to remember a traumatic experience.

In progressively increasing order, *validation* occurs when we do one or more of the following with another person: listen, are interested, make eye contact, are attentive, hear, understand, are supportive, mirror, identify, accept, are real, validate, agree, are loyal, love and love unconditionally.

When we do any one or more of these, the other person usually feels validated to some degree. When our experience is validated, we usually feel safe enough to continue to open up, explore, work through and eventually heal around the memory of a painful experience.

Difficulty Hearing Others' Pain

But many people have difficulty when another talks about a traumatic experience. Most people are not trained or very experienced in the importance of validation and how to do it. Some reasons for this are that they likely grew up in a dysfunctional family and therefore had inadequate role models, and that they don't understand how difficult it is to accurately comprehend the details of another person's inner life and experience.

Humility

People who are not in recovery or self-actualized may have an especially difficult time validating another's experience. One of the most positive after effects of the recovery process is humility. Not simply being passive or a "doormat," humility means being open to learning and experiencing more about self, others and the God of our understanding. Humility is a healthy state of consciousness. So when you tell me about your experience, if I remain open to what you are telling me about your experience, I will be able to validate you spontaneously. It will come naturally.

The only way that I know to be humble is to be real, i.e., to live and act as my Real Self. That is where humility naturally resides. But if I am living as my false self, I will likely have great difficulty either being humble or being able to validate your experience. In fact, attached to my false self I probably can't even know the fullness of my own inner life experience.

The false self

One of the characteristics of the false self (also called the ego) is that it always wants to be right, in control and "win." With anything it hears that threatens it in any way, it takes an oppositional stance. It says "No." If validation says "Yes" to the other in the relationship, our ego says "No" and thereby invalidates the other person's experience. We invalidate, even though there is no way that we can ever know another's inner life experience completely.

Table 27.1. A Spectrum of Validation and Invalidation

16	Loving unconditionally	
15	Loving	
14	Being loyal	
13	Agreeing	
12	Validating	**Validation** = healing
11	Being real	↑
10	Accepting	
9	Identifying	
8	Mirroring	
7	Being supportive	
6	Understanding	
5	Hearing	
4	Being attentive	**Safe**
3	Making eye contact	
2	Being interested	
1	Listening	

————Being Neutral————

-1	Not listening	
-2	Uninterested	
-3	No eye contact	
-4	Not being attentive	
-5	Not hearing	**Unsafe**
-6	Not understanding	
-7	Not being supportive	
-8	Not identifying	
-9	Not accepting	
-10	Unhealthy Teasing	
-11	Not being real	↓
-12	Invalidating	**Invalidation** = wounding
-13	Neglecting	
-14	Abandoning	
-15	Disagreeing	
-16	Rejecting	
-17	Betraying	
-18	Attacking	

Invalidation

Invalidation says "No" to the other's experience and thus often to a part of the relationship. Because I don't accept their experience, to the other person it frequently feels like I don't accept them, their very Being or Soul. Because I don't allow them to have and talk about their own personal experience, they may feel psychologically invisible, as though they don't even exist.[68a] When this dynamic happens repeatedly in a relationship, it tends to erode, and the feeling of closeness or intimacy is lost. If the experiencer wants to heal around their trauma, it will likely not be possible to do so with this other person present. It may not feel safe enough.

Being invalidated feels unsafe, and it hurts. It is one of the most crippling things a person can do in and to a relationship. Behaviors that tend to induce a feeling of being invalidated include, in progressively increasing order: not listening, being uninterested, not making eye contact, not being attentive, not hearing, not understanding, not being supportive, not identifying with the experience, not accepting it, unhealthy teasing, not being real, outright verbal invalidating, neglecting, abandoning, disagreeing, rejecting, betraying and attacking. As shown in Table 27.1 above, invalidation is wounding because it injures the person's True Self, and if repeated, may induce it to go into hiding.

When another says that my memory, which is an important part of my own personal experience, is wrong, I may begin to doubt my own experience. But unless I tell them of it when I feel psychologically safe, how can another know about my authentic experience, and thus know more about me as an individual and about my experience in our relationship?

A conflict may result when two or more people have different experiences of the same or a similar event. As part of that disagreement, how can I reconcile my own experience with theirs, especially if theirs is diametrically opposed to mine? Do we agree to disagree? Sorting out these questions is a major task of the recovery process. It takes dedication, persistence and patience. Psychotherapists and psychoanalysts who have practiced using Freud's oedipal theory, which says that the child was only fantasizing about having been abused, have subtly invalidated their patients for 100 years.[327, 570] Could this be a factor in lowering their success rate at helping people heal? If so, how might this observation apply to our relationships with others, whether they are our colleagues, friends or family?

Validation Versus Enabling

With all that we have learned about the healing power of feeling safe, validated and accepted, it would be a mistake to agree with and not question and at times even challenge what people say in their expressions and stories. In most relationships and exchanges, including individual and group psychotherapy, there is room for response and feedback. In group therapy we know that the most helpful and healing feedback includes saying to the person who has just told a part of their story:

- This is what I see. This is how I identify with you.
- This is what I hear. This is what is coming up for me in my inner life as I hear your story.

Advice and suggestions are usually less helpful. Of course, being defensive, judgmental or attacking are often destructive to the relationship.

In addition to giving feedback, in relationships outside of therapy I may just want to respond and relate to another by expressing what comes up for me in my inner life, either spontaneously or planned. If during this time I stay real, i.e., live and express as my True Self, then I will tend not to invalidate another's experience—especially if they are also real with me. But if I let my false self speak for me, there is a good chance that I will sooner or later invalidate their experience.

In a relationship I don't have to "walk on eggshells" around the person. I can be real. In fact, being spontaneous, which is part of being real, is a healthy way to be in most close relationships. Not trying to change the other, including their shared experiences, is a way to let them be themselves.

Most things in life have double-edged sword qualities. The downside of validating is enabling. An "enabler" is a person who unconsciously—and sometimes consciously—facilitates the destructive behavior of a dysfunctional person. This facilitating may include repeated attempts to rescue or fix the dysfunctional person.[689] A difference is that validating supports healthy being and growth, and enabling supports inappropriate and dysfunctional behavior.

Healing the Conflict when Accused

A question with a built-in conflict arises when a person who is accused of abusing another cannot remember the abuse or denies it.

They may ask their accuser, "What's wrong with you that you would make up such a story?" Rather than simply listen to the accuser with a non-defensive attitude, the accused often attacks with an invalidating posture and statement. This behavior immediately sets the stage for an adversarial relationship, wherein both may feel unsafe.

A way out for the accused person would be to just listen, mull it over, pray about it and talk to someone neutral, such as a psychotherapist who has experience with working with dysfunctional families and who has done their own personal healing. After a sufficient number of sessions, the accused person may then choose to explore the possibility of asking their accuser to have a joint session with a different and neutral therapist with the same qualifications as above—and one that neither of them has seen for counseling.

This kind of approach is far healthier and more loving and constructive than an immediate adversarial one. It demonstrates humility, sincerity and caring by both parties, all of which frees them to step back and reflect on their own reaction. Here we are more likely, although not guaranteed, to have two people who speak their truth, yet validate one another's experience. For the accused to take responsibility for honest self-reflection and self-examination is a great act of courage, as well as being an unselfish and loving act. Just seeing and experiencing this happen may be healing to some degree for the accuser. (See also pages 170 and 172 for further information and approaches.)

But the above scenario does not usually happen. Given the natural history of abusers, especially those with certain Stage Zero disorders such as advanced personality disorders, pedophilia and other extreme forms of sexual deviance, their likelihood for authentic introspection and risking to ask for assistance is low. Currently, only court-mandated long-term comprehensive treatment for pedophiles and other violent people appears to produce even a small percentage of lasting success.[67, 202] A problem with these programs is that they are either not comprehensive enough and not delivered by competent therapists, or the court mandate is too weak. These people tend to need a minimum of five years in a Stage One full recovery program for their specific Stage Zero disorder, followed by strong Stage Two recovery work for a similar duration or longer.

While it may be somewhat easier for the co-abuser to work through their denial, as for the abuser, those with certain Stage Zero disorders such as advanced personality disorders may be strongly resistant to healing their own wounds. Many co-abusers will also have been abused themselves, and this can often make their healing paradoxically easier and more difficult at the same time, as shown in the following history.

> Mary is a 60-year-old divorced woman. A year ago her 38-year-old daughter Christine confronted her with having abused her physically, mentally and emotionally as a child, and on at least one occasion sexually abused her. On hearing this information, Mary felt crushed. While talking with her best friend about it she began to remember that her father had similarly abused her except for the sexual abuse, and so had her mother. This confused her. She felt guilty and ashamed about having been abused and then for having abused her own daughter, although she would not share this with Christine, and they remained alienated. Two months ago she began to work on her pain with a therapist.

Mary appears to be at an early stage of her healing process. The more that she and Christine work on themselves separately, the greater will be the likelihood that they will be able to reconcile.

Abusers and some co-abusers appear to have much difficulty introspecting and owning their own behavior. They do not seem to get the message, the simple request that would likely allow them to make amends to their accuser, which is to acknowledge that the abuse happened and to apologize for having done it. Any accused abuser and co-abuser who has read this far in this book may be on the right road. I congratulate you and invite you to explore this potentially healing possibility that I have described in the paragraphs above.

While it is uncommon, occasionally after years of pain and work to heal, a kind of acknowledgement and apology happens spontaneously, as shown in the following history.

> Barbara is a 50-year-old survivor of severe physical and mental abuse. She has been in recovery off and on for the last 19 years. Her mother had a long history of chemical dependence and physical and mental illness. Barbara had never thought to try to be validated by her abusive mother until it happened spontaneously in a recent conversation with her brother present.
>
> She explains: "My brother was talking about the students he works with at his school who have been abused. With her usual far-off look, my mother said in a confused voice, 'Why would anyone do that to a child?' I knew this was my one chance, my one moment in time. And I knew from my reading and working with survivors of abuse myself that I had to do it.

"I looked intently at her and said, 'You abused us, mother. You abused Marshall and me.' She looked at me and said, 'I did?' 'Yes, you did' I answered. She thought again for quite a while and, with what seemed like true sincerity, said, 'I'm sorry.' 'Accepted' I answered, and a burden was lifted from me.

"It happened fast and in the context of our next move that day—going to see my dying father—it seemed not so important. But it's a year now and I remember that scene in the restaurant vividly and often. I have explained that scene to many people. It didn't erase the years of pain and years of psychotherapy for me. I was afraid of her for years and I hated her. I got through that and slowly worked on trying to forgive her, praying for help. Her apology, as short and simple as it was, has made my forgiveness and even my love for my mother feel authentic now."

While Barbara still had more work to do in her healing, this experience freed her to be able to let go of a lot of fear, shame and anger about her having been abused by her mother.

Guidelines for Survivors

An additional reason for confronting our abuser(s) and asking for their acknowledgment and apology is so that we can know we have tried everything to help heal the unfinished business of our abuse experience. Even though a survivor may express their experience to their abuser and co-abuser, it is common for them to deny the existence of the abuse and to try to invalidate their experience. They may also try to shame them about their recovery work and, as has happened frequently with many, even attack their methods of healing.

Because of the above, it is often difficult for the survivor to work through and heal the pain that is associated with the rejection and invalidation of their experience. To assist them in handling this pain, I have made several suggestions, as shown in Table 27.2.

Knowing the age-old statement, "The only person that I can change or heal is myself," I can begin or continue a program of recovery to heal my own wounds from the abuse. During this time I can also work on and set healthy boundaries and limits with others, especially any family members or others who have abused me or may still be mistreating or abusing me.[691]

As I heal, I can identify any people in my family of origin, or any close to it, who validate and support me. If they are otherwise safe, I can get

Table 27.2 Some Guidelines for Abuse Survivors Whose Abuser(s) Deny the Abuse or Try to Invalidate Their Experience

1) Work a program of recovery to heal your woundedness from the abuse.

2) Work on and set healthy boundaries and limits with others, especially any family members or others who may have abused you or may be still abusing you.

3) Is there anyone in your family of origin who validates and supports you? If they are otherwise safe, get appropriate psychological nourishment (healthy contact, sharing, validation and support) from them.

4) Find validation in a safe "family of choice."

5) Make a "family tree" and share it with someone safe.

6) Differentiate who is safe from who is not.

7) Find and share your story with safe people in recovery. Keep speaking your truth to safe people.

8) Learn what you can that is true about memory and abuse.

9) Do all you can for yourself, and if you choose, turn the rest over to the God of your understanding.

appropriate psychological nourishment from them, consisting of healthy contact, sharing, validation and support. If my own family of origin cannot provide this, I can find validation and support in a safe "family of choice," such as a therapy group, spouse, best friends sponsor and the like.

I can also sort out and identify what went on in my family of origin by making a "family tree," also called a genogram, as described on pages 271-274. To help myself process this information, I can then share it with someone safe. As I learn to differentiate who is safe from who is not safe, I can find and share my story of my experience of having been mistreated or abused.

All the while, I am learning what I can about memory and abuse. People who are not in recovery have a hard time hearing about abuse and its painful after effects. A reason is that to hear about and face this pain might push me to face my own wounds from having been abused. Those who are accused usually find it even more difficult. They have to not only bear their own wounds but also face their guilt, shame and fear from having abused another. These two realizations combined may be overwhelming and it may be easier for them just to dissociate from both.

As I heal I can also practice "co-creation", which means that I do all that I can for myself, and then if I choose, turn the rest over to the God of my understanding. This is close to what Ben Franklin meant when he said, "The Lord helps those that help themselves."

I cannot fix my abuser(s) or my family.

With the assistance of safe others and my Higher Power, I can heal myself.

28

SPIRITUALITY AND MEMORY

*God gave us
memories so that
we might have
roses in December*

—James M. Barrie
1860-1937

Spirituality is about our relationships with our self, others and the God of our understanding. Spirituality transcends, yet enfolds and nurtures the positive aspects of religion, and it has characteristics that include an experiential exploration of the Divine Mystery, paradoxicality and our levels of awareness and being. While I have written about the spiritual aspects of recovery elsewhere,[687-689, 691, 692] in this closing chapter I will address some aspects of the relationship between spirituality and memory.

Several questions may have already come to the mind of the survivor of abuse. Some of them may include: Why did this happen to me? If there is a Higher Power or God, why didn't that God protect me? Can I find any meaning in all of my pain? Can I ever let go of my pain or forgive my abuser(s) and co-abuser(s)? And even though I was a victim, can I forgive myself for what I thought I did wrong? Answering these kinds of questions is not easy. While I believe that we each have to explore and answer them in our own way and in our own time, some of the following reflections may be useful.

Why Me?

Why did this happen to me? I think we might begin to explore some background to this question by asking a few age-old questions. These include: Who am I? What am I doing here (on Earth)? And, Where am I going? While it all appears to be a Divine Mystery, and these questions usually take a lifetime of experiential and intellectual enquiry, we can consider some possibilities. Some may include:

> I am a child of God. Therefore I am a minute but important part of God. I am here to explore and experience the Mystery in a deeper and richer way than I have done so far. I am here to experientially find my True Identity, to learn to give and receive love, and to enjoy and be successful in living my life. And as I am doing all of the above in my own way and my own time, I am "returning" to God—whom I never left and who never left me.

This is but one possible scenario that I find personally comforting. You may not find one or more parts of it to be comforting or even possible for you. That is for you to determine, and not for me or anyone else to do.

Can I Find any Meaning in My Pain?

But why would a loving God allow me to be abused? If there is a Higher Power or God, why didn't that God protect me? While these are complex and difficult questions, could it be that the pain and confusion of the abuse are part of our finding our True Self and eventually working out this part of the Mystery? I don't know the answer for you. All I can do is explore the answer for me and to assist others, should they ask me, as they explore and arrive at their own answers.

In the movie *Shadowlands*, which is about the loving relationship between the children's writer C.S. Lewis and Joy Gresham, Joy got cancer and slowly died. During this time they both said that "The pain is part of the happiness." As we heal our woundedness from having been abused, we at last feel the pain that we had stuffed for so long in order to survive, and we grieve. Remembering what happened to us when we were mistreated or abused helps us to grieve, and reciprocally, grieving helps us to remember more about our experience of what happened. These both help us to find and be our Real Self. This process of grieving and remembering takes a long time, usually in the range of several years.

Letting Go

Eventually we can begin to let go of our pain. Some people may call doing so "forgiveness," but I prefer to use a term like *letting go* instead. This is because forgiveness often feels forced to me, and because it is often so difficult to do it. Indeed, many people find that before they can actually let go of something, they have to first know *experientially* exactly what it is that they are letting go of. The following case history is an example.

Robert is a 52-year-old dentist, divorced and a father of three. He suffered from low self-esteem, PTSD and alcoholism, the latter in successful recovery for over 10 years. Two years ago he began recovery for these and for other wounds from being an adult child of a dysfunctional family. Before joining group therapy he had begun to have glimpses of memories of his uncle sexually abusing him when he was ages two through 10. His memories became progressively clearer, even though he had attacks of fear (anxiety attacks) and nightmares for several months as the memories were emerging. He had forgotten those abusive experiences from around age 10 until about three years ago.

With the above internal corroboration (alcoholism, PTSD, age regressions and memory characteristics), Robert was also able to find external corroboration when his younger sister told him that their uncle had also sexually abused her as a child, and an aunt who said she had had to keep her two children away from him for fear of the uncle "trying something funny." More internal corroborations came when he remembered at age four having his head forced into the cushions of a sofa with rough dark blue fabric and being held by someone's hand who had two missing fingers. His aunt reminded him that his uncle had two missing fingers on his left hand.

Later in group therapy he spoke of his uncle's being on his death bed and his now having an urge to go and forgive him, even though he was still angry and hurt from his uncle's having abused him. "When I think of doing it, though, I feel frozen and glued to my chair." The group helped him consider his possibilities and some healthy choices.

Robert had difficulty letting go, and he said that over the course of the next several weeks and months he could feel some movement. His uncle slowly worsened and he finally visited him in the hospital and said, "I'm here to forgive you for what you did to me when I was a child." His uncle gasped, and the "beeps" on the heart monitor became faster. Robert knew that his uncle's response was a kind of internal corroboration, perhaps in the form of a somatic memory, that was coming from his uncle and at the same time some more external corroboration for him. His uncle never answered him verbally and they never discussed it again. He died two weeks later, and Robert felt some relief for having expressed himself.

Robert had traumatically forgotten having been abused by his uncle until the past four years, when his memories of it began to return and during which he grieved his previously ungrieved pain.

Dictionary definitions usually define forgiveness as letting go of anger or resentment, but it is actually letting go of all of our stored pain that we never got to grieve before. Forgiving another—or letting go of the pain that was associated with part of our relationship—may be a way that we learn to forgive ourselves. We can then eventually let go of the pain, which may include self-blame, shame and guilt that somehow we caused and deserved to have been mistreated or abused.

Forgiveness releases the forgiver more than it does the forgiven. After the letting go, core issues may come up, such as difficulty trusting, feelings—including anger, fear, shame and guilt—and difficulty being our Real Self with the forgiven. But now we have a greater awareness of both our inner life *and* what is going on outside of us. To assist us in working through any of these core issues or any other conflicts, we can also consider using the process of co-creation.

The Process of Co-creation

Benjamin Franklin summarized co-creation in his saying, "The Lord helps those that help themselves." We do all that we can do and then turn the rest over to our Higher Power. Figure 28.1 shows a map of the process of co-creation. The first half of the process, shown on the left side of the figure, is what we do. It is our work. The remaining half is what we surrender and let God do.

Name the Feeling, Dynamic or Issue

Whenever we have a problem, upset, hurt or loss, it is important to become fully aware of what is coming up for us from moment to moment in our inner life and then, if useful, to give it an accurate name. When we heal our wounds we will be "tuned in" and fully aware of our inner life, and thus able to know what it is that we are experiencing. We can now give an accurate name to anything in that inner life: any belief, thought, feeling, want, need, intuition pattern or anything else—including our memories.

For example, we can name ourselves as an adult child of a dysfunctional family. I remember how enlightening and empowering that was for me when I realized and accepted that I was an adult child. Another example is when I am angry, and fully feel it. Doing so tells me several

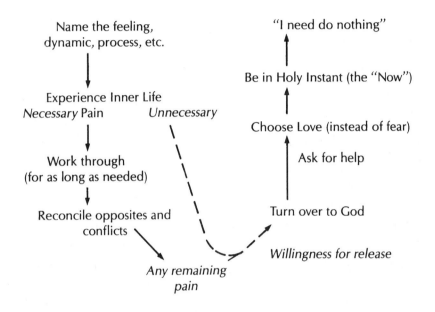

Figure 28.1. Some Steps in the Process of Co-Creation

things—that I may be being mistreated or have lost something important, and that I may need to set some healthy boundaries or take some other action.

Experience My Inner Life

Before we can work through any of our pain, we have to both name it and experience it. To experience something, we open ourselves and allow whatever might be in our inner life right now to come up into our awareness. We cannot usually name something accurately unless we can experience it. And when we name it, that helps us experience it more authentically and completely. These feed one another in a positive reciprocation.

As we experience our inner life, we will learn that some of our pain is necessary—for example when we grieve a loss. We also learn that some of our pain is *not necessary*. We don't actually need to experience it—for example, when we "beat ourselves up" for getting a parking ticket. In reality, being upset for longer than a few minutes is unnecessary in that kind of situation.

Work Through the Pain

As we experience *necessary* suffering, such as the loss of a loved one, we *begin* to work through it. And as we work through it we experience it more accurately and completely. This shows how the process of experiencing, naming and working through can act together in a healthy way, as we work through the pain or upset. And it is work. It takes a lot of energy, grief and time to do this work and to complete it. We cannot rush our grief work, our necessary pain.

Reconcile Opposites and Conflicts

Part of our work will eventually involve beginning to identify, sort out and reconcile opposites and conflicts on which we are working. For example, do I stay in this relationship or leave it? Do I stay with this job, or go elsewhere? Should I risk being real or continue not to be? Yes or no?

Once we have identified the opposites, one of the first core issues that we can work through is all-or-none. Remember that in working through any all-or-none conflict, we usually have more choices than we may think. So for each conflict, we ask ourselves, "What are my choices?" For example, I may not need to choose "all" (stay in this relationship, job or be false) or "none" (leave, work elsewhere or always be real with everyone). In fact, I may be able to do something in between. So I consider what I want to do, share it all with safe others and take plenty of time to work it through.

Any Remaining Pain

Having done "our part" of the co-creation process, we can now more strongly involve our Higher Power. This does not mean that we can't stay in conscious contact with the God of our understanding from the *beginning* of working through our upset, issue or concern. We can. Doing that is certainly appropriate, useful and empowering.

Turn It Over and Let It Go

However, now we are ready to assess how much, if any, pain may be remaining. How much do we still hurt? When we sense that we have done all that we can do for now, we can then take any remaining pain and turn it over to our Higher Power. We let go of it. We let it go.

But to do this, to let go, we must be willing. The "Big Book" of AA and its equivalents in other Twelve-Step fellowships speak of the importance of being willing to let go and to change. *A Course in Miracles* talks repeatedly of the healing power of just "a little willingness." All we need, then, is to be willing to have remaining pain removed.[145] The *Course*, one of the most sophisticated, detailed and practical writings that I have ever seen on psychological and spiritual recovery, says that taking away our pain is precisely one of the major jobs of the Holy Spirit, which other faiths call Divine Energy or Spirit, Prana, Chi or Ki. It takes the pain, outshines it and it is gone.*

And so, being willing to have our pain removed, we ask that the Holy Spirit remove it. And then we let it go.

If we feel stuck in any ways, we can assess whether we have done all we can do to work through our conflict. If there is more for us to do, we can do it, and then let go of any remaining pain. And throughout this entire process we can ask our Higher Power for help.

When we have done all our work, and when we let go of any remaining pain, we can actually feel the pain lifted from us. It disappears. It is gone.

Choose Love

Just as we let go of the pain, we can now choose Love. Many holy books describe Unconditional Love as being the most powerful, creative and healing energy in the universe. And so we choose to experience It, to have It flood our body, mind and spirit. We experience Love in our Total Being.

Thus when we experientially choose Love, we are pure Serenity,

---

* Written from a higher level of our awareness, *A Course in Miracles* also addresses the concept of memory and the experience of remembering from that higher level. These sections are in the *Text* on pages 169-170, 203, 218, 261, 512 and 547-549, the *Workbook* on pages 376 and 413 and the *Teachers Manual* on page 61. The *Course* refers to forgetting throughout.[145]

complete peace and joy, which is God's Will for us.[145] The *Course* calls it the Holy Instant, others called it Nirvana, and Christ called it the Kingdom of Heaven. It is all the same state of pure, Unconditional Love.

Have you walked into a room that was pitch black, completely dark, and searched for the light switch—and finally turned on the light? When you flipped the switch, what happened to the darkness? It probably completely disappeared. That is what happens when we choose Love over fear or any other pain. The pain simply disappears. The Light outshines the dark.

"I Need Do Nothing"

In recovery we peel away the layers of our false self in a search for our True Self. In the early stages of our journey and our recovery—Stages Zero and One—we may feel confused, numb, in pain. We may feel at times like a victim or a martyr. We may sense that there is something wrong, that something is missing, and we seek an answer. And as we search, although it may take a long time, sooner or later we will begin to peel away the first layer. What we discover underneath may be any one or more of a variety of addictions, compulsions and other physical, mental, emotional and spiritual disorders. These are our Stage Zero conditions.

After working through a Stage One recovery program for whatever condition or disorder we found, we may be ready to peel that one away also. And what is underneath it? I suggest that it is the after effects of the mistreatment or abuse, which may also be called the adult child condition, with its two most paralyzing feelings: fear and shame. When others try to inflict these on us by trying to invalidate our memories of having been abused, it can be a reminder of what it might have been like to have grown up under these circumstances. Not only might it take a long time to recognize this condition and these toxic feelings, it might also take even longer to work through them. We can work through them in a Stage Two full recovery program.

As we heal our wounds at this layer, we can see that both of the other layers of the onion are also part of (or perhaps more precisely manifestations of) that adult child wounding, which are often dominated by fear and shame. The fear seems to be mostly of abandonment and of the unknown, and the shame is mostly the paralyzing feeling that we are at our core inadequate, bad, not enough, imperfect, flawed and rotten. It can take a long time to work through this stage and discover the startling truth: that at the core of our being we are neither confused, numb,

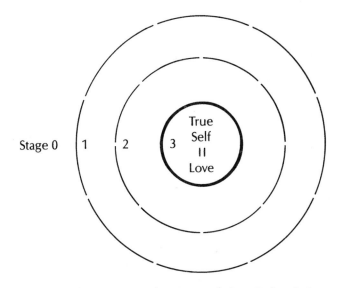

Figure 28.2. The Core of Our Being is Love

hurting, addicted, compulsive, disordered, co-dependent, scared, ashamed or any other such thing. Although any of these may come up to block our True Self, our Child Within, we learn that we are none of them. What we realize is that we are Love, at the *core* of our Being.

That Love that I am is connected to comes from and is empowered by the Unconditional Love of my Higher Power. When I tap into both of these sources of Love, I am co-creating my life. As you read this now, how do you feel? Can you sense that Love in your heart? Can you sense its healing power? Can you let yourself "do nothing" and just savor It and be It?

I wish you the best in your recovery and your life.

Charles L Whitfield

Appendix A

A NOTE ON MEMORIES AND REPORTS ABOUT SEXUAL ABUSE OF CHILDREN

While in this book I have focused primarily on traumatic memory in adults, the process most often begins with traumatic experiences in childhood. Estimates of how often children may give an untrue report or have an untrue memory are similar to those made for adults, as shown in Table A-1. Note that these are not based on proven cases, but on estimates made by helping professionals who work with children and are based on their impressions from their individual caseloads only. Child protective service workers tend to estimate a lower figure for untrue memories and reports of abuse and judges and law enforcement workers tend to estimate a higher figure. They both tend to rank adolescent girls the highest.

One of the most common conflicts in this area occurs in divorce and child custody contests, wherein there is said to be a common claim of child sexual abuse by one parent or parent-figure to try to gain custody. Either the parent is exaggerating and/or encouraging the child to exaggerate or make up a story of abuse, or the child was actually abused and the accused parent denies having committed the abuse. An especially painful outcome may occur if the accusing parent loses the custody and the child is court-ordered to the care of an actual abuser, sometimes called "court-ordered rape," or they are court-ordered to allow visits with an abuser without supervision.

Note also the section on "infantile amnesia" in Chapter 3, pages 24 through 26, where I describe how very young children *do* remember traumatic experiences. This is contrary to the "infantile amnesia" defense that FMS advocates try to use when they defend people who are accused of child abuse.

Table A-1. Studies on the Truthfulness of Sexual Abuse Reports among Children and Adolescents as Judged by Evaluators

(compiled from Everson & Boat 1989[207])

Number Studied	Study	True or Untrue Reports
64	First examined in emergency department, then had comprehensive psychiatric & medical evaluations. The selection process was unclear. (Peters 1979)	**94**% (60/64) determined to be true. No distinction was made between reports by children and those by adults on their behalf.
46	Evaluation by a child abuse agency. Number of children who actually reported abuse is not provided. (Goodwin et al 1979)	**96**% true, i.e., One false report by a child. Two others were false reports by mothers with "severe mental disturbances."
92	92 of 181 referred children reporting sexual abuse (Horowitz et al 1984 cited in Everson & Boat 1989)	**93**% true. No child under 8 y.o. made untrue reports.
576	576 *complaints* of sexual abuse among children & adolescents. (Jones & Macgraw 1987)	True findings were differentiated as to confirmed (53%), legitimate suspicion (17%), or insufficient evidence (24%), leaving 6% *untrue*, with *less than 2% untrue* by children.
142	142 children reporting abuse were evaluated in a child abuse program. (Faller 1988)	3% of children's reports determined *untrue* (older child or adolescent for revenge or to avoid punishment, young child to gain approval of interviewer)
1,249	1,249 estimated reports (1/3 each were: under age 6, 6 to 12, & adolescents) evaluated by child protective services workers who were then surveyed by the authors (Everson & Boat 1989)	*Untrue*: 1.6% under age 3; 1.7% 3 to 6; 4.3% 6 to 12; 8% 12 to 18. Authors suspected these may be inflated due to some CPS workers' bias against believing children's reports.
2,169 total	2,169 children and adolescents were evaluated.	**98**% (generally younger children) to **93**% (usually older) were determined to be true.

Appendix B

ADDITIONAL REPRESSED MEMORY GUIDELINES

BY T.F. NAGY Ph.D.

(FROM *THE NATIONAL PSYCHOLOGIST* 1994)

The following are taken from guidelines written by psychologist T.F. Nagy in 1994. I have found them to be useful.

1. Always provide thorough informed consent before beginning therapy, considering the following in your discussion of treatment:

- Provide a general indication of how therapy will proceed.
- Describe how any specialized techniques for memory retrieval, such as hypnosis or guided imagery, will be integrated into therapy.
- Describe how such specialized techniques as adjuncts can contribute to therapy, but that they do not constitute the whole of therapy.
- Explain both potential benefits and risks of engaging in such specialized techniques.
- Consult the American Psychological Association (APA) Ethics Code, with a focus on Standards 4.01 (Structuring the Relationship) and 4.02 (Informed Consent to Therapy).

2. Document your professional activities with all clients by keeping accurate records of ongoing psychotherapy.

- Use signed consent forms or contracts if appropriate; consult an attorney about risks and benefits of such a practice.
- Consult APA's "Record-Keeping Guidelines" for a current and comprehensive outline of what to include in your case notes (cf. American Psychologist, September 1993, pp. 984-984).

3. Be competent in your use of specialized techniques, such as hypnosis, guided imagery or dream analysis, to name a few. Enter these potentially intense areas with caution and thoroughness, through a formal course of study, and consultation and supervision with experienced health-care professionals. Continue to upgrade your skills by attending workshops, reading journals, joining a peer supervisory group and in other ways.

- Consult the APA Ethics Code with particular emphasis on Standards 1.04 (Boundaries of Competence) and 1.05 (Basis for Scientific and Professional Judgments).

4. Make no assumptions about the historical accuracy of hypnotic or non-hypnotic recall. Also, do not imply that hypnotically experienced "events" necessarily happened. Remember; your personal convictions about the validity of emerging "memories" are highly contagious to many patients and are communicated directly or indirectly in a variety of ways.

- Refrain from using the words "memories" or "facts" when referring to material which may emerge in treatment.

It might be wiser to use such concepts as impressions, hypnotic experiences, sensations, etc., which allow the patient to retain the dignity of their private experiences, without elevating their status to that of "evidence" or "historic fact."

5. Never attempt an uncovering technique for the first time without taking a careful history and employing your usual and customary methods of gathering information, including psychological testing, as appropriate. In spite of any felt pressure from the patient to explore the past, therapists should not compromise their standards concerning this important phase of treatment.

- Use or develop your own standardized history forms if possible.
- The decision to utilize a specialized technique such as hypnosis should be informed by the therapist's wisdom and competence, not by the patient's wishes.

6. It is wise to have an explanatory interview in which the phenomenon of hypnosis or other specialized intervention is thoroughly explored. In this discussion, be sure to include the salient aspects of the intervention. And, as with every professional contact, document these discussions thoroughly in your case notes; better still, audiotape or videotape this part of the work.

- Use printed handouts, when possible, given out early in treatment, that explain the technique to be used.
- Address the patient's preconceptions, questions, fears about the technique to be used.
- Include information about the potential usefulness of material that emerges — that it can be very helpful to the therapy process. Also include some statement about its limitations — that experiences in hypnosis are not necessarily historically accurate for everyone.
- Inform patients about the risks of using abreactive techniques or interventions where material may surface that may be distressing.

7. When conducting an exploratory session, it is wise to audiotape or videotape. This may provide a good documentation against claims of implanting memories in patients. It is also important to document each session in your case notes.

8. Use a consent form for a specialized technique, carefully drawn up, which includes the essence of the topics discussed. Consult with an attorney or senior psychologist familiar with these matters in preparing this form.

- Consent forms can be a double-edged sword, promising services or results which, in reality, could not be guaranteed. Such language could increase one's vulnerability to an ethics complaint or lawsuit. Be cautious in working all consent forms.

9. Always allow time for a thorough debriefing following the exploratory session. Continue to audiotape or videotape this for a permanent record.

- Discuss the patient's thoughts and feelings about the sessions, as appropriate.
- Explore the patients' beliefs about the historical accuracy of the session.
- Process the emerging material in any way appropriate, consistent with your theoretical base and the patient's needs.
- Inquire about any unpleasant or uncomfortable sensations or experiences, that had not yet been reported by the patient.
- Provide reminders that hypnotic events do not always reflect literal reality, but are very useful as metaphors or clues to explore new directions in therapy.

Appendix C

OVERVIEW OF OFFENDER PSYCHOLOGY AND BEHAVIOR

Nearly all experts agree that pedophilia is not curable, and they differ in opinion about whether this is even treatable.

—Alice Vachss, 1993

The following is an outline taken from the work of Robert Emerick, a therapist who specializes in assisting offenders in recovery.[202] While offenders vary in their backgrounds, offenses, and other manifestations and dynamics, as indicated on pages 79, 117, 168 and 285, this outline is helpful in our understanding of offender psychology and behavior. Emerick divides the phases of overt offending into four: engagement, grooming, assault and concealment.

The Offender's Process of Sexually Abusing A Child

Phase	Social Objective	Offender's Behavior	Victim's Perception
Engagement	Create the illusion of being a non-offender.	Befriend parents and/or guardians of children.	View the offender as a trusted family member or friend.
	Seek out a child who is perceived to be vulnerable and/or controllable.	Compliment child about personal and social characteristics.	View the offender as a trusted friend and/or caretaker.

The Offender's Process of Sexually Abusing A Child (cont.)

Phase	Social Objective	Offender's Behavior	Victim's Perception
Engagement (cont.)		Extend special privileges to the child and/or help the child achieve a special goal.	View the offender as both helpful and nurturing: a special friend.
		Verbally and/or physically abuse others in the child's presence. Or, verbally and/or physically abuse the child.	View the offender as a threat to mental, emotional and physical health.
Grooming	Invite others to view him or her as a person who is loving and responsible.	Use normative physical and social contacts that occur between adults and children to become sexually excited and desensitize the child to physical contact.	View the offender as an affectionate person who enjoys being with children. Feel loved, important and protected.
	Cultivate a sense of shared responsibility within the victim and normalize the assault behavior.	Misrepresent social morals and encourage the victim to view adult-child sexual relations as healthy or a normal outcome of an external factor (i.e., social problems, alcohol abuse, the victim, etc.).	Misinterpret paraphilic behavior to be either normal or caused by an external factor. Feel mature and view the offender as a peer.
	Measure the victim's risk of reporting the assaults.	Exploit the child's innocence and violate the child's privacy while committing "hands-off" offenses.	View the offender as threatening and feel confused about his behavior.

	Social Objective	Offender's Behavior	Victim's Perception
Assaults	Use victim to fulfill deviant sexual interests while minimizing the risk of being reported.	Ask the child for permission to touch his/her genitals. Or, use the child's curiosity to direct him/her to touch the offender's genitals.	Perceive the assault as consensual and normal. Feel mature and "loved."
		Initiate the assault behavior when the victim is unable to be self-protective (i.e., sleeping, bathing, etc.).	Perceive the assault as abusive. Feel powerless, frightened and confused.
		Direct the child's hand or mouth to his genitals. Overtly offend against the child: grope the child's genitals and/ or penetrate the child's mouth, vagina and/or rectum.	Perceive the assault as abusive and possibly feel both ashamed and threatened. May dissociate or forget the experience.
Concealment	Maintain the illusion of being a respectful community member who is loving and responsible.	Remind the child of the "special" nature of their relationship. Assert feelings of attachment to the child.	Perceive the offender as a responsible adult and feel special, important and loved.
		Make emotional, social and/or financial commitments to the child.	Perceive the offender as abusive and feel anxious, dirty and ashamed about the assaults.
		Threaten the child emotionally, physically and/or socially.	Perceive the offender as violent and feel helpless, frightened and intimidated.

Concealment (cont.)	Social Objective	Offender's Behavior	Victim's Perception
		Commonly denies the abuse if confronted. May dissociate or forget parts or all of the experience.	May dissociate or forget parts or all of the experience.

Identifying and treating offenders is a major obstacle in the prevention of child sexual abuse. Adolescent offenders are a crucial group that are just beginning to receive attention. Most people who sexually abuse children start their offending behavior during their adolescence or early adulthood. While female pedophiles are not well researched or accurately identified, we know that about half of male pedophiles have become sexually aroused toward children by age 15 to 17, and most begin offending by their mid-20s. Some children abuse younger children.

It is thus important to screen for sex and other offenses in adolescence and young adulthood. When this behavior is identified, it is crucial to initiate comprehensive and long-term treatment to prevent further offending. If Father James Porter had been so identified and treated during his adolescence, the lives of over 100 people could have been prevented from being damaged.

The average sex offender abuses and thus inflicts disabling wounds upon an average of five children (for non-pedophile offenders) to 135 (for male-preference pedophiles) with a range of one to hundreds of victims.

With each episode of abuse, the offender robs the child of their self-awareness, self-esteem and their childhood.

A growing problem today is that of offenders and co-offenders using the "false memory" defense to avoid facing their abusive behavior. Groups like the FMS Foundation are known to support convicted offenders, and admit that they have no way to accurately screen their members. As each offender uses this defense, more children will be abused. We must stop enabling child abusers.

The above information concerns only sexual abuse, which is 15 percent of all child abuse. The remaining 85 percent of child abuse involves physical, mental, emotional and spiritual abuse. Most offenders and many co-offenders who sexually abuse children also abuse them in these other ways.

Appendix D

ADDENDUM TO GUIDELINES AND LEGAL ASPECTS CHAPTERS (18, 19 AND 20)

The delayed discovery rule applies in cases of traumatic forgetting.

—Ferris v. Compton

D.C. Court of Appeals, 1994 (Also demonstrated in numerous other rulings.)

Contrary to criminal cases, in most civil cases a lawsuit must be filed within a certain number of years following the event that results in the lawsuit. Although states vary, lawsuits alleging child sexual abuse usually must be filed within one to three years after the victim reaches the age of majority, which is usually age 18 or 21, depending on the state. However, exceptions may exist under the "delayed discovery rule," first applied by the U.S. Supreme Court in 1949 in *Urie v. Thompson.*[344, 581, 654] The classic case is when a patient discovers years after surgery that a sponge was left in their abdomen during an operation, but would have no way of knowing that until they developed symptoms or signs.[344, 444] Thus, they may not know it during and for a long time after the statute of limitations period.

Delayed Discovery

Until the mid 1980s, survivors of child sexual abuse were held to this first limitation. Sensing the reality of traumatic forgetting, plaintiffs' (accusers') lawyers then urged courts to apply the delayed discovery rule to their cases of delayed memory of child sexual abuse. In 1986 in the case of *Tyson v. Tyson,* the Washington State Supreme Court narrowly (by a 5 to 4 decision) ruled that the lack of empirical, verifiable evidence, combined with the possibility of distorting the truth in repressed memory cases, made it impossible to determine the facts with substantial certainty.[581] While some states have followed this result, a general trend has developed toward *applying* the delayed discovery rule to repressed memory cases, based on important cases in California, Michigan, New Hampshire, Rhode Island and Washington state, which in 1989 set a precedent by allowing lawsuits to be filed within three years of the time the victim discovered that the act caused the injury for which the claim was brought.[344, 581]

Washington State has since been a model for similar legislation in nearly half the states, including Colorado, Connecticut, Florida, Illinois, Maine, Maryland, Minnesota, Oregon and Virginia, plus those listed above. In 1994, Representatives Pat Schroeder and Connie Morella co-sponsored a congressional resolution urging all states to adopt the delayed discovery rule.

Doctrine of Concealment

Courts may also apply the "doctrine of concealment" to calculate a limitations period from the moment that efforts to conceal the crime have ceased. Any coercion designed to inhibit a child from disclosing the abuse may apply, although some courts have not been willing to apply this doctrine of concealment or "continuing crimes."[344]

High Publicity Cases

During this time several cases have received high publicity, including the George Franklin case (see pages 161 and 218), the Paul Ingram case (pages 220) and more recently the case of Gary Ramona (see Chapter 19). But most cases appear to have been variations on the themes illustrated in Chapter 20. Since the Gary Ramona case, there have been up to 32 new cases filed against therapists by third parties, and before that there have been an estimated 4,000 cases filed against therapists by retractors and others. Some of these involve trivial accusations, while others are more serious. Many are settled out of court and many don't get to court. Of course, *Holly Ramona v. Gary Ramona* is scheduled for 1996.

The Gary Ramona case, whose result appears to have opened the gates for the 32 lawsuits against therapists mentioned above, was allowed into court after a trial court judge used a 14-year-old California case wherein a physician diagnosed syphilis in a woman and asked her husband to be tested also. The husband later sued the physician's hospital for inflicting emotional distress upon him.[470] It was later learned that the couple had each had a positive blood test for syphilis before the physician first saw the woman,[351] although this information was not brought up in the trial.

Just as they made up the term "false memory syndrome," FMS advocates have coined another one that has not been described in the trauma literature: "recovered memory therapy" (RMT).[215, 497] While they may like to lump all ways and techniques that helping professionals may use to assist people in their remembering and healing from the detrimental effects of abusive experiences, they have so far focused on only a few. Even though hypnosis, sodium amytal interviews and other methods of assisting a trauma survivor's memory have been used with success for decades (and for over a century for hypnosis), FMS advocates and their lawyers are currently attacking these methods above others.

Hypnosis

While they generally frown upon hypnosis, states and courts vary in the ways that they treat it. Based mostly on *criminal* cases, about half the states have ruled that a witness who has been hypnotized to help refresh their memory is *per se* incompetent to testify on any subject discussed while they were hypnotized, because the scientific evidence does not support the reliability of hypnosis. They here use the term "enhanced" to mean that the memories were *augmented*, as opposed to "refreshed," which denotes *revived*. They say that *anything remembered* from the hypnosis forward is also inadmissible.[581] If lawyers try to transpose this kind of thinking to civil cases, this places therapist and patient in a double bind, since hypnosis, which helps a person remember traumatic experiences, (thus resulting in a potential lawsuit,) may severely undermine a survivor's ability to win their case.[581]

Some courts have viewed hypnotically refreshed memory as admissible, allowing the jury to decide how much weight to give it. Others have the judge review the details of the hypnotist, the procedure and the memories, and then decide its admissibility. Still others require certain procedural safeguards, including that (1) the hypnotist be a qualified psychiatrist or psychologist experienced in using hypnosis, and who is (2) working independently of either side involved in the lawsuit, (3) the subject describes the facts to the hypnotist before hypnosis, (4) all information given the hypnotist before the hypnosis session is recorded, (5) all contact is recorded, preferably on videotape, and (6) no other person is present during any of their contact.[581] This is because hypnotized people are vulnerable to suggestion* and may lose critical judgment and may be too confident about their memories, which they may confuse with the contents of prior memory.[581]

Nearly all of these decisions have occurred in criminal cases, wherein police have hypnotized eyewitnesses, and not in therapeutic cases. Civil cases may be viewed more favorably since they seek only monetary damages and not jail time. There is also less risk of suggestibility when the hypnosis is used in therapy before any accusation is made. It is not fair to expect that such safeguards as described above will be used in therapy when there is no reason for therapist or patient to believe that the hypnotically refreshed memory may be needed in a lawsuit.[581] Even so, courts may still require that the hypnotist be qualified, avoid adding to the patient's memory, record the procedure, and that other evidence is submitted to corroborate the hypnotically refreshed testimony.[581]

Short-acting Barbiturates

The sodium amytal procedure is used an estimated 10 to 15 times each year in some hospital psychiatry units that specialize in assisting trauma survivors.[640] It was used often in military combat trauma and is now more often used to assist people with their traumatic memories of other origins, including all varieties of child abuse. While it has distinct therapeutic usefulness, when brought into court it can be used against a survivor and their therapist, as was illustrated in the Gary Ramona case. Before using any short-acting barbiturate procedure, such as sodium amytal, the psychiatrist should probably take similar precautions as described above for hypnosis.

---

* While safeguards are required for therapists and patients, attorneys are allowed to make suggestions to the jury and judge regularly, even though they may be inappropriate, untrue, over-ruled, asked to clarify, hypothetical statements or questions, or nearly any other statement or behavior. FMS advocates also regularly drop and push their own suggestions as their claims and attacks, frequently in the name of science. When addressing this issue, many in the media, advertising, organized religion, politics and others do so as well. Everyone and everything suggests regularly.

Other Therapeutic Aids

Another technique to help refresh traumatic memory has recently been the target of FMS advocates: Eye Movement Desensitization and Reprocessing (EMDR).[105] Although this procedure was only recently discovered and its clinical usefulness is in early evolution, some therapists and survivors are finding it to be helpful. It should not be used outside of a safe and ongoing therapeutic setting with a trained therapist, and we await formal reports of its results. With the large number of lawsuits that are now being filed and tried, because it was used by a recovering sexual abuse survivor it will likely eventually be attacked in court, as will other helpful therapeutic aids.

This does not mean that we will have to stop using these techniques. But we will have to be more cautious and more carefully document our work as we assist people in recovering from *traumatic experiences.* The highest risk for a *lawsuit* alleging *malpractice* against a therapist is in the case of a *retractor,* wherein there is usually great family turmoil associated with a person's *recovery* - something that may be difficult to avoid. While there have so far been few malpractice cases involving "false memory" that have proceeded through trial, the number of filed cases is rising.[344, 581]

In any lawsuit by a survivor against an accused abuser or a therapist, the therapist's qualifications, techniques and records will be closely examined and probably brought out in court. And at that time, if the therapist has been in therapy, their personal records may be subpoenaed. An experienced and competent attorney for the therapist can file a motion to "quash" the subpoena, giving clear reasons why such a subpoena is inappropriate. It will be then up to the judge to determine whether the subpoena is valid. The therapist should consult their attorney for the laws in their state and how to proceed.[444]

As therapists or survivors, we can use the above information to strengthen our work and our recovery. Neither is trained to negotiate the *expense, rigidity, unpredictability* and sometimes *mistreatment* of the legal and court systems. These characteristics can even remind us of our dysfunctional family of origin.

In this setting hypnosis and other recovery aids have gotten an unfair assessment. For example, hypnosis and guided imagery provide a setting in which a person can relax and focus on what is coming up for them in their inner life. These therapeutic aids tend to facilitate the re-experiencing and evaluating of that which the person has already experienced—although perhaps dissociated. They are time honored ways of helping people heal from traumatic experiences. But when some critics find psychological trauma and recovery, they want to debunk it. I am not aware of any sound published clinical evidence that hypnosis or any other recovery aid significantly distorts the veracity of traumatic memory.

From our knowledge of the psychology of *offenders* and their enablers, they will usually try to silence their victim any way they can.[39, 57, 67, 202, 250, 294, 295, 385, 429, 529] This may include attacking not only their memories, but any person or method that may assist them in remembering what happened and talking about it. FMS advocates are trying to "chill" or inhibit the assistance that therapists are providing for survivors of child sexual abuse. Their effectiveness will be determined by a number of factors, including our individual and collective responses. A way to begin will be to support and participate in such organizations as the *American Coalition for Abuse Awareness* (see the *Resources* section at the end of this book).

Appendix E

SOME POTENTIALLY DAMAGING SUGGESTIONS THAT MAY BE MADE ABOUT A POSSIBLE HISTORY OF CHILD SEXUAL ABUSE

(compiled from Yapko 1994)

1. **Direct**—Your symptoms seem to fit the profile of someone who was sexually abused as a child. Were you? *or* I have reason to believe you were sexually abused as a child. Can you think of any experiences you might have had that would be considered evidence of abuse?

2. **Presupposition**—The pain you had to endure is obvious from your symptoms. It seems clear to me that you were sexually abused and have repressed it. Try and remember what was done to you and by whom. *Or* I saw another client with the same symptoms that you have, and it turns out that she was sexually abused as a child and repressed it.

3. **Redefine resistance as cooperation**—When client says they were not abused, therapist says—Good, good. Denial is the first step on the road to acceptance and recovery. *Or,* I wonder what terrible things

must have happened in your childhood—things you probably can't even remember—that would cause these problems you have now.

4. **Confrontation and threat**—If you won't face facts about your past, then I can no longer work with you.

5. **Praise**—I know you have the strength to come to terms with what I know must have happened to you.

6. **Bribery**—You're so bright and sensitive, I'd sure like to have you help me with others like you once you have worked through your issues.

7. **Guilt**—How can you be a good mother if you haven't fully explored your relationship with your own mother and father?

8. **Providing biased information or misinformation**—Ambiguous pieces of "evidence," such as dreams and so called "body memories" that many therapists accept as valid purely on the basis of personal bias. A client is told, "I think you were abused as a child." They deny it. The therapist smiles knowingly, like a parent patiently waiting for the child to come to their senses. The therapist then offers matter-of-factly, a set of process suggestions: "When you're ready to get well, you may have dreams about the abuse at first. Then when you're ready to progress, you'll have images and daydreams. When you're ready to work through your problems once and for all, you'll have full-blown, vivid memories when you awaken." There is, apparently, a correct order: denial, then dreams then images, then memories.

9. **Using suggestions in hypnosis, guided imagery, guided meditations, or visualization exercises (or the equivalent).** The therapist asks suggestive questions, such as "Who are you with? What is he doing to you? Do you sense he has an erection? Where is he touching you? Don't you feel dirty and used? What is that look on his face telling you?" Up come images of abuse—surprise! Right in line with the theories the therapist has presented as fact. (Yapko 1994)

(See page 189 for explanation of this appendix.)

Appendix F

THE PROCESS OF OFFENDERS WORKING THROUGH DENIAL

(from Laflen and Sturm 1994)

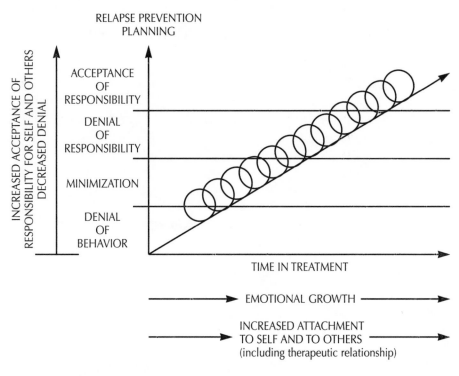

See text on page 126 for reference to this figure and Laflen and Sturm's article for a full explanation.[391a]

REFERENCES

1. Abel GG et al: Sexual offenders. in Ben-Aron MH (ed) *Clinical Criminology*. M & M Graphics, Toronto, 1985

2. Adams CBL: Examining questionable child sex abuse allegations. *Journal of Child Sexual Abuse* 3(3): 21-36, 1994

3. Adams CM: Women as perpetrators of child sexual abuse: recognition barriers. in Horton et al (eds): *The Incest Perpetrator:* A family member no one wants to treat. pp 108-125, Sage Publications, Newbury Park, CA, 1990

4. Adams JA: Significance of medical findings in suspected sexual abuse: moving towards consensus. *Journal of Child Sexual Abuse* 1(3): 91-99, 1992

5. Adler S: *The Jury:* Trial and error in the American courtroom. NY, 1994

6. Ainsworth M et al: *Patterns of Attachment:* A psychological study of the strange situation. Lawrence Erlbaum Associates, Hillsdale, NJ, 1978

7. Alkon DL: Memory storage and neural systems. *Scientific American* pp 42-50, July 1989

8. American Medical Association, Council on Scientific Affairs: Mental health consequences of interpersonal and family violence: implications for the practitioner. CSA Report (BCA-93) Chicago, 1993

9. American Medical Association Council on Scientific Affairs: Memories of childhood sexual abuse. CSA Report (5-A-94), Chicago, 1994

---

* Indicates writings with a "false memory syndrome" advocacy or point of view.

10.   American Professional Society on the Abuse of Children: *The Advisor* (a long news journal updating information about child abuse). 332 S. Michigan, Suite 1600, Chicago IL 60604
(312) 554-0166

11.   American Psychiatric Association: *Diagnostic and Statistical Manual* of mental disorders (DSM-4). American Psychiatric Press, Washington DC, 1994

12.   American Psychiatric Association, personal communication with ethics section, Washington, DC, September 1994

13.   American Psychiatric Association: Statement on memories of sexual abuse. Washington, DC, reprinted in *Moving Forward* 6(2):
8-9, 1994

14.   American Humane Association: *National Study* on child neglect and abuse reporting. AHA, Denver, 1978

15.   Anonymous: Coming out: my experience as a mental patient. *Journal of Psychosocial Nursing* 31: 17-20, 1993

16.   Arnold RP et al: Medical problems of adults who were sexually abused in childhood. *British Medical Journal* 300: 705-708, 1990

17.   Australian *60 Minutes* newsprogram: Witness [ie., Ralph Underwager] for "Mr. Bubbles." Australia, 5 August 1990

18.   Bachman G et al: Childhood sexual abuse and the consequences in adult women. *Obstetrics and Gynecology* 71: 631-642, 1988

19.   Backus J, Stannard B: Your memories are not false: A reply to the False Memory Syndrome Foundation. Private printing, available free for a self-addressed envelope and $.65 in postage from the authors at Box 16014, San Francisco, CA 94116, revised edition, 1994

20.   Baddeley A: The psychology of remembering and forgetting. (pages 33-61) in Butler T (ed): *Memory:* History, culture and the mind. Basil Blackwell, NY, 1989

21.   Bagley C: The prevalence and mental health sequels of child abuse in a community sample of women aged 18-27. *Canadian Journal of Community Mental Health* 10(1): 103-116, 1991

22.   Baillargeon R et al: Location memory in 8 month old infants in a non-search AB task: further evidence. *Cognitive Development* 4: 345-367, 1989

23.   Ballard-Scott R, Stoudemire A: Factitious apraxia. *International Journal of Psychiatry in Medicine* 22(3): 275-280, 1992

24.   Banks WP, Pezdek K (eds): The Recovery of Lost Childhood Memories for Traumatic Events. Special issues of *Consciousness & Cognition,* Summer 1994 and Winter 1995

25.   Barabal R et al: The social-cognitive development of abused children.

Journal of Consulting and Clinical Psychology 49: 508-516, 1981

26.   Barbaree H, Marshall W: Deviant sexual arousal, offense history and demographic variables as predictors of reoffense among child molesters. *Behavioral Sciences and the Law* 6: 267-280, 1988

27.   Barber TX: *Hypnosis: A Scientific Approach*. Van Nostrand Reinhold, NY, 1969

28.   Barclay CR, DeCooke PA: Ordinary everyday memories. (pp 92-125) in Neisser U, Winograd E: *Remembering Reconsidered:* Ecological and traditional approaches to the study of memory. Cambridge University Press, NY, 1988

29.   *Barden RC: A proposal to finance preparation of model legislation titled Mental Health Consumer Protection Act. sponsored by Illinois FMS Society, Hoffman Estates, IL, August 1994

30.   Barker LR, Whitfield CL: Chapter 21 - Alcoholism. in Barker LR et al (eds): *Principles of Ambulatory Medicine*. Williams & Wilkins, Baltimore, 1991

31.   Barrett MJ: Mothers' role in incest. *Journal of Child Sexual Abuse* 2(3): 141-143, 1993

32.   Barrett MJ, Scott W: Commentary 1 (on Schissler reference). *Family Therapy Networker* pp 73-76, Mar/Apr, 1994

33.   Barsalou LW: The content and organization of autobiographical memories. (pp 193-243) in Neisser U, Winograd E: *Remembering Reconsidered:* Ecological and traditional approaches to the study of memory. Cambridge University Press, NY, 1988

34.   Barstow D: A critical examination of the "false memory syndrome." *Family Violence & Sexual Assault Bulletin* 9(4): 21-23, 1994

35.   Bass A: Medical board sets rules for psychotherapists. *Boston Globe* p27, 25 May 1994

36.   Bass E, Davis L: Honoring the Truth, from the 3rd ed of *The Courage to Heal*. Harper Collins, NY, 1994

37.   Bateson G: *Steps to an Ecology of Mind*. Ballentine, NY 1972.

38.   Beck J, van der Kolk B: Reports of childhood incest and current behavior of chronically hospitalized psychotic women. *American Journal of Psychiatry* 144: 1474-1476, 1987

39.   Becker JV: Offenders: Characteristics and treatment. *The Future of Children* 4(2): 176-197, 1994

40.   Begelman DA: McHugh's psychiatric misadventures. Revised from paper given at the Tenth International Conference on Multiple Personality & Dissociative States, Nov 15-17, Chicago, 1993

41.   Behrman RE (ed): *Sexual Abuse of Children*. The future of children 4(2), Summer/Fall 1994

42.   Beisel DR: America in denial. *Journal of Psychohistory* 21(3): 245-256, 1994

43.   Beitchman JH et al: A review of the long term effects of child sexual abuse. *Child Abuse and Neglect* 16: 101-118, 1992

43a.   Belkin DS et al: Psychopathology and a history of sexual abuse. *Journal of Interpersonal Violence* 9(4): 535-547, 1994

44.   Benedek EP, Schetky DH: Allegations of sexual abuse in child custody cases. Paper given in 1984, cited in Everson and Boat 1989.

45.   Benedek EP, Schetky DH: Problems in validation of allegations of sexual abuse: parts 1 & 2. *Journal of American Academy of Child and Adolescent Psychiatry* 6: 112-115, 116-121, 1987

46.   Berendzen R: Interview on *Larry King Live*, CNN, 17 Sept. 1993

47.   Berendzen R: *Come Here*. Villard, NY, 1993

48.   Berghold J: The social trance: psychological obstacles to progress in history. *Journal of Psychohistory* 19(2): 221-243, Fall, 1991

49.   Berliner L, Wheeler JR: Treating the effects of sexual abuse on children. *Journal of Interpersonal Violence* 2: 415-434, 1987

50.   Berliner L et al: Coping with a hostile media. *The (APSAC) Advisor* 3(4): 8-9, Fall 1990

51.   Berliner L, Conte J: The process of victimization: the victim's perspective. *Child Abuse and Neglect* 14(1): 29-40, 1990

52.   Berliner L, Conte J: Sexual abuse evaluations: conceptual and empirical obstacles. *Child Abuse and Neglect* 1993

53.   Bernstein AEH, Blacher RS: The recovery of a memory from three months of age. *The Psychoanalytic Study of the Child* 22: 156-161, 1967

54.   Birrell P: An open letter to the professional advisory board of the FMSF. *Moving Forward* Sept 2(5): 4-5 1993

55.   Bissell L: Dynamics of denial in addictions. Personal communication, Springfield, IL, 1975

56.   Blake DD: Treatment outcome research on PTSD. *Clinical Newsletter*, National Center for Post-Traumatic Stress Disorder, Spring 1993

57.   Blanchard GT: Differential diagnosis of sex offenders: distinguishing characteristics of the sex addict. *American Journal of Preventive Psychiatry & Neurology* 2(3): 45-47, 1990

58.   Bliss EL: Multiple personalities. *Archives of General Psychiatry* 147: 887-892, 1990

59.   Bloom SL: Hearing the survivor's voice: sundering the walls of denial. *Journal of Psychohistory* 21(4): 461-477, Spring 1994

59a.   Bloom SL: When good people do bad things: Meditations on the "backlash." *Journal of Psychohistory* 22(3): 273-304 (Winter), 1994

60.   *Body Memories:* Radical perspectives on child sexual abuse. Issue 5/6,

Spring/Summer 1993

60a.   Boland PL, Quirk SA: Repressed memories: should child abuse be prosecuted decades after an alleged incident occurred? *American Bar Association Journal*, p 42, September 1994

61.   Bolen JS: *Crossing to Avalon:* A woman's midlife pilgrimage. Harper Collins, San Francisco, 1994

62.   Bolen JS: Wise-woman archetype. (audiotape) Sounds True, 1993

63.   Boodman SG: Cover story of Kathy O'Connor; the professional debate over an emotional issue; advocacy group for "aggrieved" parents fights back. *Washington Post* Health section, April 12 1994

63a.   Bor J: Articles on FMSF conference. *Baltimore Sun*, December 9 & 11, 1994

64.   Borden TA, LaTerz JD: Mother/daughter incest and ritual abuse: the ultimate taboos. *Treating Abuse Today* 3(4) 5-8, 1994

65.   *Boss K: True doubter. *Pacific* from the *Seattle Times*, September 1994

65a.   Boswell J: *The Kindness of Strangers:* The Abandonment of Children in Western Europe from Late Antiquity to the Renaissance. Vintage Books, NY 1990

66.   Botash AS et al: Acute care of sexual assault victims. *Patient Care* pp 112-137, 15 August 1994

67.   Bowen D: personal communication, Merritt Island, FL, 22 June 1994

68.   Bower GH: Mood and memory. *American Psychologist* 36(2): 129-148, Feb 1981

68a.   Branden N: *The Psychology of Romantic Love*. Bantam, NY, 1981

69.   Braun BG: BASK model of dissociation (parts 1 & 2). *Dissociation* 1: 4-23, 1: 16-23, 1988

70.   Braun BG: Psychotherapy of the survivor of incest with a dissociative disorder. *Psychiatric Clinics of North America* 12(2): 307-324, 1989

71.   Bregan PR: *The War Against Children*. St. Martin's Press, NY, 1993

72.   Bregan PR: *Talking Back to Prozac*. Thomas Dunne/St. Martin's, NY, 1994

73.   Bregan PR: *Toxic Psychiatry:* Why therapy, empathy and love must replace the drug, ECT and biochemical theories of the "new psychiatry." St Martins Press, NY, 1994

74.   Breier A et al: Early parental loss and development of adult psychopathology. *Archives of General Psychiatry* 45: 987-993, 1988

75.   Brende JO: The use of hypnosis in post-traumatic conditions. In Kelly WE (ed): *Post-Traumatic Stress Disorder and the War Veteran Patient*. Brunner/Mazel, NY, 1985

76.   Bremner JD et al: Neurobiology of PTSD. in Pynoos RS (ed): *Posttraumatic Stress Disorder*. Sidran Press, Lutherville, MD, 1993

77.   Bremner JD et al: Use of the structured clinical interview for DSM-4 dissociative disorders for systematic assessment of dissociative symptoms of PTSD. *American Journal of Psychiatry* 150 (7): 1011-1014, 1993

78.   Brenner I: A twentieth century demonologic neurosis. *Journal of Psychohistory* 21(4): 501-504, 1994

79.   Brenner JD et al: *Believe the Children Newsletter:* Ritual child abuse: definitions, typology and prevalence. (Box 26-8462, Chicago, 60626) vol 10, Fall 1993

80.   Brett EA, Ostroff R: Imagery and PTSD: an overview. *American Journal of Psychiatry* 142(4): 417-424, 1985

81.   Brewer WF: What is autobiographical memory? (pp 25-50). in Rubin DC (ed): *Autobiographical Memory.* Cambridge University Press, London, 1986

82.   Briere J: Adult memories of childhood trauma: current controversies. Talk given at American Psychiatric Association annual convention, San Francisco, 1993; and personal communication, June, 1994

83.   Briere J: Medical symptoms, health risk and child sexual abuse. *Mayo Clinic Proceedings* 67: 6034, 1992

84.   Briere J, Conte J: Self-reported amnesia for abuse in adults molested as children. *Journal of Traumatic Stress* 6(1): 21-31, 1993

85.   Briere J, Runtz M: Post sexual abuse trauma. *Journal of Interpersonal Violence* 2(4): 367-379, 1987

86.   Briere J, Runtz M: Symptomatology associated with childhood sexual victimization in a nonclinical adult sample. *Child Abuse and Neglect* 12: 51-59, 1988

87.   Briere J, Zaidi LY: Sexual abuse histories and sequelae in female psychiatric emergency room patients. *American Journal of Psychiatry* 146: 1602-1606, 1989

88.   Briere JN, Elliott DM: Immediate and long-term impacts of child sexual abuse. *The Future of Children* 4(2): 54-69, 1994

89.   Brisentine R: cited in Hechler D: Who's telling the truth? When memories tear families apart. *First,* 18 April 1994

89a.   Brown D: Pseudomemories, the standard of science and the standard of case in trauma treatment. *American Journal of Clinical Hypnosis* 37:1-24, 1995

90.   Brown GR, Anderson B: Psychiatric morbidity in adult inpatients with childhood histories of sexual and physical abuse. *American Journal of Psychiatry* 148: 55-61, 1991

91.   Brown S: *Treating Adult Children of Alcoholics:* A developmental perspective. Wiley, NY, 1988

92.   Browne A, Finkelhor D: Impact of child sexual abuse: a review of the

literature. *Psychological Bulletin* 99(1): 66-77, 1986

93.   Bruhn AR: *Earliest Childhood Memories.* Praeger, NY, 1990

94.   Bruhn AR: The Early Memories Procedure. Available from the author at 7910 Woodmont Ave, Suite 1300, Bethesda, MD 20814 (301-654-2255), 1989

95.   Bruhn AR: The Early Memories Procedure: a projective test of autobiographical memory, parts 1 & 2. *Journal of Personality Assessment* 58(1): 1-15 and 58(2): 326-346, 1992

96.   Bruhn AR: *The Interpretation of Autobiographical Memories.* Praeger, NY, in process for 1995

97.   Bruhn AR: Chapter 20. Early memories in personality. in J Butcher (ed): *Practical Considerations in Personality Assessment.* Oxford University Press (in press)

98.   Bryer JB et al: Childhood sexual and physical abuse as factors in adult psychiatric illness. *American Journal of Psychiatry* 144: 1426-1430, 1987

99.   Burgess A, Holmstrom L: Rape trauma syndrome. *American Journal of Psychiatry* 131: 981-986, 1974

100. Burgess A, Holmstrom LL: Sexual trauma of children and adolescents: pressure, sex, and secrecy. *Nursing Clinics of North America* 10(3): 551-563, 19?

101. Burgess AW et al: Abused to abuser: antecedents of socially deviant behavior. *American Journal of Psychiatry* 144: 1431-1436, 1987

102. Burgess A et al: Memory presentations of childhood sexual abuse. Submitted for publication, Philadelphia, 1994

103. Burgess A, Hartman CR: Children's drawings. *Child Abuse and Neglect* 17: 161-168, 1993

104. Bunge N: Child abuse and creativity: a new look at Sherwood Anderson's breakdown. *Journal of Psychohistory* 20(4): 413-426, 1993

105. Butler K: Too good to be true? EMDR's supporters are reporting dramatic results. *Family Therapy Networker* November/December, pp 19-31, 1993

106. Butler K: Memory on trial. *San Francisco Chronicle,* This World. 24 July 1994

107. Butler K: Clashing memories, mixed messages. *Los Angeles Times Magazine,* 26 June, 1994

107a. Bybee D, Mowbray CT: An analysis of allegations of sexual abuse in a multi-victim daycare center case. *Child Abuse and Neglect* 17: 767-786, 1993

108. Caffey J: Multiple fractures in the long bones of infants suffering from chronic subdural hematoma. *American Journal of Roentgenology.* 56:

163-73, 1946

109. Calof DL: A century of progress. *Treating Abuse Today* 1:1, Mar/Apr 1991

110. Calof D: Facing the truth about false memory. *Family Therapy Networker* 17: 38-45 (Sept/Oct) 1993a

111. Calof D: An interview with the FMSF, Inc, parts 1 & 2 (an interview with Pamela Freyd). *Treating Abuse Today* 3(3 & 4), 1993b

112. Calof D: Long letter to producer at KOMO-TV. Unpublished, Seattle 18 May 1994a

113. Calof DL: From traumatic dissociation to repression: origins of the "false memory syndrome" hypothesis. *Treating Abuse Today* 4(4): 24-34, 1994

114. Calof D: It's the dissociation, stupid! How the "false memory syndrome" lobby ignores traumatic dissociation and sets up "robust repression" as its strawman. *Treating Abuse Today* 4(5), 1994b

115. Calof DL: A conversation with Michael D Yapko PhD, Parts 1 & 2. *Treating Abuse Today* 4(5&6), 1994c

116. Calof DL: Personal Communications, Seattle, WA, 1994

116a. Calof DL: Debate with E. Loftus on "False Memories." Seattle, June 5 1994

117. Calvi B: The sexual abuse of males: current literature and research recommendations. *Treating Abuse Today* 4 (5&6), 1994

118. Cameron C: Women survivors confronting their abusers: issues, decisions and outcomes. *Journal of Child Sexual Abuse* 3(1): 7-35, 1994

119. Cameron N: *Personality Development and Psychopathology.* Houghton Mifflin, Boston, 1963

120. Cameron W: Personal communication. Miami, July 16, 1994

121. Carmen EJ et al: Victims of violence and psychiatric illness. *American Journal of Psychiatry* 141: 378-383, 1984

122. Carnes P: Workshop on sexual addiction and trauma. Philadelphia, 13 & 14 September 1993

122a. Cashdan S: *Object Relations Therapy:* Using the Relationship. W.W. Norton, NY, 1988

123. *Ceci SJ: Cognitive and social factors in children's testimony. Paper from talk given at APA, 1993

124. *Ceci SJ et al: Recalling nonevents: an experimental investigation of source misattribution errors. *Consciousness & Cognition* 9(4), Summer 1994

125. Cerma LS: *Human Memory:* Research and theory. Ronald Press, NY, 1972

126. Chaffin M: Assessment and treatment of child sexual abusers. *Journal of Interpersonal Violence* 9(2): 224-237, 1994

127. Chamberlain D: *Babies Remember Birth*. Tarcher, Los Angeles, 1988

128. Charney DS et al: Psychobiologic mechanisms of PTSD. *Archives of General Psychiatry* 50(4): 294-305, 1993

128a. Chafetz GS and Chafetz ME: *Obsession*, Crown, New York, 1994

129. Chu J: Ten traps for therapists in the treatment of trauma survivors. *Dissociation* 1: 24-32, 1990

130. Chu JA, Dill DL: Dissociative symptoms in relation to childhood physical and sexual abuse. *American Journal of Psychiatry* 147: 887-892, 1990

131. Classen C et al: Trauma and dissociation. *Bulletin of the Meninger Clinic*. 57(2): 178-194, 1993

132. Clute S: Adult survivor litigation as an integral part of the therapeutic process. *Journal of Child Sexual Abuse* 2(1) 121-127, 1993

132a. Cole NJ: Therapy as Grief. *Center for Trauma and Dissociation Newsletter* 2(8) Dcember 1994

133. Cole P, Putnam FW: Effect of incest on self and social functioning: a developmental psychopathology perspective. *Journal of Consulting and Clinical Psychology* 60: 174-184, 1992

134. Collet L: Hard lessons from the [Gary] Ramona case. *Treating Abuse Today* 4(5): 11-14, 1994

135. Comstock CM: Believe it or not: the challenge to the therapist of patient memory. *Treating Abuse Today* 2(6): 23-26, 1992

136. Concensus working committee (ad hoc) on internal corroboration of abuse memories, *American Coalition for Abuse Awareness,* Annual Meeting, Chicago, 30 April & 1 May 1994

136a. Connors ME, Morse W: Sexual abuse and eating disorders: A review. *International Journal of Eating Disorders* 13(1): 1-11, 1993

137. Conte JR: Child sexual abuse: Awareness and backlash. *The Future of Children* 4(2): 224- 232, 1994

138. Conte JR, Schuerman JR: The effects of sexual abuse on children. *Journal of Interpersonal Violence* 2: 380-390, 1988

139. Conte JR, Schuerman JR: Factors associated with an increased impact of child sexual abuse. *Child Abuse and Neglect* 11(2): 201-211, 1987

140. Coons PM: Psychiatric problems associated with child abuse: a review in Jacobsen JJ (ed): *Psychiatric Sequelae of Child Abuse*. CC Thomas, Springfield, IL, 1986

141. Coons PM et al: Multiple personality disorder. *Journal of Nervous and Mental Diseases* 176: 519-527, 1988

142. Coons PM et al: Posttraumatic aspects of the treatment of victims of sexual abuse and incest. *Psychiatric Clinics of North America* 12: 335-338, 1989

143.   Coons PM, Millstein V: Self-mutilation associated with dissociative disorders. *Dissociation* 3(2): 81-87, 1990

144.   Corwin DL, Olafson E: Clinical recognition of sexually abused children. Special issue of *Child Abuse and Neglect* 17(1), 1993

144a.   Cotton P: Biology enters repressed memory fray. *Journal of the American Medical Association* 272:1925-1726, 1994

145.   *A Course in Miracles.* Foundation for Inner Peace, Tiburon, CA, 1976

146.   Courtois CA: The memory retrieval process in incest survivor therapy. *Journal of Child Sexual Abuse* 1(1): 15-31, 1992

147.   Courtois CA: Adult survivors of sexual abuse. *Primary Care* 20(2): 433-446, June 1993

148.   Courtois CA: Vicarious traumatization of the therapist. *Clinical Newsletter* National Center for PTSD pp 8-9, Spring 1993

149.   Courtois C: *Healing the Incest Wound:* Adult survivors in therapy. WW Norton, NY, 1989

150.   Courtois CA, Watts DL: Counseling adult women who experienced incest in childhood or adolescence. *Personnel and Guidance Journal* pp 275-279, January, 1982

151.   Courtois CA: Walking a fine line: Issues of assessment and diagnosis of women molested in childhood. in Classen C (ed) *Treating Women Molested in Childhood.* in press for publication

151a: *Crews F: The revenge of the repressed: Part II. *The New York Review* December 1, 1994

152.   Craine LS et al: Prevalence of a history of sexual abuse among female psychiatric patients in a state hospital system. *Hospital and Community Psychiatry* 39: 300-304, 1988

152a.   Crawford C: *Mommie Dearest.* William Morrow, NY 1978; Berkley Publishing Group, 1984

153.   Crick F: Interview on *Thinking Allowed* by J Mishlove, PBS, 6 August 1994

153a.   Crimmins B: Memory, media and justice. *The Boston Phoenix,* 9 April 1993

154.   Crnich JE, Crnich KA: *Shifting the Burden of Truth:* Suing child sexual abusers - a legal guide for survivors and their supporters. Recollex Publishing, 1992

155.   Cronin J: False memory: The controversy surrounding "false memory" and child abuse. Z *Magazine* pp 31-37, April 1994

156.   Cronin J: personal communications, Baltimore, June and July 1994

157.   Crook L: personal communications. Baltimore, 1 April and 23 May 1994

158.   Cross TP, Saxe L: A critique of the validity of polygraph testing in child sexual abuse cases. *Journal of Child Sexual Abuse* 1(4): 19-33, 1992

159. Cruz Lat E: Holly takes the stand. *Napa Valley Register,* April 1994
160. Cruz Lat E: Ramona family psychiatrist takes stand. *Napa Valley Register,* 27 April 1994
161. Cruz Lat E: Ramona trial. *Napa Valley Register,* Coverage from March, April & May 1994
162. Cunningham J et al: Childhood sexual abuse and medical complaints in adult women. *Journal of Interpersonal Violence* 3: 131-144, 1988
163. Curtis D: Trauma expert testifies to validity of memories. *San Francisco Chronicle,* April 1994
164. Cutting LK: Hers: give and take. *New York Times Sunday Magazine,* 31 October, pp 52 & 54, October 1993
165. Dalenberg CJ: Making and finding memories: a commentary on the "represssed memory" controversy. *Journal of Child Sexual Abuse* 3(3): 109-118, 1994
166. Dare C: Denial and childhood sexual abuse. *Journal of Forensic Psychology* 4(1): 1-4, 1993
167. The darkest secret. *People,* pp 88-94, 10 June 1991
168. Darnton N: The pain of the last taboo. *Newsweek,* pp 70-72, 7 October 1991
169. Davidoff DA et al: Neurobehavioral sequelae of minor head injury: a consideration of post-concussive syndrome vs PTSD. *Cognitive Rehabilitation* 6(2): 8-13, 1988
169a. Davidson J: Issues in the diagnosis of post-traumatic stress disorder. in Pynois RS (ed): *Post-Traumatic Stress Disorder: A Clinical Review.* Sidran Press, Lutherville, MD, 1993
170. Deaton W et al: *The Child Sexual Abuse Custody Dispute Annotated Bibliography.* Sage, Thousand Oaks, CA, 1994
171. Deblinger E et al: The impact of a history of child sexual abuse on maternal response to allegations of sexual abuse concerning her child. *Journal of Child Sexual Abuse* 3(3): 67-75, 1994
172. Defense expert resigns. *Believe the Children* Newsletter, Fall 1993
173. deJong AR, Rose M: Frequency and significance of physical evidence in legally proven cases of child sexual abuse. *Pediatrics* 84(6): 1022-1026, 1989
174. deMause L: The universality of incest. *Journal of Psychohistory* 19(2): 123-164, Fall 1991
175. deMause L: It's time to sacrifice...our children. *Journal of Psychohistory* 18(2), Fall 1990
176. deMause L: The history of child abuse. *Sexual Addiction and Compulsivity* 1(1): 77-91, 1994
177. Dembo R et al: Physical abuse, sexual victimization and illicit drug use.

Violence and Victims 4: 121-138, 1989

178.   Dewald PA: Effects on an adult of incest in childhood. *Journal of the American Psychoanalytic Association* 37(4): 997-1014, 1989

179.   deYoung M: Self-injurious behavior in incest victims: a research note. *Child Welfare* 61: 577-584, 1982

180.   Dissociation and dissociative disorders: Part 1 8(9) and Part 2 8(10). *The Harvard Mental Health Letter*, March and April 1992

181.   *Doe J (written by Pamela Freyd): How could this happen? Coping with a false accusation of incest and rape. *Issues in Child Abuse Accusations,* 3: 154-165, 1991

181a.   Doehr E: The false memory movement's political agenda. *Treating Abuse Today* 4(6): 14-20, 1994

182.   Dollard J, Miller N: *Personality and Psychotherapy.* McGraw-Hill, NY, 1950

183.   Dolon YM: *Resolving Sexual Abuse:* Solution focused and Ericksonian hypnosis for adult survivors. WW Norton, NY, 1991

184.   Dolon Y: "only once...": brief treatment of a previously dissociated [forgotten] incest case. *Journal of Strategic and Systemic Therapies* 8(4): 3-8, 1989

185.   Domino JV, Haber, JD: Prior physical and sexual abuse in women with chronic headache: clinical correlates. *Headache* 27: 310-14, 1987

186.   Donaldson MA, Gardner R: Diagnosis and treatment of traumatic stress among women after childhood incest. in Figley C (ed): *Trauma and Its Wake.* Brunner/Mazel, NY, 1985

187.   Donovan DM: Darkness invisible. *Journal of Psychohistory* 19(2): 165-184, Fall 1991

188.   Donovan DM: Traumatology: What's in a name? *Journal of Traumatic Stress* 6(3) 409-411, 1993

189.   Donovan DM, McIntyre D: *Healing the Hurt Child.* WW Norton, NY, 1990

190.   Drossman DA et al: Sexual and physical abuse in women with functional or organic gastrointestinal disorders. *Annals of Internal Medicine* 113: 828-833, 1990

191.   Dutton D, Painter SL: Traumatic bonding: the development of emotional attachment in battered women and other relationships of intermittent abuse. *Victimology* 6: 139-155, 1981

192.   Earls CM, David H: Early family and sexual experiences of male and female prostitutes. *Canada's Mental Health* 38: 7-11, 1990

193.   Edwall GE et al: Psychological correlates of sexual abuse in adolescent girls in chemical dependency treatment. *Adolescence* 24: 279-288, 1989

194.   Efran JS et al: *Language, Structure and Change:* Frameworks of mean-

ing in psychotherapy. WW Norton, NY, 1990

195.   Efran JS, Greene MA: Overpromised, underresearched. Book review in
        Family Therapy Networker, Sept/Oct, pp 97-102, 1994

195a.   Egendorf et al: Cited in reference 326 below.

196.   Einbender AJ, Friedrich WN: Psychological functioning and behavior of
        sexually abused girls. *Journal of Consulting and Clinical Psychology* 57:
        155-157, 1989

197.   Ellenberger HF: *The Discovery of The Unconscious.* Basic Books, NY,
        1970

198.   Ellenson GS: Detecting a history of incest: a predictive syndrome. *Social
        Casework* 66: 525-532, 1985

199.   Elliot DM, Briere J: Sexual abuse trauma among professional women:
        validating the trauma symptom checklist - 40 (TSC-40). *Child Abuse and
        Neglect* 16: 391-398, 1992

200.   Elliott DM: Impaired object relations in professional women molested as
        children. *Psychotherapy* 31: 79-86, 1984

201.   Elvik SL: Professionals under fire - delayed memories vs. the false mem-
        ory syndrome. *Journal of Child Sexual Abuse* 3(3): 123-125, 1994

202.   Emrick RL: Child sexual abuse: a closer look at offenders, offense cycle,
        process of abuse, and victim trauma. Unpublished manuscript, 1994

203.   Emrick RL: *Sexual Offenders:* A provider's handbook for a structural
        cognitive behavioral intervention. Sage Publications, in review

204.   Engle B: *The Right to Innocence:* Healing the trauma of childhood sexu-
        al abuse. Ivy Books, NY, 1989

205.   Erdelyi MH: Repression, reconstruction and defense. in Singer JL (ed):
        Repression and Dissociation. University Chicago Press, 1990

206.   *Ernsdorf GM, Loftus EF: Let sleeping memories lie? words of caution
        about tolling the statute of limitations in cases of memory repression.
        Journal of Criminal Law and Criminology 84(1): 129-174, 1993

207.   Everson MD, Boat BW: False allegations of sexual abuse by children
        and adolescents. *Journal of American Academy of Child and Adolescent
        Psychiatry* 28: 230-235, 1989

208.   Everson MD et al: Beliefs among professionals about rates of false alle-
        gations of child sexual abuse. Psychiatry Dept, NC, Chapel Hill (submit-
        ted for publication) 1994

209.   Everson MD et al: Maternal support following disclosure of incest.
        Annual Progress in Child Psychiatry and Child Development 9: 292-306,
        1990

210.   Fact Sheet and other compiled data: National Center on Child Abuse
        and Neglect, Gaithersburg, MD, 1993

211.   Faller KC: Is the child victim of sexual abuse telling the truth? *Child

Abuse and Neglect 8: 473-481, 1984

212. Faller KC: Child Sexual Abuse: An interdisciplinary manual for diagnosis, case management and treatment. Columbia University Press, NY, 1988

213. Faller KC: Can therapy induce false allegations of sexual abuse? *The APSAC Advisor* 5(3- summer): 3-6, 1992

214. Faller KC: Ritual abuse: a continuum of belief. *Believe the Children Newsletter* vol 10, Fall 1993

215. *False Memory Syndrome Foundation *newsletter.* 1991-present (from December 8, 1991 to February 29, 1992 it was not named or called the FMS newsletter), 3401 Market St, Philadelphia, PA, 19104

216. False prophets of the false memory syndrome. Videotape from *Cavalcade Productions,* Ukiah, CA, 1993

217. Famularo R et al: Psychiatric diagnoses of maltreated children: preliminary findings. *Journal of the American Academy of Child and Adolescent Psychiatry* 31: 863-867, 1992

218. Felitti VJ: Long-term medical consequences of incest, rape, and molestation. *Southern Medical Journal* 84(3): 328-331, 1991

219. Felitti VJ et al: Women abused as children. *Patient Care.* pp169-180, 15 November 1993

220. Felitti VJ: Childhood sexual abuse, depression and family dysfunction in adult abuse patients. *Southern Medical Journal* 86(7): 732-736, 1993

221. Ferenczi S: Confusion of tongues between adults and the child: the language of tenderness and passion. In Balint M (ed): *Final contributions to the Problems and Methods of Psychoanalysis.* (pp 156-167) Hogarth Press, London, 1955 and reproduced in Masson 1984 below

222. Figley CR (ed): *Trauma and its Wake:* The study and treatment of posttraumatic stress disorder, vol 2. Brunner/Mazel, NY, 1986

223. Finkelhor D: Risk factors in the sexual victimization of children. *Child Abuse & Neglect* 4: 265-273, 1980

224. Finkelhor D et al: Sexual abuse in a national survey of adult men and women: Prevalence, characteristics, and risk factors. *Child Abuse and Neglect* 14: 19-28, 1990

225. Finkelhor D: Current information on the scope and nature of child sexual abuse. *The Future of Children* 4(2): 31-53, 1994

226. Fitzpatrick FL: *The Survivor Activist.* (52 Lyndon Rd, Cranston, RI 02905-1121), vol 2(3), Summer issue 1994

227. Fitzpatrick FL: Isolation and silence: a male survivor speaks out about clergy abuse. *Moving Forward* 3(1): 4-8, 1994

228. Fivush R, Hamond NC: Autobiographical memory across the preschool years: toward reconceptualizing childhood amnesia. in Fivush R,

Hudson J (eds): *Knowing and Remembering in Young Children.* Cambridge University Press, NY, 1990

229. Ford CW: *Compassionate Touch:* The role of human touch in healing and recovery. Fireside/Parkside, Simon & Schuster, 1993

230. Forward S, Buck C: *Toxic Parents.* Bantam, NY, 1989

231. Franklin E: Repressed memories and the legal system. Talk given in Seattle, WA, May 1994

232. Franklin E, Wright W: *Sins of the Father.* Crown, NY, 1991

232a. Fraser S: Freud's final seduction. *Saturday Night.* March 1994

233. Fredrickson R: *Repressed Memories:* A journey to recovery from sexual abuse. Simon & Schuster Fireside/Parkside, NY, 1992

234. Fredrickson R: The offender system. Talk given at annual meeting of the American Coalition for Abuse Awareness, Chicago, 1 May 1994

235. Fredrickson R: personal communications, May 1994

236. Freud A: *The Ego and the Mechanisms of Defense.* International University Press, 1966

237. Freud S: The aetiology of hysteria. Reprinted in Masson, 1984

238. Freyd JJ: Theoretical and personal perspectives on the delayed memory debate. Paper presented at Center for Mental Health at Foote Hospital's continuing education conference: Controversies Around Recovered Memories, Ann Arbor, MI, 7 August 1993

239. Freyd JJ: Dr Jennifer Freyd goes public: parents are FMSF founders. *Moving Forward* 2(5): 6-11, 1993

240. Freyd JJ: personal communications. Eugene, OR, 1993 and 1994

241. Freyd JJ: Betrayal—trauma: traumatic amnesia as an adaptive response to childhood abuse. *Ethics and Behavior.* in press 4(4), 1994

242. Freyd JJ: *Betrayal Trauma.* Harvard University Press, Cambridge, MA, (in preparation)

243. Freyd JJ, Birrell P: Memo to psychology faculty, Eugene, OR, 9 Aug 1993

244. *Freyd PJ et al: "FMS" discussion. 700 Club, The Family Channel, 10 August, 1993

245. Freyd PJ, Crimmins B: Radio interview on WRKO AM680, Boston, 31 March 1994

246. *Freyd PJ: personal communication (letter to and from her), April 1994

247. *Freyd PJ: Dear friends. *FMSF Newsletter,* May 1994

248. Fried S: War of remembrance: how the problems of one Philadelphia family created the False Memory Syndrome Foundation. *Philadelphia,* January 1994

249. Friedman SA: personal communication, Baltimore, MD, 1994

250. Friedman S: Outpatient treatment of child molesters. Practitioner's

Resource Series, Professional Resource Exchange, Sarasota, FL, 1991

251. Friedrich WN et al: Behavior problems in sexually abused young children. *Journal of Pediatric Psychology* 11: 47-57, 1986

252. Friedrich WN et al: Behavior problems in young sexually abused boys. *Journal of Interpersonal Violence* 3: 21-27, 1988

253. Friedrich WN: *Casebook of Sexual Abuse Treatment*. WW Norton, NY, 1991

254. Fritz G et al: A comparison of males and females who were sexually molested as children. *Journal of Sex and Marital Therapy* 7: 54-59, 1981 (60% of 412 male & 10% of 540 female college students identified a female perpetrator of sexual abuse)

255. Fromuth M, Burkhart B: Childhood sexual victimization among college men. *Violence and Victims* 2(4): 241-253, 1987

256. Frumuth ME: The relationship of childhood sexual abuse with later psychological and sexual adjustment in a sample of college women. *Child Abuse and Neglect* 10: 5-15, 1986

257. Fryer GE et al: The child protective service worker: a profile of needs, attitudes, and utilization of professional resources. *Child Abuse and Neglect* 12: 481-490, 1988

258. Gagnon J: Female child victims of sex offenses. *Social Problems* 13: 176-192, 1965

259. Gale J et al: Sexual abuse in young children. *Child Abuse and Neglect* 12: 163-170, 1988

260. Ganaway GK: personal communications, Atlanta, GA, 19 March and 17 October 1994

261. *Ganaway GK: Dissociative disorders and psychodynamic theory: trauma vs conflict and deficit. paper presented at the FMS Foundation symposium, Valley Forge, PA 17, April 1993

262. *Ganaway GK: Historical v. narrative truth: Clarifying the role of exogenous trauma in the etiology of MPD and its variants. *Dissociation* 2: 205-220, 1989

263. *Ganaway GK: cited in article below by Wylie 1993

264. *Gardner M: The false memory syndrome. *Skeptical Inquirer* 17: 370-375, Summer 1993

265. *Gardner RA: Belated realization of child sexual abuse by an adult. *Issues in Child Sexual Abuse Accusations* 4(4): 177-195, 1992

266. *Gardner RA: Sexual abuse hysteria: diagnosis, etiology, pathogenesis, and treatment. *Academy Forum* 37(3): 2-5, 1993

267. *Gardner RA: personal communication, Creskill, NJ, 5 April 1994

268. *Garry M et al: Memory: a river runs through it. *Consciousness and Cognition* 9(4), Summer 1994

269. Gayford JJ: Wife-battering: a preliminary survey of 100 cases. *British Medical Journal* pp 194-197, 1975

270. Gelinas D: The persisting negative effects of incest. *Psychiatry* 43: 312-332, 1983

271. Gembala FA, Serritella WJ: Three recent U.S. Supreme Court decisions for professionals who testify in child sexual abuse cases. *Journal of Child Sexual Abuse* 1(3): 15-30, 1992

272. Gil E: *Treatment of Adult Survivors of Childhood Abuse.* Launch Press. Walnut Creek, CA, 1989

273. Gleaves DH, Eberenz KP: Eating disorders and additional psychopathology in women: the role of prior sexual abuse. *Journal of Child Sexual Abuse* 2(3): 71-80, 1993

274. Goddard CR, Stanley JR: Viewing the abusive parent and the abused child as captor and hostage. *Journal of Interpersonal Violence* 9(2): 258-269, 1994

275. Goff DC et al: Self-reports of childhood abuse in chronically psychotic patients. *Psychiatry - Research* 37(1): 73-80, 1991

276. Gold ER: Long-term effects of sexual victimization in childhood: an attributional approach. *Journal of Consulting and Clinical Psychology* 54: 471-475, 1986

277. Goldfarb L: Sexual abuse antecedent to anorexia neurosa, bulimia, and compulsive overeating *International Journal of Eating Disorders* 6: 625-680, 1987

278. *Goldstein E, Farmer K: *True Stories of False Memories,* SIRS, Boca Raton, FL, 1993

279. Gomes-Schwartz B et al: *Child Sexual Abuse:* The initial effects. Sage, Thousand Oaks, CA, 1990

280. Gonsiorek JC et al: *Male Sexual Abuse:* A trilogy of intervention strategies. Sage, Thousand Oaks, CA, 1994

281. Goodman GS, Quas J: Children's memory for traumatic events: implications for adults' repressed memories. *Consciousness & Cognition,* Summer 1994

282. Goodwin J: Credibility problems in multiple personality disorder patients and abused children. in Kluft R (ed): *Childhood Antecedents of Multiple Personality,* American Psychiatric Press, Washington, DC, 1985

283. Goodwin J et al: Findings reported in *Bulletin of the American Academy of Psychiatry Law* 5: 269-275, 1979

284. Gravitz J: *Trauma and Excellence.* Book in process, JP Tarcher

285. Gravitz HL, Bowden, J: *Guide to Recovery:* a book for adult children of alcoholics. Simon & Schuster, NY 1985

286. Green AH: Self-destructive behavior in battered children. *American*

Journal of Psychiatry 135: 579-582, 1978

287. Green AH: True and false allegations of sexual abuse in child custody disputes. *Journal of the American Academy of Child Psychiatry* 4: 449-456, 1986

288. Greenacre P: A contribution to the study of screen memories. *Psychoanalytic Study of the Child* 3/4: 73-84, 1949

289. Greenacre P: Reconstruction: its nature and therapeutic value. *Journal of the American Psychoanalytic Association* 29: 386-402, 1982

290. Greenwood CH et al: Prevalence of sexual abuse, physical abuse, and concurrent traumatic life events in a general medical population. *Mayo Clinic Procedures* 65: 1067-1071, 1990

291. Grinfeld MJ, Duffy JF: Jury awards father $500,000 in recovered memories trial. *Psychiatric Times,* June 1994

292. Gross RJ et al: Borderline syndrome and incest in chronic pelvic pain patients. *International Journal of Psychiatry in Medicine* 10(1): 79-96, 1980-81

293. Grosskurth P: The Secret Ring: Freud's inner circle and the politics of psychoanalysis. Addison-Wesley, Reading, MA, 1991

294. Groth A et al: Undetected recidivism among rapists and child molesters. *Crime and Delinquency* 28: 450-458, 1983

295. Groth AN: *Men Who Rape:* The psychology of the offender. Plenum, NY, 1979

296. *Gutheil TG: True or false memories of sexual abuse? A forensic psychiatric view. *Psychiatric Annals* 23(9): 527-531, 1993

297. Haber JD, Roos C: Effects of spouse abuse and or sexual abuse in the development and maintenance of chronic pain in women. *Advances in Pain Research and Therapy* 9: 889- 895, 1985

298. Haber RN: How we remember what we see. *Scientific American* 104-112, 1970

299. Hall R C et al: Sexual abuse in patients with anorexia nervosa and bulimia. *Psychosomatics* 30: 37-79, 1989

300. Hamilton D, Ondrovik J: Forensic issues: "False memory syndrome" *ISSMP & D News,* August 1993

301. Hamilton JR: Violence and victims: the contributions of victimology to forensic psychiatry. *Lancet* 1: 147-150, 1987

302. Hammar RR et al: *Reducing the Risk of Child Sexual Abuse in Your Church.* Christian Ministry Resources, Matthews, NC, 1993

303. Hankes L, Bissell L: Chapter 68. Health professionals. in Lowinson JH et al (eds): *Substance Abuse:* A comprehensive Textbook. pp 897-908.Williams and Wilkins, Baltimore, 1992

304. Hanson RF et al: Characteristics of fathers in incest families. *Journal of*

Interpersonal Violence 9(2): 155-169, 1994

305. Harmine-Giddens ME, Berson NL: Harmful genital care practices on children: a type of abuse. *Journal of the American Medical Association* 261(2): 571-579, 1989

306. Harris BS: personal communication. Baltimore, 29 April 1994

307. Harris BS: *Spiritual Awakening:* Insights of the near-death experience and other doorways to our soul. Health Communications, Inc., Deerfield Beach, FL, 1995

308. *Harrison BG: Desperately seeking Susan. *Mirabella,* December 1993

309. Harrop-Griffiths J et al: The association between chronic pelvic pain, psychiatric diagnoses, and childhood sexual abuse. *Obstetrics and Gynecology* 71: 589-594, 1988

310. Harter S et al: Long-term effects of incestuous child abuse in college women: social adjustment, social cognition, and family characteristics. *Journal of Consulting and Clinical Psychology* 56: 5-8, 1988

311. Harvey MR, Herman JL: Amnesia, partial amnesia, and delayed recall among adult survivors of childhood trauma. *Consciousness & Cognition,* Summer 1994

312. Haynes-Seman C, Krugman R: Sexualized attention: normal interactions or precursors to sexual abuse? *American Journal of Orthopsychiatry* 59(2): 238-245, 1989

313. Hebb DO: *Organization of Behavior.* Wiley, NY, 1949

314. Hechler D: *The Battle and the Backlash:* The child sexual abuse war. DC Heath, Lexington, MA, 1988

315. Hechler D: Who's telling the truth? When memories tear families apart. *First,* 18 April 1994

316. Hedges LE: *Remembering, Repeating and Working Through Childhood Trauma.* Jason Aronson, NY, 1994

317. Heiman ML: Putting the puzzle together: validating allegations of child sexual abuse. *Journal of Child Psychology and Psychiatry* 33(3): 311-329, 1992

318. Henderson DJ: Incest. in Freedman AH et al (eds): *Comprehensive Textbook of Psychiatry* 2nd ed, Williams & Wilkins, Baltimore, 1975

319. Henderson R: The tangled net of memory. *Common Boundary,* pp 38-45, Nov/Dec 1993

320. Hendricks-Matthews MK, Hoz DM: Pseudocyesis in an adolescent incest survivor. *Journal of Family Practice* 36(1) 97: 101-103, 1993

321. Henry G et al: Influence of affective states and psycho-active drugs on verbal learning and memory. *American Journal of Psychiatry* 130: 966-971, 1973

322. Herbart JF: [Discussion of repression in 1806 and 1824] cited in

Laplanch and Pontalis, referenced below, 1973

323.   Herman JL et al: Long-term effects of incestuous abuse in childhood. *American Journal of Psychiatry* 143: 1293-1296, 1986

324.   Herman JL et al: Childhood trauma in borderline personality disorder. *American Journal of Psychiatry* 146: 490-495, 1989

325.   Herman JL: Complex PTSD: A syndrome in survivors of prolonged and repeated trauma. *Journal of Traumatic Stress* 5(3): 377-391, 1992

326.   Herman JL: *Trauma and Recovery.* Basic Books, NY, 1992

327.   Herman JL: *Father-Daughter Incest.* Harvard University Press, Cambridge, MA, 1981

328.   Herman JL, Harvey MR: The false memory debate: social science or social backlash? *Harvard Mental Health Letter* 9(10) 4-6, April 1993

329.   Herman JL, Schatzow E: Recovery and verification of memories of childhood sexual trauma. *Psychoanalytic Psychology* 4: 1-14, 1987

329a.   Herman J: Presuming to know the truth. *Nieman Reports: A special report to the editors of the nation's newspapers.* Ethics on trial. The Nieman Foundation of Harvard University, Spring 1994

330.   Hewitt B, Austin B: She could not keep silent. *People,* 28 October 1991, p 43

331.   Hewitt S, Friedrich WD: Assessment and abuse allegations with very young children. in Ney T (ed): *Allegations of Sexual Abuse:* Assessment and case management. Brunner/Mazel, NY, in press for 1995

332.   Hewitt SK: Preverbal sexual abuse: what two children report in later years. *Child Abuse and Neglect* 18(10): 819-824, 1994

333.   Hibbard R, Hartman G: Genitalia in human figure drawings: child rearing practices and child sexual abuse. *Journal of Pediatrics* 116: 822-828, 1990

334.   Hibbard RA et al: Abuse, feelings, and health behaviors in a student population. *American Journal of Diseases of Childhood* 142: 326-330, 1988

335.   Hilberman E, Munson M: Sixty battered women. *Victimology* 2: 460-461, 1978

336.   Hilgard ER: *Divided Consciousness:* Multiple controls in human thought and action. Wiley, NY, 1977

337.   Hilgard JR: *Personality and Hypnosis:* A study of imaginative involvement. University of Chicago Press, 1970

338.   Hislop IG: Childhood deprivation: an antecedent of the irritable bowel syndrome. *Medical Journal of Australia* 1: 372-374, 1979

339.   *Hochman J: Buried memories challenge the law. *National Law Journal* 16: 17, 1994

340.   *Holmes D: The evidence for repression: an examination of sixty years

of research. in Singer JL (ed): *Repression and Dissociation*: Implications for personality, theory, psychopathology, and health, pp 85-102, University Chicago Press, 1990

341.   Hopkins J: Daughter wins sex abuse suit: dentist ordered to pay $600,000. Seattle P-I, June 1994

342.   Horn M: Memories lost and found. *US News & World Report,* pp 52-63, 29 November 1993

343.   Horowitz MJ et al: A classification theory of defense. pp 61-84. In Singer JL (ed): *Repression and Dissociation*: Implications for personality, theory, psychopathology, and health. University Chicago Press, 1990

344.   Horowitz MJ, Bulkley JA: The statute of limitations and legal remedies for adults abused as children. *The APSAC Advisor* 7(2): 1, 6-8, Summer 1994

345.   Horney K: *The Neurotic Personality of Our Time.* Norton, NY, 1950

346.   Horowitz MJ et al 1984: cited in Everson & Boat 1989

347.   Howe ML et al: How can I remember when "I" wasn't there? Long term retention of traumatic experiences and emergence of the cognitive self. *Consciousness & Cognition,* Summer 1994

347a.   Howe ML, Courage ML: On resolving the enigma of infantile amnesia. *Psychological Bulletin* 113(2): 305-326, 1993

348.   Hunt P, Baird M: Children of sex rings. *Child Welfare* 69(3): 195-207, 1990

349.   Hunter M: *Abused boys:* the neglected victims of sexual abuse. DC Heath, Lexington, MA, 1990

350.   Incidence and prevalence of child sexual abuse from the National Incidence Study: National Resource Center on Child Sexual Abuse. *News:* 1:1 May/June 1992

351.   Isabella M: personal communications, Baltimore, 28 & 29 May, 5 June 1994

352.   Ito Y et al: Increased prevalence of electrophysiological abnormalities in children with psychological, physical and sexual abuse. *Journal of Neuropsyc. and Clinical Neuroscience* 5: 401-408, 1993

353.   Jackson L: *LaToya.* Dutton, NY 1992

354.   Jackson L: Interview on *Larry King Live,* CNN, 17 Sept 1993

355.   Jacobs JL: Child sexual abuse victimization and later sequelae during pregnancy and childbirth. *Journal of Child Sexual Abuse* 1(9): 103-112, 1992

356.   Jacobson A et al: The failure of routine assessment to detect histories of assault experienced by psychiatric patients. *Hospital and Community Psychiatry* 38(4): 386-389, 1987

357.   Jacobson A: Physical and sexual assault histories among psychiatric outpatients.

patients. *American Journal of Psychiatry* 146: 755-758, 1989

358. Jacobson A, Richardson B: Assault experiences of 100 psychiatric inpatients: evidence of the need for routine inquiry. *American Journal of Psychiatry* 144: 7, 1987

359. James J, Myerding J: Early sexual experience as a factor in prostitution. *Archives of Sexual Behavior* 7: 31-42, 1977

360. James J, Myerding J: Early sexual experience and prostitution. *American Journal of Psychiatry* 134: 1381-1385, 1977

361. Janet P: *Psychological Healing* [1919]. trans E & C Paul, Macmillan, NY, 1925

362. Janet P: *The Major Symptoms of Hysteria*. Hafner, NY, 1965

363. Jay J: Terrible knowledge. *Family Therapy Networker* pp 18-29, Nov/Dec 1991

364. Johnson D: *Body*. Beacon Press, Boston, 1983

365. Johnson R, Schrier D: Past sexual victimization by females of male patients in an adolescent medicine clinic population. *American Journal of Psychiatry* 144: 650-662, 1987

366. Jones DPH, McGraw JM: Reliable and ficticious accounts of sexual abuse of children. *Journal of Interpersonal Violence* 2: 27-45, 1987

367. Jones JG: Sexual abuse of children: current concepts. *American Journal of Diseases of Children* 136: 142-146, 1982

368. Josephson G, Fong-Beyette M: Factors assisting female clients' disclosure of incest during counseling. *Journal of Counseling and Development* 65: 475-478, 1987

369. Kahr B: The sexual molestation of children: historical perspectives. *Journal of Psychohistory* 19(2): 191-214, Fall 1994

370. Kantor D: Statement on memories. *Good Morning America,* ABC Television, 27 January 1994

371. Kardiner A, Spiegel H: *War, Stress and Neurotic Illness.* (revised edition of the Traumatic Neuroses of War) Hoeber, NY, 1947

372. Kaufman J: Depressive disorders in maltreated children. *Journal of the American Academy of Child and Adolescent Psychiatry* 30(2): 257-265, 1991

373. Keith-Spiegel P, Koocher G: APA principle no 6. in: *Ethics in Psychology,* Random House, NY, 1985

374. Kelley SJ et al: Sexual abuse of children in day care. *Child Abuse and Neglect* 17: 71-89, 1993

375. Kempe CH et al: The battered child syndrome. *Journal of the American Medical Association.* 181: 17-24, 1962

376. Kendall JC: "Psychopsychiatry": unreality and cruelty in traditional psychiatric treatments for survivors of childhood sexual abuse. *Treating*

Abuse Today 4(4): 38-43, 1994

377. Kendall JC: Anne Sexton's failed psychotherapies: the tragic fate of "her kind." *Treating Abuse Today,* scheduled for March/April 5(2) 1995

378. Kendall-Tackett KA, Simon AF: Molestation and the onset of puberty: data from 365 adults molested as children. *Child Abuse and Neglect* 12: 73-81, 1988

379. Kendall-Tackett KA et al: Impact of sexual abuse on children: a review and synthesis of recent empirical studies. *Psychological Bulletin* 113: 168-80, 1993

380. Kerns DL et al: The role of physicians in reporting and evaluating child sexual abuse cases. in Behrman RE (ed): Sexual Abuse of Children in *The Future of Children* 4(2), 1994

380a. Kerr, ME, Bowen, M: *Family Evaluation:* An approach based on Bowen theory. W.W. Norton, NY, 1988

381. Kingsbury SJ: Strategic psychotherapy for trauma: hypnosis & trauma in context. *Journal of Traumatic Stress* 5(1): 85-101, 1992

382. Kinsey A et al: *Sexual Behavior in the Human Male,* WB Saunders, Philadelphia, 1948; and ... *in the Human Female,* Saunders, 1953

383. Kluft RD: *Dissociation* and subsequent vulnerability: a preliminary study. Dissociation 3(3): 167-173, 1990

384. Knaster M: Re-membering through the body. *Massage Therapy Journal* 33(1): 46-59, 1994

385. Knopp FH: *Retraining Adult Sex Offenders:* Methods and models. Safer Society Press, Orwell, VT, 1984

386. Kolb LC: The psychobiology of PTSD: perspectives and reflections on the past, present and future. *Journal of Traumatic Stress* 6(3): 293-304, 1993

387. Kolko DJ et al: Behavioral/emotional indications of sexual abuse in child psychiatric inpatients: a controlled comparison with physical abuse. *Child Abuse and Neglect* 12: 529- 542, 1988

388. KOMO Town Meeting television show on the memory controversy, Seattle, 29 June 1994

389. Kristiansen CM et al: The recovered memory debate: science, social values or self-interest? Talk given at Canadian Psychological Association convention, Penicton, Canada, BC, July 1994

389a. Kritsberg W: *The ACoA Syndrome:* Bantam, NY, 1988

390. Lacoursiere RB: Diverse motives for fictitious post-traumatic stress disorder. *Journal of Traumatic Stress* 6(1): 141-149, 1993

391. Ladwig GB, Anderson MD: Substance abuse in women: relationship between chemical dependency and past reports of physical and sexual abuse. *International Journal of the Addictions* 24: 739-754, 1989

391a.   Laflen B, Sturm WR: Understanding and working with denial in sexual offenders. *Journal of Child Sexual Abuse* 3(4): 19-36, 1994

392.   Lamb S, Edgar-Smith S: Aspects of disclosure: mediators of outcome of childhood sexual abuse. *Journal of Interpersonal Violence* 9(3): 307-326, 1994

393.   Landsberg M: False memory label invented by lobby group. *Toronto Star,* reprinted in *Moving Forward* 2(6): 3, 6, 1994

394.   Lane RD, Schwartz GE: Levels of emotional awareness: a cognitive-development theory and its application to psychopathology. *American Journal of Psychiatry* 144: 33-43, 1988

395.   Lanktree CB et al: Incidence and impacts of sexual abuse in a child out-patient sample: the role of direct inquiry. *Child Abuse and Neglect* 15: 447-453, 1991

395a.   Lanning K: Statement on *Good Morning America.* 7 April 1994

396.   Laplanche J, Pontalis JB: *The language of Psycho-analysis* (trans. by D Nicholson-Smith), Hogarth Press, NY, 1973

396a.   Larsen E: *Stage II Recovery:* Life Beyond Addiction. Harper & Row, San Francisco, 1985

397.   Lawrence JR, Perry C: Hypnotically created memory among highly hyp-notizable subjects. *Science* 222: 523-524, 1983

398.   Lawrence LR: Resignation from FMSF Advisory Board. *Moving Forward* 2(5): 3-5, 1993

399.   Lawrence LR: personal communication, Baltimore, September 1993

399a.   LeDoux JE: Emotion, memory and the brain. *Scientific American,* June 1994

400.   Lefton LA: Chapter 6 Memory. in *Psychology.* Fifth Edition, Allyn & Bacon, Boston, 1994

401.   Lew M: *Victims No Longer.* Harper & Row, NY, 1988

402.   Lewis DO: From abuse to violence: psychophysiological consequences of maltreatment. *Journal of American Academy of Child and Adolescent Psychiatry* 31: 383-391, 1992

403.   Lief HI: Letter to the editor. *Psychology of Women,* p8, Summer 1994

404.   Lindberg FH, Distad L: Post-traumatic stress disorders in women who experienced childhood incest. *Child Abuse and Neglect* 9: 329-334, 1985

405.   Lindy JD: PTSD and transference. *Clinical Newsletter* for the National Center for PTSD, Menlo Park, CA, Spring 1993

406.   Linton M: Ways of searching and the contents of memory. (pp 50-67) in Rubin DC (ed): *Autobiographical Memory.* Cambridge University Press, London, 1986

407.   Lipovsky JA et al: Depression, anxiety and behavior problems among victims of father-child sexual assault and nonabused siblings. *Journal of*

Interpersonal Violence 4: 452-458, 1989

408. Lipshires L: Female perpetration of child sexual abuse: an overview of the problem. *Moving Forward* 2(6): 1, 12-14, 1994

409. Lloyd DW: Ritual child abuse: definitions and assumptions. *Journal of Child Sexual Abuse* 1(3): 1-14, 1992

410. Lobel CM: Relationship between childhood sexual abuse and borderline personality disorder in women psychiatric inpatients. *Journal of Child Sexual Abuse* 1(1): 63-80, 1992

411. *Loftus EF: Excerpted transcript in *Gary Ramona vs. Stephanie Ramona, Marche Isabella, etc.* No 61898, pp 1-104, Napa, CA, 7 April 1994

412. *Loftus EF: Memories of childhood sexual abuse: remembering and repressing. *Psychology of Women Quarterly* 18: 67-84, 1994c

413. *Loftus E, Ketcham K: *The Myth of Repressed Memory.* St Martin's Press, NY, 1994

413a. Loftus E, Ketcham K: *Witness for the Defense.* St. Martin's Press, NY, 1991

414. *Loftus EF, Yapko MD: Psychotherapy and the recovery of repressed memories. Unpublished manuscript, 1994b

415. *Loftus EF et al: The reality of illusory memories. Unpublished paper, 6 March 1994a

416. *Loftus EF: Deposition No 91-2-01102-5 and verbatim court testimony for the defense in *Crook v. Murphy,* Superior Court of the State of Washington, Benton Co, 24 January and 17 February, 1994

417. *Loftus EF: The reality of repressed memories. *American Psychologist* 48: 518-537, 1993

418. *Loftus EF: deposition in Carol C. *Smith v. Richard Alton Smith,* Case no 67 52 64, Superior Court of the State of California, in and for the County of Orange, pp 39-40, 18 January 1993

419. *Loftus EF, Rosenwald LA: Buried memories, shattered lives. *American Bar Association Journal* pp 70-73, November 1993b

420. *Loftus EF, Kaufman L: Why do traumatic experiences sometimes produce good memory (flashbulbs) and sometimes no memory (repression)? (pp 212-223) In Winograd & Neisser (eds): *Affect and Accuracy in Recall.* Cambridge University Press, NY, 1992

421. Lowenstein RJ: Somatoform disorders in victims of incest and child abuse. in Kluft (ed): *Incest Related Syndrome of Adult Psychopathology,* pp 75-112, American Psychiatric Press, Washington, DC, 1990

423. Lowenstein RJ: Psychogenic amnesia and psychogenic fugue: a comprehensive review. pp 45-77, in Pynoos RS (ed): *PTSD: A clinical review.* Sidran Press, Lutherville, MD, 1993

424. Lundberg-Love PK et al: The long-term consequences of childhood

incestuous victimization upon adult women's psychological symptoma-tology. *Journal of Child Sexual Abuse* 1(1): 81-102, 1992

425. Lustig N et al: Incest: a family group survival pattern. *Archives of General Psychiatry* 14: 31-40, 1966

426. Machotka P et al: Incest as a family affair. *Family Process* 6: 98-116, 1967

427. MacVicar K: Psychotherapeutic issues in the treatment of sexually abused girls. *Journal of the American Academy of Child Psychiatry* 18: 342-353, 1979

428. Males M: False media syndrome: "recovered memory," child abuse and media escapism. *Extra,* pages 10 & 11, September/October 1994

429. Maletsky B: *Treating the Sexual Offender.* Sage, Thousand Oaks, CA, 1990

430. Maltz W, Holman B: *Incest and sexuality:* A guide to understanding and healing. Lexington Books, Lexington, MA, 1987

431. Marin BV et al: The potential of children as eyewitnesses. *Law and Human Behavior* 4: 295-305, 1979

432. Marmar CR et al: Chapter 5. An integrated approach for treating post-traumatic stress. in Pynoos RS (ed) PTSD: *A clinical review.* Sidran Press, Lutherville, MD, 1994

433. Marsella AJ et al: Denial in political process. in Edelstein EL et al (eds): *Denial: A clarification of concepts and research.* Plenum Press, NY, 1989

434. Martinovich S: Rose says... *Napa Valley Register,* 17 April 1994

435. Masson JM: *The Assault on Truth:* Freud's suppression of the seduction theory. Farrar, Straus, & Giroux, NY, 1984

436. Masson JM: *Final Analysis:* The making and unmaking of a psychoana-lyst. Addison-Wesley, NY, 1990

437. Masterson JF: *The Search for the Real Self:* Unmasking the personality disorders of our age. Free Press/MacMillan, NY, 1988

438. Mate G: Fifth column-medicine [on FMS]. *The Globe and Mail,* Canada's National Newspaper, 25 July, 1 August, 8 August, p A18, 1994

439. Matthews R et al: *Female Sex Offenders.* Safer Society Press, Orwell, VT, 1989

440. Matousek M: America's darkest secret. *Common Boundary* pp 16-25, March/April 1991

441. Matz EM: A review of portions of an interview with Ralph Underwager and Hollida Wakefield in *Paidika,* a journal of pedophilia. *Family Violence & Sexual Assault Bulletin* 9(4): 23-25, 1994

442. Mayer J, Abramson J: *Strange Justice:* The selling of Clarence Thomas. Houghton Mifflin, NY, 1994

443.   Mayer J, Abramson J: Interviews on *Turning Point,* ABC News, 2 November and *Larry King Live,* CNN, 3 November, 1994

443a.   MacEwen KE: Refining the integrational transmission hypothesis. *Journal of Interpersonal Violence* 9(3): 350-365, 1994

444.   McCadden J: Personal communication, Baltimore, MD, March 1994

445.   McCahill T, Meyer LC, Fischman A: *The Aftermath of Rape.* Lexington Books, Lexington, MA 1979

446.   McCann E, Pearlman LA: Vicarious traumatization: a framework for understanding the psychological effects of working with victims. *Journal of Traumatic Stress* 3: 131-149, 1990

447.   McCann E, Pearlman L: *Psychological Trauma in the Adult Survivor.* Bruner/Mazel, NY, 1991

448.   McCulley D, McCulley B: Disinformation, media manipulation, and public perception. *Survivorship,* 3181 Mission Street #139, San Francisco 94110, 1993

449.   *McDowell J: Lies of the mind. *Time,* pp 52-59 29 November, 1993

450.   McFarland R: The children of God. *Journal of Psychohistory* 21(4): 497-499, 1994

451.   McFarlane K, Korbin J: Confronting the incest secret long after the fact. *Child Abuse and Neglect* 7: 225-237, 1983

452.   *McHugh PR: "Recovered memory": exploring the confusion. (review of *Suggestions of Abuse* by Michael Yapko) *Long Island Newsday,* Nassau, NY, 30 June, 1994a

453.   *McHugh P: Talk at FMSF seminar. Annapolis, MD, November, 1993; and Memories and pseudomemories. *The Nature of Memory* symposium, Sheppard Pratt Hospital, Baltimore, 12 March, 1994

454.   McLeer SV et al: PTSD in sexually abused children. *Journal of the American Academy of Child and Adolescent Psychiatry* 27: 650-654, 1988

455.   McLeer SV et al: Sexually abused children at high risk for PTSD. *Journal of the American Academy of Child and Adolescent Psychiatry* 31: 875-879, 1992

456.   Medawar PB: *Induction and Intuition in Scientific Thought.* American Philosophical Society, Philadelphia, 1969; also discussed in the subsequent book *Pluto's Republic:* Incorporating the Arts of the Soluble and Induction and Intuition in Scientific Thought. Oxford University Press, Oxford 1982

457.   Meiselman KC: *Incest:* A psychological study. Jossey-Bass, San Francisco, 1981 (See also 1978 book with similar title)

458.   Meiselman KC: *Resolving the Trauma of Incest.* Jossey-Bass, San Francisco, 1990

459. Mellott RN, Wagner WG: A follow-up pilot study of the psychological adjustment of a sample of sexually abused girls. *Journal of Child Sexual Abuse* 2(1): 37-45, 1993

460. Meltzoff AN: Infant imitation and memory: 9 month olds in immediate and deferred tests. *Child Development* 59: 217-225, 1988

461. Mendel MP: *The Male Survivor.* The impact of sexual abuse. Sage, Thousand Oaks, CA, 1994

462. Menninger K: *The Human Mind.* Literary Guild of America, NY, 1930

463. Meyers NA et al: When they were very young: almost - threes remember 2 years ago. *Infant Behavior and Development* 10: 123-132, 1987

464. Miller A: *Thou Shalt Not Be Aware:* Society's betrayal of the child. Farrar, Straus and Giroux, NY, 1984

465. Miller JJ: The unveiling of traumatic memories and emotions through mindfulness and concentration meditation: clinical implications and three case reports. *Journal of Transpersonal Psychology* 25: 169-181, 1994

466. Mills T et al: Hospitalization experiences of victims of abuse. *Victimology* 9: 436-459, 1984

467. Milner JS, Robertson KR: Comparison of physical abusers, intra-familial sexual child abusers and child neglecters. *Journal of Interpersonal Violence* 5(1): 37-48, 1990

468. Mischel W: *Introduction to Personality: A new look.* 4th ed. Holt, Rinehart & Winston, NY 1986

469. Mitchell J: Memories of a disputed past. *The Oregonian* 8 August 1993

470. *Molien v. Kaiser Foundation Hospitals.* 616 p2d 813, 817 (Cal 1980)

471. Monesi L: Reports of a private investigator, Falcon International Inc, Columbus, OH, 1992, cited in Loftus 1993

472. Morgan E, Froning ML: Child sexual abuse sequelae and body-image surgery. *Plastic and Reconstructive Surgery,* 86: 475-480, 1990

473. Morrison J: Childhood sexual histories of women with somatization disorder. *American Journal of Psychiatry* 146: 239-241, 1989

474. Moss DC: "Abuse scale." *American Bar Association Journal,* 1 December 1988

475. Mullen PE et al: Impact of sexual and physical abuse on women's mental health. *Lancet* 1: 841-845, 1988

476. Myers G: *History of the Great American Fortunes.* Random House/Modern Library, NY, 1907

477. Myers JEB: Legal evidence of physical child abuse. *The Advisor* 2(4): 3-4, 1989

478. Myers JEB (ed): *The Backlash:* Child protection under fire. Sage, Thousand Oaks, CA, 1994

479. Nagy TF: personal communication. Palo Alto, CA, 9 September 1994

480. Nagy TF: Repressed memories: Guidelines and directions. *The National Psychologist,* July/August 1994

481. Naifeh SW: *The Best Doctors in America.* Woodward/White, Aiken, SC (803-648-0300), 1993

482. Nakken C: *The Addictive Personality.* Hazelden, Center City, MN, 1988

483. National Child Abuse and Neglect Data System, working paper 2. US Deptartment HHS, Gaithersburg, MD, 1991

484. Neisser U: What is ordinary memory? in Neisser U & Winograd E (eds): *Remembering Reconsidered.* (p356-373) Cambridge University Press, NY, 1988

485. Nelson E: Personal communication, San Diego, CA. January 1994

486. Nelson K: The ontogeny of memory for real events. (pp 244-276) in Neisser U & Winograd E (eds): *Remembering Reconsidered.* Cambridge University Press, NY, 1988

487. Nelson K: The psychological and social origins of autobiographical memory. *Psychological Science* (American Psychological Society) 4(1): 7-14, 1993

488. Nemiah JC: Dissociative disorders. in Freedman & Kaplan (eds): *Comprehensive Textbook of Psychiatry* (3rd ed), Williams & Wilkins, Baltimore, 1981

489. Norman DA: *Learning and Memory.* WH Freeman, San Francisco, 1982

490. Oates RK: Personality development after physical abuse. *Archives of Disease in Childhood* 59: 147-150, 1984

491. Oates RK et al: Self-esteem of abused children. *Child Abuse and Neglect* 9: 159-163, 1985

492. O'Brien E: Pushing the panic button: the enigma of EMDR. *Family Therapy Networker* p33-39, November/December 1993

493. O'Connor D: personal communication, Maryland, 14 August 1994

494. O'Connor K: personal communication, Arlington, VA, 6 August 1994

495. *Ofshe RJ: letter to Gary Tabor on the Paul Ingram case. April 2, 1989

496. *Ofshe R: Inadvertent hypnosis during interrogation: false confession due to dissociative state, mis-identified multiple personality, and the satanic cult hypothesis. *International Journal of Clinical and Experimental Hypnosis* 3: 125-156, 1992

497. *Ofshe RJ, Watters E: *Making Monsters.* Scribners, NY, 1994

498. *Ofshe R: Making grossly damaging but avoidable errors: the pitfalls of the Olio/Cornell thesis. *Journal of Child Sexual Abuse* 3(3): 95-108, 1994

499. Ogata SN et al: Childhood sexual and physical abuse in adult patients with borderline personality disorder. *American Journal of Psychiatry* pp

1008-1013, 1990

500. Olafson E et al: Modern history of child sexual abuse awareness: cycles of discovery and suppression. *Child Abuse and Neglect* 17: 7-24, 1993

501. Oliver JE: Intergenerational transmission of child abuse: rates, research and clinical implications. *American Journal of Psychiatry* 150(9): 1315-1324, 1993

502. Olio KA: Memory retrieval in the treatment of adult survivors of sexual abuse. *Transactional Analysis Journal* 19: 93-100, 1989

503. Olio KA: Ending the silence: a model for family confrontation in treatment with adult survivors of sexual abuse. Unpublished paper, 1992

504. Olio KA: Facts, fiction, and fantasy [about traumatic memory]. (adapted from a talk at the American Ortho-Psychiatric Association, NY, May 1993) *The Healing Woman* Box 3038, Moss Beach, CA 94038 2: 4, 1993

505. Olio KA: Truth in memory: *American Psychologist* pp 442-443, May 1994 (this issue contains four other writers' comments and Loftus' response)

506. Olio KA, Cornell WF: The Ingram case: pseudomemory or pseudo-science? *Violence Update*, Sage Press, July 1994

507. Olio KA, Cornell WF: Making meaning, not monsters: reflections on the delayed memory controversy. *Journal of Child Sexual Abuse* 3(3): 77-94, 1994

508. Olio KA, Cornell WF: The facade of scientific documentation: a case study of Ofshe's analysis of the Paul Ingram case. *American Journal of Clinical Hypnosis,* in press, 1994

509. Olio KA, Cornell WF: The therapeutic relationship as the foundation for treatment with adult survivors of sexual abuse. *Psychotherapy* 30(3): 512-523, 1993

510. Orne MT: The use and misuse of hypnosis in court. *International Journal of Clinical & Experimental Hypnosis* 27: 311-341, 1979

511. Parents of abused children: responses and coping styles. *Believe the Children Newsletter* 10: 1, 4-5, Winter 1993

512. Pennebaker JW et al: Disclosure of traumas and immune function: Health implications for psychotherapy. *Journal of Consulting and Clinical Psychology* 56: 239-245, 1988

513. Perry NE: Letter to the editor. ISSMP&D News, August 1993

514. Perry NW: How children remember and why they forget. The APSAC *Advisor* 5(3- Summer): 1-2, 13-15, 1992

515. Peters J et al: Why prosecute child abuse? *South Dakota Law Review* 34: 649-659, 1989

516. Peters SD: Child sexual abuse and later psychological problems. in Wyatt GE & Powell GJ (eds): *The Lasting Effects of Child Sexual Abuse.*

Sage, Thousand Oaks, CA, 1988

517.   Peterson J, Sachs R, Steele MN: Mastering traumatic memories. Videotape instruction and book. Cavelcade, Ukiah, CA, 1-800-345-5530, 1993

518.   Peterson J: personal communication, Houston, TX, January 1994

518a.   Peterson R: personal communication, Seattle, WA, July, 1994

519.   Peterson RH (Judge) in: *State of Washington v. Paul R. Ingram.* Superior Court of the State of Washington in and for the County of Thurston, Report of Proceedings, volume VII, no 88-1-752-1, 1990

519a.   Peterson M: personal communication. Houston, December 16, 1994

520.   Pezdek K, Roe C Memory for Childhood events: How suggestible is it? *Consciousness & Cognition*, 9(4)Summer 1994

521.   Phelps TM, Winternitz H: *Capital Games.* Hyperion, NY, 1992

522.   Phillipp S: American Coalition for Abuse Awareness to address legal issues. *Moving Forward* 2(5): 16-17, 1993

523.   Pines AM: Early sexual exploitation as an influence in prostitution. *Social Work* 28: 285-289, 1983

524.   Pittman RK: PTSD, hormones and memory. *Biological Psychiatry* 26(3): 221-223, 1989

524a.   *Plumb D: Sebastian's dead, pass the eggs. Talk at International Transpersonal Association Conference, Atlanta, Sept. 15-22, 1991

525.   Plummer C: personal communications. Southeastern Michigan Chapter, Coalition for Accuracy About Abuse, Ann Arbor, MI, 313-930-6899, May 1994

526.   Pogrebin LC: The stolen spotlight syndrome. *MS* p96, Nov/Dec 1993

527.   *Pomeroy WB: A new look at incest. *Forum* p 9-B, Nov 1976

527a.   Pope HG, Hudson JI: Is childhood special abuse a risk factor for bulemia nervosa? *American Journal of Psychology* 149(4): 455

527b.   Pope HG, Hudson JI: Can memories of childhood sexual abuse be repressed? *Psychol Medicine* 1995 (in press)

528.   Porter J: Confession of abuse and survivor testimony at his sentencing hearing. *Court Television*, December 9, 1993

529.   Prendergast WE: *Treating Sex Offenders* in correctional institutions and outpatient clinics: a guide to clinical practice. Haworth Press, Binghamton, NY, 1994

530.   Putnam FW: Pierre Janet and modern views of dissociation. *Journal of Traumatic Stress* 2(4): 413-429, 1989

531.   Putnam FW et al: The clinical phenomenology of MPD. *Journal of Clinical Psychiatry* 47: 285-293, 1986

532.   Putnam FW, Trickett PK: Child sexual abuse: a model of chronic trauma. *Psychiatry* - Interpersonal & Biological Processes. 56: 82-95, 1993

533.   Pynoos RS (ed): *Posttraumatic Stress Disorder.* A clinical review. Sidran Press, Lutherville, MD, 1993

534.   Quina K: Editorial [on "FMS" controversy], *Psychology of Women,* pp12-13, Winter 1994; plus letters to the editor, *Psychology of Women,* pp6-9 Summer 1994

535.   Quirk SA: personal communication, Washington, DC, 31 August 1994

535a.   Quirk SA, DePrince AP: Backlash legislation targeting psychotherapists. *Journal of Psychohistory* 22(3): 258-264, Winter, 1995

536.   Quirk SA: False memories. *American Bar Association Journal* vol 80, March 1994

536a   Radbill SX: Children in a world of violence: a history of child abuse. in Kempe CH & Helfer RE: *The Battered Child.* University of Chicago Press, Chicago, 1980

537.   Ramona trial in California, *Dateline,* 18 May 1994

538.   Ramona G: my letters inviting personal communication with him, July - September 1994

539.   Ramona H: personal communication, Los Angeles, 3 June 1994

540.   Ramona S: personal communication, Napa, CA, June 14 & 22, December 12, 1994

541.   Rapaport D: *Emotions and Memory.* International Universities Press, NY, 1942, 1959

542.   Raskin D: Diagnosis in patients with chronic pelvic pain. *American Journal of Psychiatry* 141: 824, 1984

543.   Recovered Memory Task Group. Women's Place, 241 Bruyere, Ottowa, ON, 1994

544.   Reece RM: Making meaning - a pediatrician's view. *Journal of Child Sexual Abuse* 3(3): 119-122, 1994

545.   *Reiff D: Victims All? *Harpers,* pp49-56 October 1991

545a.   Reilly MA, Pedigo MK: personal communication. Washington, DC, 1994

546.   Reinhard PG: US Court of Appeals, 7th circuit, No 93-2422, Underwager case, Decision of 25 April 1994

547.   *The Retractor: Newsletter for Survivors of False Memories. (apparently now defunct) Box 5012, Reno, NV 89503

548.   Riggs S et al: Health risk behaviors and attempted suicide in adolescents who report prior maltreatment. *Journal of Pediatrics* 116: 815-821, 1990

549.   Rimsza ME et al: Sexual abuse: somatic and emotional reactions. *Child Abuse and Neglect* 12: 201-208, 1988

549a.   Ring K., Rosing C: The Omega Project. *Journal of Near-Death Studies* 8(4) 1990

550.   Roberts J, Hawton K: Child abuse and attempted suicide. *British*

Journal of Psychiatry 137: 319-323, 1980

551. Robin M (ed): *Assessing Child Maltreatment Reports*: The problem of false allegations. Haworth Press, Binghamton, NY, 1991

551a. Roe CM et al: Memories of previously forgotten childhood sexual abuse: a descriptive study. Unpublished, from Masters and Johnson Sexual Trauma and Compulsivity Programs, St. Louis, MO, 1995

552. Roesler TA, Wind TW: Telling the secret: adult women describe their disclosures of incest. *Journal of Interpersonal Violence* 9(3): 327-338, 1994

553. *Rogers M: Evaluating adult litigants who allege injuries from sexual abuse: clinical assessment methods for traumatic memories. *Issues in Child Abuse Accusations* 4(4): 221-238, 1992

554. Rolfe R: When you're the only one in recovery. (booklet) Health Communications, Deerfield Beach, FL, 1991

555. Root MPP: Treatment failures: the role of sexual victimizations in women's addictive behavior. *American Journal of Orthopsychiatry* 59: 542-549, 1989

555a. Rorty A et al: Childhood sexual, physical and psychological abuse in bulimia nervosa. *American Journal of Psychiatry* 151:1122-1126, 1994

556. Rosenfeld AA: Incidence of a history of incest among 18 female psychiatric patients. *American Journal of Psychiatry* 136: 791-795, 1979

557. Ross CA: *The Osiris Complex*. University of Toronto Press, 1994

558. Ross CA et al: Dissociation and abuse among multiple-personality patients, prostitutes, and exotic dancers. *Hospital and Community Psychiatry* 41(3): 328-330, 1990

558a Rossi E: *The Psychology of Mind-Body Healing*. W.W. Norton, NY, 1986

559. Roth D, Rehm LP: Relationships among self-monitoring processes, memory and depression. *Cognitive Therapy and Research* 4: 149-158, 1980

560. Rowan AB, Foy DW: PTSD in child sexual abuse. in Pynoos RS (ed): *PTSD: A clinical review.* Sidran Press, Lutherville, MD, 1994

561. Rowan AB, Foy DW: PTSD in child sexual abuse. *Journal of Traumatic Stress* 6: 3-20, 1993

562. Roy M (ed): *Battered women*: A psychosociological study of domestic violence. Van Nostrand Reinhold, NY, 1977

563. Roy M: *Children in the crossfire*: Violence in the home—How does it affect our children? Health Communications, Deerfield Beach, FL, 1988

564. Roy M: *The Abusive Partner*: An analysis of domestic battering. Van Nostrand Reinhold, NY, 1982

565. Rubin DC (ed): *Autobiographical Memory*. Cambridge University Press, London, 1986

566. Runtz M, Briere J: Adolescent "acting out" and childhood history of

sexual abuse. *Journal of Interpersonal Violence* 1: 326-334, 1986

567. Rush F: *The Best Kept Secret.* Prentice Hall, NY, 1980

568. Rush F: The Freudian cover-up. *Chrysalis* 1: 31-45, 1977

569. Russell DEH: The incidence and prevalence of intrafamilial and extrafamilial sexual abuse of female children. *Child Abuse & Neglect* 7: 133-146, 1983

570. Russell DEH: *The Secret Trauma.* Basic Books, NY, 1986

570a Ryle G: *The Concept of Mind.* University of Chicago Press, 1984

571. Sachs R, Peterson J & Steele K: *Mastering Traumatic Memories.* Videotape Presentation, Cavalcade Productions, Ukiah, CA, 1992

572. Salter AC: Accuracy of expert testimony in child sexual abuse cases: a case study of Ralph Underwager and Hollida Wakefield. Unpublished 83-1 page manuscript, the study sponsored by the New England Commissioners of Child Welfare Agencies (Directors of Social Services for each New England state), 1991

573. Satir V: *The New Peoplemaking.* Science and Behavior Books, Mt View, CA, 1988

574. Saunders BE et al: Child sexual assault as a risk factor for mental disorders among women: a community survey. *Journal of Interpersonal Violence* 7: 189-204, 1992

575. Sauzier M: Disclosure of child sexual abuse: For better or for worse. *Psychiatric Clinics of North America* 12(2): 455-489, 1989

576. Saywitz KJ, Moan-Hardie S: Reducing the potential for distortion of childhood memories. *Consciousness and Cognition* 9(4), Summer 1994

577. Saywitz KJ: Enhancing children's memory with the cognitive interview. The APSAC *Advisor* 5(3-summer): 9-10, 1992

578. Schatzow E, Herman JL: Breaking secrecy: adult survivors disclose to their families. *Psychiatric Clinics of North America* 12(2): 337-349, 1989

579. Schecter JO et al: Sexual assault and anorexia nervosa. *International Journal of Eating Disorders* 5: 313-16, 1987

580. Schissler H: Avoiding the truth trap: responding to allegations (and denials) of sexual abuse. *Family Therapy Networker* pp69-73, Mar/Apr 1994

581. Schneider JG: A legal update on "repressed memory" of childhood sexual abuse. *The Psychologist's Legal Update,* Washington, DC, 1994

582. Schnitt JM: Traumatic stress studies: what's in a name? *Journal of Traumatic Stress* 6(3) 405-408, 1993

583. Schonberg IJ: The distortion of the role of mother in child sexual abuse. *Journal of Child Sexual Abuse* 1(3) 47-61, 1992

584. Schudson CB: Antagonistic parents in family courts: false allegations or false assumptions about true allegations of child sexual abuse? *Journal*

of Child Sexual Abuse 1(2): 113-116, 1992

585.   Schwartz MF: False memory blues. *Masters and Johnson Report,* New Orleans, 1993

586.   Schwartz MF: [Talk on treatment of sexual abusers] given at conference on Advances in Treating Survivors of Sexual Abuse. Reston, VA, 6 November 1993

587.   Sedney MA, Brooks B: Factors associated with a history of childhood sexual experiences in a non-clinical female population. *Journal of the American Academy of Child Psychiatry* 23, 215-218, 1984

587a.   Seidman BT et al: An examination of intimacy and loneliness in sex offenders. *Journal of Intergenerational Violence* 9(4) 518-534, 1994

587b.   Shapiro N: attorney for the defense of *The Courage to Heal,* personal communication, 5 October, 1994

588.   Shapiro R: Evaluating sexually transmitted diseases in children. *The* APSAC *Advisor* 7(2): 11-14, 1994

589.   Sheiman JA: "I've always wondered if something happened to me:" Assessment of child sexual abuse survivors with amnesia. *Journal of Child Sexual Abuse* 2(2): 13-21, 1993

590.   Shengold L: Child abuse and deprivation: Soul murder. *Journal of the American Psychoanalytic Association.* 27: 533-599, 1979

591.   Sherman R: Gardner's "law." *National Law Journal,* 16 August 1993

592.   *Sifford D: When tales of sex abuse aren't true. *The Philadelphia Inquirer* 1I, 8I, 5 January 1991; Accusations of sex abuse, years later. 24 November 1F, 5F, 1992

593.   Silver RL et al: Searching for meaning in misfortune: making sense of incest. *Journal of Social Issues* 39: 81-102, 1983

594.   Silverman F: The roentgen manifestations of unrecognized skeletal trauma. *American Journal of Roentgenology,* Radium Therapy & Nuclear Medicine G9: 413-27, 1953

595.   Simons RL, Whitbeck LB: Sexual abuse as a precursor to prostitution. *Journal of Family Issues* 12: 361-379, 1991

596.   *Simons J and FMSF staff: Third party vs therapist, interpreting Illinois law. *FMSF Newsletter,* May 1994

597.   *Simons J and FMSF staff: Analysis of the Ramona decision [and related decisions]. *FMSF Newsletter,* June, July, August, October, November 1994, January-March, 1995

598.   Simos BG: *A Time to Grieve.* Loss as a universal human experience. Family Services Association of America, NY, 1979

599.   Singer MI et al: The relationship between sexual abuse and substance abuse among psychiatrically hospitalized adolescents. *Child Abuse and Neglect* 4: 121-138, 1989

600. Singer JA, Salovey P: *The Remembered Self:* Emotion and memory in personality. Lexington Books, NY, 1993

601. Singer JL, Sincoff JB: Beyond repression and the defenses. in Singer JL (ed): *Repression and Dissociation:* Implications for personality, theory, psychopathology, and health, pp471- 496, University of Chicago Press, 1990

602. Singer JL: Preface: A fresh look at repression, dissociation, and the defenses as mechanisms and as personality styles. in Singer JL (ed): *Repression and Dissociation:* Implications for personality, theory, psychopathology, and health. University of Chicago Press, 1990

603. Smith W: *American Daughter Gone to War.* W. Morrow, NY, 1992

604. Smyth J: Testimony of extreme mental, emotional and sexual abuse by a therapist. *Court Television,* November 1993

605. Snowden N: personal communication, Oakland, CA, 17 September 1994

606. Somers S: *Keeping Secrets.* Warner NY, 1988

607. Spear J: Can I trust my memory? A handbook for partial or no memories of childhood sexual abuse. 16-page booklet from Hazelden (1-800-328-9000), Center City, Mn, 1992

608. Spencer M, Dunklee P: Sexual abuse of boys. *Pediatrics* 78: 113-138, 1986

609. Spiegel D: Hypnosis in the treatment of victims of sexual abuse. *Psychiatric Clinics of North America* 12(2): 295-306, 1989

610. Spiegel D: Hypnosis, dissociation and trauma: hidden and overt observers. in Singer JL (ed): *Repression and Dissociation:* Implications for personality, theory, psychopathology, and health. University of Chicago Press, 1990

611. Spiegel D: Dissociation and trauma, in Speigel D (ed): *Dissociative Disorders:* A clinical review. Sidran Press, Lutherville, Md, 1993

612. Spitz R: Hospitalism. *Psychoanalytic Study of the Child:* 64-72, 1945

613. Springs FE, Friedrich WN: High risk behaviors and medical sequelae of childhood sexual abuse. *Mayo Clinic Proceedings* 67: 527-532, 1992

614. Sroufe A, Ward M: Seductive behavior of mothers of toddlers. *Child Development* 9: 1222-1229, 1980

615. Standing Bear L: *Land of the Spotted Eagle.* University of Nebraska Press, Lincoln, NB, 1993

616. Stannard D: *American Holocaust.* Oxford University Press, NY, 1992

617. Stanton M: *Sandor Ferenczi:* Reconsidering active intervention. Jason Aronson, Northvale, NJ, 1991

618. A Star Cries Incest, *People,* pp84-88, 7 October 1991

619. Starr R, Wolfe D (Eds): *The Effects of Child Abuse and Neglect.* Guilford, NY, 1991

619a   *State v. Maule*, 35 Wn. App. 287, 667 p. 2d 96, 1983

620.   *State v. Swan*, 114 Wash. 2d 613, 655-56, 790 P. 2d 610, 632, 1990
    In the *Swan* case, psychologist and founding FMSF board member Ralph Underwager was disqualified from testifying as an expert witness: "The Court remains convinced that the psychologist did not have the qualifications to testify as a doctor. The trial court ruled that the psychologist's proposed testimony was not proper because there was no indication that the result of the doctor's work had been accepted in the scientific community." A similar ruling occurred in *Timmons v. Indiana.* Speaking on the Australian *60 Minutes* news program, Dr. Anna Salter said about Ralph Underwager: *Salter*—What he says in court does not necessarily fairly represent the literature. *60 Minutes*—He distorts the facts? *Salter*—Frequently. Sometimes he quotes specific studies and is frequently wrong about what the studies say. 17,[572] other FMSF board members, such as Richard Ofshe, have also been admonished by the courts,[519, 572, 591, 635, 646, 718] as described on pages 204 and 221.

621.   *Stayton RP: Making meaner monsters: the polarization of the delayed/false memory controversy. *Journal of Child Sexual Abuse* 3(3): 127-134, 1994

622.   Steele KH: Concepts and techniques in traumatic memory work. Talk given at conference on Advances in Treating Survivors of Sexual Abuse. Reston, VA, 6 November, 1993

623.   Stempke R: Clinical experience in child abuse. *48 Hours,* CBS TV, 8 September 1993

624.   Stern P: Surviving in the courtroom: ten rules of testifying as an expert witness. *The APSAC Advisor* 4(1): 3-4, Winter 1991

625.   Steward MS: Preliminary findings from V.C. Davis, child memory study: development and testing of interview protocols for young children. *The APSAC Advisor* 5(3-summer): 11-13, 1992

626.   Stone MH: Incest in the borderline patient. in Kluft RP (ed): *Incest Related Syndromes in Adult Psychopathology.* American Psychiatric Press, pp183-204, Washington, DC, 1990

627.   Sullivan EJ: Association between chemical dependency and sexual problems in nurses. *Journal of Interpersonal Violence* 3: 323-330, 1988

628.   Sullivan HS: *Clinical Studies in Psychiatry.* Norton, NY, 1956

629.   Summit RC: The child sexual abuse accommodation syndrome. *Child Abuse and Neglect* 7: 177-193, 1983

630.   Summit RC: The centrality of victimization. *Psychiatric Clinics of North America* 12(2): 413-430, 1989

631.   Summit RC: Too terrible to hear: barriers to perception of child sexual abuse. Unpublished paper, Torrance, CA, updated 1991

631a.   Surrey J et al: Reported history of physical and sexual abuse and severity of symptomatology in women psychiatric outpatients. *American Journal of Orthopsychiatry* 60: 412-4 17, 1990

632.   *Survivors of Female Incest Emerge* (SOFIE) newsletter for survivors and therapists (Box 2794, Renton, WA 98056-0794). Special issue on repressed memory, 2(4), February 1994

633.   Swett C, Halpert M: Reported history of physical and sexual abuse in relation to dissociation and other symptomatology in women psychiatric inpatients. *Journal of Interpersonal Violence* 8(4): 545-555, 1993

634.   Swett C et al: Sexual and physical abuse histories and psychiatric symptoms among male psychiatric outpatients. *American Journal of Psychiatry* 147: 632-636, 1990

635.   Tabor G: Personal communication, Olympia, WA, 25 October 1994

635a.   Talley NJ et al: Self-reported abuse and gastrointestinal disease in outpatients: association with irritable bowel-type symptoms. *American Journal of Gastroenterology* 90 (3): 366-371, 1995

636.   Taub K (District Attorney in NY): Statements on unreliability of polygraph. *Court TV*, October 1, 1993

637.   Terr L: What happens to the memories of early childhood? *Journal of the American Academy of Child and Adolescent Psychiatry* 27: 96-104, 1988

638.   Terr LC: Childhood traumas: An outline and overview. *American Journal of Psychiatry* 148: 10-20, 1991

639.   Terr L: *Too Scared to Cry:* Psychic trauma in childhood. Basic Books, NY, 1990

640.   Terr L: Deposition, volume 2, pp205-358. in: *Gary Ramona v. Stephanie Ramona, Marche Isabella,* etc, 28 May 1993

641.   Terr L: *Unchained Memories:* True stories of traumatic memories, lost and found. Basic Books, NY, 1994

642.   Terr L: *Talk on traumatic memories.* Philadelphia, March 1994

643.   Tessler M, Nelson K: Making memories: the influence of joint encoding and later recall. *Consciousness & Cognition,* Summer 1994

644.   Thompson L: Supplemental officer's report on *Richard Ofshe* (literature review and background) in the Paul Ingram case. No 88-27067-11, Thurston County, Washington, 10 July 1989

645.   Threlkeld ME, Thyer BA: Sexual and physical abuse histories among child and adolescent psychiatric outpatients, unpublished, 1989

646.   *Timmons v. Indiana,* 584 N.E. 2d 1108 (Ind.) 1992

647.   Timnick L: Children's abuse reports reliable, most believe. *Los Angeles Times* A1, 1985

648.   Todd T: The false memory debate: Is it real or is it...? *Just Us* 4(3): 1-14, May/June 1994

649. Tomkins S: *Affect, Imagery and Consciousness.* Vols 1 & 2, Springer, NY, 1962 & 3

650. Tsai M, Wagner NN: Therapy groups for women sexually molested as children. *Archives of Sexual Behavior* 7: 417-427, 1978

651. Tyler A: 2.5 year controlled study of abusers, with multidiscriminate analysis, finding highly statistically significant (94%) predictability for abusing was having been abused as a child. Reported by author in testimony on *Court TV,* 14 October 1993

652. Uddo M et al: Memory and attention in combat-related PTSD. *Journal of Psychopathology and Behavioral Assessment* 15(1): 43-52, 1993

653. *United States v. Frye,* 293 F. 1013, DC Cir 1923

654. *Urie v. Thompson,* 337 U.S. 163, 1949 Washington Review Code Annotation 4.16.340 (West 1993)

655. Vachss A: Comment on "The universality of incest." *Journal of Psychohistory* 19(2): 219-220, Fall 1991

656. Vachss A: You carry the cure [for emotional abuse] in your own heart. *Parade—the Sunday Newspaper Magazine,* 28 August 1994

657. Vaillant GE: *Adaptation to Life.* Little Brown, NY, 1977

658. Vaillant GE (ed): *Ego Mechanisms of Defense.* American Psychiatric Press, Washington DC, 1992

659. van der Hart O, van der Horst R: The dissociation theory of Pierre Janet. *Journal of Traumatic Stress* 2: 399-414, 1989

660. van der Kolk BA: The compulsion to repeat the trauma. *Psychiatric Clinics of North America* 12(2): 389-411, 1989

661. van der Kolk BA: Trauma and Memory. Guest transcript, *Practical Reviews in Psychiatry* vol 18-2, Mar 1994

662. van der Kolk BA, van der Hart O: The intrusive past: the flexibility of memory and the engraving of trauma. *American Imago* 48(4): 425-454, 1991

663. van der Kolk BA: The body keeps the score: Memory and the evolving psychobiology of post traumatic stress. *Harvard Review of Psychiatry* 1(3), 1994

664. van der Kolk BA et al: Cavalcade Productions (videotape commentary on PTSD), Ukiah, CA, (1-800-345-5530), 1994

665. van der Kolk BA et al: Childhood origins of self-destructive behavior. *American Journal of Psychiatry* 148: 1665-1671, 1991

666. van der Kolk BA et al: Field trials for the DSM-4, Post Traumatic Stress Disorder II: Disorders of extreme stress. American Psychiatric Association, Washington, DC, 1992

667. Victor M: Treatment of alcoholic intoxication and the withdrawal syndrome. *Psychosomatic Medicine* 25: 636-650, 1966

668. Vittone BT: Personal communication, Alexandria, VA, 12 July 1994
669. *Wakefield H, Underwager R: Uncovering memories of alleged sexual abuse: the therapists who do it. *Issues in Child Abuse Accusations* 4(4): 197-210, 1992
670. *Wakefield H, Underwager R: Recovered memories of alleged sexual abuse. Fourth American Psychological Society convention, San Diego, CA, 20 June 1992
671. *Wakefield H, Underwager R: Interview on pedophilia. *Paidika: The Journal of Paedophilia* 3(1): 2-12, Winter 1993
672. Walker AG: Checklist for interviewing/questioning children. *NRCCSA News,* July/August, 1994
673. Walker E et al: Relationship of chronic pelvic pain to psychiatric diagnoses and childhood sexual abuse. *American Journal of Psychiatry* 145: 75-80, 1988
674. Walker L: *The Battered Woman.* Harper & Row, NY, 1979
675. Wallace J: Alcoholism from the inside out: a phenomenological analysis. in Estes & Heinemann (eds): *Alcoholism: Development, Consequences, and Interventions.* C.V. Mosby, St Louis, 1977
676. Wallen J, Berman K: Possible indicators of childhood sexual abuse for individuals in substance abuse treatment. *Journal of Child Sexual Abuse* 1(3): 63-74, 1992
677. Walsh B: Interviewing versus interrogation. *NRCCSA News* July/August, 1994
678. Walsh BW, Rosen P: *Self-mutilation:* Theory, research, and treatment. Guilford Press, NY, 1988
679. *Wartik N: A question of abuse. *American Health.* May 1993, pp62-67
679a. Waugh and Norman: Cited in Norman 1982 above.
680. Wegsheider S: *Another Chance:* Hope and Health for the Alcoholic Family. Science and Behavior Books, Palo Alto, CA, 1981
680a. Wegsheider S et al: *Experiential Psychotherapy Techniques,* Basic Books, 1990
681. Weingartner H et al: Mood-state-dependent retrieval of verbal associations. *Journal of Abnormal Psychology* 86: 276-284, 1977
682. Wells FL: *Mental Adjustments.* Appleton, NY, 1922
683. Westen D et al: Physical and sexual abuse in adolescent girls with borderline personality disorder. *American Journal of Orthopsychiatry* 60(1): 55-66, 1990
684. Westermeyer J: Incest in psychiatric practice: a description of patients and incestuous relationships. *Journal of Clinical Psychiatry* 39: 643-648, 1978
685. Whitfield CL: *The Patient with Alcoholism and Other Drug Problems.*

Unpublished book, Baltimore, 1980

686.   Whitfield CL: Who is safe to talk to? in Whitfield CL: *A Gift to Myself:* a personal workbook and guide to healing the true self. Health Communications, Deerfield Beach, FL, 1990

687.   Whitfield CL: *Healing the Child Within:* Discovery and recovery for adult children of dysfunctional families. Health Communications, Deerfield Beach, FL, 1987

688.   Whitfield CL: *A Gift to Myself* (Workbook & guide for healing). Health Communications, Deerfield Beach, FL, 1990

689.   Whitfield CL: *Co-dependence - Healing the Human Condition:* the new paradigm for helping professionals and people in recovery. p45, and chap 21. Health Communications, Deerfield Beach, FL, 1991

690.   Whitfield CL: Denial of the truth: political and psychological dysfunction in the Anita Hill/Clarence Thomas hearings. *Journal of Psychohistory,* 19(3) p.269-279, Winter 1992

691.   Whitfield CL: *Boundaries and Relationships:* Knowing, protecting and enjoying the self. Health Communications, Deerfield Beach, FL, 1993

692.   Whitfield CL: My Recovery Plan for Stage Two Recovery (booklet, 95 cents, from 1-800-851-9100). Health Communications, Deerfield Beach FL, 1992

693.   Whitfield CL: The forgotten difference: ordinary memory versus traumatic memory. *Consciousness and Cognition,* 4, Winter 1995

693a.   Whitfield CL: How common is traumatic forgetting? (Modified and expanded from Chapter 7 of this book.) *Journal of Psychohistory,* Summer 1995; and author's commentary on articles in response in Fall 1995

694.   Whitfield CL: Internal verification and corroboration of traumatic memories. Submitted for publication to *Journal of Child Sexual Abuse,* 1995

695.   Whitfield CL: Survey on 2,000 adult children of dysfunctional families, 1988 through 1994, Baltimore, 1994

696.   Wiehe VR: Religious influence on parental attitude toward the use of corporal punishment. *Journal of Family Violence* 5(2): 173-186, 1990

697.   Wilber K: *Quantum Questions.* Shambhala, Boston, 1984

697a.   Wilber K: *Eye to Eye:* The quest for the new paradigm. Anchor/ Doubleday, NY, 1983

698.   Wild NJ: Prevalence of child sex rings. *Pediatrics* 83(4): 553-558, 1989

699.   Williams LM: Recovered memories of abuse in women with documented child sexual victimization histories. *Consciousness & Cognition,* 4 Fall 1994

700.   Williams LM: Recall of childhood trauma: a prospective study of women's memories of child sexual abuse. Paper presented at American

Society of Criminology annual meeting, Phoenix, 27 October 1993. revision in press for *Journal of Consulting and Clinical Psychology* for 1994

701. Williams MB: Assessing the traumatic impact of child sexual abuse: What makes it more severe? *Journal of Child Sexual Abuse* 2(2): 41-59, 1993

702. Wilson JP, Raphael B (eds): *International Handbook on Traumatic Stress Syndromes.* Plenum Press, NY, 1993

703. Wimberly L: The perspective from Victims of Child Abuse Laws (VOCAL), in Myers JEB: *The Backlash.* Sage, Thousand Oaks, CA, 1994

704. Winell M: *Leaving the Fold:* A guide for former fundamentalists and others leaving their religion. New Harbinger, Oakland, CA, 1993

705. Winograd E, Neisser U: *Affect and Accuracy in Recall:* Studies of "flashbulb" memories. Cambridge University Press, NY, 1992

706. Wolf J: Adult reports of sexual abuse during childhood, 1992. Cited in Finkelhor 1994

706a. Wood BL: *Children of Alcoholism:* The struggle for self and intimacy in adult life. University Press, NY, 1987

707. *Woodward KL et al: Was it real or memories? *Newsweek,* pp54-55, 14 March 1994

708. Wozencraft T et al: Depression and suicidal ideation in sexually abused children. *Child Abuse and Neglect* 15: 505-511, 1991

709. Wyatt GE: The sexual abuse of Afro-American and White American women in childhood. *Child Abuse and Neglect* 9: 507-519, 1985

710. Wylie MS: The shadow of a doubt. *Family Therapy Networker* 17: 18-29, 70-73 (September/October), 1993.

711. *Yapko M: The seductions of memory. *Family Therapy Networker* 17: 31-37 (September/October), 1993.

712. *Yapko M: *Suggestions of abuse.* Simon & Schuster, NY, 1994

713. *Yapko M: Appearance on *Maury Povich* talk show, 18 May 1994

714. Yapko M: *Trancework,* cited in Calof 1994a

715. Yates A et al: Drawings by child victims of incest. *Child Abuse and Neglect* 9: 183-189, 1985

716. Yates JL, Nasby W: Dissociation, affect, and network models of memory: an integrative proposal. *Journal of Traumatic Stress* 6(3): 305-326, 1993

717. Young EB: The role of incest in relapse. *Journal of Psychoactive Drugs* 22: 249-258, 1990

718. Zaragosa MS: *Memory and Testimony in the Child Witness.* Sage, Thousand Oaks, CA, 1994

719. Zeitlin SB, McNally RJ: Implicit and explicit memory bias for threat in PTSD. *Behavior Research and Therapy* 29(5): 451-457, 1991

RESOURCES FOR INFORMATION AND NETWORKING

Adults Molested as Children United (AMAC): groups for survivors; nationwide referrals. PO Box 952, San Jose, CA 95108. (408) 280-5055.

Advocates for Abuse Recovery: bimonthly newsletter supporting survivors, therapists and involved others. PO Box 161, Malvern, PA 19355-161. (610) 524-1499, fax 269-9467.

American Bar Association Center on Children and the Law: For lawyers and other professionals; education, training and program evaluation. 1800 M St. NW, Ste 200 So, Washington, DC 20036. (202) 331-2250.

American Coalition for Abuse Awareness (ACAA): national organization lobbies for enactment of federal and state legislation on childhood sexual abuse issues and educates the public and media about abuse. PO Box 27959, Washington DC 20038-7959. (202) 462-4688, 4689 (fax)

American Professional Society on the Abuse of Children (APSAC): organization for professionals in child abuse treatment and prevention; offers information, guidelines, referral services to professionals. 332 S Michigan Ave, Ste 1600, Chicago, IL 60604. (312) 554-0166.

Believe the Children: newsletter on child abuse. Box 797, Cary, IL 60013. Voice mail phone (708) 515-5432.

Center for Abuse Recovery and Empowerment: Inpatient treatment. Psychiatric Institute of Washington, DC. 4228 Wisconsin Ave, NW, Washington, DC 20016. (800) 369-2273.

The Center for Trauma and Dissociation: Treatment and information on trauma and dissociation. 4400 E. Iliff Ave., Denver, CO 80222. (800) 441-6921.

Childhelp USA—National Hot Line: (800) 422-4453: offers a 24-hour crisis hot line, national information and referral network for support groups and therapists and for reporting suspected abuse. Sponsors Adult Survivors of Child Abuse Anonymous meetings. c/o NSCAAP, PO Box 630, Hollywood, CA 90028.

The Counseling Connection: national mental health referral, educational and advocacy service. Free referrals to consumers and instruction in the interviewing and screening process. (404) 516-0941.

European Response to the Backlash Network (ENBAR): newsletter to combat the isolating effect of the backlash. F. Clockstraat 167, 9665 BJ, Oude Pekela, Netherlands.

False Memory Syndrome Foundation: newsletter: focuses on the support of people accused of child sexual abuse. 3401 Market St, Philadelphia, PA, 19104.

Family Violence and Sexual Assault Bulletin: published by the Family Violence and Sexual Assault Institute, 1310 Clinte Dr., Tyler, TX 75701. (903) 525-6600.

The Healing Woman: monthly newsletter for women survivors of childhood sexual abuse. Box 3038, Moss Beach, CA 94038. (415) 728-0330 (fax)-1324.

Incest Survivor Information Exchange (I.S.I.E.): newsletter for survivors' writings, artwork and exchange of information. PO Box 3399, New Haven, CT 06515. (203) 389-5166.

Incest Survivors Resource Network International: Quaker peace witness offering educational resources and networking for survivors of mother/son incest. PO Box 7375, Las Cruces, NM 88006-7375. (505) 521-4260.

International Society for the Study of MPD and Dissociative Disorders: educational organization; conferences and literature. 5700 Old Orchard Rd, Skokie, IL 60077-1024. (708) 966-4322.

Journal of Child Sexual Abuse: research, treatment and program innovations for victims, survivors and offenders. Haworth Press, 10 Alice St, Binghamton, NY 13904-1580.

Journal of Interpersonal Violence: concerned with the study and treatment of victims and perpetrators of physical and sexual violence. Sage Publications, 2455 Teller Rd, Thousand Oaks, CA 91320.

Journal of Psychohistory: addresses past and current child abuse from many dimensions. 140 Riverside Dr, Ste 14 H, New York, NY 10024.

Justus Unlimited: newsletter for MPD and ritual abuse issues. Box 1121, Parker, CO 80134 (303) 643-8698.

Liegebeest (Children of Yesterday, Today and Tomorrow): Publication of the Association for Legal Protection and Rights of Molested and Abused Children, Box 217, 5750 AE Deurne, Netherlands.

Moving Forward: a news journal for survivors of sexual child abuse and those who care for them. Box 4426, Arlington, VA 22204. (703) 271-4024, 4025 (fax).

National Center on Child Abuse and Neglect: Federal policy, part of DHHS. Three information resources include the *National Resource Centers* on: *Child Abuse and Neglect; Child Sexual Abuse* and *The Clearinghouse,* whose addresses are respectively—63 Inverness Drive E., Englewood, CO 80112-5117 (800) 227-5242; 107 Lincoln St., Huntsville, AL 35801 (800) 543-7006; and Box 1182, Washington, DC 20013-1182 (800) 394-3366.

National Center for Prosecution of Child Abuse: a central resource for training and expert legal assistance, court reform and state-of-the-art information on criminal child abuse investigations and prosecutions. Publishes a one-page *Update* newsletter. 99 Canal Center Plaza, Ste 510, Alexandria, VA 22314. (703) 739-0321, fax 549-6259.

National Legal Resource for Child Advocacy and Protection: Legal resources and information. 1800 M St, Washington, DC 20036. (202) 331-2250.

One Voice—National Center for Redress of Incest and Sexual Abuse: national organization addresses legal needs of survivors, provides advocacy and educational information, is establishing a network of legal professionals. PO Box 27958, Washington, DC 20038-7958. (202) 371-6056.

Parents United International (and Daughters and Sons United): for children, parents and adults who were molested as children, as well as others who are concerned with child sexual abuse and related problems. PO Box 952, San Jose, CA 95108-0952. (408) 453-7616. Crisis line: (408) 279-8228.

S.O.F.I.E.: Survivors of Female Incest Emerge: bi-monthly newsletter, PO Box 2794, Renton, WA 98056.

Survivor CONNECTIONS: international activist organization for nonoffending survivors. Quarterly newsletters, support groups and perpetrator database. Frank & Sara Fitzpatrick, 52 Lyndon Rd, Cranston, RI 02905-1121. (401) 941-2548.

Survivors Network for Those, Who as Children, Were Sexually Abused by Priests (S.N.A.P.): grass-roots organization; provides self-help support/resources and organizes for political action. 8025 S Honore, Chicago, IL 60620. (312) 483-1059.

Survivors of Abusive Rituals (SOAR): dedicated to researching abusive rituals perpetrated by cults, pseudo-cults and individuals; publishes a newsletter by and for survivors of these rituals. PO Box 1776, Cahokia, IL 62206-1776.

Survivors of Incest Anonymous (SIA): international network with self-help meetings, literature, pen pals, speakers, meeting information and bimonthly bulletin. Send a self-addressed, stamped envelope (two first-class stamps) for information about support groups. PO Box 26870, Baltimore, MD 21212. (410) 433-2365. Michigan residents: call (313) 459-3090.

The Sidran Foundation: resource, referral service and books for people with dissociative disorders, their supporters, and mental health professionals. 2328 W Joppa Rd, Ste 15, Lutherville, MD 21093. (410) 825-8888.

Treating Abuse Today: international news journal of abuse survivorship and therapy. 2722 Eastlake Ave, Ste 300, Seattle, WA 98102. (800) 847-3964 fax (206) 329-8462.

Truth about Abuse: bi-monthly news journal that corrects the disinformation from the backlash. Box 2794, Renton, WA 98056-0794.

VOICES In Action (Victims of Incest Can Emerge Survivors): international organization for survivors and partners. Conferences, special interest groups and newsletter. PO Box 148309, Chicago, IL 60614. (800) 786-4238; (312) 327-1500.

Varied Directions International: resource catalog, educational materials, consultation and networking for survivors and therapists. (800) 888-5236.

Victims of Clergy Abuse Linkup: network of survivors and professionals to support and assist victims. PO Box 1268, Wheeling, IL 60090.

Victims of Child Abuse Laws (VOCAL): appears to be more evolved and constructive in their writings than FMSF. Box 1314, Orangeville, CA, 95662.

INDEX

ABOUT THE AUTHOR

Charles L. Whitfield, M.D., has a private practice in Baltimore, MD, and Atlanta, GA, where he assists trauma survivors in their recovery. He also assists people with alcoholism, and other addictions and disorders.

Certified in addiction medicine by the American Society of Addictions Medicine, Dr. Whitfield was a founding board member of the National Association for Children of Alcoholics. He is on the faculty of the Rutgers University Advanced Summer School on Alcohol and Drug Studies. He is a member of the American Professional Society on the Abuse of Children and gives talks and workshops nationally.

To be on Dr. Whitfield's mailing list, or to explore having him give a talk or workshop on a recovery related topic, send a self-addressed stamped envelope to him at P.O. Box 420487, Atlanta, GA 30342.